MEREDITH'S
BIG BOOK OF
BIBLE
LISTS

MEREDITH'S BIG BOOK OF BIBLE LISTS

THE ULTIMATE COLLECTION OF BIBLE FACTS

J. L. MEREDITH

Inspirational Press ♦ New York

First Galahad Books edition pubished in 1998.

Inspirational Press
A division of BBS Publishing Corporation
450 Raritan Center Parkway
Edison, New Jersey 08837

Inspirational Press is a registered trademark of
BBS Publishing Corporation.

Published by arrangement with Betahny House Publishers.

Distributed by World Publishing
Nashville, TN 37214
www.worldpublishing.com

Library of Congress Catalog Card number: 97-77404

ISBN: 0-88486-349-2

Printed in the United States of America.

CONTENTS

MEREDITH'S BOOK OF BIBLE LISTS

A One-of-a-Kind Collection
of Bible Facts
Presented in List Form

Dedication

This book is dedicated to my wife, Lorraine.

Preface

The purpose of *Meredith's Book of Bible Lists* is to entertain, interest, fascinate, stimulate and, most of all, to educate. Many people have complained that the Bible is dull reading and that they can't get past all the "begats" (i.e., "Abraham begat Isaac," etc.). Here's a fresh and informative look at some of the interesting and helpful portions of the Scriptures, showing that the Bible is certainly not a dull book. And if this book gets the reader back into *The Book*, its real purpose will be fulfilled.

Many people have complained also that religion, and thus the Bible, has too many "thou shalt nots." While *Meredith's Book of Bible Lists* does include such negatives when necessary, you will realize from a quick perusal of the contents that the great weight of Christianity and the Bible is on the positive side—what God has done and is doing for His creation. There are 452 promises from the Bible listed in this book, with special attention paid to conditions for acquiring those promises.

All Bible references quoted here are from the King James Version. All scriptures which are not exact quotes are paraphrased by the compiler in the interest of condensing longer passages, etc.

If you have suggestions for further lists, you may send them to the publisher.

Mr. Meredith's preparation for this monumental project included a thorough familiarity with the Bible; he has read the Old Testament through 16 times; the New Testament, 34 times. His hope is that you will enjoy reading *Meredith's Book of Bible Lists* as much as he enjoyed putting it all together.

Table of Contents

1

Commandments

Laws form the foundation of civilized society. One of the wonders of history is that so much was summed up in the list known as the Ten Commandments. When Jesus lived on earth He offered His selection of the two greatest commandments and, in so doing, produced an even more concise statement. In the final analysis, governing man's attitude and behavior toward God and his fellow human beings can be summed up in one word—love.

Though this truth is found also in the Old Testament, when Jesus came 2,000 years ago He further revealed the nature of God: a God who is a Judge and yet a Father, a King who is also a Savior. We are able to find as many as 250 New Testament commandments. These do not replace the Ten Commandments of the Old Testament but are a more detailed, further unfolding of God's expectations for the way people should live. Included here is a list of Old Testament laws with Jesus' commentary and application of them.

You will also find: Jesus' exhortation to the unconverted, His commandments concerning human relationships, fifty ways to please God, the apostles' exhortations about how to treat others, warnings about other spirits, principles for good family relationships, and guidelines for church leaders.

1. The Ten Commandments

1. Thou shalt have no other gods before me (Ex. 20:3).
2. Thou shalt not make unto thee any graven image (Ex. 20:4, 5).

Moses Giving the Law

3. Thou shalt not take the name of the Lord thy God in vain (Ex. 20:7).
4. Remember the Sabbath day, to keep it holy (Ex. 20:8-11).
5. Honour thy father and thy mother (Ex. 20:12).
6. Thou shalt not kill (Ex. 20:13).
7. Thou shalt not commit adultery (Ex. 20:14).
8. Thou shalt not steal (Ex. 20:15).
9. Thou shalt not bear false witness against thy neighbour (Ex. 20:16).
10. Thou shalt not covet . . . anything that is thy neighbour's (Ex. 20:17).

2. *The Two Greatest Commandments and the New Commandment*

1. Thou shalt love the Lord thy God with all thy heart, and

with all thy soul, and with all thy mind (Matt. 22:36-38).
2. Thou shalt love thy neighbour as thyself (Matt. 22:39).
3. A new commandment I give unto you, That ye love one another; as I have loved you, that ye also love one another. By this shall all men know that ye are my disciples, if ye have love one to another (John 13:34, 35).

3. The "Ten Commandments" As Stated in the New Testament

1. According to Jesus
    A. Matthew 19:17-19
        1. Thou shalt do no murder.
        2. Thou shalt not commit adultery.
        3. Thou shalt not steal.
        4. Thou shalt not bear false witness.
        5. Honour thy father and thy mother.
        6. Thou shalt love thy neighbour as thyself.
    B. Mark 10:19
        1. Do not commit adultery.
        2. Do not kill.
        3. Do not steal.
        4. Do not bear false witness.
        5. Defraud not.
        6. Honour thy father and mother.
    C. Luke 18:20
        1. Do not commit adultery.
        2. Do not kill.
        3. Do not steal.
        4. Do not bear false witness.
        5. Honour thy father and thy mother.
2. According to Paul (Rom. 13:9)
    A. Thou shalt not commit adultery.
    B. Thou shalt not kill.
    C. Thou shalt not steal.
    D. Thou shalt not bear false witness.
    E. Thou shalt not covet.
    F. Thou shalt love thy neighbour as thyself.

4. Jesus' Interpretation of Old Testament Law

1. Thou shalt not kill. But I say unto you, That whosoever is

angry with his brother without a cause shall be in danger of the judgment (Matt. 5:21, 22).

2. Thou shalt not commit adultery: But I say unto you, That whosoever looketh on a woman to lust after her hath committed adultery with her already in his heart (Matt. 5:27, 28).

3. Whosoever shall put away his wife, let him give her a writing of divorcement. But I say unto you, Whosoever shall put away his wife, saving for the cause of fornication, causeth her to commit adultery: and whosoever shall marry her that is divorced committeth adultery (Matt. 5:31-32).

4. Thou shalt not forswear thyself, but shalt perform unto the Lord thy oaths: But I say unto you, Swear not at all (Matt. 5:33, 34).

5. An eye for an eye, and a tooth for a tooth: But I say unto you, That ye resist not evil: but whosoever shall smite thee on thy right cheek, turn to him the other also (Matt. 5:38, 39).

6. Thou shalt love thy neighbour, and hate thine enemy. But I say unto you, Love your enemies (Matt. 5:43, 44).

7. Be ye therefore perfect, even as your Father which is in heaven is perfect (Matt. 5:48).

8. Whatsoever ye would that men should do to you, do ye even so to them: for this is the law and the prophets (Matt. 7:12).

9. Why do thy disciples transgress the tradition of the elders? for they wash not their hands when they eat bread. . . . And he called the multitude, and said unto them, Hear, and understand: Not that which goeth into the mouth defileth a man; but that which cometh out of the mouth, this defileth a man (Matt. 15:2-11).

10. Moses because of the hardness of your hearts suffered you to put away your wives: but from the beginning it was not so. And I say unto you, Whosoever shall put away his wife, except it be for fornication, and shall marry another, committeth adultery: and whoso marrieth her which is put away doth commit adultery (Matt. 19:8, 9).

11. Moses suffered to write a bill of divorcement, and to put her away. Jesus answered and said unto them, For the hardness of your heart he wrote you this precept. But from the beginning of the creation God made them male and female. . . . What therefore God hath joined together, let not man put asunder (Mark 10:4-9).

12. Why do ye that which is not lawful to do on the sabbath days? . . . And he said unto them, That the Son of man is

Lord also of the sabbath. . . . I will ask you one thing; Is it lawful on the sabbath days to do good, or to do evil? to save life, or to destroy it? (Luke 6:2-10).

13. Is it lawful to heal on the sabbath day? And he took him, and healed him (Luke 14:3, 4).

14. Moses wrote unto us, If any man's brother die, having a wife, and he die without children, that his brother should take his wife, and raise up seed unto his brother. . . . Jesus answering said unto them, The children of this world marry, and are given in marriage (Luke 20:28-34).

15. The Jews persecuted Jesus, and sought to slay him, because he had done these things on the sabbath day. But Jesus answered them, My Father worketh hitherto, and I work (John 5:16, 17).

16. Do not think that I will accuse you to the Father: there is one that accuseth you, even Moses, in whom ye trust. For had ye believed Moses, ye would have believed me: for he wrote of me. But if ye believe not his writings, how shall ye believe my words? (John 5:45-47).

17. Did not Moses give you the law, and yet none of you keepeth the law? Why go ye about to kill me? (John 7:19).

18. Master, this woman was taken in adultery, in the very act. Now Moses in the law commanded us, that such should be stoned: but what sayest thou? . . . When they continued asking him, he lifted up himself, and said unto them, He that is without sin among you, let him first cast a stone at her (John 8:4-7).

19. It is written in your law, that the testimony of two men is true. I am one that bears witness of myself, and the Father that sent me beareth witness of me (John 8:17, 18).

20. We know that God spake unto Moses: as for this fellow, we know not from whence he is. The man answered and said unto them, Why herein is a marvelous thing, that ye know not from whence he is, and yet he hath opened mine eyes. . . . If this man were not of God, he could do nothing. . . . And they cast him out. Jesus heard that they had cast him out; and when he had found him, he said unto him, Dost thou believe on the Son of God? . . . Thou hast both seen him, and he it is that talketh with thee (John 9:29-37).

21. For a good work we stone thee not; but for blasphemy; and because that thou, being a man, makest thyself God. Jesus answered them, Is it not written in your law, I said, Ye are

gods? If he called them gods, unto whom the word of God came, and the scripture cannot be broken; say ye of him, whom the Father hath sanctified, and sent into the world, Thou blasphemest; because I said, I am the Son of God? (John 10:33-36).

22. I know that he shall rise again in the resurrection at the last day. Jesus said unto her, I am the resurrection, and the life (John 11:24, 25).

23. We have heard out of the law that Christ abideth for ever: and how sayest thou, The Son of Man must be lifted up? who is this Son of man? Then Jesus said unto them, Yet a little while is the light with you. Walk while ye have the light, lest darkness come upon you (John 12:34, 35).

24. We have a law, and by our law he ought to die, because he made himself the Son of God. . . . Then said Pilate unto him, Speakest thou not unto me? knowest thou not that I have power to crucify thee, and have power to release thee? Jesus answered, Thou couldest have no power at all against me, except it were given thee from above: therefore he that delivered me unto thee hath the greater sin (John 19:7-11).

5. *The Four Commandments for Gentile Converts (Acts 15:29)*

1. Abstain from meats offered to idols.
2. Abstain from blood.
3. Abstain from things strangled.
4. Abstain from fornication.

6. *Exhortations to the Unconverted from the Gospel of Matthew*

1. Bring forth fruits meet for repentance (Matt. 3:8).
2. Every tree which bringeth not forth good fruit is hewn down, and cast into the fire (Matt. 3:10, 7:19).
3. He will burn up the chaff with unquenchable fire (Matt. 3:12).
4. Repent: for the kingdom of heaven is at hand (Matt. 4:17).
5. Except your righteousness shall exceed the righteousness of the scribes and Pharisees, ye shall in no case enter into the kingdom of heaven (Matt. 5:20).
6. It is profitable for thee that one of thy members should per-

ish, and not that thy whole body should be cast into hell (Matt. 5:29).

7. No man can serve two masters; for either he will hate the one, and love the other; or else he will hold to the one, and despise the other. Ye cannot serve God and mammon (Matt. 6:24).

8. Enter ye in at the strait gate: for wide is the gate, and broad is the way, that leadeth to destruction, and many there be which go in thereat: because strait is the gate and narrow is the way, which leadeth unto life, and few there be that find it (Matt. 7:13, 14).

9. Not every one that saith unto me, Lord, Lord, shall enter into the kingdom of heaven; but he that doeth the will of my Father which is in heaven (Matt. 7:21).

10. Then will I profess unto them, I never knew you: depart from me, ye that work iniquity (Matt. 7:23).

11. Every one that heareth these sayings of mine, and doeth them not, shall be likened unto a foolish man, which built his house upon the sand (Matt. 7:26).

12. Many shall come from the east and west, and shall sit down with Abraham, and Isaac, and Jacob, in the kingdom of heaven. But the children of the kingdom shall be cast out into outer darkness: there shall be weeping and gnashing of teeth (Matt. 8:11, 12).

13. Follow me; and let the dead bury their dead (Matt. 8:22).

14. That ye may know that the Son of man hath power on earth to forgive sins, (then saith he to the sick of the palsy,) Arise, take up thy bed, and go into thy house (Matt. 9:6).

15. I am not come to call the righteous, but sinners to repentance (Matt. 9:13).

16. Fear not them which kill the body, but are not able to kill the soul: but rather fear him which is able to destroy both soul and body in hell (Matt. 10:28).

17. Whosoever shall confess me before men, him will I confess also before my Father which is in heaven. But whosoever shall deny me before men, him will I also deny before my Father which is in heaven (Matt. 10:32, 33).

18. He that taketh not his cross, and followeth after me, is not worthy of me. He that findeth his life shall lose it: and he that loseth his life for my sake shall find it (Matt. 10:38, 39).

19. If the mighty works, which were done in you, had been done

in Tyre and Sidon, they would have repented long ago in sackcloth and ashes (Matt. 11:21).

20. He that is not with me is against me; and he that gathereth not with me scattereth abroad (Matt. 12:30).

21. How can ye, being evil, speak good things? for out of the abundance of the heart the mouth speaketh (Matt. 12:34).

22. Every idle word that men shall speak, they shall give account thereof in the day of judgment. For by thy words thou shalt be justified, and by thy words thou shalt be condemned (Matt. 12:36, 37).

23. In the time of harvest I will say to the reapers, Gather ye together first the tares, and bind them in bundles to burn them: but gather the wheat into my barn (Matt. 13:30).

24. The Son of man shall send forth his angels, and they shall gather out of his kingdom all things that offend, and them which do iniquity; and shall cast them into a furnace of fire: there shall be wailing and gnashing of teeth (Matt. 13:41, 42).

25. So shall it be at the end of the world: the angels shall come forth, and sever the wicked from among the just, and shall cast them into the furnace of fire (Matt. 13:49, 50).

26. This people draweth nigh unto me with their mouth, and honoureth me with their lips; but their heart is far from me (Matt. 15:8).

27. Every plant which my heavenly Father hath not planted, shall be rooted up (Matt. 15:13).

28. If the blind lead the blind, both shall fall into the ditch (Matt. 15:14).

29. Those things which proceed out of the mouth come forth from the heart: and they defile the man. For out of the heart proceed evil thoughts, murders, adulteries, fornications, thefts, false witness, blasphemies: these are the things which defile a man (Matt. 15:18-20).

30. I am not sent but unto the lost sheep of the house of Israel (Matt. 15:24).

31. If any man will come after me, let him deny himself, and take up his cross, and follow me. For whosoever will save his life shall lose it: and whosoever will lose his life for my sake shall find it. For what is a man profited, if he shall gain the whole world, and lose his own soul? (Matt. 16:24-26).

32. Except ye be converted, and become as little children, ye shall not enter into the kingdom of heaven (Matt. 18:3).

33. It is better for thee to enter into life halt or maimed, rather than having two hands or two feet to be cast into everlasting fire. . . . It is better for thee to enter into life with one eye, rather than having two eyes to be cast into hell fire (Matt. 18:8, 9).
34. The Son of man is come to save that which was lost (Matt. 18:11).
35. It is not the will of your Father which is in heaven, that one of these little ones should perish (Matt. 18:14).
36. If thou wilt be perfect, go and sell that thou hast, and give to the poor, and thou shalt have treasure in heaven: and come and follow me (Matt. 19:21).
37. It is easier for a camel to go through the eye of a needle, than for a rich man to enter into the kingdom of God (Matt. 19:24).
38. Every one that hath forsaken houses, or brethren, or sisters, or father, or mother, or wife, or children, or lands, for my name's sake, shall receive an hundredfold, and shall inherit everlasting life (Matt. 19:29).
39. The publicans and the harlots go into the kingdom of God before you. For John came unto you in the way of righteousness, and ye believed him not: but the publicans and the harlots believed him: and ye, when ye had seen it, repented not afterward, that ye might believe him (Matt. 21:31, 32).
40. Whosoever shall fall on this stone shall be broken: but on whomsoever it shall fall, it will grind him to powder (Matt. 21:44).
41. Friend, how camest thou in hither not having a wedding garment? And he was speechless. Then said the king to the servants, Bind him hand and foot, and take him away, and cast him into outer darkness (Matt. 22:13).
42. Render therefore unto Caesar the things which are Caesar's; and unto God the things that are God's (Matt. 22:21).
43. Ye shut up the kingdom of heaven against men: for ye neither go in yourselves, neither suffer ye them that are entering to go in. . . . Ye devour widows' houses, and for a pretense make long prayer: therefore ye shall receive the greater damnation. . . . Ye compass sea and land to make one proselyte, and when he is made, ye make him twofold more the child of hell than yourselves (Matt. 23:13-15).
44. Ye pay tithe of mint and anise and cummin, and have omitted the weightier matters of the law, judgment, mercy, and

faith: these ought ye to have done, and not to leave the other undone (Matt. 23:23).

45. Ye make clean the outside of the cup and of the platter, but within they are full of extortion and excess. . . . Cleanse first that which is within the cup and platter, that the outside of them may be clean also (Matt. 23:25, 26).

46. Ye are like unto whited sepulchres, which indeed appear beautiful outward, but are within full of dead men's bones, and of all uncleanness. Even so ye also outwardly appear righteous unto men, but within ye are full of hypocrisy and iniquity (Matt. 23:27, 28).

47. Ye be witnesses unto yourselves, that ye are the children of them which killed the prophets (Matt. 23:31).

48. Ye serpents, ye generation of vipers, how can ye escape the damnation of hell? (Matt. 23:33).

49. He that shall endure unto the end, the same shall be saved (Matt. 24:13).

50. Watch therefore, for ye know neither the day nor the hour wherein the Son of man cometh (Matt. 25:13).

51. Cast ye the unprofitable servant into outer darkness: there shall be weeping and gnashing of teeth (Matt. 25:30).

52. Depart from me, ye cursed, into everlasting fire, prepared for the devil and his angels (Matt. 25:41).

53. These shall go away into everlasting punishment: but the righteous into life eternal (Matt. 25:46).

54. This is my blood of the new testament, which is shed for many for the remission of sins (Matt. 26:28).

55. All they that take the sword shall perish with the sword (Matt. 26:52.)

7. Fifty Ways to Please God

1. It becometh us to fulfill all righteousness (Matt. 3:15).

2. Man shall not live by bread alone, but by every word that proceedeth out of the mouth of God (Matt. 4:4).

3. Thou shalt worship the Lord thy God, and him only shalt thou serve (Matt. 4:10).

4. Seek ye first the kingdom of God, and his righteousness (Matt. 6:33).

5. Pray that the Lord of the harvest will send forth labourers into his harvest (Matt. 9:38).

6. Ye must be born again (John 3:7).

7. Worship God in spirit and in truth (John 4:24).
8. Repent and be baptized (Acts 2:38).
9. Obey God rather than man (Acts 5:29).
10. Reckon yourselves to be dead indeed unto sin, but alive unto God through Jesus Christ our Lord (Rom. 6:11).
11. Present your bodies a living sacrifice unto God (Rom. 12:1).
12. Glorify God in your body, and in your spirit (1 Cor. 6:20).
13. Desire spiritual gifts (1 Cor. 14:1).
14. Stand fast in the faith (1 Cor. 16:13).
15. Do not grieve the Holy Spirit of God (Eph. 4:30).
16. Be filled with the Spirit (Eph. 5:18).
17. Pray in the Spirit (Eph. 6:18).
18. Rejoice in the Lord (Phil. 3:1).
19. Set your affection on things above, where Christ sits at the right hand of God, and not on things on earth (Col. 3:1, 2).
20. Let the peace of God rule in your heart (Col. 3:15).
21. Let the word of Christ dwell in you richly in all wisdom (Col. 3:16).
22. Whatsoever ye do in word or deed, do all in the name of the Lord Jesus, giving thanks to God and the Father by him (Col. 3:17).
23. Pray without ceasing (1 Thess. 5:17).
24. In everything give thanks (1 Thess. 5:18).
25. Do not neglect your spiritual gift (1 Tim. 4:14).
26. Lay hold on eternal life (1 Tim. 6:12).
27. Be not ashamed of the testimony of our Lord (2 Tim. 1:8).
28. Labour to enter into the rest of the people of God (Heb. 4:11).
29. Hold fast to your profession of faith without wavering (Heb. 10:23).
30. The just shall live by faith (Heb. 10:38).
31. But without faith it is impossible to please him: for he that cometh to God must believe that he is, and that he is a rewarder of them that diligently seek him (Heb. 11:6).
32. Despise not thou the chastening of the Lord, for whom the Lord loveth he chasteneth, and scourgeth every son whom he receiveth (Heb. 12:5, 6).
33. Make straight paths for your feet (Heb. 12:13).
34. Refuse not him that speaketh (Heb. 12:25).
35. Offer the sacrifice of praise to God continually, that is, the fruit of our lips giving thanks to his name (Heb. 13:15).
36. Receive with meekness the engrafted word, which is able to save your souls (James 1:21).

37. Submit yourselves to God (James 4:7).
38. Is any among you afflicted? Let him pray (James 5:13).
39. Is any merry? Let him sing psalms (James 5:13).
40. Fear God (1 Pet. 2:17).
41. Sanctify the Lord God in your heart (1 Pet. 3:15).
42. Commit the keeping of [your soul] to God in well doing (1 Pet. 4:19).
43. Casting all your care upon him, for he careth for you (1 Pet. 5:7).
44. Looking for and hasting unto the coming of the day of God (2 Pet. 3:12).
45. Believe on the name of the Son of God; that ye may know that ye have eternal life (1 John 5:13).
46. Build up yourselves on your most holy faith, praying in the Holy Ghost (Jude 20).
47. Keep yourselves in the love of God (Jude 21).
48. Remember from whence thou art fallen, and repent, and do the first works (Rev. 2:5).
49. Fear God, and give glory to him (Rev. 14:7).
50. Worship him that made heaven, and earth, and sea, and the fountains of waters (Rev. 14:7).

8. Jesus' Commandments and Comments Concerning Relationships

1. I will make you fishers of men (Matt. 4:19).
2. Blessed are the peacemakers: for they shall be called the children of God (Matt. 5:9).
3. Blessed are ye, when men shall revile you, and persecute you, and shall say all manner of evil against you falsely, for my sake (Matt. 5:11).
4. Ye are the light of the world (Matt. 5:14).
5. Let your light so shine before men, that they may see your good works, and glorify your Father (Matt. 5:16).
6. Be reconciled to thy brother, and then come and offer thy gift (Matt. 5:24).
7. Agree with thine adversary quickly, while thou art in the way with him (Matt. 5:25).
8. If any man will sue thee at the law, and take away thy coat, let him have thy cloak also (Matt. 5:40).
9. Whosoever shall compel thee to go a mile, go with him twain (Matt. 5:41).

10. Give to him that asketh thee, and from him that would borrow of thee turn not thou away (Matt. 5:42).

11. If ye love them which love you, what reward have ye? do not even the publicans the same? And if ye salute your brethren only, what do ye more than others? do not even the publicans so? (Matt. 5:46, 47).

12. When thou doest thine alms, do not sound a trumpet before thee (Matt. 6:2).

13. When thou prayest, thou shalt not be as the hypocrites are: for they love to pray standing in the synagogues and in the corners of the streets, that they may be seen of men (Matt. 6:5).

14. If ye forgive men their trespasses, your heavenly Father will also forgive you (Matt. 6:14).

15. When ye fast, be not, as the hypocrites, of a sad countenance: for they disfigure their faces, that they may appear unto men to fast (Matt. 6:16).

16. Judge not, that ye be not judged (Matt. 7:1).

17. Thou hypocrite, first cast out the beam out of thine own eye; and then thou shalt see clearly to cast out the mote out of thy brother's eye (Matt. 7:5).

18. Give not that which is holy unto the dogs, neither cast ye your pearls before swine, lest they trample them under their feet, and turn again and rend you (Matt. 7:6).

19. Whatsoever ye would that men should do to you, do ye even so to them: for this is the law and the prophets (Matt. 7:12).

20. By their fruits ye shall know them (Matt. 7:20).

21. Go thy way, show thyself to the priest, and offer the gift that Moses commanded, for a testimony unto them (Matt. 8:4).

22. Follow me; and let the dead bury their dead (Matt. 8:22).

23. They said unto his disciples, Why eateth your Master with publicans and sinners? But when Jesus heard that, he said unto them, They that be whole need not a physician, but they that are sick (Matt. 9:11, 12).

24. Pray ye therefore the Lord of the harvest, that he will send forth labourers into his harvest (Matt. 9:38).

25. Go rather to the lost sheep of the house of Israel. And as ye go, preach (Matt. 10:6, 7).

26. Heal the sick, cleanse the lepers, raise the dead, cast out devils: freely ye have received, freely give (Matt. 10:8).

27. Whosoever shall not receive you, nor hear your words, when he depart out of that house or city, shake off the dust of your feet (Matt. 10:14).

28. I send you forth as sheep in the midst of wolves: be ye therefore wise as serpents, and harmless as doves (Matt. 10:16).

29. But beware of men: for they will deliver you up. . . . When they deliver you up, take no thought how or what ye shall speak: for it shall be given you in that same hour what ye shall speak (Matt. 10:17-19).

30. Ye shall be hated of all men for my name's sake: but he that endureth to the end shall be saved (Matt. 10:22).

31. Fear not them which kill the body, but are not able to kill the soul: but rather fear him which is able to destroy both soul and body in hell (Matt. 10:28).

32. Whosoever therefore shall confess me before men, him will I confess also before my Father which is in heaven (Matt. 10:32).

33. He that loveth father or mother more than me is not worthy of me (Matt. 10:37).

34. He that receiveth you receiveth me (Matt. 10:40).

35. Whosoever shall give to drink unto one of these little ones a cup of cold water only in the name of a disciple, verily I say unto you, he shall in no wise lose his reward (Matt. 10:42).

36. Give ye them to eat (Matt. 14:16).

37. Whoso shall receive one such little child in my name receiveth me (Matt. 18:5).

38. Whoso shall offend one of these little ones which believe in me, it were better that a millstone were hanged about his neck, and that he were drowned in the depth of the sea (Matt. 18:6).

39. If thy brother shall trespass against thee, go and tell him his fault between thee and him alone: if he shall hear thee, thou has gained thy brother. But if he will not hear thee, then take with thee one or two more, that in the mouth of two or three witnesses every word may be established. And if he shall neglect to hear them, tell it to the church: but if he neglect to hear the church, let him be unto thee as a heathen man and a publican (Matt. 18:15-17).

40. If two of you shall agree on earth as touching anything that they shall ask, it shall be done for them of my Father which is in heaven (Matt. 18:19).

41. Lord, how oft shall my brother sin against me, and I forgive him? till seven times? Jesus saith unto him, I say not unto thee, Until seven times: but, Until seventy times seven (Matt. 18:21, 22).

42. His lord was wroth, and delivered him to the tormentors, till he should pay all that was due unto him. So likewise shall my heavenly Father do also unto you, if ye from your hearts forgive not every one his brother their trespasses (Matt. 18:34, 35).

43. All men cannot receive this saying, save they to whom it is given. For there are some eunuchs, which were so born from their mother's womb: and there are some eunuchs, which were made eunuchs of men: and there be eunuchs for the kingdom of heaven's sake. He that is able to receive it, let him receive it (Matt. 19:11, 12).

44. Suffer little children, and forbid them not, to come unto me: for of such is the kingdom of heaven (Matt. 19:14, 15).

45. Every one that hath forsaken houses, or brethren, or sisters, or father, or mother, or wife, or children, or lands, for my name's sake, shall receive an hundredfold, and shall inherit everlasting life (Matt. 19:29).

46. Whosoever will be chief among you, let him be your servant: even as the Son of man came not to be ministered unto, but to minister, and to give his life a ransom for many (Matt. 20:27, 28).

47. Render unto Caesar the things which are Caesar's; and unto God the things that are God's (Matt. 22:21).

48. In the resurrection they neither marry, nor are given in marriage, but are as the angels of God in heaven (Matt. 22:30).

49. Thou shalt love thy neighbour as thyself (Matt. 22:39).

50. Whosoever shall exalt himself shall be abased; and he that shall humble himself shall be exalted (Matt. 23:12).

51. Two shall be in the field; the one shall be taken, and the other left. Two women shall be grinding at the mill; the one shall be taken, and the other left (Matt. 24:40, 41).

52. Inasmuch as ye have done it unto one of the least of these my brethren, ye have done it unto me (Matt. 25:40).

53. Put up again thy sword into his place: for all they that take the sword shall perish with the sword (Matt. 26:52).

54. Go tell my brethren that they go into Galilee, and there shall they see me (Matt. 28:10).

55. Go ye therefore, and teach all nations, baptizing them in the name of the Father, and of the Son, and of the Holy Ghost: teaching them to observe all things whatsoever I have commanded you (Matt. 28:19, 20).

56. Go home to thy friends, and tell them how great things the

Lord hath done for thee, and hath had compassion on thee (Mark 5:19).

57. A prophet is not without honour, but in his own country, and among his own kin, and in his own house (Mark 6:4).

58. Master, we saw one casting out devils in thy name, and he followeth not us: and we forbade him, because he followeth not us. But Jesus said, Forbid him not: for there is no man which shall do a miracle in my name, that can lightly speak evil of me (Mark 9:38, 39).

59. Sell whatsoever thou hast, and give to the poor (Mark 10:21).

60. Beware of the scribes, which love to go in long clothing, and love salutations in the marketplaces, and the chief seats in the synagogues, and the uppermost rooms at feasts: which devour widows' houses, and for a pretence make long prayers: these shall receive greater damnation (Mark 12:38-40).

61. When Simon Peter saw it, he fell down at Jesus' knees, saying, Depart from me; for I am a sinful man, O Lord. . . . And Jesus said unto Simon, Fear not; from henceforth thou shalt catch men (Luke 5:8-10).

62. I will ask you one thing; Is it lawful on the sabbath days to do good, or to do evil? to save life, or to destroy it? (Luke 6:9).

63. Woe unto you, when all men shall speak well of you! for so did their fathers to the false prophets (Luke 6:26).

64. Love your enemies, do good to them which hate you, bless them that curse you, and pray for them which despitefully use you (Luke 6:27, 28).

65. If ye lend to them of whom ye hope to receive, what thank have ye? for sinners also lend to sinners, to receive as much again. But love ye your enemies, and do good, and lend, hoping for nothing again; and your reward shall be great, and ye shall be the children of the Highest: for he is kind unto the unthankful and to the evil (Luke 6:34, 35).

66. Be ye therefore merciful, as your Father also is merciful (Luke 6:36).

67. Give, and it shall be given unto you; good measure, pressed down, and shaken together, and running over, shall men give into your bosom. For with the same measure that ye mete withal it shall be measured to you again (Luke 6:38).

68. Seest thou this woman? I entered into thine house, thou gavest me no water for my feet: but she hath washed my feet with tears, and wiped them with the hairs of her head. Thou gavest me no kiss: but this woman since the time I came in

hath not ceased to kiss my feet. My head with oil thou didst not anoint: but this woman hath anointed my feet with ointment. Wherefore I say unto thee, Her sins, which are many, are forgiven (Luke 7:44-47).

69. Which now of these three, thinkest thou, was neighbour unto him that fell among the thieves? And he said, He that showed mercy on him. Then Jesus said unto him, Go, and do thou likewise (Luke 10:36, 37).

70. Take heed, and beware of covetousness: for a man's life consisteth not in the abundance of the things which he possesseth (Luke 12:15).

71. When thou art bidden of any man to a wedding, sit not down in the highest room: lest a more honourable man than thou be bidden of him; and he that bade thee and him come and say to thee, Give this man place; and thou begin with shame to take the lowest room. But when thou art bidden, go and sit down in the lowest room; that when he that bade thee cometh, he may say unto thee, Friend, go up higher (Luke 14:8-10).

72. When thou makest a feast, call the poor, the maimed, the lame, the blind: and thou shalt be blessed; for they cannot recompense thee: for thou shalt be recompensed at the resurrection of the just (Luke 14:13, 14).

73. Son, thou art ever with me, and all that I have is thine. It was meet that we should make merry, and be glad: for this thy brother was dead, and is alive again; and was lost, and is found (Luke 15:31, 32).

74. If thy brother trespass against thee, rebuke him; and if he repent, forgive him (Luke 17:3).

75. Whether is greater, he that sitteth at meat, or he that serveth? is not he that sitteth at meat? but I am among you as he that serveth (Luke 22:27).

76. If I then, your Lord and Master, have washed your feet; ye also ought to wash one another's feet (John 13:14).

77. By this shall all men know that ye are my disciples, if ye have love one to another (John 13:35).

78. Greater love hath no man than this, that a man lay down his life for his friends. Ye are my friends, if ye do whatsoever I command you (John 15:13, 14).

79. Whosoever sins ye remit, they are remitted unto them: and whosoever sins ye retain, they are retained (John 20:23).

80. Jesus saith to Simon Peter, Simon, son of Jonas, lovest thou

me more than these? He saith unto him, Yea, Lord; thou knowest that I love thee. He saith unto him, Feed my lambs (John 21:15).

9. Guidelines from the Early Church Concerning Relationships

1. Thou, Lord, which knowest the hearts of all men, show whether of these two thou hast chosen, that he may take part of this ministry and apostleship. . . . And they gave forth their lots; and the lot fell upon Matthias; and he was numbered with the eleven apostles (Acts 1:24-26).
2. All that believed were together, and had all things common; and sold their possessions and goods, and parted them to all men, as every man had need (Acts 2:44, 45).
3. Silver and gold have I none; but such as I have give I thee; In the name of Jesus Christ of Nazareth rise up and walk (Acts 3:6).
4. And the multitude of them that believed were of one heart and of one soul: neither said any of them that aught of the things which he possessed was his own; but they had all things common. . . . Neither was there any among them that lacked: for as many as were possessors of lands or houses sold them, and brought the prices of the things that were sold, and laid them down at the apostles' feet: and distribution was made unto every man according as he had need (Acts 4:32-35).
5. Their widows were neglected in the daily ministration. Then the twelve called the multitude of the disciples unto them, and said, It is not reason that we should leave the word of God, and serve tables. Wherefore, brethren, look ye out seven men of honest report, full of the Holy Ghost and wisdom, whom we may appoint over this business (Acts 6:1-3).
6. He kneeled down, and cried with a loud voice, Lord, lay not this sin to their charge. And when he had said this, he fell asleep (Acts 7:60).
7. What God hath cleansed, that call not thou common (Acts 10:15).
8. Ye know how that it is an unlawful thing for a man that is a Jew to keep company, or come unto one of another nation; but God hath showed me that I should not call any man common or unclean (Acts 10:28).

9. Of a truth I perceive that God is no respecter of persons: but in every nation he that feareth him, and worketh righteousness, is accepted with him (Acts 10:34, 35).

10. Can any man forbid water, that these should not be baptized, which have received the Holy Ghost as well as we? And he commanded them to be baptized in the name of the Lord (Acts 10:47, 48).

11. As God gave them the like gift as he did unto us, who believed on the Lord Jesus Christ; what was I, that I could withstand God? (Acts 11:17).

12. When they were come, and had gathered the church together, they rehearsed all that God had done with them and how he had opened the door of faith unto the Gentiles (Acts 14:27).

13. My sentence is, that we trouble not them, which from among the Gentiles are turned to God: but that wo write unto them . . . (Acts 15:19, 20).

14. When they had read, they rejoiced for the consolation. And Judas and Silas, being prophets also themselves, exhorted the brethren with many words and confirmed them (Acts 15:31, 32).

15. Let us go again and visit our brethren in every city where we have preached the word of the Lord, and see how they do (Acts 15:36).

16. They spake unto him the word of the Lord, and to all that were in his house, and he took them the same hour of that night, and washed their stripes; and was baptized, he and all his, straightway (Acts 16:32, 33).

17. I kept back nothing that was profitable unto you, but have showed you, and have taught you publicly, and from house to house (Acts 20:20).

18. I have showed you all things, how that so labouring ye ought to support the weak, and to remember the words of the Lord Jesus, how he said, It is more blessed to give than to receive (Acts 20:35).

19. Then said Paul unto him, God shall smite thee, thou whited wall: for sittest thou to judge me after the law, and commandest me to be smitten contrary to the law? And they that stood by said, Revilest thou God's high priest? Then said Paul, I wist not, brethren, that he was the high priest: for it is written, Thou shalt not speak evil of the ruler of thy people (Acts 23:3-5).

20. Paul besought them all to take meat, saying, This is the four-teenth day that ye have tarried and continued fasting, hav-ing taken nothing. Wherefore I pray you to take some meat: for this is for your health: for there shall not a hair fall from the head of any of you (Acts 27:33, 34).

21. Paul dwelt two whole years in his own hired house, and re-ceived all that came in unto him (Acts 28:30).

10. Paul's Examples and Exhortations About How to Treat Others

1. I thank my God through Jesus Christ for you all, that your faith is spoken of throughout the whole world. For God is my witness, whom I serve with my spirit in the gospel of his Son, that without ceasing I make mention of you always in my prayers (Rom. 1:8, 9).

2. Thou art inexcusable, O man, whosoever thou art that judg-est: for wherein thou judgest another, thou condemnest thy-self; for thou that judgest doest the same things (Rom. 2:1).

3. Thou therefore which teachest another, teachest thou not thyself? (Rom. 2:21).

4. I could wish that myself were accursed from Christ for my brethren, my kinsmen according to the flesh (Rom. 9:3).

5. Brethren, my heart's desire and prayer to God for Israel is, that they might be saved (Rom. 10:1).

6. If some of the branches be broken off, and thou, being a wild olive tree, wert grafted in among them, and with them par-takest of the root and the fatness of the olive tree; boast not against the branches (Rom. 11:17, 18).

7. Be kindly affectioned one to another with brotherly love; in honour preferring one another (Rom. 12:10).

8. Distributing to the necessity of the saints; given to hospital-ity. Bless them which persecute you: bless, and curse not. Rejoice with them that do rejoice, and weep with them that weep. Be of the same mind one toward another. Mind not high things, but condescend to men of low estate. Be not wise in your own conceits. Recompense to no man evil for evil. Provide things honest in the sight of all men. If it be possible, as much as lieth in you, live peaceably with all men. Dearly beloved, avenge not yourselves, but rather give place unto wrath: for it is written, Vengeance is mine; I will repay, saith the Lord. Therefore if thine enemy hunger, feed him; if he

St. Paul Preaching to the Thessalonians

thirst, give him drink: for in so doing thou shalt heap coals of
fire on his head (Rom. 12:13-20).

9. Let every soul be subject unto the higher powers. For there is
   no power but of God: the powers that be are ordained of God.
   Whosoever therefore resisteth the power, resisteth the ordinance of God: and they that resist shall receive to themselves
   damnation (Rom. 13:1, 2).

10. Pay ye tribute also: for they are God's ministers, attending

continually upon this very thing. Render therefore to all their dues: tribute to whom tribute is due; custom to whom custom; fear to whom fear; honour to whom honour (Rom. 13:6, 7).

11. Owe no man any thing, but to love one another: for he that loveth another hath fulfilled the law (Rom. 13:8).

12. If there be any other commandment, it is briefly comprehended in this saying, namely, Thou shalt love thy neighbour as thyself. Love worketh no ill to his neighbour: therefore love is the fulfilling of the law (Rom. 13:9, 10).

13. Him that is weak in the faith receive ye, but not to doubtful disputations. For one believeth that he may eat all things: another, who is weak, eateth herbs. Let not him that eateth despise him that eateth not; and let not him which eateth not judge him that eateth: for God hath received him (Rom. 14:1, 2).

14. Who art thou that judgest another man's servant? to his own master he standeth or falleth (Rom. 14:4).

15. Why dost thou judge thy brother? or why dost thou set at nought thy brother? for we shall all stand before the judgment seat of Christ (Rom. 14:10).

16. Let us not therefore judge one another any more: but judge this rather, that no man put a stumblingblock or an occasion to fall in his brother's way (Rom. 14:13).

17. If thy brother be grieved with thy meat, now walkest thou not charitably. Destroy not him with thy meat, for whom Christ died (Rom. 14:15).

18. Let us therefore follow after the things which make for peace, and things wherewith one may edify another. . . . It is good neither to eat flesh, nor to drink wine, nor any thing whereby thy brother stumbleth, or is offended, or is made weak (Rom. 14:19-21).

19. We then that are strong ought to bear the infirmities of the weak, and not to please ourselves. Let every one of us please his neighbour for his good to edification. For even Christ pleased not himself (Rom. 15:1-3).

20. The God of patience and consolation grant you to be likeminded one toward another according to Christ Jesus: that ye may with one mind and one mouth glorify God, even the Father of our Lord Jesus Christ. Wherefore receive ye one another, as Christ also received us to the glory of God (Rom. 15:5-7).

21. I have strived to preach the gospel, not where Christ was named, lest I should build upon another man's foundation (Rom. 15:20).

22. Receive her in the Lord, as becometh saints, and ye assist her in whatsoever business she hath need of you: for she hath been a succourer of many, and of myself also (Rom. 16:2).

23. Greet Priscilla and Aquila my helpers in Christ Jesus: who have for my life laid down their own necks (Rom. 16:3, 4).

24. Greet Mary, who bestowed much labour on us. . . . Salute Urbane, our helper in Christ. . . . Salute Tryphaena and Tryphosa, who labour in the Lord. Salute the beloved Persis, which laboured much in the Lord (Rom. 16:6-12).

25. Salute one another with a holy kiss (Rom. 16:16).

26. Mark them which cause divisions and offences contrary to the doctrine which ye have learned; and avoid them (Rom. 16:17).

27. I beseech you, brethren, by the name of our Lord Jesus Christ, that ye all speak the same thing, and that there be no divisions among you; but that ye be perfectly joined together in the same mind and in the same judgment (1 Cor. 1:10).

28. Ye are yet carnal: for whereas there is among you envying, strife, and divisions, are ye not carnal, and walk as men? For while one saith, I am of Paul; and another, I am of Apollos; are ye not carnal? (1 Cor. 3:3, 4).

29. We are labourers together with God (1 Cor. 3:9).

30. We both hunger, and thirst, and are naked, and are buffeted, and have no certain dwelling place; and labour, working with our own hands: being reviled, we bless, being persecuted, we suffer it: being defamed, we entreat (1 Cor. 4:11-13).

31. In the name of the Lord Jesus Christ, when ye are gathered together, and my spirit, with the power of our Lord Jesus Christ, to deliver such an one unto Satan for the destruction of the flesh, that the spirit may be saved in the day of the Lord Jesus (1 Cor. 5:4, 5).

32. I wrote unto you in an epistle not to company with fornicators: yet not altogether with the fornicators of this world, or with the covetous, or extortioners, or with idolaters; for then must ye needs go out of the world. But now I have written unto you not to keep company, if any man that is called a brother be a fornicator, or covetous, or an idolater, or a railer, or a drunkard, or an extortioner; with such a one, no, not to eat. For what have I to do to judge them also that are with-

out? do not ye judge them that are within? But them that are without God judgeth. Therefore put away from among yourselves that wicked person (1 Cor. 5:9-13).

33. Dare any of you, having a matter against another, go to law before the unjust, and not before the saints? Do ye not know that the saints shall judge the world? and if the world shall be judged by you, are ye unworthy to judge the smallest matters? Know ye not that we shall judge angels? how much more things that pertain to this life? (1 Cor. 6:1-3).

34. Now therefore there is utterly a fault among you, because ye go to law one with another. Why do ye not rather take wrong? why do ye not rather suffer yourselves to be defrauded? (1 Cor. 6:7).

35. Take heed lest by any means this liberty of yours become a stumblingblock to them that are weak (1 Cor. 8:9).

36. If meat make my brother to offend, I will eat no flesh while the world standeth, lest I make my brother to offend (1 Cor. 8:13).

37. Let no man seek his own, but every man another's wealth (1 Cor. 10:24).

38. If any of them that believe not bid you to a feast, and ye be disposed to go; whatsoever is set before you, eat, asking no question for conscience sake. But if any man say unto you, This is offered in sacrifice unto idols, eat not for his sake that showed it (1 Cor. 10:27, 28).

39. Give none offence, neither to the Jews, nor to the Gentiles, nor to the church of God: even as I please all men in all things, not seeking mine own profit, but the profit of many, that they may be saved (1 Cor. 10:32, 33).

40. The body is not one member, but many. If the foot shall say, Because I am not the hand, I am not of the body; is it therefore not of the body? . . . But now hath God set the members every one of them in the body, as it hath pleased him (1 Cor. 12:14-18).

41. There should be no schism in the body; but that the members should have the same care one for another. And whether one member suffer, all the members suffer with it; or one member be honoured, all the members rejoice with it (1 Cor. 12:25, 26).

42. Though I bestow all my goods to feed the poor, and though I give my body to be burned, and have not charity, it profiteth me nothing (1 Cor. 13:3).

43. Concerning the collection for the saints, as I have given order to the churches of Galatia, even so do ye. Upon the first day of the week let every one of you lay by him in store, as God hath prospered him (1 Cor. 16:1, 2).
44. Submit yourselves unto such, and to every one that helpeth with us, and laboureth (1 Cor. 16:16).
45. We faint not; but have renounced the hidden things of dishonesty, not walking in craftiness, nor handling the word of God deceitfully; but by manifestation of the truth commending ourselves to every man's conscience in the sight of God (2 Cor. 4:1, 2).
46. Giving no offence in any thing, that the ministry be not blamed (2 Cor. 6:3).
47. Providing for honest things, not only in the sight of the Lord, but also in sight of men (2 Cor. 8:21).
48. Every man according as he purposeth in his heart, so let him give; not grudgingly, or of necessity: for God loveth a cheerful giver (2 Cor. 9:7).
49. Do ye look on things after the outward appearance? (2 Cor. 10:7).
50. They would that we should remember the poor; the same which I also was forward to do (Gal. 2:10).
51. There is neither Jew nor Greek, there is neither bond nor free, there is neither male nor female: for ye are all one in Christ Jesus (Gal. 3:28).
52. If ye bite and devour one another, take heed that ye be not consumed one of another (Gal. 5:15).
53. Let us not be desirous of vain glory, provoking one another, envying one another (Gal. 5:26).
54. If a man be overtaken in a fault, ye which are spiritual, restore such an one in the spirit of meekness; considering thyself, lest thou also be tempted. Bear ye one another's burdens, and so fulfil the law of Christ (Gal. 6:1, 2).
55. As we have therefore opportunity, let us do good unto all men, especially unto them who are of the household of faith (Gal. 6:10).
56. Walk worthy of the vocation wherewith ye are called, with all lowliness and meekness, with long-suffering, forbearing one another in love; endeavoring to keep the unity of the Spirit in the bond of peace (Eph. 4:1-3).
57. Putting away lying, speak every man truth with his neighbour: for we are members one of another. Be ye angry, and

sin not: let not the sun go down upon your wrath (Eph. 4:25, 26).

58. Let him that stole steal no more: but rather let him labour, working with his hands the thing which is good, that he may have to give to him that needeth. Let no corrupt communication proceed out of your mouth, but that which is good to the use of edifying, that it may minister grace unto the hearers (Eph. 4:28, 29).

59. Be ye kind one to another, tenderhearted, forgiving one another, even as God for Christ's sake hath forgiven you (Eph. 4:32).

60. Servants, be obedient to them that are your masters according to the flesh, with singleness of your heart, as unto Christ; not with eyeservice, as menpleasers; but as the servants of Christ, doing the will of God from the heart; with good will doing service, as to the Lord, and not to men (Eph. 6:5-7).

61. Ye masters, do the same things unto them, forbearing threatening: knowing that your Master also is in heaven (Eph. 6:9).

62. Stand fast in one spirit, with one mind striving together for the faith of the gospel; and in nothing terrified by your adversaries (Phil. 1:27, 28).

63. Let nothing be done through strife or vainglory; but in lowliness of mind let each esteem other better than themselves. Look not every man on his own things, but every man also on the things of others (Phil. 2:3, 4).

64. Beware lest any man spoil you through philosophy and vain deceit, after the tradition of men, after the rudiments of the world, and not after Christ (Col. 2:8).

65. Lie not one to another, seeing that ye have put off the old man with his deeds; . . . Forbearing one another, and forgiving one another, if any man have a quarrel against any: even as Christ forgave you, so also do ye (Col. 3:9-13).

66. No man go beyond and defraud his brother in any matter: because that the Lord is the avenger of all such, as we also have forewarned you and testified (1 Thess. 4:6).

67. We exhort you, brethren, warn them that are unruly, comfort the feebleminded, support the weak, be patient toward all men. See that none render evil for evil unto any man; but ever follow that which is good, both among yourselves, and to all men (1 Thess. 5:14, 15).

68. If any man obey not our word by this epistle, note that man, and have no company with him, that he may be ashamed.

Yet count him not as an enemy, but admonish him as a brother (2 Thess. 3:14, 15).

69. Let no man despise thy youth; but be thou an example of the believers, in word, in conversation, in charity, in spirit, in faith, in purity (1 Tim. 4:12).

70. Rebuke not an elder, but entreat him as a father; and the younger men as brethren; the elder women as mothers; the younger as sisters, with all purity. Honour widows that are widows indeed (1 Tim. 5:1-3).

71. Them that sin rebuke before all, that others also may fear. I charge thee before God, and the Lord Jesus Christ, and the elect angels, that thou observe these things without preferring one before another, doing nothing by partiality. Lay hands suddenly on no man, neither be partaker of other men's sins: keep thyself pure (1 Tim. 5:20-22).

72. Charge them that are rich in this world, that they be not high-minded, nor trust in uncertain riches, but in the living God, who giveth us richly all things to enjoy; that they do good, that they be rich in good works, ready to distribute, willing to communicate; laying up in store for themselves a good foundation against the time to come, that they may lay hold on eternal life (1 Tim. 6:17-19).

73. The servant of the Lord must not strive; but be gentle unto all men, apt to teach, patient, in meekness instructing those that oppose themselves; if God peradventure will give them repentance to the acknowledging of the truth (2 Tim. 2:24, 25).

74. A man that is an heretic after the first and second admonition reject; knowing that he that is such is subverted, and sinneth, being condemned of himself (Titus 3:10, 11).

11. Exhortations from Other Apostles About How to Treat Others

1. Pure religion and undefiled before God and the Father is this, To visit the fatherless and the widows in their affliction, and to keep himself unspotted from the world (James 1:27).

2. If ye have respect to persons, ye commit sin, and are convinced of the law as transgressors (James 2:9).

3. If a brother or sister be naked, and destitute of daily food, and one of you say unto them, Depart in peace, be ye warmed and filled; notwithstanding ye give them not those

things which are needful to the body; what doth it profit?
(James 2:15, 16).

4. Ye adulterers and adulteresses, know ye not that the friendship of the world is enmity with God? whosoever therefore will be a friend of the world is the enemy of God (James 4:4).

5. Speak not evil one of another, brethren. He that speaketh evil of his brother and judgeth his brother, speaketh evil of the law, and judgeth the law (James 4:11).

6. Grudge not one against another, brethren, lest ye be condemned: behold, the judge standeth before the door (James 5:9).

7. Is any sick among you? let him call for the elders of the church; and let them pray over him, anointing him with oil in the name of the Lord (James 5:14).

8. Confess your faults one to another, and pray for one another, that ye may be healed (James 5:16).

9. Seeing ye have purified your souls in obeying the truth through the Spirit unto unfeigned love of the brethren, see that ye love one another with a pure heart fervently (1 Pet. 1:22).

10. Having your conversation honest among the Gentiles: that, whereas they speak against you as evildoers, they may by your good works, which they shall behold, glorify God in the day of visitation. Submit yourselves to every ordinance of man for the Lord's sake: whether it be to the king, as supreme: or unto governors, as unto them that are sent by him for the punishment of evildoers, and for the praise of them that do well (1 Pet. 2:12-14).

11. Honour all men. Love the brotherhood. Fear God. Honour the king (1 Pet. 2:17).

12. Servants, be subject to your masters with all fear; not only to the good and gentle, but also the froward. For this is thankworthy, if a man for conscience toward God endure grief, suffering wrongfully. For what glory is it, if, when ye be buffetted for your faults, ye shall take it patiently? but if, when ye do well, and suffer for it, ye take it patiently, this is acceptable with God (1 Pet. 2:18-20).

13. Be ye all of one mind, having compassion one of another, love as brethren, be pitiful, be courteous: not rendering evil for evil, or railing for railing: but contrariwise blessing; knowing that ye are thereunto called, that ye should inherit a blessing (1 Pet. 3:8, 9).

14. If ye suffer for righteousness' sake, happy are ye: and be not afraid of their terror, neither be troubled; but sanctify the Lord God in your hearts: and be ready to give an answer to every man that asketh you a reason of the hope that is in you with meekness and fear (1 Pet. 3:14, 15).

15. Above all things have fervent charity among yourselves: for charity shall cover a multitude of sins. Use hospitality one to another without grudging. As every man hath received the gift, even so minister the same one to another, as good stewards of the manifold grace of God (1 Pet. 4:8-10).

16. Greet ye one another with a kiss of charity (1 Pet. 5:14).

17. Add to your faith virtue; and to virtue knowledge; and to knowledge temperance; and to temperance patience; and to patience godliness; and to godliness brotherly kindness; and to brotherly kindness charity (2 Pet. 1:5-7).

18. He that saith he is in the light, and hateth his brother, is in darkness even until now. He that loveth his brother abideth in the light, and there is none occasion of stumbling in him. But he that hateth his brother is in darkness, and walketh in darkness, and knoweth not whither he goeth, because that darkness hath blinded his eyes (1 John 2:9-11).

19. This is the message that ye heard from the beginning, that we should love one another (1 John 3:11).

20. We know that we have passed from death unto life, because we love the brethren. He that loveth not his brother abideth in death. Whosoever hateth his brother is a murderer: and ye know that no murderer hath eternal life abiding in him. Hereby perceive we the love of God, because he laid down his life for us: and we ought to lay down our lives for the brethren. But whoso hath this world's good, and seeth his brother have need, and shutteth up his bowels of compassion from him, how dwelleth the love of God in him? My little children, let us not love in word, neither in tongue; but in deed and in truth (1 John 3:14-18).

21. This is his commandment, That we should believe on the name of his Son Jesus Christ, and love one another, as he gave us commandment (1 John 3:23).

22. Beloved, let us love one another: for love is of God; and every one that loveth is born of God, and knoweth God. He that loveth not knoweth not God; for God is love (1 John 4:7, 8).

23. If God so loved us, we ought also to love one another. No man hath seen God at any time. If we love one another, God

dwelleth in us, and his love is perfected in us (1 John 4:11, 12).

24. If a man say, I love God, and hateth his brother, he is a liar: for he that loveth not his brother whom he hath seen, how can he love God whom he hath not seen? And this commandment have we from him, That he who loveth God love his brother also (1 John 4:20, 21).

25. If any man see his brother sin a sin which is not unto death, he shall ask, and he shall give him life for them that sin not unto death. There is a sin unto death: I do not say that he shall pray for it (1 John 5:16).

26. I beseech thee, lady, not as though I wrote a new commandment unto thee, but that which we had from the beginning, that we love one another. And this is love, that we walk after his commandments (2 John 5, 6).

27. If there come any unto you, and bring not this doctrine, receive him not into your house, neither bid him God speed; for he that biddeth him God speed is partaker of his evil deeds (2 John 10, 11).

28. Keep yourselves in the love of God, looking for the mercy of our Lord Jesus Christ unto eternal life. And of some have compassion, making a difference: and others save with fear, pulling them out of the fire; hating even the garment spotted by the flesh (Jude 21-23).

29. I know thy works, and thy labour, and thy patience, and how thou canst not bear them which are evil: and thou hast tried them which say they are apostles, and are not, and hast found them liars (Rev. 2:2).

12. Eight Warnings Concerning Evil Spirits

1. When the unclean spirit is gone out of a man, he walketh through dry places, seeking rest, and findeth none. Then he saith, I will return into my house from whence I came out; and when he is come, he findeth it empty, swept, and garnished. Then goeth he, and taketh with himself seven other spirits more wicked than himself, and they enter in and dwell there: and the last state of that man is worse than the first (Matt. 12:43-45).

2. Neither give place to the devil (Eph. 4:27).

3. Put on the whole armour of God, that ye may be able to stand against the wiles of the devil (Eph. 6:11).

4. Resist the devil, and he will flee from you (James 4:7).

5. Be sober, be vigilant; because your adversary the devil, as a roaring lion, walketh about, seeking whom he may devour: whom resist, steadfast in the faith (1 Pet. 5:8, 9).

6. Believe not every spirit, but try the spirits whether they are of God: because many false prophets are gone out into the world. Hereby know ye the Spirit of God: Every spirit that confesseth that Jesus Christ is come in the flesh is of God: and every spirit that confesseth not that Jesus Christ is come in the flesh is not of God: and this is that spirit of antichrist, whereof ye have heard that it should come; and even now already is it in the world (1 John 4:1-3).

7. If any man worship the beast and his image, and receive his mark in his forehead, or in his hand, the same shall drink of the wine of the wrath of God, which is poured out without mixture into the cup of his indignation; and he shall be tormented with fire and brimstone in the presence of the holy angels, and in the presence of the Lamb: and the smoke of their torment ascendeth up forever and ever: and they have no rest day nor night, who worship the beast and his image, and whosoever receiveth the mark of his name (Rev. 14:9-11).

8. They are the spirits of devils, working miracles, which go forth unto the kings of the earth and of the whole world, to gather them to the battle of that great day of God Almighty (Rev. 16:14).

13. Principles for Good Family Relationships

1. Let every man have his own wife, and let every women have her own husband. Let the husband render unto the wife due benevolence: and likewise also the wife unto the husband. The wife hath not power of her own body, but the husband: and likewise also the husband hath not power of his own body, but the wife. Defraud ye not one the other, except it be with consent for a time, that ye may give yourselves to fasting and prayer; and come together again, that Satan tempt you not for your incontinency (1 Cor. 7:2-5).

2. Unto the married I command, yet not I, but the Lord, Let not the wife depart from her husband: but and if she depart, let her remain unmarried, or be reconciled to her husband: and let not the husband put away his wife. . . . And the woman

The Marriage in Cana

which hath an husband that believeth not, and if he be pleased to dwell with her, let her not leave him. For the unbelieving husband is sanctified by the wife, and the unbelieving wife is sanctified by the husband: else were your children unclean; but now are they holy. But if the unbelieving depart, let him depart. A brother or a sister is not under bondage in such cases: but God hath called us to peace (1 Cor. 7:10-15).

3. I would have you know, that the head of every man is Christ; and the head of the woman is the man; and the head of Christ is God (1 Cor. 11:3).

4. Be ye not unequally yoked together with unbelievers: for what fellowship hath righteousness with unrighteousness: and what communion hath light with darkness? (2 Cor. 6:14).

5. The children ought not to lay up for the parents, but the parents for the children (2 Cor. 12:14).

6. Children, obey your parents in the Lord: for this is right. Honour thy father and mother; which is the first commandment with promise; that it may be well with thee, and thou mayest live long on the earth. And, ye fathers, provoke not your children to wrath: but bring them up in the nurture and admonition of the Lord (Eph. 6:1-4).

7. Wives, submit yourselves unto your own husband, as it is fit in the Lord. Husbands, love your wives, and be not bitter against them. Children, obey your parents in all things: for this is well-pleasing unto the Lord. Fathers, provoke not your children to anger, lest they be discouraged (Col. 3:18-21).

8. If any provide not for his own, and specially for those of his own house, he hath denied the faith, and is worse than an infidel (1 Tim. 5:8).

9. I will therefore that the younger women marry, bear children, guide the house, give none occasion to the adversary to speak reproachfully (1 Tim. 5:14).

10. Ye wives, be in subjection to your own husbands; that, if any obey not the word, they also may without the word be won by the conversation of the wives; while they behold your chaste conversation coupled with fear. Whose adorning let it not be that outward adorning of plaiting the hair, and of wearing of gold, or of putting on of apparel; but let it be the hidden man of the heart, in that which is not corruptible, even the ornament of a meek and quiet spirit, which is in the sight of God of great price. For after this manner in the old time the holy women also, who trusted in God, adorned themselves, being in subjection unto their own husbands: even as Sarah obeyed Abraham calling him lord: whose daughters ye are, as long as ye do well, and are not afraid with any amazement. Likewise, ye husbands, dwell with them according to knowledge, giving honour unto the wife, as unto the weaker vessel, and as being heirs together of the grace of life; that your prayers be not hindered (1 Pet. 3:1-7).

14. Guidelines for Church Leaders

1. Look ye out among you seven men of honest report, full of the Holy Ghost and wisdom, whom we may appoint over this business. But we will give ourselves continually to prayer, and to the ministry of the word (Acts 6:3, 4).

2. If a man desire the office of a bishop, he desireth a good work. A bishop then must be blameless, the husband of one wife, vigilant, sober, of good behaviour, given to hospitality, apt to teach; not given to wine, no striker, not greedy of filthy lucre; but patient, not a brawler, not covetous; one that ruleth well his own house, having his children in subjection with all gravity; (for if a man know not how to rule his own house, how shall he take charge of the church of God?) Not a novice, lest being lifted up with pride he fall into the condemnation of the devil. Moreover he must have a good report of them which are without; lest he fall into the reproach and snare of the devil (1 Tim. 3:1-7).

3. Likewise must the deacons be grave, not doubletongued, not given to much wine, not greedy of filthy lucre; holding the mystery of the faith in a pure conscience. And let these also first be proved; then let them use the office of a deacon, being found blameless. Even so must their wives be grave, not slanderers, sober, faithful in all things. Let the deacons be the husbands of one wife, ruling their children and their own houses well. For they that have used the office of a deacon well purchase to themselves a good degree, and great boldness in the faith which is in Christ Jesus (1 Tim. 3:8-13).

4. Let the elders that rule well be counted worthy of double honour, especially they who labour in the word and doctrine. For the scripture saith, Thou shalt not muzzle the ox that treadeth out the corn. And, the labourer is worthy of his reward. Against an elder receive not an accusation, but before two or three witnesses. Them that sin rebuke before all, that others also may fear (1 Tim. 5:17-20).

5. If any be blameless, the husband of one wife, having faithful children not accused of riot or unruly. For a bishop must be blameless, as the steward of God; not self-willed, not soon angry, not given to wine, no striker, not given to filthy lucre; but a lover of hospitality, a lover of good men, sober, just, holy, temperate; holding fast the faithful word as he hath been taught, that he may be able by sound doctrine both to

exhort and to convince the gainsayers (Titus 1:6-9).

6. Is any among you afflicted? let him pray. Is any merry? let him sing psalms. Is any sick among you? let him call for the elders of the church; and let them pray over him, anointing him with oil in the name of the Lord (James 5:13, 14).

7. The elders which are among you I exhort, who am also an elder, and a witness of the sufferings of Christ, and also a partaker of the glory that shall be revealed: feed the flock of God which is among you, taking the oversight thereof, not by constraint, but willingly; nor for filthy lucre, but of a ready mind; neither as being lords over God's heritage, but being examples to the flock. And when the chief Shepherd shall appear, ye shall receive a crown of glory that fadeth not away (1 Pet. 5:1-4).

2

Promises

There are two old gospel hymns which talk about "standing on the promises" and "every promise in the Book is mine." What are those promises? Is access to the promises automatic or are there conditions to be met?

The lists in this chapter offer a total of 452 promises. Some are unconditional, requiring no action by the receiver. Many of them are conditional; a certain course of action is required in order to be included in the promise. And there are some warnings—not as enjoyable reading but nevertheless important.

Whether it's salvation, finances, blessings, health, peace, forgiveness, or a good night's sleep, He has given promises to cover all these and more.

Some of the promises in this chapter are arranged in tabular form, giving the promise, the condition and the scripture reference. A few scripture portions have been condensed or paraphrased slightly in the interest of abbreviation.

15. Twenty-three Unconditional New Testament Promises

1. For [Jesus'] yoke is easy, and [his] burden is light (Matt. 11:30).
2. With God all things are possible (Matt. 19:26).
3. All power is given to [Jesus] in heaven and in earth (Matt. 28:18).
4. God is no respecter of persons (Acts 10:34).
5. Every one of us shall give account of himself to God (Rom. 14:12).

6. Where the Spirit of the Lord is, there is liberty (2 Cor. 3:17).
7. Godly sorrow works repentance to salvation (2 Cor. 7:10).
8. [In Christ] there is neither Greek nor Jew, circumcision nor uncircumcision, Barbarian, Scythian, bond nor free (Col. 3:11).
9. [Jesus] abides faithful (2 Tim. 2:13).
10. The Lord knows them that are his (2 Tim. 2:19).
11. Jesus Christ [is] the same yesterday, and today, and forever (Heb. 13:8).
12. God does not tempt any man (James 1:13).
13. Every good gift and every perfect gift . . . comes from the Father (James 1:17).
14. [Jesus] is gone into heaven, and is on the right hand of God; angels and authorities and powers being made subject unto him (1 Pet. 3:22).
15. The Lord is not slack concerning his promise, . . . but is longsuffering toward us, not willing that any should perish, but that all should come to repentance (2 Pet. 3:9).
16. [Jesus] comes with clouds; and every eye shall see Him (Rev. 1:7).
17. Jesus is Lord of lords, and King of kings (Rev. 17:14).
18. Satan shall be bound a thousand years, and he will not be able to deceive the nations during that time (Rev. 20:1-3).
19. The devil will be cast into the lake of fire and brimstone and shall be tormented day and night forever (Rev. 20:7-10).
20. There shall not be anything that defiles, works abomination, or makes a lie in the New Jerusalem (Rev. 21:27).
21. There shall be no more curse in the New Jerusalem (Rev. 22:3).
22. There shall be no night in the New Jerusalem (Rev. 22:5).
23. The Lord God gives light in the New Jerusalem (Rev. 22:5).

16. Twenty-nine New Testament Promises About the Future

PROMISE	CONDITION	REFERENCE
1. You shall inherit the earth.	If you are meek.	Matt. 5:5
2. Great is your reward in heaven.	When men shall revile and persecute you for Jesus' sake.	Matt. 5:11, 12
3. The Son of Man shall reward every man.	According to his works.	Matt. 16:27
4. The end shall come.	When the gospel of the kingdom shall be preached in all the world for a witness to all nations.	Matt. 24:14
5. God shall make him ruler over all His goods.	Be a faithful and wise servant.	Matt. 24:45-47
6. He shall not lose his reward.	Whosoever shall give you a cup of water to drink in my name, because you belong to Christ.	Mark 9:41
7. Jesus shall change our vile body that it may be fashioned like unto His glorious body.	If we stand fast in the Lord.	Phil. 3:20, 21; 4:1
8. When Christ shall appear, you shall appear with Him in glory.	If you then be risen with Christ.	Col. 3:1, 4
9. The dead in Christ shall rise first. Then we which are alive and remain shall be caught up together with them in the clouds, to meet the Lord in the air: and so shall we ever be with the Lord.	If we believe that Jesus died and rose again.	1 Thess. 4:14-17

PROMISE	CONDITION	REFERENCE
10. There is laid up a crown of righteousness, which the Lord shall give at that day.	To all them that love His appearing.	2 Tim. 4:8
11. We may serve God acceptably.	With reverence and godly fear.	Heb. 12:28
12. He shall receive the crown of life.	The man that endures temptation and loves the Lord.	James 1:12
13. Elders (pastors) shall receive a crown of glory that fades not away.	Feed the flock of God among you, taking the oversight, not by constraint, but willingly; not for filthy lucre, but of a ready mind; neither as being lords over God's heritage, but being examples to the flock.	1 Pet. 5:1-4
14. When [Jesus] shall appear, we shall be like Him.	If we are sons of God.	1 John 3:2
15. We shall receive a full reward.	Confess that Jesus Christ is come in the flesh.	2 John 7, 8
16. [Jesus] will give to eat of the tree of life which is in the midst of the paradise of God.	To him that overcomes.	Rev. 2:7
17. [Jesus] will give you a crown of life.	Be faithful unto death.	Rev. 2:10
18. He shall not be hurt of the second death.	He that overcomes.	Rev. 2:11

PROMISE	CONDITION	REFERENCE
19. [Jesus] will give to eat of the hidden manna and will give a white stone, and in the stone a new name written, which no man knows save he that receives it.	To him that overcomes.	Rev. 2:17
20. [Jesus] will give to every one of you.	According to your works.	Rev. 2:23
21. [Jesus] will give power over the nations, and will give the morning star.	To him that overcomes and keeps [Jesus'] works to the end.	Rev. 2:26-28
22. He shall be clothed in white raiment, and [Jesus] will not blot out his name out of the book of life.	He that overcomes.	Rev. 3:5
23. [Jesus] will confess his name before the Father and before His angels.	He that overcomes.	Rev. 3:5
24. [Jesus] will make him a pillar in the temple of God and he shall go out no more: and [Jesus] will write upon him the name of God, and the name of the city of God, which is new Jerusalem. [Jesus] will write upon him [His] new name.	Him that overcomes.	Rev. 3:12
25. [Jesus] will grant to sit with Him in His throne.	To him that overcomes.	Rev. 3:21

PROMISE	CONDITION	REFERENCE
26. They are before the throne of God, and serve Him day and night in His temple: and He that sitteth on the throne shall dwell among them. They shall hunger no more; neither shall the sun light on them, nor any heat. For the Lamb which is in the midst of the throne shall feed them, and shall lead them unto living fountains of waters: and God shall wipe away all tears from their eyes.	They have washed their robes and made them white in the blood of the Lamb.	Rev. 7:14-17
27. They shall live and reign with Christ a thousand years.	They which had not worshiped the beast, neither his image, neither had received his mark.	Rev. 20:4
28. He shall inherit all things.	He that overcomes.	Rev. 21:7
29. They shall enter into the holy Jerusalem.	They which are written in the Lamb's book of life.	Rev. 21:10, 27

17. Twenty-nine New Testament Promises for Prosperity

PROMISE	CONDITION	REFERENCE
1. They shall be comforted.	They that mourn.	Matt. 5:4
2. They shall obtain mercy.	The merciful.	Matt. 5:7

PROMISE	CONDITION	REFERENCE
3. Your Father shall reward you openly.	When you give alms, let not your left hand know what your right hand does. When you pray, enter into your closet, and when you have shut your door, pray to your Father.	Matt. 6:3-6
4. What you shall eat, what you shall drink, what you shall put on.	Seek first the kingdom of God and His righteousness.	Matt. 6:25-33
5. It shall be given you.	Ask.	Matt. 7:7
6. You shall find.	Seek.	Matt. 7:7
7. It shall be opened unto you.	Knock.	Matt. 7:7
8. You shall say to this mountain, "Remove hence to yonder place," and it shall remove.	If you have faith as a grain of mustard seed.	Matt. 17:20
9. You shall receive a hundredfold and shall inherit everlasting life.	Everyone that has forsaken houses, or brethren, or sisters, or father, or mother, or wife, or children, or lands, for [Jesus] name's sake.	Matt. 19:29
10. You shall receive all things.	Whatever you shall ask in prayer, believing.	Matt. 21:22
11. He shall be exalted.	He that shall humble himself.	Matt. 23:12
12. Your reward shall be great, and you shall be the children of the Highest.	Love your enemies and do good, and lend, hoping for nothing again.	Luke 6:35

PROMISE	CONDITION	REFERENCE
13. It shall be given unto you; good measure, pressed down, and running over.	Give.	Luke 6:38
14. [Jesus] will do it.	Ask anything in [Jesus'] name.	John 14:14
15. You shall ask what you will, and it will be done unto you.	If you abide in me [Jesus] and my words abide in you.	John 15:7
16. You shall receive that your joy may be full.	Ask the Father in [Jesus'] name.	John 16:23, 24
17. You shall live.	If you through the Spirit do mortify the deeds of the body.	Rom. 8:13
18. All things work together for good.	To them that love God and are called according to His purpose.	Rom. 8:28
19. No one can be against you.	If God is for you.	Rom. 8:31
20. God is able to make all grace abound toward you; that you, having all sufficiency in all things, may abound in every good work.	Be a cheerful giver.	2 Cor. 9:7, 8
21. I can do all things.	Through Christ who strengthens me.	Phil. 4:13
22. You may know how you ought to answer every man.	Let your speech be always with grace, seasoned with salt.	Col. 4:6
23. You may walk honestly toward them that are without, and have lack of nothing.	Love one another; study to be quiet and to do your own business and to work with your own hands.	1 Thess. 4:9-12

60

PROMISE	CONDITION	REFERENCE
24. You may be perfect and entire, wanting nothing.	Let patience have her perfect work.	James 1:4
25. Wisdom shall be given.	Ask of God . . . in faith.	James 1:5, 6
26. The prayer of faith shall save the sick, and the Lord shall raise him up.	Call for the elders of the church; and let them pray over you, anointing you with oil in the name of the Lord. Confess your faults one to another and pray for one another, that you may be healed.	James 5:14-16
27. He will love life and see good days.	Let him refrain his tongue from evil, and his lips that they speak no guile. Let him eschew evil, and do good; let him seek peace, and ensue it.	1 Pet. 3:10
28. Whatsoever we ask, we receive of [God].	We keep His commandments and do those things that are pleasing in His sight.	1 John 3:22
29. [God] hears us, whatever we ask, and we know that we have the petitions that we desired of Him.	If we ask anything according to His will.	1 John 5:15

18. One Hundred Ten New Testament Promises for Spiritual Blessings

PROMISE	CONDITION	REFERENCE
1. Theirs is the kingdom of heaven.	The poor in spirit.	Matt. 5:3

PROMISE	CONDITION	REFERENCE
2. They shall be filled with righteousness.	They which do hunger and thirst after righteousness.	Matt. 5:6
3. They shall see God.	The pure in heart.	Matt. 5:8
4. They shall be called the children of God.	The peacemakers.	Matt. 5:9
5. Him will I confess before my Father which is in heaven.	Whosoever therefore shall confess me [Jesus] before men.	Matt. 10:32
6. You shall find rest unto your soul.	If you take my [Jesus'] yoke upon you and learn of me.	Matt. 11:29
7. The same is my brother, and sister, and mother.	Whosoever shall do the will of my Father.	Matt. 12:50
8. You shall enter into the kingdom of heaven.	Be converted and become as little children.	Matt. 18:3
9. Be greatest in the kingdom of heaven.	Humble yourself as a little child.	Matt. 18:4
10. You shall receive Jesus.	If you receive a little child in Jesus' name.	Matt. 18:5
11. Anything that they shall ask it shall be done for them of my Father which is in heaven.	If two of you shall agree on earth as touching anything.	Matt 18:19
12. There am I in the midst of them.	Where two or three are gathered in my [Jesus'] name.	Matt. 18:20
13. He shall be saved.	He that shall endure unto the end.	Matt. 24:13
14. You can minister unto Jesus.	If you minister unto one of the least of His brethren.	Matt. 25:40

PROMISE	CONDITION	REFERENCE
15. I [Jesus] am with you always, even unto the end of the world.	Go and teach all nations, baptizing them . . . teaching them to observe all things whatsoever I have commanded you.	Matt. 28:19, 20
16. You shall not be judged.	Judge not.	Luke 6:37
17. You shall not be condemned.	Condemn not.	Luke 6:37
18. You shall be forgiven.	Forgive.	Luke 6:37
19. Your heavenly Father shall give the Holy Spirit.	To them that ask Him.	Luke 11:13
20. The Son of Man shall confess [you] before the angels of God.	Whosoever shall confess me [Jesus] before men.	Luke 12:8
21. You shall have everlasting life.	Believe in the only begotten Son of God.	John 3:16
22. You shall have eternal life.	Eat my [Jesus'] flesh and drink my blood.	John 6:54
23. He shall not walk in darkness, but shall have the light of life.	He that follows [Jesus].	John 8:12
24. You shall know the truth, and the truth shall set you free.	If you continue in [Jesus'] word.	John 8:31, 32
25. You shall be free indeed.	If the Son therefore shall make you free.	John 8:36
26. Him will my [Jesus'] Father honour.	If any man serve me.	John 12:26
27. The works that I [Jesus] do shall he do also; and greater works than these shall he do also.	He that believeth on me.	John 14:12.

PROMISE	CONDITION	REFERENCE
28. I [Jesus] will pray the Father, and He shall give you another Comforter that He may abide with you forever.	Love me [Jesus] and keep my commandments.	John 14:15, 16
29. He that loves me [Jesus] shall be loved of my Father, and I will love him, and will manifest myself to him.	He that has my [Jesus] commandments and keeps them.	John 14:21
30. He brings forth much fruit.	He that abides in me [Jesus], and I in him.	John 15:5
31. You are [Jesus'] friend.	If you do whatsoever I [Jesus] command you.	John 15:14
32. You shall receive power.	After the Holy Ghost is come upon you.	Acts 1:8
33. You shall receive the gift of the Holy Ghost.	Repent and be baptized every one of you in the name of Jesus Christ for the remission of sins.	Acts 2:38
34. Receive remission of sins.	Believe in Jesus.	Acts 10:43
35. There is therefore now no condemnation.	To them which are in Christ Jesus, who walk not after the flesh, but after the Spirit.	Rom. 8:1
36. He that raised up Christ from the dead shall quicken your mortal body.	If the Spirit of Him who raised up Jesus from the dead dwell in you.	Rom. 8:11
37. They are the sons of God.	As many as are led by the Spirit of God.	Rom. 8:14
38. We are joint-heirs with Christ.	If we are children of God.	Rom. 8:17

PROMISE	CONDITION	REFERENCE
39. In all these things we are more than conquerors.	Through Him that loved us.	Rom. 8:37
40. Christ is the end of the law for righteousness.	To everyone that believes.	Rom. 10:4
41. You shall be saved.	If you shall confess with your mouth the Lord Jesus, and shall believe in your heart that God has raised Him from the dead.	Rom. 10:9
42. You shall have faith.	By hearing the Word of God.	Rom. 10:17
43. Preaching of the cross is the power of God.	To us who are saved.	1 Cor. 1:18
44. Jesus is made unto us wisdom, righteousness, sanctification, and redemption.	If you are in Christ Jesus.	1 Cor. 1:30
45. We can know the things that are freely given to us of God.	We have received the Spirit which is of God.	1 Cor. 2:12
46. You are one spirit with the Lord.	He that is joined unto the Lord.	1 Cor. 6:17
47. Your labor is not in vain.	In the Lord.	1 Cor. 15:58
48. He is a new creature; old things are passed away; behold, all things are become new.	If any man be in Christ.	2 Cor. 5:17
49. The weapons of our warfare are not carnal but mighty to the pulling down of strongholds.	Through God.	2 Cor. 10:4

PROMISE	CONDITION	REFERENCE
50. We are justified.	By the faith of Jesus Christ.	Gal. 2:16
51. You have put on Christ.	As many of you as have been baptized into Christ.	Gal. 3:27
52. You are Abraham's seed and an heir according to the promise.	If you are Christ's.	Gal. 3:29
53. You shall not fulfill the lust of the flesh.	Walk in the Spirit.	Gal. 5:16
54. You are not under the law.	If you are led of the Spirit.	Gal. 5:18
55. In due season we shall reap.	If we faint not.	Gal. 6:9
56. You were sealed with the Holy Spirit.	After you believed [in Jesus].	Eph. 1:13
57. We have access by one Spirit to the Father.	Through [Jesus].	Eph. 2:18
58. The peace of God, which passes all understanding, shall keep your heart and mind through Christ Jesus.	In everything by prayer and supplication with thanksgiving let your requests be made known unto God.	Phil. 4:6, 7
59. Jesus has reconciled you, in the body of His flesh through death, to present you holy and unblameable and unreprovable in His sight.	If you continue in the faith and are not moved away from the hope of the gospel.	Col. 1:21-23
60. You shall both save yourself and them that hear you.	Take heed to yourself and to the doctrine; continue in them.	1 Tim. 4:16

PROMISE	CONDITION	REFERENCE
61. We shall live with [Jesus].	If we be dead with him.	2 Tim. 2:11
62. We shall reign with [Jesus].	If we suffer.	2 Tim. 2:12
63. He shall be a vessel unto honour, sanctified, and meet for the Master's use, and prepared unto every good work.	If a man therefore purge himself from [iniquity].	2 Tim. 2:19, 21
64. The man of God may be perfect, thoroughly furnished unto all good works.	If scripture is used for doctrine, for reproof, for correction, for instruction in righteousness.	2 Tim. 3:16, 17
65. We may obtain mercy and find grace to help in time of need.	Come boldly unto the throne of grace.	Heb. 4:16
66. [Jesus] is able to save them to the uttermost.	Those that come to God by [Jesus].	Heb. 7:25
67. Jesus has perfected you forever.	If you are sanctified.	Heb. 10:14
68. You will receive the promise.	Have patience after you have done the will of God.	Heb. 10:36
69. It is possible to please God.	Believe that He is, and that He is a rewarder of them that diligently seek Him.	Heb. 11:6
70. God deals with you as with a son.	If you endure chastening.	Heb. 12:7
71. This man shall be blessed in his deed.	Whoso looks into the perfect law of liberty and continues therein, being not a forgetful hearer, but a doer of the work.	James 1:25
72. God gives grace.	To the humble.	James 4:6

PROMISE	CONDITION	REFERENCE
73. God will draw nigh to you.	Draw nigh to God.	James 4:8
74. God shall lift you up.	Humble yourself in the sight of the Lord.	James 4:10
75. You are kept by the power of God.	Through faith.	1 Pet. 1:5
76. Receive the end of your faith, even the salvation of your soul.	Whom [Jesus] having not seen, you love, in whom, though now you see Him not, yet believing, you rejoice with joy unspeakable.	1 Pet 1:8, 9
77 Husbands, your prayers will not be hindered.	Dwell with your wife according to knowledge, giving honor unto the wife, as unto the weaker vessel, and as being heirs together of the grace of life.	1 Pet. 3:7
78. The eyes of the Lord are over you, and His ears are open to your prayers.	Be righteous.	1 Pet. 3:12
79. You are happy and Christ is glorified.	If you are reproached for the name of Christ.	1 Pet. 4:14
80. The spirit of glory and of God rests upon you.	If you are reproached for the name of Christ.	1 Pet. 4:14
81. God gives grace to you.	Be clothed with humility.	1 Pet. 5:5
82. God will exalt you in due time.	Humble yourself under the mighty hand of God.	1 Pet. 5:6

PROMISE	CONDITION	REFERENCE
83. You shall be fruitful in the knowledge of our Lord Jesus Christ.	If these things be in you and abound: faith, virtue, knowledge, temperance, patience, godliness, brotherly kindness, and love.	2 Pet. 1:5-8
84. You shall never fall.	Give diligence to make your calling and election sure.	2 Pet. 1:10
85. The Lord knows how to deliver you out of temptations.	Be godly.	2 Pet. 2:9
86. We have fellowship with one another, and the blood of Jesus cleanses us from all sin.	If we walk in the light as He [God] is in the light.	1 John 1:7
87. [God] is faithful and just to forgive us our sins and to cleanse us from all unrighteousness.	If we confess our sins.	1 John 1:9
88. We do know that we know Him [Jesus].	If we keep His commandments.	1 John 2:3
89. In him verily is the love of God perfected.	Whoever keeps His word.	1 John 2:5
90. He abides in the light and there is no occasion of stumbling in him.	He that loves his brother.	1 John 2:10
91. Ye need not that any man teach you.	The anointing which ye have received of Him [the Holy Spirit] abideth in you.	1 John 2:27
92. He cannot sin.	Whosoever is born of God.	1 John 3:9

PROMISE	CONDITION	REFERENCE
93. We know that we have passed from death unto life.	Because we love the brethren.	1 John 3:14
94. We have confidence toward God.	If our heart does not condemn us.	1 John 3:21
95. You dwell in Jesus, and He dwells in you.	Keep Jesus' commandments.	1 John 3:24
96. He that knows God hears you.	If you are of God.	1 John 4:6
97. God dwells in us, and His love is perfected in us.	If we love one another.	1 John 4:12
98. God dwells in you, and you dwell in God.	Confess that Jesus is the Son of God.	1 John 4:15
99. You dwell in God, and God dwells in you.	Dwell in love.	1 John 4:16
100. You are born of God.	Believe that Jesus is the Christ.	1 John 5:1
101. We know that we love the children of God.	When we love God and keep His commandments.	1 John 5:2
102. You overcome the world.	Whatsoever is born of God. Believe that Jesus is the Son of God.	1 John 5:4. 5
103. He has eternal life.	He that has the Son.	1 John 5:11, 12
104. [God] shall give him life for them that sin not unto death.	If any man see his brother sin a sin not unto death, he shall ask [God].	1 John 5:16
105. He sins not, he keeps himself, and the wicked one touches him not.	Whoever is born of God.	1 John 5:18

70

PROMISE	CONDITION	REFERENCE
106. He has both the Father and the Son.	He that abides in the doctrine of Christ.	2 John 9
107. I [Jesus] have set before you an open door, and no man can shut it.	You have a little strength, have kept my [Jesus'] word, and have not denied my name.	Rev. 3:8
108. [Jesus]will keep you from the hour of temptation, which shall come upon all the world, to try them that dwell upon the earth.	Keep the word of Jesus' patience.	Rev. 3:10
109. I [Jesus] will come in to him, and will sup with him.	If any man hear my [Jesus'] voice and open the door.	Rev. 3:20
110. Overcome the accuser of our brethren.	By the blood of the Lamb, and by the word of their testimony, and they loved not their lives unto death.	Rev. 12:10, 11

19. Eighteen New Testament Warnings

WARNING	CONDITION	REFERENCE
1. [Jesus] will deny us.	If we deny Him.	2 Tim. 2:12
2. You shall suffer persecutions.	Live godly in Christ.	2 Tim. 3:12
3. There remains no more sacrifice for sins.	If we sin willfully after that we have received the knowledge of the truth.	Heb. 10:26
4. He is guilty of breaking all the commandments.	Whosoever shall keep the whole law, and yet offend in one point.	James 2:10

WARNING	CONDITION	REFERENCE
5. You have not.	Because you ask not.	James 4:2
6. You ask and receive not.	Because you ask amiss, that you may consume it upon your lusts.	James 4:3
7. He is blind and cannot see afar off, and has forgotten that he was purged from his old sins.	He that lacks faith, virtue, knowledge, temperance, patience, godliness, brotherly kindness, and love.	2 Pet. 1:5-9
8. The latter end is worse with them than the beginning.	If after they have escaped the pollutions of the world through the knowledge of the Lord and Saviour Jesus Christ, they are again entangled therein, and overcome.	2 Pet. 2:20
9. We deceive ourselves, and the truth is not in us.	If we say that we have no sin.	1 John 1:8
10. We make [God] a liar, and His word is not in us.	If we say that we have not sinned.	1 John 1:10
11. He is in darkness, and walks in darkness, and knows not where he goes, because that darkness has blinded his eyes.	He that hates his brother.	1 John 2:11
12. The love of the Father is not in him.	If any man love the world.	1 John 2:15
13. He is a liar.	He that denies that Jesus is the Christ.	1 John 2:22
14. He has not God.	Whoever transgresses and abides not in the doctrine of Christ.	2 John 9

WARNING	CONDITION	REFERENCE
15. All that dwell upon the earth shall worship [the beast].	All whose names are not written in the book of life of the Lamb.	Rev. 13:8
16. The same shall drink of the wine of the wrath of God and . . . be tormented with fire and brimstone. And the smoke of their torment ascends up forever, and they have no rest day nor night.	If any man worship the beast and his image and receive his mark in his forehead or in his hand.	Rev. 14:9-11
17. He was thrown into the lake of fire.	Whosoever was not found in the book of life.	Rev. 20:15
18. They shall have their part in the lake which burns with fire and brimstone: which is the second death.	The fearful, and unbelieving, and the abominable, and murderers, and whoremongers, and sorcerers, and idolaters, and all liars.	Rev. 21:8

20. Forty-three Unconditional Old Testament Promises

1. God's way is perfect (2 Sam. 22:31).
2. God controls the weather (Job 37:3-13).
3. You shall be judged righteously by God (Ps. 9:8).
4. The Lord will be a refuge in times of trouble (Ps. 9:9).
5. The Lord is King forever and ever (Ps. 10:16).
6. The Lord's throne is in heaven (Ps. 11:4).
7. The Lord loves righteousness (Ps. 11:7).
8. The heavens declare the glory of God (Ps. 19:1).
9. All the ends of the world shall remember and turn unto the Lord: and all the kindreds of the nations shall worship before thee (Ps. 22:27).
10. The Lord will bless His people with peace (Ps. 29:11).

11. God makes wars to cease unto the end of the earth (Ps. 46:9).
12. God is for me (Ps. 56:9).
13. God knows my foolishness, and my sins are not hidden from [Him] (Ps. 69:5).
14. [God says], My covenant will I not break (Ps. 89:34).
15. The Lord's enemies shall perish (Ps. 92:9).
16. The Lord knows the thoughts of man (Ps. 94:11).
17. [God's] truth endures to all generations (Ps. 100:5).
18. The Lord is merciful (Ps. 103:8).
19. The Lord is gracious (Ps. 103:8).
20. The Lord is slow to anger (Ps. 103:8).
21. The Lord will not keep His anger forever (Ps. 103:9).
22. Precious in the sight of the Lord is the death of His saints (Ps. 116:15).
23. The earth is full of [the Lord's] mercy (Ps. 119:64).
24. [God's] faithfulness is unto all generations (Ps. 119:90).
25. The entrance of God's words gives understanding to the simple (Ps. 119:130).
26. God neither slumbers nor sleeps (Ps. 121:3, 4).
27. Children are a heritage from the Lord (Ps. 127:3).
28. The Lord is good (Ps. 135:3).
29. God has magnified His word above all His name (Ps. 138:2).
30. You cannot flee from God's presence (Ps. 139:7, 8).
31. God's understanding is infinite (Ps. 147:5).
32. Love covers all sins (Prov. 10:12).
33. The Lord of hosts will defend Jerusalem (Isa. 31:5).
34. The word of our God shall stand forever (Isa. 40:8).
35. There is none that can deliver out of God's hand (Isa. 43:13).
36. God's counsel shall stand, and, He will do all His pleasure (Isa. 46:10, 11).
37. [God's] righteousness shall not be abolished (Isa. 51:6).
38. Jesus was wounded for our transgressions (Isa. 53:5).
39. [God's] word shall not return unto [Him] void, but it shall accomplish that which [He] pleases and it shall prosper in the thing whereto [He] sent it (Isa. 55:11).
40. God will bring upon you the good that He has promised you (Jer. 32:42).
41. The Lord your God in the midst of you is mighty (Zeph. 3:17).

42. The Lord changes not (Mal. 3:6).
43. From the rising of the sun even unto the going down of the same, my [God's] name shall be great among the Gentiles (Mal. 1:11).

21. Seven Old Testament Promises for Families

PROMISE	CONDITION	REFERENCE
1. Blessed shall be the fruit of your body.	If you shall hearken unto the voice of the Lord.	Deut. 28:2, 4
2. God's righteousness is unto your children's children.	To such as keep His covenant and to those that remember His commandments to do them.	Ps. 103:17
3. Your wife shall be as a fruitful vine by the sides of your house; your children like olive plants round about your table. You shall see your children's children.	The man that fears the Lord.	Ps. 128:1-6
4. The Lord relieves the fatherless and widow.	He that has the God of Jacob for his help, whose hope is in the Lord.	Ps. 146:5, 9
5. Your children shall be delivered.	If you are righteous.	Prov. 11:21
6. You shall leave an inheritance to your children's children.	[If you are a] good man.	Prov. 13:22
7. When a child is old, he will not depart from the way he should go.	Train up a child in the way he should go.	Prov. 22:6

22. Seven Old Testament Promises Concerning Nations

PROMISE	CONDITION	REFERENCE
1. [God] will bless them.	That bless [Israel].	Gen. 12:3
2. All the nations of the earth shall be blessed in [Abraham].	Unconditional	Gen. 18:18
3. [God] will hear from heaven, and will forgive their sin, and will heal their land.	If my [God's] people, which are called by my name, shall humble themselves, and pray, and seek my face, and turn from their wicked ways.	2 Chron. 7:14
4. Blessed is the nation.	Whose God is the Lord.	Ps. 33:12
5. Happy is that people.	Whose God is the Lord.	Ps. 144:15
6. A nation is exalted.	By righteousness.	Prov. 14:34
7. Blessed art thou, O land.	When thy king is the son of nobles, and thy princes eat in due season, for strength, and not for drunkenness.	Eccles. 10:17

23. Ninety-three Promises to the Individual from the Psalms

PROMISE	CONDITION	REFERENCE
1. He shall be like a tree planted by the rivers of water, that brings forth his fruit in his season; his leaf also shall not wither; whatever he does shall prosper.	The man that walks not in the counsel of the ungodly, nor stands in the way of sinners, nor sits in the seat of the scornful. But his delight is in the law of the Lord and in his law does he meditate day and night.	Ps. 1:1-3
2. The Lord has set you apart and will hear you when you call to Him.	If you are godly.	Ps. 4:3
3. He shall abide in [the Lord's] tabernacle.	He that walks uprightly, and works righteousness, and speaks the truth in his heart.	Ps. 15:1, 2
4. I shall not be moved. Therefore my heart is glad, and my glory rejoices; my flesh also shall rest in hope.	I have set the Lord always before me.	Ps. 16:8, 9
5. Your flesh shall rest in hope.	Set the Lord always before you.	Ps. 16:8, 9
6. There is fulness of joy.	In [God's] presence.	Ps. 16:11
7. The Lord shall deliver you.	If He delights in you.	Ps. 18:19
8. The Lord shall reward you.	According to your righteousness.	Ps. 18:20
9. [The Lord] will show himself merciful.	With the merciful.	Ps. 18:25
10. There is great reward.	In keeping the law of the Lord.	Ps. 19:11

PROMISE	CONDITION	REFERENCE
11. I shall not want.	The Lord is my shepherd.	Ps. 23:1
12. [The Lord] restores my soul: He leads me in the paths of righteousness.	The Lord is my shepherd.	Ps. 23:3
13. Though I walk through the valley of the shadow of death, I will fear no evil.	The Lord is my shepherd.	Ps. 23:4
14. Goodness and mercy shall follow me all the days of my life.	The Lord is my shepherd.	Ps. 23:6
15. I will dwell in the house of the Lord forever.	The Lord is my shepherd.	Ps. 23:6
16. He shall receive the blessing from the Lord and righteousness from the God of his salvation.	He that has clean hands, and a pure heart; who has not lifted up his soul to vanity, nor sworn deceitfully.	Ps. 24:4, 5
17. God will guide in judgment, and will teach His ways.	To the meek.	Ps. 25:9
18. All of the paths of the Lord are mercy and truth unto such.	Keep His covenant and His testimonies.	Ps. 25:10
19. His soul shall dwell at ease.	He that fears the Lord.	Ps. 25:12, 13
20. [The Lord] shall strengthen your heart.	Wait upon the Lord.	Ps. 27:14
21. [The Lord] shall strengthen your heart.	Be of good courage.	Ps. 31:24
22. Blessed is he.	He whose transgression is forgiven, whose sin is covered.	Ps. 32:1

PROMISE	CONDITION	REFERENCE
23. Mercy shall compass him about.	He that trusts in the Lord.	Ps. 32:10
24. Our heart shall rejoice in [the Lord].	Because we have trusted in His holy name.	Ps. 33:21
25. The Lord delivered me from all my fears.	I sought the Lord.	Ps. 34:4
26. The angel of the Lord encamps round about them and delivers them.	Them that fear Him.	Ps. 34:7
27. See that the Lord is good.	Taste [Him].	Ps. 34:8
28. They shall not want any good thing.	Seek the Lord and fear Him.	Ps. 34:9, 10
29. The Lord delivers them out of all of their troubles.	The righteous.	Ps. 34:17
30. Not one of his bones is broken.	The righteous.	Ps. 34:19, 20
31. None shall be desolate.	Trust in [the Lord].	Ps. 34:22
32. You shall dwell in the land, and you shall be fed.	Trust in the Lord and do good.	Ps. 37:3
33. [The Lord] shall give you the desires of your heart.	Delight yourself also in the Lord.	Ps. 37:4
34. [The Lord] shall bring it to pass.	Commit your way unto the Lord; trust also in Him.	Ps. 37:5
35. They shall inherit the earth.	Those that wait upon the Lord.	Ps. 37:9
36. They shall delight themselves in the abundance of peace.	The meek.	Ps. 37:11

PROMISE	CONDITION	REFERENCE
37. A little is better than the riches of many wicked.	Be righteous.	Ps. 37:16
38. The Lord upholds them.	The righteous.	Ps. 37:17
39. In the days of famine they shall be satisfied.	The upright.	Ps. 37:19
40. His steps are ordered by the Lord.	A good man.	Ps. 37:23, 24
41. None of his steps shall slide.	The law of his God is in his heart.	Ps. 37:31
42. [The Lord] is their strength in the time of trouble.	The righteous.	Ps. 37:39
43. The Lord shall deliver them from the wicked.	Because they trust in Him.	Ps. 37:40
44. God will incline unto you and hear your cry.	Wait patiently for the Lord.	Ps. 40:1
45. Blessed is he; the Lord shall deliver him in time of trouble.	He that considers the poor.	Ps. 41:1
46. The Lord will preserve him and keep him alive.	He that considers the poor.	Ps. 41:1, 2
47. God has anointed you with the oil of gladness above your fellows.	Love righteousness and hate wickedness.	Ps. 45:7

80

PROMISE	CONDITION	REFERENCE
48. We will not fear, though the earth be removed, and though the mountains be carried into the midst of the sea; though the waters roar and be troubled, though the mountains shake.	God is our refuge and strength.	Ps. 46:1, 2
49. God will be your guide even unto death.	If He is your God.	Ps. 48:14
50. I [God] will deliver you, and you shall glorify me.	Offer unto God thanksgiving, pay your vows unto the Most High, and call upon Him in the day of your trouble.	Ps. 50:14, 15
51. He glorifies God.	Whoso offers praise.	Ps. 50:23
52. You can offer a sacrifice to God that He will not despise.	Offer a broken spirit and a broken and contrite heart.	Ps. 51:17
53. [God] shall hear my voice.	Evening, and morning, and at noon, will I pray.	Ps. 55:17
54. [The Lord] will sustain you.	Cast your burden upon the Lord.	Ps. 55:22
55. I will not be afraid what man can do unto me.	In God have I put my trust.	Ps. 56:11
56. The earth shall yield her increase, and God shall bless us.	Let all the people praise Thee, O God.	Ps. 67:5, 6
57. God gives strength and power.	To His people.	Ps. 68:35
58. [God] will fill your mouth.	Open your mouth wide.	Ps. 81:10

PROMISE	CONDITION	REFERENCE
59. No good thing will He withhold.	From them that walk uprightly.	Ps. 84:11
60. He shall abide under the shadow of the Almighty.	He that dwells in the secret places of the Most High.	Ps. 91:1
61. God shall deliver you from the snare of the fowler and from the noisome pestilence.	He that dwells in the secret place of the Most High.	Ps. 91:1, 3
62. You shall not be afraid for the terror by night.	He that dwells in the secret place of the Most High.	Ps. 91:5
63. You shall not be afraid for the arrow that flies by day.	He that dwells in the secret place of the Most High.	Ps. 91:5
64. You shall not be afraid for the pestilence that walks in darkness.	He that dwells in the secret place of the Most High.	Ps. 91:6
65. You shall not be afraid for the destruction that wastes at noonday.	He that dwells in the secret place of the Most High.	Ps. 91:6
66. A thousand shall fall at your side, and ten thousand at your right hand; but it shall not come nigh you.	He that dwells in the secret place of the Most High.	Ps.91:7
67. There shall no evil befall you, neither shall any plague come near your dwelling.	Because you have made the Lord your habitation.	Ps. 91:10
68. [God] shall give His angels charge over you, to keep you in all your ways.	Because you have made the Lord your habitation.	Ps. 91:11

PROMISE	CONDITION	REFERENCE
69. With long life will I [God] satisfy him and show him my salvation.	Because he has set his love upon me.	Ps. 91:14, 16
70. He shall flourish like the palm tree.	The righteous.	Ps. 92:12
71. You are blessed.	If the Lord chastens you.	Ps. 94:12
72. As the heaven is high above the earth, so great is [God's] mercy toward them.	That fear Him.	Ps. 103:11
73. The mercy of the Lord is from everlasting to everlasting upon them.	That fear Him.	Ps. 103:17
74. [God] sent His word and healed them.	They cry unto the Lord in their trouble.	Ps. 107:19, 20
75. Wealth and riches shall be in his house, and his righteousness endures forever.	Fear the Lord, delight greatly in His commandments.	Ps. 112:1, 3
76. He shall not be afraid of evil tidings.	His heart is fixed, trusting in the Lord.	Ps. 112:7
77. A young man shall cleanse his way.	By taking heed according to [God's] word.	Ps. 119:9
78. You shall not perish in your affliction.	Make God's law your delight.	Ps. 119:92
79. I shall live.	Get understanding of the righteousness of God's testimonies.	Ps. 119:144
80. Great peace have they, and nothing shall offend them.	They which love Thy law.	Ps. 119:165

PROMISE	CONDITION	REFERENCE
81. The sun shall not smite you by day.	If the Lord is your keeper.	Ps. 121:5, 6
82. The moon shall not smite you by night.	If the Lord is your keeper.	Ps. 121:5, 6
83. The Lord shall preserve you from all evil.	If the Lord is your keeper.	Ps. 121:5, 7
84. They shall prosper.	Pray for the peace of Jerusalem.	Ps. 122:6
85. They shall be as Mount Zion which cannot be removed, but abides forever.	Trust in the Lord.	Ps. 125:1
86. The rod of the wicked shall not rest on [your] lot.	[If you are] righteous.	Ps. 125:3
87. They shall reap in joy.	That sowed in tears.	Ps. 126:5
88. [God] gives them sleep.	His beloved.	Ps. 127:2
89. It is good and pleasant for brethren to dwell together.	Dwell together in unity.	Ps. 133:1
90. The Lord is nigh unto all.	To all that call upon Him in truth.	Ps. 145:18
91. The Lord preserves all.	All them that love Him.	Ps. 145:20
92. The Lord loves you.	If you are righteous.	Ps. 146:8
93. God will beautify them with salvation.	The meek.	Ps. 149:4

24. Eighty-six Other Old Testament Promises to the Individual

PROMISE	CONDITION	REFERENCE
1. [God] will bless your bread and your water and will take sickness away from you.	Serve the Lord.	Ex. 23:25
2. You will prolong your days upon the earth, which the Lord gives you.	Keep His statutes and His commandments.	Deut. 4:40
3. It will be well with you and you will increase mightily.	Observe to do [all His statutes and commandments].	Deut. 6:3
4. The Lord will take away from you all sickness.	Keep the commandments, and the statutes, and the judgments which I [God] command you.	Deut. 7:11, 15
5. You shall be blessed in the city and in the field.	Hearken to the voice of the Lord your God.	Deut. 28:2, 3
6. Your crops and your herds shall be blessed.	Hearken unto the voice of the Lord your God.	Deut. 28:2, 4
7. You shall be blessed when you come in and go out.	Hearken to the voice of the Lord your God.	Deut. 28: 2, 6
8. The Lord shall cause your enemies to be smitten before your face. They shall come against you one way, and flee from you seven ways.	Hearken to the voice of the Lord your God.	Deut. 28:2, 7
9. The Lord shall establish you a holy people unto himself.	Keep the commandments of the Lord your God, and walk in His ways.	Deut. 28:9

PROMISE	CONDITION	REFERENCE
10. The Lord shall give you rain in His season, and bless all the work of your hand.	Keep the commandments of the Lord your God, and walk in His ways.	Deut. 28:9, 12
11. The Lord shall make you the head and not the tail.	If you hearken to the commandments of the Lord to observe and to do them.	Deut. 28:13
12. One man of you shall chase a thousand.	Cleave unto the Lord your God.	Josh. 23:8, 10
13. God will honour them.	Them that honour God.	1 Sam. 2:30
14. You shall prosper.	Take heed to fulfill the statutes and judgments which the Lord charged Moses with.	1 Chron. 22:13
15. The Lord is with you.	While you be with Him.	2 Chron. 15:2
16. [God] will be found of you.	If you seek Him.	2 Chron. 15:2
17. God made him to prosper.	As long as he sought God.	2 Chron. 26:5
18. He shall be stronger and stronger.	He that has clean hands.	Job 17:9
19. They shall spend their days in prosperity and their years in pleasures.	If they obey and serve [God].	Job 36:11
20. I [God] will pour out my Spirit unto you, I will make known my words unto you.	Turn you at my reproof.	Prov. 1:23
21. The Lord lays up sound wisdom for them.	The righteous.	Prov. 2:7

PROMISE	CONDITION	REFERENCE
22. [The Lord] shall direct your paths.	Trust in the Lord with all your heart, and lean not unto your own understanding. In all your ways acknowledge Him.	Prov. 3:5, 6
23. Your barns shall be filled with plenty.	Honour the Lord with your substance and with the firstfruits of all your increase.	Prov. 3:9, 10
24. When you lie down, you shall not be afraid; your sleep shall be sweet.	Keep sound wisdom and discretion.	Prov. 3:21-24
25. The Lord shall be your confidence and shall keep your foot from being taken.	Keep sound wisdom and discretion.	Prov. 3:21, 26
26. You shall find wisdom.	Love wisdom and seek it early.	Prov. 8:17
27. Have wisdom and understanding.	Have the fear of the Lord and the knowledge of the Holy.	Prov. 9:10
28. The years of your life shall be increased.	Have the fear of the Lord and the knowledge of the Holy.	Prov. 9:10, 11
29. You shall be made rich and have no sorrow with your riches.	Have the blessing of the Lord.	Prov. 10:22
30. Their desire shall be granted.	The righteous.	Prov. 10:24
31. He is delivered out of trouble.	The righteous.	Prov. 11:8
32. The just shall be delivered.	Through knowledge.	Prov. 11:9
33. To him shall be a sure reward.	Sow righteousness.	Prov. 11:18

PROMISE	CONDITION	REFERENCE
34. He shall be made fat [figuratively: satisfied].	The liberal soul.	Prov. 11:25
35. He is wise.	He that wins souls.	Prov. 11:30
36. He shall obtain favour of the Lord.	A good man.	Prov. 12:2
37. His house shall stand.	The righteous.	Prov. 12:7
38. To [them] is joy.	Counselors of peace.	Prov. 12:20
39. There shall no evil happen to them.	The just.	Prov. 12:21
40. He shall be honoured.	He that regards reproof.	Prov. 13:18
41. He shall be wise.	He that walks with wise men.	Prov. 13:20
42. Happy is he.	He that has mercy on the poor.	Prov. 14:21
43. You shall turn away wrath.	Give a soft answer.	Prov. 15:1
44. In his house is much treasure.	The righteous.	Prov. 15:6
45. Your thoughts shall be established.	Commit your works unto the Lord.	Prov. 16:3
46. Men depart from evil.	By the fear of the Lord.	Prov. 16:6
47. The Lord makes your enemies to be at peace with you.	Please the Lord.	Prov. 16:7
48. A man that has friends.	Must show himself friendly.	Prov. 18:24
49. The Lord will repay you.	Have pity on the poor.	Prov. 19:17

88

PROMISE	CONDITION	REFERENCE
50. He finds life, righteousness, and honour.	He that follows after righteousness and mercy.	Prov. 21:21
51. He keeps his soul from troubles.	Whoso keeps his mouth and his tongue.	Prov. 21:23
52. You shall have riches, honour, and life.	By humility and the fear of the Lord.	Prov. 22:4
53. He falls seven times, and rises up again.	A just man.	Prov. 24:16
54. You shall heap coals of fire upon your enemy's head, and the Lord shall reward you.	If your enemy be hungry, give him bread to eat; and if he be thirsty, give him water to drink.	Prov. 25:21, 22
55. He shall have good things.	The upright.	Prov. 28:10
56. He shall have mercy.	Whoso confesses and forsakes [his sins].	Prov. 28:13
57. He shall have plenty of bread.	He that tills his land.	Prov. 28:19
58. He shall not lack.	He that gives unto the poor.	Prov. 28:27
59. He shall be safe.	Whoso puts his trust in the Lord.	Prov. 29:25
60. God gives to a man wisdom, knowledge, and joy.	To a man that is good in His sight.	Eccles. 2:26
61. Though your sins be as scarlet, they shall be white as snow.	Reason together with the Lord.	Isa. 1:18
62. You shall eat the good of the land.	If you are willing and obedient.	Isa. 1:19
63. Thou [God] will keep him in perfect peace.	Whose mind is stayed on Thee.	Isa. 26:3

PROMISE	CONDITION	REFERENCE
64. Blessed are they.	They that wait for [the Lord].	Isa. 30:18
65. He shall dwell on high.	He that walks righteously, speaks uprightly, despises the gain of oppression, shakes his hand from holding bribes, stops ears from hearing blood, and shuts his eyes from seeing evil.	Isa. 33:15, 16
66. They shall renew their strength.	They that wait upon the Lord.	Isa. 40:31
67. They shall run and not be weary.	They that wait upon the Lord.	Isa. 40:31
68. They shall walk and not faint.	They that wait upon the Lord.	Isa. 40:31
69. God will help you and strengthen you.	If God is your God.	Isa. 41:10
70. When you pass through the waters, the Lord will be with you; and through the rivers, they shall not overflow you; when you walk through the fire, you shall not be burned.	If you are God's.	Isa. 43:2
71. I have righteousness and strength.	In the Lord.	Isa. 45:24
72. You shall go out with joy, and be led forth with peace.	Seek the Lord while He may be found.	Isa. 55:6, 12

PROMISE	CONDITION	REFERENCE
73. God will have mercy; He will abundantly pardon.	Seek the Lord while He may be found, call upon Him while He is near. Let the wicked forsake his way and the unrighteous man his thoughts and let him return unto the Lord.	Isa. 55:7
74. God dwells with him to revive the spirit and the heart.	Him that is of a humble and contrite heart.	Isa. 57:15
75. You shall eat, drink, rejoice, and sing for joy.	[God's] servants.	Isa. 65:13, 14
76. They shall not labour in vain.	The seed of the blessed of the Lord.	Isa. 65:23
77. Before they call, I [God] will answer, and while they are yet speaking, I will hear.	The seed of the blessed of the Lord.	Isa. 65:23, 24
78. You shall find rest for your soul.	Ask for the old paths, where is the good way, and walk therein.	Jer. 6:16
79. It shall be well with you.	Walk in all the ways that I [God] have commanded you.	Jer. 7:23
80. [The Lord] will show you great and mighty things which you know not.	Call unto [the Lord].	Jer. 33:3
81. [God] will return unto you.	Return unto [God].	Mal. 3:7

PROMISE	CONDITION	REFERENCE
82. The Lord of hosts will open you the windows of heaven, and pour you out a blessing that there shall not be room enough to receive it.	Bring all the tithes into the storehouse.	Mal. 3:10
83. I [the Lord] will rebuke the devourer for your sakes, and He shall not destroy the fruits of your ground.	Bring all the tithes into the storehouse.	Mal. 3:10, 11
84. All nations shall call you blessed, for you shall be a delight-some land.	Bring all the tithes into the storehouse.	Mal. 3:10, 12
85. A book of remembrance was written before God for them.	Them that feared the Lord and that thought upon His name.	Mal. 3:16
86. Unto you shall the Sun of righteousness arise with healing in His wings.	Fear [the Lord's] name.	Mal. 4:2

25. Eight Old Testament Warnings

WARNING	CONDITION	REFERENCE
1. You shall surely perish, and you shall not prolong your days upon the land.	If thine heart turn away, so that thou wilt not hear, but shalt be drawn away.	Deut. 30:17, 18
2. [The Lord] will forsake you.	If you forsake Him.	2 Chron. 15:2
3. The Lord will not hear me.	If I regard iniquity in my heart.	Ps. 66:18

WARNING	CONDITION	REFERENCE
4. They labour in vain that build.	Except the Lord build the house.	Ps. 127:1
5. Contention will come.	By pride.	Prov. 13:10
6. Evil shall not depart from his house.	Whoso rewards evil for good.	Prov. 17:13
7. He shall fall into mischief.	He that hardens his heart.	Prov. 28:14
8. The people perish.	Where there is no vision.	Prov. 29:18

3

New Testament Proverbs and Facts

Many sayings of Jesus and the apostles nicely fit the pattern of the Old Testament book of Proverbs.

The dictionary definition of the word "proverb" and the content of the Old Testament book of Proverbs do not necessarily agree. Thus, the proverbs of this chapter are categorized in the spirit of the Old Testament example, if not the definition in Webster's. If there were a New Testament book called "Proverbs," it might have been a lot like this chapter!

The facts in this chapter are unusual, in that most of them can be proven only by the Bible, and many have to be understood in the realm of faith.

26. Twenty-one New Testament Proverbs Concerning God

1. [Your Father] maketh his sun to shine on the evil and on the good, and he sendeth rain on the just and on the unjust (Matt. 5:45).
2. In the beginning was the Word, and the Word was with God, and the Word was God. The same was in the beginning with God. All things were made by him; and without him was not anything made that was made. In him was life; and the life was the light of men. And the light shineth in darkness; and the darkness comprehended it not (John 1:1-5).
3. The times of this ignorance God once winked at; but now commandeth all men every where to repent (Acts 17:30).
4. Why should it be thought a thing incredible with you, that God should raise the dead? (Acts 26:8).

5. The invisible things of [God] from the creation of the world are clearly seen, being understood by the things that are made, even his eternal power and Godhead (Rom. 1:20).

6. The foolishness of God is wiser than men; and the weakness of God is stronger than men (1 Cor. 1:25).

7. God has sealed us, and has given the earnest of the Spirit in our hearts (2 Cor. 1:22).

8. In God are hid all the treasures of wisdom and knowledge (Col. 2:2, 3).

9. God hath not appointed us to wrath, but to obtain salvation by our Lord Jesus Christ, who died for us, that, whether we wake or sleep, we should live together with him (1 Thess. 5:9, 10).

10. It is a righteous thing with God to recompense tribulation to them that trouble you (2 Thess. 1:6).

11. Without controversy, great is the mystery of godliness: God was manifest in the flesh, justified in the Spirit, seen of angels, preached unto the Gentiles, believed on in the world, received up into glory (1 Tim. 3:16).

12. God resisteth the proud and giveth grace to the humble (1 Pet. 5:5).

13. One day is with the Lord as a thousand years, and a thousand years as one day (2 Pet. 3:8).

14. The Lord is not slack concerning his promise, as some men count slackness; but is longsuffering to us-ward, not willing that any should perish, but that all should come to repentance (2 Pet. 3:9).

15. God is light, and in him is no darkness at all (1 John 1:5).

16. All that is in the world, the lust of the flesh, and the lust of the eyes, and the pride of life, is not of the Father, but is of the world (1 John 2:16).

17. Behold, what manner of love the Father hath bestowed upon us, that we should be called the sons of God: therefore, the world knoweth us not, because it knew him not (1 John 3:1).

18. Ye are of God, little children, and have overcome them: because greater is he that is in you, than he that is in the world (1 John 4:4).

19. Hereby know ye the Spirit of God: Every spirit that confesseth that Jesus Christ is come in the flesh is of God: and every spirit that confesseth not that Jesus Christ is come in the flesh is not of God: and this is the spirit of antichrist, whereof ye have heard that it should come; and even now already is it

in the world (1 John 4:2, 3).

20. Herein is love, not that we loved God, but that he loved us, and sent his Son to be the propitiation for our sins (1 John 4:10).

21. We love him, because he first loved us (1 John 4:19).

27. Sixty New Testament Proverbs Concerning Man

1. The light of the body is the eye: if therefore thine eye be single, thy whole body shall be full of light. But if thine eye be evil, thy whole body shall be full of darkness. If therefore the light that is in thee be darkness, how great is that darkness! (Matt. 6:22, 23).

2. Take therefore no thought for the morrow: for the morrow shall take thought for the things of itself. Sufficient unto the day is the evil thereof (Matt. 6:34).

3. Ask, and it shall be given you; seek, and ye shall find; knock, and it shall be opened to you: for everyone that asketh receiveth; and he that seeketh findeth; and to him that knocketh it shall be opened (Matt. 7:7, 8).

4. If ye, then, being evil, know how to give good gifts unto your children, how much more shall your Father which is in heaven give good things to them that ask him? (Matt. 7:11).

5. By their fruits ye shall know them (Matt. 7:20).

6. Jesus said unto him, Follow me; and let the dead bury their dead (Matt. 8:22).

7. How can one enter into a strong man's house, and spoil his goods, except he first bind the strong man? and then he will spoil his house (Matt. 12:29).

8. Those things which proceed out of the mouth come forth from the heart; and they defile the man. For out of the heart proceed evil thoughts, murders, adulteries, fornications, thefts, false witness, blasphemies: these are the things which defile a man (Matt. 15:18-20).

9. Whatsoever thou shalt bind on earth shall be bound in heaven: and whatsoever thou shalt loose on earth shall be loosed in heaven (Matt. 16:19).

10. Wherefore [a man and his wife] are no more twain, but one flesh. What therefore God hath joined together, let not man put asunder (Matt. 19:5, 6).

11. Whosoever shall put away his wife, except it be for fornication, and shall marry another, committeth adultery: and

whoso marrieth her which is put away commits adultery (Matt. 19:9).

12. Watch and pray, that ye enter not into temptation: the spirit indeed is willing, but the flesh is weak (Matt. 26:41).

13. Remember Lot's wife (Luke 17:32).

14. If I have told you earthly things, and ye believe not, how shall ye believe, if I tell you of heavenly things? (John 3:12).

15. Everyone that doeth evil hateth the light, neither cometh to the light, lest his deeds should be reproved. But he that doeth truth cometh to the light, that his deeds may be made manifest, that they are wrought in God (John 3:20, 21).

16. What shall we do, that we might work the works of God? This is the work of God, that ye believe on him whom he hath sent (John 6:28, 29).

17. Judge not according to the appearance, but judge righteous judgment (John 7:24).

18. Whosoever commiteth sin is the servant of sin (John 8:34).

19. It is not for you to know the times or the seasons, which God hath put in his own power (Acts 1:7).

20. If this counsel or this work be of men, it will come to nought: but if it be of God, ye cannot overthrow it; lest haply ye be found even to fight against God (Acts 5:38, 39).

21. Blessed is the man to whom the Lord will not impute sin (Rom. 4:8).

22. He that is dead is freed from sin (Rom. 6:7).

23. Know ye not, that to whom ye yield yourselves servants to obey, his servants ye are to whom ye obey; whether of sin unto death, or of obedience unto righteousness? (Rom. 6:16).

24. To be carnally minded is death; but to be spiritually minded is life and peace (Rom. 8:6).

25. If any man have not the Spirit of Christ, he is none of his (Rom. 8:9).

26. Let him that thinketh he standeth take heed lest he fall (1 Cor. 10:12).

27. The spirits of the prophets are subject to the prophets (1 Cor. 14:32).

28. The last enemy that shall be destroyed is death (1 Cor. 15:26).

29. Godly sorrow worketh repentance to salvation not to be repented of: but the sorrow of the world worketh death (2 Cor. 7:10).

30. He that glorieth, let him glory in the Lord. For not he that

commendeth himself is approved, but whom the Lord commendeth (2 Cor. 10:17, 18).

31. The law was our schoolmaster to bring us unto Christ, that we might be justified by faith. But after that faith is come, we are no longer under a schoolmaster. For ye are all the children of God by faith in Christ Jesus (Gal. 3:24-26).

32. The law is good, if a man use it lawfully (1 Tim. 1:8).

33. If a man desire the office of a bishop, he desireth a good work (1 Tim. 3:1).

34. Every creature of God is good, and nothing to be refused, if it be received with thanksgiving: for it is sanctified by the word of God and prayer (1 Tim. 4:4, 5).

35. If a man also strive for masteries, yet is he not crowned, except he strive lawfully (2 Tim. 2:5).

36. Those that oppose themselves . . . are taken captive by [the devil] at his will (2 Tim. 2:25, 26).

37. In the last days, perilous times shall come (2 Tim. 3:1).

38. Evil men and seducers shall wax worse and worse, deceiving, and being deceived (2 Tim. 3:13).

39. The time will come when they will not endure sound doctrine; but after their own lusts shall they heap to themselves teachers, having itching ears; and they shall turn away their ears from the truth, and shall be turned unto fables (2 Tim. 4:3, 4).

40. Unto the pure all things are pure: but unto them that are defiled and unbelieving is nothing pure; but even their mind and conscience is defiled (Titus 1:15).

41. For everyone that useth milk is unskillful in the word of righteousness: for he is a babe. But strong meat belongeth to them that are of full age, even those who by reason of use have their senses exercised to discern both good and evil (Heb. 5:13-14).

42. It is impossible for those who were once enlightened, and have tasted of the heavenly gift, and were made partakers of the Holy Ghost, and have tasted the good word of God, and the powers of the world to come, if they shall fall away, to renew them again unto repentance; seeing they crucify to themselves the Son of God afresh, and put him to an open shame (Heb. 6:4-6).

43. The law . . . can never with those sacrifices which they offered year by year continually make the comers thereunto perfect (Heb. 10:1).

44. It is a fearful thing to fall into the hands of the living God (Heb. 10:31).

45. Now faith is the substance of things hoped for, the evidence of things not seen (Heb. 11:1).

46. Ye have not resisted unto blood, striving against sin (Heb. 12:4).

47. No chastening for the present seemeth to be joyous, but grievous: nevertheless afterward it yieldeth the peaceable fruit of righteousness unto them which are exercised thereby (Heb. 12:11).

48. A double minded man is unstable in all his ways (James 1:8).

49. Every man is tempted, when he is drawn away of his own lust, and enticed. Then when lust hath conceived, it bringeth forth sin: and sin, when it is finished, bringeth forth death (James 1:14, 15).

50. If any man among you seem to be religious, and bridleth not his tongue, but deceiveth his own heart, this man's religion is vain (James 1:26).

51. Thou believest that there is one God; thou doest well: the devils also believe and tremble (James 2:19).

52. The tongue is a little member, and boasteth great things. Behold, how great a matter a little fire kindleth! And the tongue is a fire, a world of iniquity: so is the tongue among our members, that it defileth the whole body, and setteth on fire the course of nature; and it is set on fire of hell. The tongue no man can tame; it is an unruly evil, full of deadly poison (James 3:5, 6, 8).

53. Where envying and strife is, there is confusion and every evil work (James 3:16).

54. There is one lawgiver, who is able to save and to destroy: who art thou that judgest another? (James 4:12).

55. Ye know not what shall be on the morrow . . . For that ye ought to say, If the Lord will, we shall live, and do this, or that (James 4:14, 15).

56. He that saith he is in the light, and hateth his brother, is in darkness even until now (1 John 2:9).

57. He that loveth his brother abideth in the light, and there is none occasion of stumbling in him (1 John 2:10).

58. You have an unction from the Holy One, and ye know all things (1 John 2:20).

59. All unrighteousness is sin (1 John 5:17).

60. Whosoever transgresseth, and abideth not in the doctrine of

Christ, hath not God. He that abideth in the doctrine of Christ, he hath both the Father and the Son (2 John 9).

28. Nine New Testament Proverbs Concerning Scripture

1. Man shall not live by bread alone, but by every word that proceedeth out of the mouth of God (Matt. 4:4).
2. Till heaven and earth pass, one jot or one tittle shall in no wise pass from the law, till all be fulfilled (Matt. 5:18).
3. He that is of God heareth God's words: ye therefore hear them not, because ye are not of God (John 8:47).
4. Faith cometh by hearing, and hearing by the word of God (Rom. 10:17).
5. The natural man receiveth not the things of the Spirit of God: for they are foolishness unto him: neither can he know them, because they are spiritually discerned (1 Cor. 2:14).
6. The holy scriptures are able to make thee wise unto salvation through faith which is in Christ Jesus (2 Tim. 3:15).
7. No prophecy of the scripture is of any private interpretation (2 Pet. 1:20).
8. He that hath an ear, let him hear what the Spirit saith unto the churches (Rev. 3:22).
9. The testimony of Jesus is the spirit of prophecy (Rev. 19:10).

29. Twenty-six New Testament Proverbs Concerning Eternal Life

1. Except your righteousness shall exceed the righteousness of the scribes and Pharisees, ye shall in no case enter into the kingdom of heaven (Matt. 5:20).
2. With what judgment ye judge, ye shall be judged (Matt. 7:2).
3. Strait is the gate, and narrow is the way which leadeth unto life, and few there be that find it (Matt. 7:14).
4. He that endureth to the end shall be saved (Matt. 10:22).
5. Fear not them which kill the body, but are not able to kill the soul: but rather fear him which is able to destroy both soul and body in hell (Matt. 10:28).
6. Out of the abundance of the heart the mouth speaketh. A good man out of the good treasure of the heart bringeth forth good things: and an evil man out of the evil treasure bringeth

forth evil things. . . . Every idle word that men shall speak, they shall give account thereof in the day of judgment. For by thy words thou shalt be justified, and by thy words thou shalt be condemned (Matt. 12:34-37).

7. Whosoever hath, to him shall be given, and he shall have more abundance: but whosoever hath not, from him shall be taken away even that he hath (Matt. 13:12).

8. What is a man profited, if he shall gain the whole world, and lose his own soul? or what shall a man give in exchange for his soul? (Matt. 16:26).

9. Many that are first shall be last; and the last shall be first (Matt. 19:30).

10. Rejoice not that the spirits are subject unto you; but rather rejoice, because your names are written in heaven (Luke 10:20).

11. Whosoever shall seek to save his life shall lose it; and whosoever shall lose his life shall preserve it (Luke 17:33).

12. He that believeth on the Son hath everlasting life: and he that believeth not the Son shall not see life; but the wrath of God abideth on him (John 3:36).

13. We must through much tribulation enter into the kingdom of God (Acts 14:22).

14. As many as have sinned without law shall also perish without law: and as many as have sinned in the law shall be judged by the law (Rom. 2:12).

15. All have sinned, and come short of the glory of God (Rom. 3:23).

16. The wages of sin is death; but the gift of God is eternal life through Jesus Christ our Lord (Rom. 6:23).

17. If, in this life only we have hope in Christ, we are of all men most miserable (1 Cor. 15:19).

18. If our gospel be hid, it is hid to them that are lost (2 Cor. 4:3).

19. We must all appear before the judgment seat of Christ; that everyone may receive the things done in his body, according to that he hath done, whether it be good or bad (2 Cor. 5:10).

20. To live is Christ, and to die is gain (Phil. 1:21).

21. Bodily exercise profiteth little: but godliness is profitable unto all things, having promise of the life that now is, and of that which is to come (1 Tim. 4:8).

22. Some men's sins are open beforehand, going before to judgment; and some men they follow after. Likewise also the good works of some are manifest beforehand; and they that

are otherwise cannot be hid (1 Tim. 5:24, 25).

23. It is appointed unto men once to die, but after this the judgment (Heb. 9:27).

24. Blessed are they which are called unto the marriage supper of the Lamb (Rev. 19:9).

25. Blessed and holy is he that hath part in the first resurrection: on such the second death hath no power, but they shall be priests of God and of Christ, and shall reign with him a thousand years (Rev. 20:6).

26. The Spirit and the bride say, Come. And let him that heareth say, Come. And let him that is athirst come. And whosoever will, let him take the water of life freely (Rev. 22:17).

30. Eleven New Testament Proverbs Concerning Stewardship

1. Where your treasure is, there will your heart be also (Matt. 6:21).

2. Give not that which is holy unto the dogs, neither cast ye your pearls before swine, lest they trample them under their feet, and turn again and rend you (Matt. 7:6).

3. Freely ye have received, freely give (Matt. 10:8).

4. Render therefore unto Caesar the things which are Caesar's; and unto God the things that are God's (Matt. 22:21).

5. Unto whomsoever much is given, of him shall be much required: and to whom men have committed much, of him they will ask the more (Luke 12:48).

6. He that is faithful in that which is least is faithful also in much: and he that is unjust in the least is unjust also in much. If therefore ye have not been faithful in unrighteous mammon, who will commit to your trust the true riches? And if ye have not been faithful in that which is another man's, who shall give you that which is your own? (Luke 16:10-12)

7. Remember the words of the Lord Jesus, how he said, It is more blessed to give than to receive (Acts 20:35).

8. If any provide not for his own, and specially for those of his own house, he hath denied the faith, and is worse than an infidel (1 Tim. 5:8).

9. Godliness with contentment is great gain. For we brought nothing into this world, and it is certain we carry nothing out (1 Tim. 6:6, 7).

10. The love of money is the root of all evil (1 Tim. 6:10).

11. What doth it profit, my brethren, though a man say he hath faith, and have not works? Can faith save him? If a brother or sister be naked, and destitute of daily food, and one of you say unto them, Depart in peace, be ye warmed and filled; notwithstanding ye give them not those things which are needful to the body; what doth it profit? Even so faith, if it hath not works, is dead, being alone (James 2:14-17).

31. Ten New Testament Proverbs Concerning Witnessing

1. Jesus said unto them, Follow me, and I will make you fishers of men (Matt. 4:19).

2. Ye are the salt of the earth: but if the salt have lost his savor,

Job and His Friends

wherewith shall it be salted? It is thenceforth good for nothing, but to be cast out, and to be trodden under foot of men (Matt. 5:13).

3. Let your light so shine before men, that they may see your good works, and glorify your Father which is in heaven (Matt. 5:16).
4. The disciple is not above his master, nor the servant above his lord. It is enough for the disciple that he be as his master, and the servant as his lord (Matt. 10:24, 25).
5. A prophet is not without honour, save in his own country, and in his own house (Matt. 13:57).
6. The servant is not greater than his lord; neither is he that is sent greater than he that sent him (John 13:16).
7. Greater love hath no man than this, that a man lay down his life for his friends (John 15:13).
8. Whether it be right in the sight of God to hearken unto [men] more than unto God, judge ye. For we cannot but speak the things which we have seen and heard (Acts 4:19, 20).
9. [God] hath made us able ministers of the new testament; not of the letter, but of the spirit: for the letter killeth, but the spirit giveth life (2 Cor. 3:6).
10. Marvel not, my brethren, if the world hate you (1 John 3:13).

32. Thirteen Special Facts About God the Father

1. Your Father knoweth what things ye have need of before ye ask him (Matt. 6:8).
2. Of that day and hour knoweth no man, no, not the angels, but my Father only (Matt. 24:36).
3. God is a Spirit (John 4:24).
4. Jesus said, My Father is greater than I (John 14:28).
5. God that made the world and all things therein, seeing that he is Lord of heaven and earth, dwelleth not in temples made with hands; neither is worshiped with men's hands, as though he needed anything, seeing he giveth to all life, and breath, and all things; and hath made of one blood all nations of men for to dwell on all the face of the earth, and hath determined the times before appointed, and the bounds of their habitation; that they should seek the Lord, if haply they might feel after him, and find him, though he be not far from every one of us: for in him we live, and move, and have our being (Acts 17:24-28).

6. God is not the author of confusion, but of peace, as in all churches of the saints (1 Cor. 14:33).

7. There is . . . one God and Father of all, who is above all, and through all, and in you all (Eph. 4:6).

8. God cannot lie (Titus 1:2).

9. Thou art the same, and thy years shall not fail (Heb. 1:12).

10. Neither is there any creature that is not manifest in his sight: but all things are naked and opened unto the eyes of him with whom we have to do (Heb. 4:13).

11. God is not unrighteous to forget your work and labour of love, which ye have showed toward his name, in that ye have . . . , and do, minister to the saints (Heb. 6:10).

12. Our God is a consuming fire (Heb. 12:29).

13. There are seven Spirits of God (Rev. 4:5).

33. Fifty-four Special Facts About Jesus

1. [Jesus said], not everyone that saith unto me, Lord, Lord, shall enter into the kingdom of heaven; but he that doeth the will of my Father which is in heaven. Many will say to me in that day, Lord, Lord, have we not prophesied in thy name, and in thy name have cast out devils, and in thy name done many wonderful works? And then will I profess unto them, I never knew you: depart from me, ye that work iniquity (Matt. 7:21-23).

2. [Jesus said], I will have mercy, and not sacrifice: for I am not come to call the righteous, but sinners to repentance (Matt. 9:13).

3. The Son of man is Lord even of the sabbath day (Matt. 12:8).

4. [Jesus said], Think not that I am come to send peace on earth: I came not to send peace, but a sword. For I am come to set a man at variance against his father, and the daughter against her mother, and the daughter-in-law against her mother-in-law. And a man's foes shall be they of his own household (Matt. 10:34-36).

5. [Jesus said], He that loveth father or mother more than me is not worthy of me: and he that loveth son or daughter more than me is not worthy of me (Matt. 10:37).

6. [Jesus said], All things are delivered unto me of my Father: and no man knoweth the Son, but the Father; neither knoweth any man the Father, save the Son, and he to whomsoever the Son will reveal him (Matt. 11:27).

7. The Son of man shall send forth his angels, and they shall gather out of his kingdom all things that offend, and them which do iniquity; and shall cast them into a furnace of fire: there shall be wailing and gnashing of teeth. Then shall the righteous shine forth as the sun in the kingdom of their Father (Matt. 13:41-43).

8. [Jesus said], Heaven and earth shall pass away, but my words shall not pass away (Matt. 24:35).

9. The Word was made flesh, and dwelt among us, (and we beheld his glory, the glory as of the only begotten of the Father,) full of grace and truth (John 1:14).

10. The law was given by Moses, but grace and truth came by Jesus Christ (John 1:17).

11. [Jesus] is he which baptizeth with the Holy Ghost (John 1:33).

12. Hereafter ye shall see heaven open, and the angels of God ascending and descending upon the Son of man (John 1:51).

13. Jesus said . . . I am the bread of life: he that cometh to me shall never hunger; and he that believeth on me shall never thirst (John 6:35).

14. [Jesus said], All that the Father giveth me shall come to me; and him that cometh to me I will in no wise cast out. No man can come to me, except the Father which hath sent me draw him: and I will raise him up at the last day (John 6:37, 44).

15. [Jesus said], The words that I speak unto you, they are spirit and they are life (John 6:63).

16. [Jesus said], If ye believe not that I am he, ye shall die in your sins (John 8:24).

17. Jesus said, For judgment I am come into this world, that they which see not might see; and that they which see might be made blind (John 9:39).

18. [Jesus said], I am the good shepherd, and know my sheep, and am known of mine. And other sheep I have, which are not of this fold: them also I must bring, and they shall hear my voice; and there shall be one fold, and one shepherd (John 10:14, 16).

19. [Jesus said], If I then, your Lord and Master, have washed your feet; ye also ought to wash one another's feet. For I have given you an example, that ye should do as I have done to you (John 13:14, 15).

20. [Jesus said], I will come again, and receive you unto myself; that where I am, there ye may be also (John 14:3).

21. Jesus said . . . I am the way, the truth, and the life: no man cometh unto the Father but by me (John 14:6).
22. [Jesus said], In the world ye shall have tribulation; but be of good cheer; I have overcome the world (John 16:33).
23. To [the apostles] he shewed himself alive after his passion by many infallible proofs, being seen of them forty days, and speaking of the things pertaining to the kingdom of God (Acts 1:3).
24. Heaven must receive [Jesus] until the times of restitution of all things, which God hath spoken by the mouth of all his holy prophets since the world began (Acts 3:21).
25. Him hath God exalted with his right hand to be a Prince and a Saviour, for to give repentance to Israel, and forgiveness of sins (Acts 5:31).
26. Be it known unto you therefore, men and brethren, that through [Jesus] is preached unto you the forgiveness of sins: and by him all that believe are justified from all things, from which you could not be justified by the law of Moses (Acts 13:38, 39).
27. The gospel of Christ . . . is the power of God unto salvation to every one that believeth (Rom. 1:16).
28. Christ is the end of the law for righteousness to every one that believeth (Rom. 10:4).
29. [God] hath made [Jesus], who knew no sin, to be sin for us; that we might be made the righteousness of God in him (2 Cor. 5:21).
30. Ye know the grace of our Lord Jesus Christ, that, though he was rich, yet for your sakes he became poor, that ye through his poverty might be rich (2 Cor. 8:9).
31. If righteousness come by the law, then Christ is dead in vain (Gal. 2:21).
32. Christ hath redeemed us from the curse of the law, being made a curse for us: for it is written, Cursed is everyone that hangeth on a tree (Gal. 3:13).
33. God also hath highly exalted [Jesus] and given him a name which is above every name: that at the name of Jesus every knee should bow, of things in heaven, and things in earth, and things under the earth; and that every tongue should confess that Jesus Christ is Lord, to the glory of God the Father (Phil. 2:9-11).
34. [Jesus] is the image of the invisible God, the firstborn of every creature: for by him were all things created (Col. 1:15, 16).

35. In [Christ] dwelleth all the fulness of the Godhead bodily (Col. 2:9).
36. The Lord Jesus shall be revealed from heaven with his mighty angels, in flaming fire taking vengeance on them that know not God, and that obey not the gospel of our Lord Jesus Christ (2 Thess. 1:7, 8).
37. There is one God, and one mediator between God and men, the man Christ Jesus (1 Tim. 2:5).
38. Our Saviour Jesus Christ hath abolished death and hath brought life and immortality to light through the gospel (2 Tim. 1:10).
39. The Lord Jesus Christ shall judge the quick and the dead at his appearing (2 Tim. 4:1).
40. [Jesus] is the brightness of [God's] glory, and is the express image of his person, and upholding all things by the word of his power, when he had by himself purged our sins, sat down on the right hand of the Majesty on high (Heb. 1:3).
41. [Jesus was] made so much better than the angels. The angels of God worship him (Heb. 1:4, 6).
42. [Jesus], the captain of [our] salvation, [was made] perfect through sufferings (Heb. 2:10).
43. Through death, [Jesus] destroyed him that had the power of death, that is, the devil (Heb. 2:14).
44. In all things it behoved [Jesus] to be made like unto his brethren, that he might be a merciful and faithful high priest in things pertaining to God, to make reconciliation for the sins of the people (Heb. 2:17).
45. Though [Jesus] were a Son, yet learned he obedience by the things which he suffered; and being made perfect, he became the author of eternal salvation unto all them that obey him (Heb. 5:8, 9).
46. But [Jesus], because he continueth ever, hath an unchangeable priesthood (Heb. 7:24).
47. How much more shall the blood of Christ, who through the eternal Spirit offered himself without spot to God, purge your conscience from dead works to serve the living God? (Heb. 9:14).
48. [We have the] boldness to enter into the holiest by the blood of Jesus (Heb. 10:19).
49. Yet a little while, and he that shall come will come, and will not tarry (Heb. 10:37).
50. Wherefore Jesus also, that he might sanctify the people with his own blood, suffered without the gate. Let us go forth

therefore unto him without the camp, bearing his reproach (Heb. 13:12, 13).

51. [By the Spirit, Christ] went and preached unto the spirits in prison; which sometime were disobedient, when once the longsuffering of God waited in the days of Noah, while the ark was a preparing (1 Pet. 3:18-20).

52. [Jesus has] the keys of hell and of death (Rev. 1:18).

53. Jesus is holy and true, and he has the key of David. He opens, and no man can shut. He shuts, and no man opens (Rev. 3:7).

54. [Jesus is] the beginning of the creation of God (Rev. 3:14).

34. Seven New Testament Facts About Man

1. The light of the body is the eye (Matt. 6:22).

2. No man can serve two masters: for either he will hate the one, and love the other; or else he will hold to the one, and despise the other. Ye cannot serve God and mammon (Matt. 6:24).

3. In the resurrection they neither marry, nor are given in marriage (Matt. 22:30).

4. If I pray in an unknown tongue, my spirit prayeth (1 Cor. 14:14).

5. [The Hebrews] could not enter in [to the rest of God] because of unbelief (Heb. 3:7-19).

6. Every man is tempted, when he is drawn away of his own lust, and enticed (James 1:14).

7. If any man offend not in word, the same is a perfect man, and able to bridle the whole body (James 3:2).

35. Eleven New Testament Facts About Angels

1. Children have personal angels (Matt. 18:10).

2. Angels do not marry (Matt. 22:30).

3. There is joy in the presence of the angels of God over one sinner that repenteth (Luke 15:10).

4. Satan himself is transformed into an angel of light (2 Cor. 11:14).

5. God maketh his angels spirits, and his ministers a flame of fire (Heb. 1:7).

6. [Angels are] all ministering spirits, sent forth to minister for them who shall be heirs of salvation (Heb. 1:14).

7. God spared not the angels that sinned, but cast them down to hell, and delivered them into chains of darkness, to be reserved unto judgment (2 Pet. 2:4).

8. The angels which kept not their first estate, but left their own habitation, [God] hath reserved in everlasting chains under darkness unto the judgment of the great day (Jude 6).

9. Michael the archangel, when contending with the devil he disputed about the body of Moses, durst not bring against him a railing accusation, but said, The Lord rebuke thee (Jude 9).

10. [Jesus] sent and signified the revelation by his angel unto his servant John (Rev. 1:1).

11. There was war in heaven: Michael and his angels fought against the dragon; and the dragon fought and his angels, and prevailed not; neither was their place found any more in heaven (Rev. 12:7, 8).

36. Seventeen New Testament Facts About Bible Characters

1. Herod laid hold upon John [the Baptist] and bound him in prison for Herodias' sake, his brother Philip's wife: for he had married her. For John had said unto Herod, It is not lawful for thee to have thy brother's wife (Mark 6:17, 18).

2. The woman with the issue of blood whom Jesus healed, had been ill twelve years, and had spent all her living on physicians (Luke 8:43).

3. Peter fell into a trance and saw a vision (Acts 10:10-16).

4. Agabus gave two recorded prophecies which were fulfilled: (1) There should be a great dearth throughout all the world: which came to pass in the days of Claudius Caesar (Acts 11:28); (2) He took Paul's girdle, and bound his own hands and feet, and said, Thus saith the Holy Ghost, So shall the Jews at Jerusalem bind the man that owneth this girdle, and shall deliver him into the hands of the Gentiles (Acts 21:11).

5. At Lycaonia, the people called Barnabas "Jupiter," and Paul, "Mercurius" (Acts 14:11, 12).

6. Paul circumcised Timothy (Acts 16:3) even though Paul held circumcision to be unnecessary (Gal. 2).

7. Philip the evangelist had four daughters, virgins, who could prophesy (Acts 21:8, 9).

8. Paul was in a trance and saw a vision (Acts 22:17-21).

9. [Paul could] deliver . . . unto Satan for the destruction of the flesh, that the spirit may be saved in the day of the Lord Jesus (1 Cor. 5:5).

10. Paul (whether in the body or out of the body; he could not tell) was caught up to the third heaven, into paradise, and heard unspeakable words, which it is not lawful for a man to utter (2 Cor. 12:2-4).

11. [Paul said], There was given to me a thorn in the flesh, the messenger of Satan to buffet me, lest I should be exalted above measure (2 Cor. 12:7).

12. Adam was first formed, then Eve. And Adam was not deceived, but the woman being deceived was in the transgression. Notwithstanding she shall be saved in childbearing, if they continue in faith and charity and holiness with sobriety (1 Tim. 2:13-15).

13. [Timothy received a gift] which was given [him] by prophecy, with the laying on of the hands of the presbytery (1 Tim. 4:14).

14. Timothy's grandmother was named Lois, and his mother's name was Eunice (2 Tim. 1:5). His mother was a Jewess, and his father was a Greek (Acts 16:1).

15. Melchisedec was better than Abraham (Heb. 7:7).

16. The devil, as a roaring lion, walketh about, seeking whom he may devour (1 Pet. 5:8).

17. John heard the voices of over 100 million angels (Rev. 5:11).

37. Six New Testament Facts About the Holy Spirit

1. [Jesus said], All manner of sin and blasphemy shall be forgiven unto men: but the blasphemy against the Holy Ghost shall not be forgiven unto men. Whosoever speaketh a word against the Holy Ghost, it shall not be forgiven him, neither in this world, neither in the world to come (Matt. 12:31, 32).

2. The wind bloweth where it listeth, and thou hearest the sound thereof, but canst not tell whence it cometh, and whither it goeth: so is every one that is born of the Spirit (John 3:8).

3. [Jesus said], He that believeth on me, as the scripture hath said, out of his belly shall flow rivers of living water. (This spake he of the Spirit, which they that believe on him should receive) (John 7:38, 39).

4. [Jesus said], I will send [the Holy Spirit] unto you. And

when he is come, he will reprove the world of sin, and of righteousness, and judgment. When the Spirit of truth is come, he will guide you into all truth: for he shall not speak of himself; but whatsoever he shall hear, that shall he speak: and he will show you things to come. He shall glorify me: for he shall receive of mine, and shall show it unto you (John 16:7, 8, 13, 14).

5. [Jesus] through the Holy Ghost had given commandments unto the apostles (Acts 1:2).
6. [The 120 disciples] were all filled with the Holy Ghost, and began to speak with other tongues, as the Spirit gave them utterance (Acts 2:1-4).

The Descent of the Spirit

4

Supernatural Events

The Bible, the best seller of all time, is in itself a "supernatural event." And within its pages is found a marvelous record of hundreds of unusual occurrences. Some may think of a miracle as only a positive action which God does for a person. The Bible, though, includes accounts of people who were supernaturally struck blind, deaf, or even dead. This chapter lists some of those "negative" miracles, as well as "Ten Accounts of People Raised from the Dead" and "Fourteen Supernatural Journeys."

For more on the supernatural, see chapter fourteen, "Miracle Workers and Their Deeds."

38. Eleven Visions of God

1. Jacob dreamed of "a ladder set up on the earth, and the top of it reached to heaven. . . . And, behold, the Lord stood above it" (Gen. 28:12, 13).
2. Moses, and Aaron, Nadab, and Abihu, and seventy of the elders of Israel . . . saw the God of Israel (Ex. 24:9, 10).
3. Moses saw the back of God (Ex. 33:23).
4. Micaiah "saw the Lord sitting upon his throne" (2 Chron. 18:18).
5. Isaiah "saw also the Lord sitting upon a throne, high and lifted up, and his train filled the temple" (Isa. 6:1).
6. Ezekiel saw "the likeness of a throne, as the appearance of a sapphire stone: and . . . the likeness as the appearance of a man above it" (Ezek. 1:26).
7. Ezekiel again had a similar vision (Ezek. 10:1).
8. Daniel "beheld till the thrones were cast down, and the Ancient of days did sit" (Dan. 7:9).
9. Stephen "looked up stedfastly into heaven, and saw the glory

Jacob's Dream

of God, and Jesus standing on the right hand of God" (Acts 7:55).

10. Paul wrote that he "knew a man" (likely himself), who was "caught up to the third heaven" (2 Cor. 12:2).

11. John "was in the spirit; and behold, a throne was set in heaven, and one sat on the throne" (Rev. 4:2).

39. People Who Were Struck Blind

1. Many men of Sodom were struck blind by two angels who came to rescue Lot and his family before Sodom was destroyed (Gen. 19:11).

2. The Syrian army was struck blind at the word of Elisha when the army came to capture him (2 Kings 6:18).

3. Paul was struck blind on the road to Damascus (Acts 9:8).

4. Elymas the sorcerer was blinded when Paul spoke the word, because Elymas tried to turn Sergius Paulus from the faith (Acts 13:7-11).

40. Two Men Who Were Struck Dumb

1. Ezekiel was struck dumb by the Lord on occasion and then could speak only when the Lord gave him something to say (Ezek. 3:25-27).
2. The angel Gabriel struck Zecharias dumb for about nine months until his son, John the Baptist, was born and named (Luke 1:5-20, 62-64).

41. People Whom the Bible Says God Killed and Three Other Accounts of Strange Deaths

1. God destroyed the entire world population, except Noah and seven others, when He caused the great flood (Gen. 6:7).
2. God killed all the people in Sodom and Gomorrah when He rained fire and brimstone. Only Lot and his daughters escaped (Gen. 19:24, 25).
3. God slew Er for being wicked (Gen. 38:7).
4. God slew Onan for not producing offspring with his widowed sister-in-law (Gen. 38:9, 10).
5. God killed all the firstborn of Egypt, and Pharaoh and his soldiers that pursued Israel into the Red Sea (Ex. 12:29; 14:16-19; 24-27).
6. Fire from the Lord devoured Nadab and Abihu when they offered strange fire (Lev. 10:1, 2).
7. Korah, his family, and all his men were swallowed up by the earth, and 250 other men were consumed by fire from the Lord because they sought the priesthood beyond the duties they already had (Num. 16:1-35).
8. When Israel murmured about the incident in item 7, the Lord killed 14,700 more people with a plague (Num. 16:41-50).
9. The Lord killed an unknown number of Amorites battling against Israel by casting down great hailstones from heaven (Josh. 10:8-14).
10. Jael, the wife of Heber, killed Sisera, the captain of the host of the Canaanites, by hammering a tent peg through his temples while he slept in her tent (Judges 4:18-21).
11. God killed Uzzah for touching the ark of God (2 Sam. 6:6, 7).
12. The Lord sent a pestilence upon Israel, killing 70,000 people, because David numbered Israel and Judah (2 Sam. 24:1-15).
13. God killed 102 soldiers by sending fire down from heaven

when they came to capture Elijah (2 Kings 1:10, 12).

14. Bears tore up 42 children when Elisha cursed them in God's name for making fun of his bald head (2 Kings 2:23, 24).

15. Haman was hanged on the gallows that he had prepared for hanging Mordecai, and Mordecai was set over the house of Haman (Esther 7:10-8:2).

16. Ananias and Sapphira dropped dead after it was supernaturally revealed that they had lied about the price received for a possession they sold (Acts 5:1-10).

42. Ten Biblical Accounts of People Raised from the Dead

1. Elijah raised the son of the Zarephath widow from the dead (1 Kings 17:17-22).

2. Elisha raised the son of the Shunammite woman from the dead (2 Kings 4:32-35).

3. A man was raised from the dead when his body touched Elisha's bones (2 Kings 13:20, 21).

4. Many saints rose from the dead at the resurrection of Jesus (Matt. 27:50-53).

5. Jesus rose from the dead (Matt. 28:5-8; Mark 16:6; Luke 24:5, 6).

6. Jesus raised the son of the widow of Nain from the dead (Luke 7:11-15).

7. Jesus raised the daughter of Jairus from the dead (Luke 8:41, 42, 49-55).

8. Jesus raised Lazarus from the dead (John 11:1-44).

9. Peter raised Dorcas from the dead (Acts 9:36-41).

10. Eutychus was raised from the dead by Paul (Acts 20:9, 10).

43. The Only Times the Sun Stood Still or Changed Direction

1. Then spake Joshua to the Lord in the day when the Lord delivered up the Amorites before the children of Israel, and he said in the sight of Israel, Sun, stand thou still upon Gibeon; and thou, Moon, in the valley of Ajalon. And the sun stood still, and the moon stayed, until the people had avenged themselves upon their enemies. Is not this written in the book of Jasher? So the sun stood still in the midst of heaven, and hasted not to go down about a whole day (Josh. 10:12, 13).

2. And Hezekiah said unto Isaiah, What shall be the sign that the Lord will heal me, and that I shall go up into the house of the Lord the third day? And Isaiah said, This sign shalt thou have of the Lord, that the Lord will do the thing that he hath spoken: shall the shadow go forward ten degrees, or go back ten degrees? And Hezekiah answered, It is a light thing for the shadow to go down ten degrees: nay, but let the shadow return backward ten degrees. And Isaiah the prophet cried unto the Lord: and he brought the shadow ten degrees backward, by which it had gone down in the dial of Ahaz (2 Kings 20:8-11).

44. Animals God Used Miraculously

1. God provided Abraham a *ram* to be sacrificed instead of Isaac (Gen. 22:13).
2. Moses' rod became a *serpent* (Ex. 4:3).
3. God filled Egypt with *frogs* (Ex. 8:6).
4. God sent *lice* upon the Egyptians (Ex. 8:17).
5. The Lord sent *flies* upon Egypt (Ex. 8:22).
6. God sent *locusts* upon Egypt (Ex. 10:13).
7. God sent *quail* to the Israelites after they murmured (Ex. 16:13).
8. God sent *fiery serpents* among the Israelites (Num. 21:6).
9. Balaam's *ass* spoke to him (Num. 22:28).
10. The Philistines hitched *two cows*, separated from their calves, to the cart holding the ark of the covenant. The cows went straight to Israel (1 Sam. 6:7-12).
11. A prophet who disobeyed God's command was told, "Thy carcase shall not come into the sepulchre of thy fathers." Riding on an ass, he was killed by a *lion* that did not devour him, and never touched the ass (1 Kings 13:24, 28).
12. When Elijah hid from Ahab at the brook Cherith, *ravens* brought him bread and flesh, morning and evening (1 Kings 17:6).
13. *Horses of fire*, pulling a chariot, parted Elijah and Elisha when Elijah was taken up by a whirlwind into heaven (2 Kings 2:11).
14. Elisha cursed children at Bethel, in the name of the Lord, that taunted him for his baldness. Two she *bears* appeared and tore 42 of the children (2 Kings 2:24).
15. *Dogs* ate the flesh of Jezebel, as prophesied (2 Kings 9:36).

16. The mouths of *lions* were shut when Daniel was cast into their den because he worshiped God (Dan. 6:22).
17. The Lord prepared a great *fish* to swallow up Jonah (Jonah 1:17).
18. God prepared a *worm* to kill the vine that shaded Jonah (Jonah 4:7).
19. God provided Peter a *fish* with money in its mouth to pay tribute (Matt. 17:27).
20. Jesus rode into Jerusalem on an *ass* and its *colt*, fulfilling Zechariah's prophecy (Zech. 9:9; Matt. 21:7).
21. The *cock* crowed after Peter denied Jesus three times, as Jesus prophesied (Matt. 26:74, 75).
22. Jesus sent unclean spirits into a herd of *swine* (Mark 5:13).
23. Jesus fed four thousand with seven loaves and a few small *fish* (Mark 8:6-9).
24. Jesus gave Simon a great catch of *fish* after he had failed to catch any all night (Luke 5:5, 6).
25. Jesus fed the five thousand men with two *fish* and five barley loaves (John 6:9-12).
26. Jesus, after His resurrection, caused seven of the disciples to catch more *fish* than they could draw in, though they had caught none all night (John 21:2-6).
27. Paul was bitten by a venomous *viper*, but was unharmed (Acts 28:3-6).

45. Fourteen Supernatural Journeys

1. Israel crossed the Red Sea on dry ground while the water stood as a wall on their right and on their left (Ex. 14:19-28).
2. Israel crossed the Jordan River on dry ground while the water stood in a heap (Josh. 3).
3. Elijah outran Ahab's chariot all the way from the top of Mount Carmel to the entrance of Jezreel (about ten miles) (1 Kings 18:41-46).
4. Elijah traveled 40 days in the strength of a cake and water brought to him by an angel (1 Kings 19:5-8).
5. Elijah went up by a whirlwind into heaven (2 Kings 2:11).
6. Elijah and Elisha walked across the Jordan River on dry ground after Elijah smote the waters with his mantle (2 Kings 2:8).
7. Elisha walked across the Jordan River alone on dry ground

Elijah's Ascent in a Chariot of Fire

after smiting the waters with Elijah's mantle (2 Kings 2:14).

8. A spirit took Ezekiel by a lock of his head and lifted him up between heaven and earth (Ezek. 8:1-3).

9. The devil took Jesus up into a high mountain and showed Him all the kingdoms of the world in a moment. He then brought Jesus to Jerusalem and set Him on a pinnacle of the temple (Matt. 4; Luke 4).

10. Jesus and Peter walked on water in the midst of a storm (Matt. 14:22-32).

11. After Jesus got into the boat after walking on water, the ship was immediately at the land where they were headed (John 6:15-21).
12. Jesus was caught up to heaven as the apostles watched (Acts 1:9).
13. The Spirit of the Lord carried Philip from Gaza to Azotus (Acts 8:39, 40).
14. Paul knew a man (probably himself) who was caught up to the third heaven. He didn't know whether he was there bodily or not (2 Cor. 12:1-7).

46. Supernatural Fire in the Bible

1. And [God] placed at the east end of the garden of Eden Cherubims, and a flaming sword which turned every way (Gen. 3:24).
2. The Lord rained upon Sodom and Gomorrah brimstone and fire from the Lord of heaven (Gen. 19:24).
3. The angel of the Lord appeared unto [Moses] in a flame of fire out of a bush . . . and the bush was not consumed (Ex. 3:2).
4. The Lord sent thunder and hail, and the fire ran along upon the ground (Ex. 9:23).
5. The Lord went before them . . . by night in a pillar of fire (Ex. 13:21).
6. The Lord descended upon [Mount Sinai] in fire (Ex. 19:18).
7. There came a fire out from before the Lord, and consumed upon the altar the burnt offering and the fat (Lev. 9:24).
8. There went out fire from the Lord, and devoured [Nadab and Abihu] (Lev. 10:2).
9. There was upon the tabernacle as it were the appearance of fire, until morning (Num. 9:15).
10. When the people complained . . . the fire of the Lord burnt among them and consumed them (Num. 11:1).
11. There came out a fire from the Lord, and consumed the two hundred and fifty men that offered incense (Num. 16:35).
12. The angel of the Lord put forth the end of the staff that was in his hand . . . and there rose up fire out of the rock, and consumed the flesh of the unleavened cakes (Judges 6:21).
13. The fire of the Lord fell, and consumed the burnt sacrifice (1 Kings 18:38).
14. There came down fire from heaven, and consumed [the captain of fifty] and his fifty (2 Kings 1:10).

15. The fire of God came down from heaven, and consumed [another captain of fifty] and his fifty (2 Kings 1:12).
16. There appeared a chariot of fire and horses of fire (2 Kings 2:11).
17. The mountain was full of horses and chariots of fire round about Elisha (2 Kings 6:17).
18. David . . . called upon the Lord; and he answered him from heaven by fire upon the altar of burnt offering (1 Chron. 21:26).
19. When Solomon had made an end of praying, the fire came down from heaven (2 Chron. 7:1).
20. The fire of God is fallen from heaven, and hath burned up the sheep, and the servants, and consumed them (Job 1:16).
21. While I [David] was musing the fire burned: then spake I with my tongue (Ps. 39:3).
22. Then flew one of the seraphims unto me, having a live coal in his hand, which he had taken with the tongs from off the altar (Isa. 6:6).
23. Behold, a whirlwind came out of the north, a great cloud, and a fire infolding itself, and a brightness was about it, and out of the midst thereof as the colour of amber, out of the midst of the fire (Ezek. 1:4).
24. I beheld, and lo a likeness as the appearance of fire: from the appearance of his loins even downward, fire (Ezek. 8:2).
25. Go in between the wheels, even under the cherub, and fill thine hand with coals of fire from between the cherubims, and scatter them over the city (Ezek. 10:2).
26. [The Ancient of days'] throne was like the fiery flame, and his wheels as burning fire (Dan. 7:9).
27. [The rich man] cried . . . I am tormented in this flame (Luke 16:24).
28. There appeared unto them cloven tongues like as of fire, and it sat upon each of them (Acts 2:3).
29. His eyes were as a flame of fire (Rev. 1:14).
30. There were seven lamps of fire burning before the throne, which are the seven Spirits of God (Rev. 4:5).
31. And the angel took the censer and filled it with fire of the altar, and cast it into the earth (Rev. 8:5).
32. The first angel sounded, and there followed hail and fire mingled with blood (Rev. 8:7).
33. And thus [John] saw the horses in the vision, and them that sat on them, having breastplates of fire . . . and out of [the

The Flight of Lot

horses'] mouths issued fire and smoke and brimstone (Rev. 9:17).

34. [John] saw another mighty angel . . . and his feet as pillars of fire (Rev. 10:1).

35. And if any man hurt [the two witnesses], fire proceedeth out of their mouth, and devoureth their enemies (Rev. 11:5).

36. [The second beast] doeth great wonders, so that he maketh fire come down from heaven on the earth in the sight of men (Rev. 13:13).

37. And [John] saw as it were a sea of glass intermingled with fire (Rev. 15:2).
38. The fourth angel poured out his vial upon the sun; and power was given unto him to scorch men with fire (Rev. 16:8).
39. His eyes were as a flame of fire, and on his head were many crowns (Rev. 19:12).
40. [The beast and the false prophet] were cast alive into a lake of fire burning with brimstone (Rev. 19:20).
41. Fire came down from God out of heaven, and devoured them. And the devil that deceived them was cast into the lake of fire and brimstone. . . . And death and hell were cast into the lake of fire. . . . And whosoever was not found written in the book of life was cast into the lake of fire (Rev. 20:9, 10, 14, 15).

47. Dividing of Waters in the Bible

1. The children of Israel went through the Red Sea "upon the dry ground: and the waters were a wall unto them on their right hand, and on their left" (Ex. 14:22).
2. The waters of the Jordan were cut off before the ark of the covenant of the Lord (Josh. 4:7).
3. Elijah took his mantle, and wrapped it together, and smote the waters, and they were divided hither and thither, so that they two went over on dry ground (2 Kings 2:8).
4. When [Elisha] also had smitten the waters, they parted hither and thither (2 Kings 2:14).
5. The Lord shall utterly destroy the tongue of the Egyptian sea; and with his mighty wind shall he shake his hand over the river, and shall smite it in the seven streams, and make men go over dryshod (Isa. 11:15).

5

Word Power

Where would we be without words? Without them, it's nearly impossible to communicate. Some even theorize that we can't really think without words!

God reveals himself to man through His Word. This chapter is about God's Word, whether written, spoken through prophecy, or delivered by angels. This chapter also covers other aspects of word power, such as wisdom, rules for exhortation, yardsticks for measuring prophecy, names that Jesus called the scribes and Pharisees, the seven last sayings of Jesus, and benedictions.

One further note: no attempt was made to list all of the prophecies concerning Jesus' first and second coming. However, in the list of Old Testament prophecies fulfilled by Jesus, the passages found there are specifically quoted by New Testament writers as having been fulfilled by Jesus. For very special Old Testament prophecies concerning Jesus, see Psalm 22 and Isaiah 52:13-15 and 53:1-12.

48. Twenty-five Facts About God's Word

1. Man doth not live by bread only, but by every word that proceedeth out of the mouth of the Lord (Deut. 8:3).
2. The word is very nigh unto thee, in thy mouth, and in thy heart, that thou mayest do it (Deut. 30:14).
3. The word of the Lord is right (Ps. 33:4).
4. By the word of the Lord were the heavens made (Ps. 33:6).
5. [Angels] hearken unto the voice of [God's] word (Ps. 103:20).
6. [God] sent his word and healed them (Ps. 107:20).
7. Wherewithal shall a young man cleanse his way? by taking heed thereto according to [God's] word (Ps. 119:9).
8. For ever, O Lord, thy word is settled in heaven (Ps. 119:89).

124

9. [God's] word is a lamp unto my feet and a light unto my path (Ps. 119:105).
10. [God's] word is true (Ps. 119:160).
11. Thou [God] hast magnified thy word about all thy name (Ps. 138:2).
12. [God's] word runneth very swiftly (Ps. 147:15).
13. Every word of God is pure (Prov. 30:5).
14. [God's word] shall not return unto [Him] void, but it shall accomplish that which [God] pleases, and it shall prosper in the thing whereto [He] sent it (Isa. 55:11).
15. Is not my word like as a fire? saith the Lord; and like a hammer that breaketh the rock in pieces? (Jer. 23:29)
16. The word that [God] shall speak shall come to pass (Ezek. 12:25).
17. The Word was made flesh and dwelt among us (John 1:14).
18. The word of God is the sword of the Spirit (Eph. 6:17).
19. The word of God is not bound (2 Tim. 2:9).
20. The word of God is quick (Heb. 4:12).
21. The word of God is powerful (Heb. 4:12).
22. The word of God is sharper than any twoedged sword, piercing even to the dividing asunder of soul and spirit (Heb. 4:12).
23. The word of God is a discerner of the thoughts and intents of the heart (Heb. 4:12).
24. The worlds were framed by the word of God (Heb. 11:3).
25. The word of God liveth and abideth forever (1 Pet. 1:23).

49. Twenty-three Old Testament Prophecies Fulfilled by Jesus

NO.	OLD TESTAMENT REFERENCE	NEW TESTAMENT FULFILLMENT
1.	For thou wilt not leave my soul in hell; neither wilt thou suffer thine Holy One to see corruption (Ps. 16:10).	Whom God hath raised up, having loosed the pains of death: because it was not possible that he should be holden of it (Acts 2:24).
2.	They part my garments among them, and cast lots upon my vesture (Ps. 22:18).	They crucified [Jesus], and parted his garments, casting lots (Matt. 27:35).

NO.	OLD TESTAMENT REFERENCE	NEW TESTAMENT FULFILLMENT
3.	He keepeth all his bones: not one of them is broken (Ps. 34:20).	But when they came to Jesus, and saw that he was dead already, they brake not his legs (John 19:30-36).
4.	Yea, mine own familiar friend, in whom I trusted, which did eat of my bread, hath lifted up his heel against me (Ps. 41:9).	And when [Jesus] had dipped the sop, he gave it to Judas Iscariot. . . . And after the sop Satan entered into him. Then said Jesus unto him, That thou doest, do quickly (John 13:18-30).
5.	Thou hast ascended on high, thou hast led captivity captive: thou has received gifts for men (Ps. 68:18).	But unto every one of us is given grace according to the measure of the gift of Christ (Eph. 4:7).
6.	They that hate me without a cause are more than the hairs of mine head (Ps. 69:4).	[Jesus said], But now have they both seen and hated both me and my Father (John 15:24, 25).
7.	In my thirst they gave me vinegar to drink (Ps. 69:21).	And they filled a sponge with vinegar, and put it upon hyssop, and put it to his mouth (John 19:28, 29).
8.	I will open my mouth in a parable: I will utter dark sayings of old (Ps. 78:2).	All these things spake Jesus unto the multitude in parables; and without a parable spake he not unto them (Matt. 13:34, 35).
9.	And he said, Go, and tell this people, Hear ye indeed, but understand not; and see ye indeed, but perceive not (Isa. 6:9).	I [Jesus] speak to [the multitudes] in parables: because they seeing see not; and hearing they hear not, neither do they understand (Matt. 13:13, 14).
10.	Make the heart of this people fat, and make their ears heavy, and shut their eyes; lest they see with their eyes, and hear with their ears, and understand with their heart, and convert, and be healed (Isa. 6:10).	The people could not believe Jesus because of Isaiah's prophecy (John 12:39-41).

NO.	OLD TESTAMENT REFERENCE	NEW TESTAMENT FULFILLMENT
11.	Behold, a virgin shall conceive, and bear a son, and shall call his name Immanuel (Isa. 7:14).	Jesus was born of the virgin Mary (Matt. 1:18-25).
12.	He lightly afflicted the land of Zebulun and the land of Naphtali, and afterward did more grievously afflict her by the way of the sea, beyond Jordan, in Galilee of the nations. The people that walked in darkness have seen a great light (Isa. 9:1-2).	And leaving Nazareth, he came and dwelt in Capernaum, which is upon the sea coast, in the borders of Zebulun and Naphtali (Matt. 4:12-16).
13.	Behold my servant whom I uphold; mine elect, in whom my soul delighteth; I have put my spirit upon him: he shall bring forth judgment to the Gentiles. He shall not cry, nor lift up, nor cause his voice to be heard in the street. A bruised reed shall he not break, and the smoking flax shall he not quench: he shall bring forth judgment unto truth (Isa.42:1-3).	But when Jesus knew [the Pharisees were plotting to destroy Him], he withdrew himself from thence: and great multitudes followed him, and he healed them all; and charged them that they should not make him known (Matt. 12:14-21).
14.	Who hath believed our report? and to whom is the arm of the Lord revealed? (Isa. 53:1).	But though [Jesus] had done so many miracles before them, yet they believed not on him (John 12:37, 38).
15.	Surely he hath borne our griefs and carried our sorrows (Isa. 53:4).	Jesus cast out spirits with his word, and healed all that were sick (Matt. 8:16, 17).
16.	He was numbered with the transgressors (Isa. 53:12).	And with him they crucify two thieves (Mark 15:27, 28).
17.	The Spirit of the Lord is upon me; because the Lord hath anointed me to preach good tidings unto the meek; he hath sent me to bind up the brokenhearted, to proclaim liberty to the captives, and the opening of the prison to them that are bound; to proclaim the acceptable year of the Lord (Isa.61:1,2).	And [Jesus] began to say unto them, This day is this scripture fulfilled in your ears (Luke 4:16-21).

NO.	OLD TESTAMENT REFERENCE	NEW TESTAMENT FULFILLMENT
18.	I . . . called my son out of Egypt (Hos. 11:1).	Joseph took Mary and Jesus into Egypt and stayed there until the death of Herod (Matt. 2:13-15).
19.	But thou Bethlehem Ephratah, though thou be little among the thousands of Judah, yet out of thee shall he come forth unto me that is to be ruler in Israel; whose goings forth have been from of old, from everlasting (Micah 5:2).	Jesus was born in Bethlehem of Judea (Matt. 2:1, 5, 6).
20.	Thus speaketh the Lord of hosts, saying, Behold the man whose name is The BRANCH; and he shall grow up out of his place, and he shall build the temple of the Lord (Zech. 6:12).	Jesus dwelt in Nazareth [a play on words between the BRANCH and Nazarene] (Matt. 2:23).
21.	Rejoice greatly, O daughter of Zion; shout, O daughter of Jerusalem: behold, thy King cometh unto thee: he is just, and having salvation; lowly, and riding upon an ass, and upon a colt the foal of an ass (Zech. 9:9).	Jesus made His triumphal entry into Jerusalem riding on an ass and its colt (Matt. 21:1-11).
22.	So they weighed for my price thirty pieces of silver. And the Lord said unto me, Cast it unto the potter: a goodly price that I was prised at of them. And I took the thirty pieces of silver, and cast them to the potter in the house of the Lord (Zech. 11:12, 13).	Judas . . . brought again the thirty pieces of silver to the chief priests and elders. He cast down the pieces of silver in the temple. They took counsel and bought with them the potter's field, to bury strangers in (Matt. 27:3-10).
23.	They shall look upon me whom they have pierced (Zech. 12:10).	But one of the soldiers with a spear pierced his side, and forthwith came there out blood and water (John 19:34, 37).

50. Six Old Testament Prophecies Concerning Jesus' Second Coming

1. Out of Zion, the perfection of beauty, God hath shined. Our God shall come, and shall not keep silence: a fire shall devour before him, and it shall be very tempestuous round about him. He shall call to the heavens from above, and to the earth, that he may judge his people. Gather my saints together unto me (Ps. 50:2-5).

2. For unto us a child is born, unto us a son is given: and the government shall be upon his shoulder: and his name shall be called Wonderful, Counsellor, the Mighty God, the everlasting Father, the Prince of Peace. Of the increase of his government and peace there shall be no end, upon the throne of David, and upon his kingdom, to order it, and to establish it with judgment and with justice from henceforth even for ever. The zeal of the Lord of hosts will perform this (Isa. 9:6, 7).

3. For I know their works and their thoughts: it shall come, that I will gather all nations and tongues; and they shall come, and see my glory (Isa. 66:18).

4. I saw in the night visions, and, behold, one like the Son of man came with the clouds of heaven, and came to the Ancient of days, and they brought him near before him. And there was given him dominion, and glory, and a kingdom, that all people, nations, and languages, should serve him: his dominion is an everlasting dominion, which shall not pass away, and his kingdom that which shall not be destroyed (Dan. 7:13, 14).

5. And it shall come to pass in that day, that I will seek to destroy all the nations that come against Jerusalem. And I will pour upon the house of David, and upon the inhabitants of Jerusalem, the spirit of grace and of supplications: and they shall look upon me whom they have pierced, and they shall mourn for him, as one mourneth for his only son, and shall be in bitterness for him, as one that is in bitterness for his firstborn (Zech. 12:9, 10).

6. And his feet shall stand in that day upon the mount of Olives, which is before Jerusalem on the east, and the mount of Olives shall cleave in the midst thereof toward the east and toward the west, and there shall be a very great valley; and half of the mountain shall remove toward the north, and half

of it toward the south. And ye shall flee to the valley of the mountains; for the valley of the mountains shall reach unto Azal: yea, ye shall flee, like as ye fled from before the earthquake in the days of Uzziah king of Judah: and the Lord my God shall come, and all the saints with thee. And the Lord shall be king over all the earth (Zech. 14:4, 5, 9).

51. Twenty Encounters with Angels

1. The angel of the Lord appeared to Hagar after she had been sent away by Sarai. The angel told Hagar to return to, and to submit to, Sarai. He also told Hagar that her seed would be multiplied exceedingly and that she should call her child Ishmael (Gen. 16:1-12).
2. Two angels rescued Lot, his wife, and two daughters from Sodom. The angels told them to escape to the mountains and not to look back, because the angels were going to destroy

The Angel of the Lord Appears to Abraham

Sodom. Lot convinced the angels to let him stay at Zoar (Gen. 19:1-22).

3. Abraham went up on the mountain to offer his son Isaac as a burnt sacrifice. As Abraham took the knife to slay Isaac, the angel of the Lord stopped Abraham and assured him that he had proven he feared God. The angel spoke again a little later and blessed Abraham by saying that the Lord would multiply Abraham's seed as the stars of heaven, and in his seed all the nations of the earth would be blessed (Gen. 22:1-18).

4. An angel appeared to Jacob and wrestled with him all night. Unable to prevail against Jacob, he disjointed the hollow of Jacob's thigh. The angel changed Jacob's name to Israel and blessed him (Gen. 32:24-30).

5. The angel of the Lord appeared to Moses in a burning bush. The Lord then told Moses to free the Hebrews from the bondage of Egypt (Ex. 3-4:17).

6. The angel of the Lord stood in the way of Balaam and his donkey. The donkey saw the angel, but Balaam did not. When the donkey turned aside into the field, Balaam struck the donkey. The Lord caused the donkey to speak. Then Balaam finally saw the angel, who told Balaam that he could go to Balak, but he should only speak that which God gave him to say (Num. 22:22-35).

7. Joshua was confronted by an angel who was the captain of the host of the Lord. The angel gave Joshua instructions on conquering Jericho (Josh. 5:13-15).

8. An angel of the Lord appeared to Gideon and commissioned him to save Israel from the Midianites. Gideon made a meal for the angel. The angel had Gideon put the food on a rock, then caused fire to come forth from the rock and consume it (Judges 6:11-23).

9. The angel of the Lord appeared to Samson's mother and told her she would have a son even though she had been barren. Later, the angel appeared again to both of Samson's parents and repeated his command that Samson was to be a Nazarite (Judges 13:1-20).

10. Elijah, depressed because Jezebel vowed to kill him, went into the wilderness, sat under a juniper tree, and begged God to let him die. An angel came and prepared food for Elijah. Elijah was so strengthened by those meals that he journeyed 40 days without eating again (1 Kings 19:1-8).

11. One or two angels met the woman at Jesus' tomb and announced His resurrection (Matt. 28:5-7; Mark 16:5-7; Luke 24:4-7; John 20:11-18).

12. The angel Gabriel appeared to Zacharias and announced that Elizabeth, who was old and barren, would have a son and that he should be named John. He also told Zacharias about John's future ministry. Zacharias asked for a sign; he was struck dumb and couldn't speak again until John was born and named (Luke 1:5-22, 57-64).

13. The angel Gabriel also appeared to the Virgin Mary and told her that she would give birth to Jesus and God would be the Father. He also told her about Elizabeth (Luke 1:26-38).

14. The angel of the Lord announced the birth of Jesus to the shepherds and was then joined by a multitude of the heavenly host praising God (Luke 2:8-15).

15. As Jesus ascended into heaven, two angels appeared to the apostles and said, "Ye men of Galilee, why stand ye gazing up into heaven? This same Jesus, which is taken up from you into heaven, shall so come in like manner as ye have seen him go into heaven" (Acts 1:9-11).

16. The angel of the Lord brought the apostles out of prison and said, "Go, stand and speak in the temple to the people all the words of this life" (Acts 5:17-20).

17. The angel of the Lord told Philip to go to Gaza. There Philip met and converted the Ethiopian eunuch (Acts 8:26-39).

18. An angel appeared to Cornelius, telling him that God had heard his prayers and that he should send to Joppa for Peter. The angel said Peter would tell Cornelius what he should do (Acts 10:1-8).

19. Peter was asleep in prison while other Christians were praying for his release. The angel of the Lord woke Peter and released his chains. Peter followed the angel out of the prison and through the iron gate, which opened of its own accord (Acts 12:1-19).

20. Paul, sailing to Rome to be tried before Caesar, was in a storm for two weeks. The angel of God appeared to Paul and said, "Fear not, Paul; thou must be brought before Caesar: and, lo, God hath given thee all of them that sail with thee" (Acts 27:21-25).

52. Nineteen New Testament Prayers

1. Our Father which art in heaven, Hallowed be thy name. Thy kingdom come. Thy will be done in earth, as it is in heaven. Give us this day our daily bread. And forgive us our debts, as we forgive our debtors. And lead us not into temptation, but deliver us from evil: For thine is the kingdom, and the power, and the glory, for ever. Amen (Matt. 6:9-13).

2. I thank Thee, O Father, Lord of heaven and earth, because thou hast hid these things from the wise and prudent, and hast revealed them unto babes. Even so, Father: for it seemed good in thy sight (Matt. 11:25, 26).

3. Have mercy on me, O Lord, thou son of David; my daughter is grievously vexed with a devil. . . . Lord, help me. . . . Truth, Lord; yet the dogs eat of the crumbs which fall from their master's table (Matt. 15:22, 25, 27).

4. And there came a leper to [Jesus] beseeching him, and kneeling down to him, and saying to him, If thou wilt, thou canst make me clean (Mark 1:40).

5. God be merciful to me a sinner (Luke 18:13).

6. Father, if thou be willing, remove this cup from me: nevertheless not my will, but thine, be done (Luke 22:42).

7. Father, forgive them; for they know not what they do (Luke 23:34).

8. And he said unto Jesus, Lord, remember me when thou comest into thy kingdom (Luke 23:42).

9. Father, into thy hands I commend my spirit (Luke 23:46).

10. And Jesus lifted up his eyes, and said, Father, I thank thee that thou hast heard me. And I knew that thou hearest me always: but because of the people which stand by I said it, that they may believe that thou hast sent me (John 11:41, 42).

11. Father, save me from this hour: but for this cause came I unto this hour. Father, glorify thy name (John 12:27, 28).

12. Father, the hour is come; glorify thy Son, that thy Son also may glorify thee: As thou hast given him power over all flesh, that he should give eternal life to as many as thou hast given him. And this is life eternal, that they might know thee the only true God, and Jesus Christ whom thou hast sent.

    I have glorified thee on the earth: I have finished the work which thou gavest me to do. And now, O Father, glorify thou me with thine own self with the glory which I had with thee before the world was.

I have manifested thy name unto the men which thou gavest me out of the world: thine they were, and thou gavest them me; and they have kept thy word. Now they have known that all things whatsoever thou hast given me are of thee. For I have given unto them the words which thou gavest me; and they have received them, and have known surely that I came out from thee, and they have believed that thou didst send me.

I pray for them: I pray not for the world, but for them which thou hast given me; for they are thine. And all mine are thine, and thine are mine; and I am glorified in them. And now I am no more in the world, but these are in the world, and I come to thee.

Holy Father, keep through thine own name those whom thou hast given me, that they may be one, as we are. While I was with them in the world, I kept them in thy name: those that thou gavest me I have kept, and none of them is lost, but the son of perdition; that the scripture might be fulfilled.

And now I come to thee; and these things I speak in the world, that they might have my joy fulfilled in themselves. I have given them thy word; and the world hated them, because they are not of the world, even as I am not of the world. I pray not that thou shouldest take them out of the world, but that thou shouldest keep them from the evil. They are not of the world, even as I am not of the world. Sanctify them through thy truth: thy word is truth. As thou hast sent me into the world, even so have I sent them into the world. And for their sakes I sanctify myself, that they also might be sanctified through the truth.

Neither pray I for these alone, but for them also which shall believe on me through their word; that they all may be one; as thou, Father, art in me, and I in thee, that they also may be one in us: that the world may believe that thou hast sent me. And the glory which thou gavest me I have given them; that they may be one, even as we are one: I in them, and thou in me, that they may be made perfect in one; and that the world may know that thou hast sent me, and hast loved them, as thou hast loved me.

Father, I will that they also, whom thou hast given me, be with me where I am; that they may behold my glory, which thou hast given me: for thou lovedst me before the foundation of the world. O righteous Father, the world hath not

known thee: but I have know thee, and these have known
that thou hast sent me. And I have declared unto them thy
name, and will declare it: that the love wherewith thou hast
loved me may be in them, and I in them (John 17).

13. Thou Lord, which knowest the hearts of all men, show
whether of these two thou hast chosen, that they may take
part of this ministry and apostleship, from which Judas by
transgression fell, that he might go to his own place (Acts
1:24).

14. Lord, thou art God, which hast made heaven, and earth, and
the sea, and all that in them is: who by the mouth of thy servant David hast said, Why did the heathen rage, and the
people imagine vain things? The kings of the earth stood up,
and the rulers were gathered together against the Lord, and
against his Christ. For of a truth against thy holy child Jesus,
whom thou hast anointed, both Herod, and Pontius Pilate,
with the Gentiles, and the people of Israel, were gathered together, for to do whatsoever thy hand and thy counsel determined before to be done. And now, Lord, behold their threat-
enings: and grant unto thy servants, that with all boldness
they may speak thy word, by stretching forth thine hand to
heal; and that signs and wonders may be done by the name
of thy holy child Jesus (Acts 4:24-30).

15. Lord Jesus, receive my spirit (Acts 7:59).

16. Lord, lay not this sin to their charge (Acts 7:60).

17. Lord, what wilt thou have me to do? (Acts 9:6).

18. Thanks be unto God for his unspeakable gift (2 Cor. 9:15).

19. Even so, come, Lord Jesus (Rev. 22:20).

53. Fifteen Facts About Wisdom

1. Happy is the man that findeth wisdom (Prov. 3:13).

2. [Wisdom] is more precious than rubies, and all the things
thou canst desire are not to be compared unto her (Prov.
3:15).

3. Wisdom is the principal thing; therefore, get wisdom: and
with all thy getting get understanding (Prov. 4:7).

4. Those who seek [wisdom] early shall find [it] (Prov. 8:17).

5. [Wisdom will] cause those that love [her] to inherit substance; and [she] will fill their treasures (Prov. 8:21).

6. The fear of the Lord is the beginning of wisdom: and the
knowledge of the Holy is understanding (Prov. 9:10).

Solomon

7. Wisdom that is from above is pure (James 3:17).
8. Wisdom that is from above is peaceable (James 3:17).
9. Wisdom that is from above is gentle (James 3:17).
10. Wisdom that is from above is easy to be entreated (James 3:17).
11. Wisdom that is from above is full of mercy (James 3:17).
12. Wisdom that is from above is full of good fruits (James 3:17).

13. Wisdom that is from above is without partiality (James 3:17).
14. Wisdom that is from above is without hypocrisy (James 3:17).
15. If any of you lack wisdom, let him ask of God (James 1:5).

54. Eighteen Rules of Exhortation

1. Our exhortation was not of deceit (1 Thess. 2:3).
2. Our exhortation was not of uncleanness (1 Thess. 2:3).
3. Our exhortation was not in guile (1 Thess. 2:3).
4. As you were allowed of God to be put in trust with the gospel, even so speak (1 Thess. 2:4).
5. Speak not as pleasing men (1 Thess. 2:4).
6. Speak as pleasing God (1 Thess. 2:4).
7. Use no flattering words (1 Thess. 2:5).
8. Use no cloak of covetousness (1 Thess. 2:5).
9. Do not seek glory from men (1 Thess. 2:6).
10. Be gentle, even as a nurse cherishes her children (1 Thess. 2:7).
11. Impart the gospel of God (1 Thess. 2:8).
12. Impart your own souls (1 Thess. 2:8).
13. Behave holily (1 Thess. 2:10).
14. Behave justly (1 Thess. 2:10).
15. Behave unblameably (1 Thess. 2:10).
16. Exhort as a father does his children (1 Thess. 2:11).
17. Charge everyone to walk worthy of God (1 Thess. 2:11, 12).
18. Thank God without ceasing for those who receive the exhortation (1 Thess. 2:13).

55. Five Yardsticks by which to Measure Prophecy

1. When a prophet speaketh in the name of the Lord, if the thing follow not, nor come to pass, that is the thing which the Lord hath not spoken, but the prophet hath spoken it presumptuously: thou shalt not be afraid of him (Deut. 18:22).
2. He that prophesieth speaketh unto men to edification (1 Cor. 14:3).
3. He that prophesieth speaketh unto men to . . . exhortation (1 Cor. 14:3).
4. He that prophesieth speaketh unto men to . . . comfort (1 Cor. 14:3).

5. If all prophesy, and there come in one that believeth not . . . thus are the secrets of his heart made manifest (1 Cor. 14:24, 25).

56. Seven Names That Jesus Called the Scribes and Pharisees

1. Ye blind guides (Matt. 23:16).
2. Ye fools (Matt. 23:17).
3. Woe unto you, scribes and Pharisees . . . for ye are like whited sepulchres . . . full of dead men's bones, and of all uncleanness (Matt. 23:27).
4. Ye serpents (Matt. 23:33).
5. Ye generation of vipers (Matt. 23:33).
6. Woe unto you, scribes and Pharisees, hypocrites! (Luke 11:44).
7. Ye are as graves which appear not (Luke 11:44).

57. The Last Seven Sayings of Jesus on the Cross

1. Then said Jesus, Father, forgive them; for they know not what they do (Luke 23:34).
2. Jesus said unto [the thief on the cross], Verily I say unto thee, Today shalt thou be with me in paradise (Luke 23:43).
3. He saith unto his mother, Woman, behold, thy son! Then saith he to the disciple, Behold, thy mother! (John 19:26, 27).
4. Jesus cried with a loud voice, saying, Eloi, Eloi, lama sabachthani? which is, being interpreted, My God, my God, why hast thou forsaken me? (Mark 15:34).
5. Jesus . . . saith, I thirst (John 19:28).
6. Jesus . . . said, It is finished (John 19:30).
7. And when Jesus had cried with a loud voice, he said, Father, into thy hands I commend my spirit: and having said thus he gave up the ghost (Luke 23:46).

58. Twelve Benedictions

1. The Lord bless thee, and keep thee: the Lord make his face shine upon thee, and be gracious unto thee: the Lord lift up his countenance upon thee, and give thee peace (Num. 6:24-26).
2. Grace to you and peace from God our Father, and the Lord Jesus Christ (Rom. 1:7).

3. Now the God of peace be with you all. Amen (Rom. 15:33).
4. The grace of our Lord Jesus Christ be with you all. Amen (Rom. 16:24).
5. Peace be to the brethren, and love with faith, from God the Father and the Lord Jesus Christ. Grace be with all them that love our Lord Jesus Christ in sincerity. Amen (Eph. 6:23, 24).
6. Now the Lord of peace himself give you peace always by all means. The Lord be with you all (2 Thess. 3:16).
7. Grace, mercy, and peace, from God our Father and Jesus Christ our Lord (1 Tim. 1:2).
8. The Lord Jesus Christ be with thy spirit. Grace be with you. Amen (2 Tim. 4:22).
9. Now the God of peace, that brought again from the dead our Lord Jesus, that great shepherd of the sheep, through the blood of the everlasting covenant, make you perfect in every good work to do his will, working in you that which is well-pleasing in his sight, through Jesus Christ; to whom be glory for ever and ever. Amen (Heb. 13:20, 21).
10. Peace be with you all that are in Christ Jesus. Amen (1 Pet. 5:14).
11. Grace and peace be multiplied unto you through the knowledge of God, and of Jesus our Lord (2 Pet. 1:2).
12. Grace be unto you, and peace, from him which is, and which was, and which is to come; and from the seven Spirits which are before his throne; and from Jesus Christ, who is the faithful witness, and the first begotten of the dead, and the prince of the kings of the earth (Rev. 1:4, 5).

6

Books

The Bible makes several references to books which are not contained within the Bible itself. Sometimes the reference is unusual and often intriguing. This chapter includes the following lists: Two Prophets Who Ate Books; The Most Important Directory in the Universe; Two Other Heavenly Books; Two Accounts of Book-Burning in the Bible, and Fourteen Non-Biblical Books Mentioned in the Bible.

59. Two Prophets Who Ate Books

1. Ezekiel wrote, "And when I looked, behold, an hand was sent unto me; and, lo, a roll of a book was therein; and he spread it before me; and it was written within and without: and there was written therein lamentations, and mourning, and woe. Moreover he said unto me, Son of man, eat that thou findest; eat this roll, and go speak unto the house of Israel. So I opened my mouth, and he caused me to eat that roll. And he said unto me, Son of man, cause thy belly to eat, and fill thy bowels with this roll that I give thee. Then did I eat it; and it was in my mouth as honey for sweetness" (Ezek. 2:9-3:3).

2. John wrote, "And I went unto the angel, and said unto him, Give me the little book. And he said unto me, Take it, and eat it up; and it shall make thy belly bitter, but it shall be in thy mouth sweet as honey. And I took the little book out of the angel's hand, and ate it up; and it was in my mouth sweet as honey: and as soon as I had eaten it, my belly was bitter" (Rev 10:9, 10).

60. The Most Important Directory in the Universe

1. Jesus said, "Rejoice not, that the spirits are subject unto you; but rather rejoice, because your names are written in heaven" (Luke 10:20).
2. Jesus said, "He that overcometh, the same shall be clothed in white raiment; and I will not blot out his name out of the book of life, but I will confess his name before my Father and before his angels" (Rev. 3:5).
3. And whosoever was not found in the book of life was cast into the lake of fire (Rev. 20:15).
4. There shall in no wise enter into it anything that defileth . . . but they which are written in the Lamb's book of life (Rev. 21:27).

61. Two Other Heavenly Books

1. Then they that feared the Lord spake often one to another: and the Lord hearkened, and heard it, and a book of remembrance was written before him for them that feared the Lord, and that thought upon his name. And they shall be mine, saith the Lord of hosts, in that day when I make up my jewels; and I will spare them, as a man spareth his own son that serveth him (Mal. 3:16, 17).
2. One of the elders saith to me [John], Weep not; behold, the Lion of the tribe of Judah, the Root of David, hath prevailed to open the book, and to loose the seven seals thereof (Rev. 5:5).

62. Two Accounts of Book-Burning in the Bible

1. When Jehudi read a book of God's judgments to king Jehoiakim, the king "cut it with a penknife and cast it into the fire that was on the hearth, until all the roll was consumed in the fire that was on the hearth" (Jer. 36:23).
2. And many that believed came, and confessed, and shewed their deeds. Many of them also which used curious arts brought their books together, and burned them before all men: and they counted the price of them, and found it fifty thousand pieces of silver (Acts 19:18, 19).

63. Fourteen Non-Biblical Books Mentioned in the Bible

1. It is said in the book of the wars of the Lord, What he did in the Red sea, and in the brooks of Arnon. And at the stream of the brooks that goeth down to the dwelling of Ar, and lieth upon the border of Moab (Num. 21:14, 15).
2. And the sun stood still, and the moon stayed, until the people had avenged themselves upon their enemies. Is not this written in the book of Jasher? (Josh. 10:13).
3. Three men from each of seven of the tribes of Israel "passed through the land, and described it by cities into seven parts in a book, and came again to Joshua to the host at Shiloh" (Josh. 18:9).
4. Samuel told the people the manner of the kingdom [that they would have under King Saul], and wrote it in a book, and laid it up before the Lord (1 Sam. 10:25).
5. The rest of the acts of Solomon, and all that he did, and his wisdom, are they not written in the book of the acts of Solomon? (1 Kings 11:41)
6. The acts of David the king, first and last, behold, they are written in . . . the book of Nathan the prophet (1 Chron. 29:29).
7. The acts of David the king, first and last, behold, they are written in . . . the book of Gad the seer (1 Chron. 29:29).
8. The acts of Rehoboam, first and last, are they not written in the book of Shemaiah the prophet? (2 Chron. 12:15).
9. The acts of Rehoboam, first and last, are they not written in the book . . . of Iddo the seer concerning genealogies? (2 Chron. 12:15).
10. The rest of the acts of Jehoshaphat, first and last, behold, they are written in the book of Jehu the son of Hanani, who is mentioned in the book of the Kings of Israel (2 Chron. 20:34).
11. Rehum the chancellor, and Shimshai the scribe wrote a letter to Artaxerxes the king and asked "that search may be made in the book of the records of thy fathers: so shalt thou find in the book of the records, and know that this city is a rebellious city, and hurtful unto kings and provinces, and that they have moved sedition within the same of old time: for which cause was this city destroyed" (Ezra 4:15).
12. In those days, while Mordecai sat in the king's gate, two of the king's chamberlains, Bigthan and Teresh, of those which

kept the door, were wroth, and sought to lay hand on the king Ahasuerus. And the thing was known to Mordecai who told it unto Esther the queen; and Esther certified the king thereof in Mordecai's name. And when inquisition was made of the matter, it was found out; therefore they were both hanged on a tree: and it was written in the book of the chronicles before the king (Esther 2:21-23).

13. And the decree of Esther confirmed these matters of Purim; and it was written in the book (Esther 9:32).

14. And the king Ahasuerus laid a tribute upon the land, and upon the isles of the sea. And all the acts of his power and of his might, and the declaration of the greatness of Mordecai, whereunto the king advanced him, are they not written in the book of the chronicles of the kings of Media and Persia? (Esther 10:1, 2).

7

People

The Bible, of course, is not just about God; it is also about people, many of whom were extraordinary. The people found in this chapter include inventors, kings, prophets, apostles, heroes, government employees, and polygamists. The lists here are short and contain brief interesting facts about them along with supporting scripture references.

The chapter opens with these two lists: Two Men Who Never Died and Seven Men Who Lived More Than 900 Years. Can you name them without looking at the lists?

64. Two Men Who Never Died

1. Enoch lived 365 years (Gen. 5:23, 24), and then was translated by God (Heb. 11:5).
2. Elijah was carried by a whirlwind into heaven (2 Kings 2:11).

65. Seven Men Who Lived More Than 900 Years

1. Adam lived 930 years (Gen. 5:5).
2. Seth lived 912 years (Gen. 5:8).
3. Enos lived 905 years (Gen. 5:11).
4. Cainan lived 910 years (Gen. 5:14).
5. Jared lived 962 years (Gen. 5:20).
6. Methuselah lived 969 years (Gen. 5:27).
7. Noah lived 950 years (Gen. 9:29).

66. Seven Suicides in the Bible

1. [Abimelech] called hastily unto the young man his armour-bearer, and said unto him, Draw thy sword, and slay me,

that men say not of me, A woman slew him. And his young man thrust him through, and he died (Judges 9:54).
2. And Samson said, Let me die with the Philistines. And he bowed with all his might; and the house fell . . . upon all the people that were therein (Judges 16:30).
3. Saul took a sword and fell on it (1 Sam. 31:4).
4. When [Saul's] armour-bearer saw that Saul was dead, he fell likewise upon his sword, and died (1 Sam. 31:5).
5. When Ahithophel saw that his counsel was not followed, he . . . gat him home to his house, to his city, and put his house in order, and hanged himself, and died (2 Sam. 17:23).
6. It came to pass, when Zimri saw that the city was taken, that he went into the palace of the king's house, and burnt the king's house over him with fire, and died (1 Kings 16:18).
7. [Judas] cast down the pieces of silver in the temple, and departed, and went and hanged himself (Matt. 27:5).

67. The Three Kings Who Ruled All of Israel

1. Saul ruled 40 years (Acts 13:21).
2. David ruled for 40 years (2 Sam. 5:4).
3. Solomon ruled for 40 years (1 Kings 11:42).

68. Nineteen Kings Who Ruled Judah

1. Rehoboam ruled 17 years (1 Kings 14:21).
2. Abijam ruled 3 years (1 Kings 15:2).
3. Asa ruled 41 years (1 Kings 15:10).
4. Jehoshaphat ruled 25 years (1 Kings 22:42).
5. Jehoram ruled 8 years (2 Kings 8:17).
6. Ahaziah ruled part of one year (2 Kings 8:25, 26).
   NOTE: Queen Athaliah ruled 6 years (2 Kings 11:3).
7. Jehoash ruled 40 years (2 Kings 12:1).
8. Amaziah ruled 29 years (2 Kings 14:2).
9. Uzziah (also known as Azariah) ruled 52 years (2 Kings 15:2).
10. Jotham ruled 16 years (2 Kings 15:33).
11. Ahaz ruled 16 years (2 Kings 16:2).
12. Hezekiah ruled 29 years (2 Kings 18:1, 2).
13. Manasseh ruled 55 years (2 Kings 21:1).
14. Amon ruled 2 years (2 Kings 21:19).
15. Josiah ruled 31 years (2 Kings 22:1).

16. Jehoahaz ruled 3 months (2 Kings 23:31).
17. Jehoiakim ruled 11 years (2 Kings 23:36).
18. Jehoiachin ruled 3 months (2 Kings 24:8).
19. Zedekiah ruled 11 years (2 Kings 24:18).

69. Nineteen Kings Who Ruled the Northern Kingdom of Israel

1. Jeroboam ruled 22 years (1 Kings 14:20).
2. Nadab ruled 2 years (1 Kings 15:25).
3. Baasha ruled 24 years (1 Kings 15:33).
4. Elah ruled 2 years (1 Kings 16:8).
5. Zimri ruled 7 days (1 Kings 16:15).
6. Omri ruled 12 years (1 Kings 16:23).
7. Ahab ruled 22 years (1 Kings 16:29).
8. Ahaziah ruled 2 years (1 Kings 22:51).
9. Jehoram ruled 12 years (2 Kings 3:1).
10. Jehu ruled 28 years (2 Kings 10:36).
11. Jehoahaz ruled 17 years (2 Kings 13:1).
12. Jehoash ruled 16 years (2 Kings 13:10).
13. Jeroboam ruled 41 years (2 Kings 14:23).
14. Zachariah ruled 6 months (2 Kings 15:8).
15. Shallum ruled 1 month (2 Kings 15:13).
16. Menahem ruled 10 years (2 Kings 15:17).
17. Pekahiah ruled 2 years (2 Kings 15:23).
18. Pekah ruled 20 years (2 Kings 15:27).
19. Hoshea ruled 9 years (2 Kings 17:1).

70. Gentile Kings of Israel

1. Jacob and his sons settled in Egypt under a Pharaoh (Gen. 47:1-10).
2. The Pharaoh whom God delivered Israel from was "a new king over Egypt which knew not Joseph" (Ex. 1:8).
3. King Ahaz submitted to Tiglathpileser, king of Assyria (2 Kings 16:7).
4. Shalmaneser, king of Assyria, imprisoned Hoshea, king of the northern kingdom of Israel (2 Kings 17:3, 4).
5. Sennacherib, king of Assyria, took control of Judah during Hezekiah's reign (2 Kings 18:13).
6. Esarhaddon succeeded Sennacherib (2 Kings 19:36, 37).
7. Pharaoh-nechoh made Judah pay tribute after imprisoning

king Jehoahaz (2 Kings 23:33, 34).

8. Evil-merodach, king of Babylon, brought king Jehoiachin of Judah out of prison (2 Kings 25:27).
9. Ahasuerus (Artaxerxes) became king of Persia (Ezra 4:6, 7).
10. Ahasuerus (possibly Xerxes) reigned from India to Ethiopia. Esther was his queen (Esther 1:1; 2:17).
11. Nebuchadnezzar took Jerusalem during Jehoiakim's reign (Dan. 1:1).
12. Daniel interpreted Belshazzar's vision (Dan. 5:1-28).
13. Darius conquered Babylon and assumed the rule of Israel (Dan. 5:31).
14. Darius the Mede was a son of Ahasuerus (Dan. 9:1).
15. Herod the king was king of Judea at Jesus' birth (Matt. 2:1).
16. Archelaus, son of Herod, reigned in Judea when Joseph brought Jesus and Mary to Nazareth (Matt. 2:22, 23).
17. Caesar Augustus ruled the known world at the time of Jesus' birth (Luke 2:1, 7).
18. Tiberius Caesar reigned when John the Baptist began preaching (Luke 3:1-3).
19. Herod the tetrarch put John the Baptist in prison (Luke 3:19, 20).
20. Herod the king imprisoned and killed some of the apostles (Acts 12:1-3).
21. There was a great dearth throughout the world in the reign of Claudius Caesar (Acts 11:28).
22. Paul referred to Nero when he declared, "I appeal unto Caesar" (Acts 25:11).

71. Four Major Prophets of the Old Testament

1. Isaiah prophesied of the Messiah (Isa. 52:13-53:1-12).
2. Jeremiah prophesied of the Messiah (Jer. 23:5, 6 and 33:14-16).
3. Ezekiel prophesied of the Messiah (Ezek. 37:24, 25 and 34:11-16).
4. Daniel prophesied of the Messiah (Dan. 2:44, 45 and 9:24-26).

72. Twelve Minor Prophets of the Old Testament

1. Hosea prophesied of the Messiah (Hos. 11:1).
2. Joel prophesied of the outpouring of the Holy Spirit (Joel 2:28, 29).

3. Amos rebuked Israel for its sins (Amos).
4. Obadiah prophesied against Edom (Obadiah).
5. Jonah foreshadowed the death, burial, and resurrection of Jesus (Jonah and Matt. 12:38-40).
6. Micah prophesied of the Messiah (Micah 5:2).
7. Nahum prophesied against Nineveh (Nahum).
8. Habakkuk said, "The just shall live by his faith" (Hab. 2:4).
9. Zephaniah prophesied of the day of the Lord's wrath (Zeph.).
10. Haggai prophesied of the Messiah (Hag. 2:7).
11. Zechariah prophesied of the Messiah (Zech. 6:12, 13; 9:9, 10; 13:6, 7).
12. Malachi prophesied of the Messiah (Malachi 3:1).

73. Eleven Other Prophets of the Old Testament

1. Abraham was revealed as a prophet to King Abimelech in a dream (Gen. 20:1-7).
2. Balaam prophesied of the Messiah (Num. 24:17, 19).
3. Moses prophesied of the Messiah (Deut. 18:15, 18, 19).
4. Samuel was established to be a prophet of the Lord (1 Sam. 3:19-21).
5. King Saul prophesied on two occasions (1 Sam. 10:1-13; 19:18-24).
6. Nathan the prophet declared to King David that God knew about David's sins of adultery and murder (2 Sam. 12:1-23).
7. The prophet Gad presented to King David three choices of judgment upon Israel after David sinned in numbering Israel. The choices: (1) seven years of famine, (2) three months of being pursued by enemies, or (3) three days of pestilence (2 Sam. 24:10-14).
8. Ahijah prophesied that Jeroboam would be king over ten tribes which God would take away from King Solomon (1 Kings 11:29-40).
9. Elijah the prophet (1 Kings 18:36) was translated (2 Kings 2:1-11).
10. Elisha the prophet (2 Kings 9:1) succeeded Elijah (2 Kings 2:1-15).
11. King David prophesied of the Messiah (Ps. 22:1, 6-8, 13, 16-18, 31).

74. Six New Testament Prophets

1. Jesus said that there was no greater prophet than John the Baptist (Matt. 11:7-15).
2. Jesus prophesied the destruction of Jerusalem and the events leading up to His second coming (Matt. 24).
3. Agabus prophesied that there would be a famine and that the Jews would deliver Paul into the hands of the Gentiles (Acts 11:27, 28; 21:10, 11).
4. Judas Barsabas was a prophet (Acts 15:22, 32).
5. Silas was a prophet (Acts 15:32).
6. St. John recorded the great prophetic work known as the Revelation (Rev. 1-22).

75. Eight Women Prophets

1. Miriam, Moses' sister, was a prophetess (Ex. 15:20).
2. Deborah, a judge in Israel, was a prophetess (Judges 4:4).
3. When Josiah was king of Judah, a book of the law was found during cleaning of the temple. Josiah commanded Hilkiah the high priest to inquire of the Lord for the king. Hilkiah then went to Huldah the prophetess (2 Kings 22).
4. The prophetess Anna recognized Jesus as being the Messiah when Jesus was brought to the temple to be circumcised (Luke 2:36-38).
5. The four virgin daughters of Philip the evangelist prophesied (Acts 21:8, 9).

76. The Twelve Apostles

1. Peter, James, John, Andrew, Philip, Thomas, Bartholomew, Matthew, James (son of Alphaeus), Simon, Lebbaeus Thaddaeus (Judas), and Judas Iscariot (Matt. 10:2-4).
2. Peter, James, John, Andrew, Philip, Thomas, Bartholomew, Matthew, James (son of Alphaeus), Simon, Thaddaeus, and Judas Iscariot (Mark 3:16-19).
3. Peter, James, John, Andrew, Philip, Thomas, Bartholomew, Matthew, James (son of Alphaeus), Simon Zelotes, Judas (brother of James), and Judas Iscariot (Luke 6:14-16).
4. Peter, James, John, Andrew, Philip, Thomas, Bartholomew, Matthew, James (son of Alphaeus), Simon Zelotes, Judas (brother of James), and Judas Iscariot (deceased) (Acts 1:13).

77. Eight More Apostles

1. Matthias was selected to be the apostle to replace Judas Iscariot, first by qualifications, and then by casting a prayerful lot (Acts 1:26).
2. Barnabas was an apostle and companion of Paul (Acts 14:14).
3. Paul was the apostle to the Gentiles (Rom. 11:13).
4. Paul mentioned Andronicus as an apostle (Rom. 16:7).
5. Paul mentioned Junia as an apostle (Rom. 16:7).
6. Paul mentions James, the brother of Jesus, as being an apostle (Gal. 1:19).
7. Paul called Silvanus a fellow apostle (1 Thess. 1:1; 2:6).
8. Paul called Timothy a fellow apostle (1 Thess. 1:1; 2:6).

78. Twenty-five Ways Old Testament Heroes Exercised Faith

1. Abel offered an acceptable sacrifice by faith (Heb. 11:4).
2. Enoch was translated by faith (Heb. 11:5).
3. Noah prepared the ark by faith (Heb. 11:7).
4. Abraham went into a strange land by faith (Heb. 11:8-10).
5. Sarah received strength to conceive a child in her old age by faith (Heb. 11:11, 12).
6. Abraham offered up Isaac by faith (Heb. 11:17-19).
7. Isaac blessed Jacob and Esau prophetically by faith (Heb. 11:20).
8. Jacob blessed the sons of Joseph prophetically by faith (Heb. 11:21).
9. Joseph prophesied of Israel's departure from Egypt by faith (Heb. 11:22).
10. Moses was hid as a baby by faith (Heb. 11:23).
11. Moses forsook the riches of Egypt by faith (Heb. 11:24-27).
12. Moses kept the passover by faith (Heb. 11:28).
13. The Red Sea parted by faith (Heb. 11:29).
14. The walls of Jericho fell by faith (Heb. 11:30).
15. Rahab, the harlot, saved her self and her family by faith (Heb. 11:31).
16. Gideon delivered Israel from the Midianites by faith (Heb. 11:32).
17. Barak delivered Israel from the Canaanites by faith (Heb. 11:32).

18. Samson delivered Israel from the Philistines by faith (Heb. 11:32).
19. Jephtha delivered Israel from the Ammonites by faith (Heb. 11:32).
20. David waxed valiant in fight by faith (Heb. 11:32).
21. Samuel prophesied by faith (Heb. 11:32).
22. Daniel stopped the mouths of lions by faith (Heb. 11:33).
23. Shadrach, Meshach, and Abednego quenched the violence of fire by faith (Heb. 11:34).
24. The son of the Zarephath widow was raised from the dead by faith (Heb. 11:35).
25. The son of the Shunammite woman was raised from the dead by faith (Heb. 11:35).

79. Important Servants in the Bible

1. Abraham and 318 of his servants defeated the captors of Sodom and Gomorrah (Gen. 14:14, 15).
2. Hagar, the mother of Ishmael, was Sarah's handmaid (Gen. 16:1).
3. Abraham's eldest servant found a wife for Isaac (Gen. 24).
4. Jacob served Laban for several years (Gen. 29-31).
5. Zilpah and Bilhah, Leah's and Rachel's maids, bore children for Jacob (Gen. 30).
6. Joseph was Potiphar's servant (Gen. 39:1).
7. Pharaoh's chief butler and chief baker were instrumental in Joseph's eventual promotion to the position of prime minister (Gen. 41).
8. The Egyptians made the children of Israel serve with rigor (Ex. 1:13).
9. A maid of the daughter of Pharaoh took Moses in his basket from the river (Ex. 2:5).
10. Joshua was Moses' servant (Ex. 33:11).
11. The Hivites were cursed to be Israel's servants (Joshua 9:23).
12. Abimelech's armorbearer killed him, at his request (Judges 9:54).
13. Mephibosheth's nurse dropped him while fleeing the enemy. He was permanently crippled (2 Sam. 4:4).
14. Elisha poured water on the hands of Elijah (2 Kings 3:11).
15. Gehazi was Elisha's servant (2 Kings 4:12).
16. A young girl, captured from Israel, was the maid of Naaman's wife. She advised that he go to Elisha and be healed of leprosy (2 Kings 5:2, 3).

17. Nehemiah was cupbearer for Artexerxes (Neh. 1:11).
18. The centurion's servant at Capernaum was healed by Jesus (Matt. 8:13).
19. Jesus spoke of an unforgiving servant (Matt. 18:23-34).
20. Jesus told of three servants who were each given money to invest for their master (Matt. 25:14-30).
21. Jesus told a parable of a vineyard owner, whose servants were killed or beaten by the husbandmen (Mark 12:1-5).
22. Peter cut off the ear of Malchus, the high priest's servant (John 18:10).
23. A servant girl at the house of Caiaphas asked Peter if he was one of the disciples (John 18:17).
24. Peter denied knowing Jesus the third time to a servant of the high priest (John 18:26).
25. Two of Cornelius' servants were sent to bring Peter from Joppa (Acts 10:7, 8).
26. Onesimus, a servant of Philemon, was converted by Paul (Philemon).

80. Fifteen Men in the Bible Who Had More Than One Wife

1. Lamech, who was Cain's great-great-great grandson, was the first man recorded to have two wives (Adah, Zillah) (Gen. 4:19).
2. Abraham had three wives (Sarah, Hagar, and Keturah) (Gen 23:19; 25:1; 16:3).
3. Esau had three wives (Judith, Bashemath, and Mahalath) (Gen. 26:34; 28:9).
4. Jacob had four wives (Leah, Rachel, Bilhah, and Zilpah) (Gen. 29:15-35; 30:4, 9).
5. Moses had two wives (Zipporah and the Ethiopian woman) (Ex. 18:2; Num. 12:1).
6. Gideon had many wives and 70 sons (Judges 8:30).
7. Samuel's father, Elkanah, had two wives (Hannah, Peninnah) (1 Sam. 1:1, 2).
8. King Saul had at least two wives (Ahinoam, Rizpah) (1 Sam. 14:50; 2 Sam. 3:7).
9. David had at least eight wives (Michal, Abigail, Ahinoam, Bathsheba, Maacah, Haggith, Abital, and Eglah) plus Saul's wives (2 Sam. 12:8).
10. Solomon had 700 wives and 300 concubines (1 Kings 11:3).

152

11. King Ahab had more than one wife (1 Kings 20:7).
12. King Rehoboam had 18 wives and 60 concubines (2 Chron. 11:21).
13. King Abijah who ruled over Judah had 14 wives (2 Chron. 13:21).
14. King Joash had two wives (2 Chron. 24:1-3).
15. King Ahasuerus had a harem. Two wives are mentioned by name: Vashti and Esther (Esther 1:10-12; 2:1-17).

81. Six Women in the Bible Who Had More Than One Husband

1. Tamar was married to Judah's two sons Er and Onan (Gen. 38:6-10).
2. Samson's wife was given to Samson's companion (Judges 14:20).
3. David's wife Michal was given to Phaltiel by Saul and was later reclaimed by David (2 Sam 3:13-16).
4. Ruth was married to Mahlon and to Boaz (Ruth 4:10, 13).
5. The Sadducees described to Jesus a woman who had successively married seven brothers (Mark 12:18-25).
6. The woman whom Jesus met at the well had had five husbands and was living with a sixth man to whom she was not married (John 4:6-19).

82. Widows in the Bible

1. The wives of the men of the city of Shechem, who were killed by Simeon and Levi (Gen. 34:25).
2. Tamar, the wife of Er (Gen. 38:6, 7).
3. Naomi and her daughters-in-law, Orpah and Ruth, were all widows (Ruth 1:3, 5).
4. The wife of Phinehas, Eli's son (1 Sam. 4:19).
5. Abigail, who became David's wife (1 Sam. 25:37, 39).
6. Bathsheba, whose husband was murdered (2 Sam. 11:26).
7. A woman of Tekoah pretended to be a widow before David (2 Sam. 14:2-5).
8. When David returned to Jerusalem, his ten concubines were placed in widowhood (2 Sam. 20:3).
9. Hiram's mother (1 Kings 7:13, 14).

10. Solomon, who had seven hundred wives, probably left many widows (1 Kings 11:3).
11. Zeruah, the mother of Jeroboam (1 Kings 11:26).
12. Jezebel, the wife of Ahab (1 Kings 16:31; 22:40).
13. The widow of Zarephath whom Elijah stayed with (1 Kings 17:9).
14. A certain woman of the wives of the sons of the prophets (2 Kings 4:1).
15. The Sadducees told Jesus of a woman who was widowed seven times (Mark 12:22).
16. The poor widow who gave two mites to the temple treasury (Mark 12:42).
17. Anna the prophetess (Luke 2:36, 37).
18. Many widows were in Israel in the days of Elias (Luke 4:25).
19. The widow at Nain whose son Jesus raised (Luke 7:12-15).
20. The widow in Jesus' parable who prevailed upon a judge to help her (Luke 18:2-5).
21. Sapphira was a widow for about three hours (Acts 5:5-10).
22. The Grecian widows of the church were neglected in the daily ministration (Acts 6:1).
23. Many widows received coats and garments from Dorcas (Acts 9:39).
24. There were widows in the Corinthian church (1 Cor. 7:8).
25. There were widows under Timothy's jurisdiction (1 Tim. 5:3).

83. Ten Remarkable Acts of Heroism in the Bible

1. Simeon and Levi killed all of the men of a whole city with their swords to avenge the defiling of their sister, Dinah. First they convinced the men of the city to be circumcised, and then, while the men were still recovering, they slaughtered them (Gen. 34).
2. Shamgar, the son of Anath, delivered Israel by slaying 600 Philistines with an ox goad (Judges 3:31).
3. Samson, tied up with two new cords, broke the cords after the Spirit of the Lord came upon him, and slew a thousand Philistines with the jawbone of an ass (Judges 15:9-17).
4. Jonathan and his armorbearer slew twenty Philistines and thus began a great victory for Israel (1 Sam. 14:1-14).

5. David slew the giant, Goliath, with a sling and one stone (1 Sam. 17:38-54).

David and Goliath

6. The chief captain in King David's army killed 800 men with his spear in one battle (2 Sam. 23:8).

7. Shadrach, Meshach, and Abednego defied the king's order to worship the king's golden image and were therefore thrown into the fiery furnace. God saved them even in the midst of the fire (Dan. 3).

8. Peter preached the gospel openly and boldly on the day of Pentecost under the anointing of the Holy Ghost, in spite of the fact that he had denied knowing Jesus less than two months before (Acts 2:1-41).

9. Stephen defended the gospel before the Sanhedrin, though it cost him his life. While he was dying, he forgave those who stoned him (Acts 6:9-15; 7:1-60).

10. Paul continued to preach the gospel even though he received 39 lashes on five occasions, was beaten with rods on three other occasions, was stoned once, and was shipwrecked three times. And that is not to mention the number of times he was imprisoned or otherwise persecuted (2 Cor. 11:23-28).

84. Government Employees Mentioned in the Bible

1. Joseph was *governor* over the land (of Egypt) (Gen. 42:6).

2. And David reigned over all Israel; and David executed judgment and justice unto all his people. And Joab the son of Zeruiah was *over the host*; [and Jehosphaphat the son of Ahilud was *recorder*;] and Zadok the son of Ahitub, and Ahimelech the son of Abiathar, were the priests; and Seraiah was the *scribe*; and Benaiah the son of Jehoiada was over the Cherethites and the Pelethites; and David's sons were *chief rulers* (2 Sam. 8:15-18).

3. Later, "Adoram was *over the tribute* . . . Sheva was *scribe* . . . and Ira . . . the Jairite was a *chief ruler* about David" (2 Sam. 20:24-26).

4. King Solomon was king over all Israel. And these were the *princes* which he had: Azariah the son of Zadok the priest, Elihoreph and Ahiah, the sons of Shisha, *scribes*; Jehoshaphat the son of Ahilud, the *recorder*. And Benaiah the son of Jehoiada was *over the host*: and Zadok and Abiathar were the priests: and Azariah the son of Nathan was over the *officers*: and Zabud the son of Nathan was *principal officer* and the king's friend: and Ahishar was *over the household*: and

Adoniram the son of Abda was *over the tribute.* And Solomon had twelve *officers over all Israel,* which provided victuals for the king and his household: each man his month in a year made provision. And these are their names: The son of Hur, in mount Ephraim: The son of Dekar, in Makaz, and in Shaalbim, and Bethshemesh, and Elonbethhanan: The son of Hesed, in Aruboth; to him pertained Sochoh, and all the land of Hepher: The son of Abinadab, in all the region of Dor; which had Taphath the daughter of Solomon to wife: Baana the son of Ahilud; to him pertained Taanach and Megiddo, and all Bethshean, which is by Zartanah beneath Jezreel, from Bethshean to Abelmeholah, even unto the place that is beyond Jokneam: The son of Geber, in Ramothgilead; to him pertained the towns of Jair the son of Manasseh, which are in Gilead; to him also pertained the region of Argob, which is in Bashan, threescore great cities with walls and brasen bars: Ahinadab the son of Iddo had Mahanaim: Ahimaaz was in Naphtali; he also took Basmath the daughter of Solomon to wife: Baanah the son of Hushai was in Asher and in Aloth: Jehoshaphat the son of Paruah, in Issachar: Shimei the son of Elah, in Benjamin: Geber the son of Uri was in the country of Gilead, in the country of Sihon king of the Amorites, and of Og king of Bashan; and he was the only officer which was in the land (1 Kings 4:1-19).

5. Ahab called Obadiah, which was the *governor of his house* (1 Kings 18:3).
6. The King of Israel said, Take Micaiah, and carry him back unto Amon the *governor of the city* (1 Kings 22:26).
7. Under King Hezekiah, "Eliakim the son of Hilkiah . . . was *over the household,* and Shebna (was) the *scribe,* and Joah the son of Asaph (was) the *recorder*" (2 Kings 18:18).
8. In the eighteenth year of King Josiah . . . the king sent Shaphan . . . the *scribe* to the house of the Lord (2 Kings 22:3).
9. And Satan stood up against Israel, and provoked David to number Israel. And David said to Joab and to the *rulers* of the people, Go, number Israel from Beersheba even to Dan; and bring the number of them to me, that I may know it (1 Chron. 21:1, 2).
10. Rehum the *chancellor* and Shimshai the *scribe* wrote a letter against Jerusalem to Artaxerxes the king (Ezra 4:8).
11. Nebuchadnezzar the king sent to gather together the *princes,* the *governors,* and the *captains,* the *judges,* the *treasurers,*

the *counsellors*, the *sheriffs*, and all the *rulers* of the provinces, to come to the dedication of the image which Nebuchadnezzar the king had set up (Dan. 3:2).

12. It pleased Darius to set over the kingdom an hundred and twenty *princes*, which should be over the whole kingdom; and over these three *presidents*; of whom Daniel was first (Dan. 6:1, 2).

13. And as Jesus passed forth from thence, he saw a man, named Matthew, sitting at the *receipt of custom*: and he saith unto him follow me. And he arose, and followed him (Matt. 9:9).

14. Jesus said, "When thou goest with thine adversary to the *magistrate*, as thou art in the way, give diligence that thou mayest be delivered from him; lest he hale thee to the *judge*, and the *judge* deliver thee to the *officer*, and the *officer* cast thee into prison" (Luke 12:58).

15. There was a man named Zacchaeus, which was the chief among the *publicans*, and he was rich (Luke 19:2).

16. The angel of the Lord spoke unto Philip, saying, Arise, and go toward the south unto the way that goeth down from Jerusalem unto Gaza, which is desert. And he arose and went: and, behold a man of Ethiopia, an eunuch of great authority under Candace queen of the Ethiopians, who had *charge of all her treasure* (Acts 8:26, 27).

17. There was a certain man in Caesarea called Cornelius, a *centurion* of the band called the Italian band (Acts 10:1).

18. And Herod was highly displeased with them of Tyre and Sidon: but they came with one accord to him, and, having made Blastus the king's *chamberlain* their friend, desired peace; because their country was nourished by the king's country (Acts 12:20).

19. Paul and Barnabas went to Paphos on the island of Cyprus where "the *deputy* of the country, Sergius Paulus, a prudent man . . . called for Barnabas and (Paul), and desired to hear the word of God" (Acts 13:4-7).

20. After Paul and Silas had converted the *jailor* and his household, "and when it was day, the *magistrates* sent the *sergeants*, saying, Let those men go. And the *keeper of the prison* told this saying to Paul, The magistrates have sent to let you go: now therefore depart, and go in peace" (Acts 16:35, 36).

21. When Gallio was the *deputy* of Achaia, the Jews made insurrection with one accord against Paul, and brought him before

the judgment seat . . . (But Gallio reacted by saying) I will be no judge of such matters. And he drave them from the judgment seat (Acts 18:12-16).

22. Demetrius the silversmith caused a riot in Ephesus that was directed against Paul and his companions Gaius and Aristarchus. "And when the *townclerk* had appeased the people, he said . . . If Demetrius, and the craftsmen which are with him, have a matter against any man, the law is open, and there are *deputies*: let them implead one another. But if ye enquire any thing concerning other matters, it shall be determined in a lawful assembly" (Acts 19:23-39).

85. Sixteen Traitors Mentioned in the Bible

1. When *Delilah* saw that [Samson] had told her all his heart, she . . . sent for the Lords of the Philistines. . . . Then the lords of the Philistines came up unto her, and brought money. . . . And she made [Samson] sleep upon her knees; and she called for a man, and she caused him to shave . . . his head; and she began to afflict him, and his strength went from him. . . . [Then] the Philistines took him, and put out his eyes . . . and bound him with fetters of brass; and he did grind in the prison house (Judges 16:18, 19, 21).

2. *Absalom* sent spies throughout all the tribes of Israel, saying, As soon as ye hear the sound of the trumpet, then ye shall say, Absalom reigneth in Hebron. . . . And the conspiracy was strong; for the people increased continually with Absalom. And there came a messenger to David, saying, The hearts of the men of Israel are after Absalom. And David said unto all his servants. . . . Let us flee. . . . And the king went forth, and all the people after him, and tarried in a place that was far off (2 Sam. 15:10, 12-14, 17).

3. And one told David, saying, *Ahithophel* is among the conspirators with Absalom (2 Sam. 15:31).

4. *Baasha* the son of Ahijah . . . conspired against . . . Nadab . . . (and) in the third year of Asa king of Judah did Baasha slay him, and reigned in his stead (1 Kings 15:27, 28).

5. Elah the son of Baasha (reigned) over Israel in Tirzah, two years. And his servant *Zimri*, captain of half his chariots, conspired against him, as he was in Tirzah drinking himself drunk in the house of Arza steward of his house in Tirzah. And Zimri went in and smote him, and killed him . . . and

reigned in his stead (1 Kings 16:8-10).

6. It came to pass ... that [*Hazael*] took a thick cloth, an dipped it in water, and spread it on [the face of Benhadad the king of Syria] so that he died; and Hazael reigned in his stead (2 Kings 8:15).

7. *Jehu* the son of Jehoshaphat the son of Nimshi conspired against Joram. ... And it came to pass when Joram saw Jehu, that he said, Is it peace, Jehu? And he answered, What peace, so long as the whoredoms of thy mother Jezebel and her witchcrafts are so many? And Joram turned his hands, and fled, and said to Ahaziah, There is treachery, O Ahaziah. And Jehu drew a bow with his full strength, and smote Jehoram between his arms and the arrow went out at his heart, and he sunk down in his chariot. ... But when Ahaziah the king of Judah saw this, he fled by the way of the garden house. And Jehu followed after him, and said, Smite him also in the chariot. And they did so ... (2 Kings 9:14, 22-24, 27).

8. The servants of Joash "made a conspiracy, and slew Joash in the house of Millo, which goeth down to Silla. For *Jozachar* the son of Shimeath, and *Jehozabad* the son of Shomer, his servants smote him and he died" (2 Kings 12:20, 21).

9. *Shallum* the son of Jabesh conspired against [Zachariah king of Israel], and smote him before the people, and slew him and reigned in his stead (2 Kings 15:10).

10. *Menahem* the son of Gadi went up from Tirzah, and came to Samaria, and smote Shallum the son of Jabesh in Samaria, and slew him, and reigned in his stead (2 Kings 15:14).

11. *Pekah* the son of Remaliah, a captain of [Pekahiah king of Israel], conspired against [Pekahiah] and smote him in Samaria ... and he killed him, and reigned in his room (2 Kings 15:25).

12. *Hoshea* the son of Elah made a conspiracy against Pekah the son of Remaliah, and smote him, and slew him, and reigned in his stead (2 Kings 15:30).

13. *Zabad* and *Jehozabad* "conspired against [Joash] for the blood of the sons of Jehoiada the priest, and slew him on his bed, and he died" (2 Chron. 24:25).

14. Jesus said, "Rise up, let us go; lo, he that betrayeth me is at hand. And immediately, while he yet spake, cometh *Judas*, one of the twelve, and with him a great multitude with swords and staves, from the chief priests and the scribes and

the elders. And he that betrayed him had given them a to-
ken, saying, Whomsoever I shall kiss, that same is he; take
him, and lead him away safely. And as soon as he was come,
he goeth straightway to him, and saith, Master, master, and
kissed him. And they laid their hands on him, and took him"
(Mark 14:42-46).

86. Nine of the Earliest Recorded Inventors

1. Abel invented shepherding (Gen. 4:2).
2. Cain invented farming (Gen. 4:2).
3. Cain invented the city (Gen. 4:17).
4. Jabal invented tents (Gen. 4:20).
5. Jubal invented the harp and organ (Gen. 4:21).
6. Tubal-cain invented metal working with brass and iron
   (Gen. 4:22).
7. Noah invented the ark and zoology (Gen. 6:14).
8. Noah invented wine (Gen. 9:20, 21).
9. Nimrod invented hunting (Gen. 10:8, 9).

87. People in the Bible Who Wept

1. [Hagar] sat over against him, and lift up her voice, and wept
   (Gen. 21:16).
2. Abraham came to mourn for Sarah, and to weep for her
   (Gen. 23:2).
3. Esau lifted up his voice, and wept (Gen. 27:38).
4. Jacob kissed Rachel, and lifted up his voice, and wept (Gen.
   29:11).
5. Joseph . . . entered into his chamber, and wept there (Gen.
   43:30).
6. Benjamin wept upon [Joseph's] neck (Gen. 45:14).
7. The babe [Moses] wept (Ex. 2:6).
8. Moses heard the people weep throughout their families
   (Num. 11:10).
9. The children of Israel . . . lifted up their voice, and wept
   (Judges 2:4).
10. Samson's wife wept before him (Judges 14:16).
11. They lifted up their voice, and wept again: and Orpah kissed
    [Naomi]; but Ruth clave unto her (Ruth 1:14).
12. Then said Elkanah her husband to her, Hannah, weepest
    thou? (1 Sam. 1:8).

13. All the people [of Gibeah] lifted up their voices, and wept (1 Sam. 11:4).

14. [David and Jonathan] kissed one another, and wept one with another (1 Sam. 20:41).

15. Saul lifted up his voice, and wept (1 Sam. 24:16).

16. David and the people that were with him lifted up their voice and wept (1 Sam. 30:4).

17. [Michal's] husband went with her along weeping behind her (2 Sam. 3:16).

18. [David's] sons came, and lifted up their voice and wept: and the king also and all his servants wept very sore (2 Sam. 13:36).

19. The man of God [Elisha] wept (2 Kings 8:11).

20. Joash the king of Israel came down unto [Elisha], and wept over his face (2 Kings 13:14).

21. Hezekiah wept sore (2 Kings 20:3).

22. God spoke of Josiah, that he "didst rend thy clothes and weep before me" (2 Chron. 34:27).

23. Many of the priests and Levites and chief of the fathers, who were ancient men . . . wept with a loud voice (Ezra 3:12).

24. Ezra had prayed . . . weeping and casting himself down (Ezra 10:1).

25. [Nehemiah] sat down and wept, and mourned certain days (Neh. 1:4).

26. All the people wept when they heard the words of the law (Neh. 8:9).

27. There was great mourning among the Jews, and fasting, and weeping [because of Ahasuerus' command to kill the Jews] (Esther 4:3).

28. Esther . . . fell down at [the king's] feet, and besought him with tears to put away the mischief of Haman (Esther 8:3).

29. [Eliphaz, Bildad, and Zophar] lifted up their voice, and wept (Job 2:12).

30. Job said, "Mine eye poureth out tears unto God" (Job 16:20).]

31. Isaiah said, "I will weep bitterly" (Isa. 22:4).

32. Rachel weeping for her children refused to be comforted (Jer. 31:15).

33. Ishmael the son of Nethaniah went forth from Mizpah to meet them, weeping all along as he went (Jer. 41:6).

34. Jeremiah cried, "Mine eyes do fail with tears" (Lam. 2:11).

35. Behold, there sat women weeping for Tammuz (Ezek. 8:14).

36. [Peter] went out and wept bitterly (Matt. 26:75).

37. [Jesus] cometh to the house of the ruler of the synagogue, and seeth the tumult, and [the mourners] that wept (Mark 5:38).

38. The father of the child cried out, and said with tears, Lord, I believe; help thou mine unbelief (Mark 9:24).

39. [Mary Magdalene] went and told them that had been with [Jesus], as they mourned and wept (Mark 16:10).

40. When the Lord saw [the widow of Nain], he had compassion on her, and said unto her, Weep not (Luke 7:13).

41. [A woman who was a sinner] stood at [Jesus'] feet behind him weeping, and began to wash his feet with tears (Luke 7:38).

42. Jesus turning unto them said, Daughters of Jerusalem, weep not for me (Luke 23:28).

43. Jesus saw [Mary] weeping, and the Jews also weeping (John 11:33).

44. Jesus wept (John 11:35).

45. Mary stood without at the sepulchre weeping (John 20:11).

46. All the widows [at Joppa] stood by [Peter] weeping (Acts 9:39).

47. Paul said, "I have been with you at all seasons, serving the Lord with all humility of mind, and with many tears" (Acts 20:18, 19).

48. [The elders at Ephesus] all wept sore, and fell on Paul's neck, and kissed him (Acts 20:37).

49. Paul answered, What mean ye [Paul's companions and the believers at Caesarea] to weep and to break mine heart? (Acts 21:13)

50. Paul wrote to Timothy that he was "greatly desiring to see thee, being mindful of thy tears" (2 Tim. 1:4).

51. Melchisedec . . . offered up prayers and supplications with strong crying and tears (Heb. 5:6, 7).

52. [John] wept much, because no man was found worthy to open and to read the book (Rev. 5:4).

53. [Those watching Babylon burn] cast dust on their heads, and cried, weeping and wailing (Rev. 18:19).

88. The Seven Deacons

1. Stephen was full of faith and power and did great wonders and miracles among the people (Acts 6:5, 8).

2. Philip went down to Samaria and preached Christ to them (Acts 6:5; 8:5).
3. Prochorus was of honest report, and full of the Holy Ghost and wisdom (Acts 6:3, 5).
4. Nicanor was of honest report, and full of the Holy Ghost and wisdom (Acts 6:3, 5).
5. Timon was of honest report, and full of the Holy Ghost and wisdom (Acts 6:3, 5).
6. Parmenas was of honest report, and full of the Holy Ghost and wisdom (Acts 6:3, 5).
7. Nicolas was a proselyte of Antioch (Acts 6:5).

89. The Eighteen Judges of Israel

1. Othniel judged Israel and led Israel to victory against Chushan-rish-a-thaim the king of Mesopotamia (Judges 3:10).
2. Ehud killed Eglon the king of Moab and led Israel to victory against Moab (Judges 3:15-30).
3. Shamgar slew 600 Philistines with an ox goad and delivered Israel (Judges 3:31).
4. Deborah judged Israel and helped lead Israel to victory against Canaan (Judges 4).
5. Baruk helped Deborah lead Israel to victory against Canaan (Judges 4).
6. Gideon led Israel to victory against the Midianites (Judges 6, 7, 8).
7. Abimelech killed 69 of his brothers so that he could rule (Judges 8:30-9:5).
8. Tola the son of Dodo judged Israel 23 years (Judges 10:1, 2).
9. Jair judged Israel 22 years (Judges 10:3).
10. Jephthah delivered Israel from the Ammonites and judged Israel six years (Judges 11 and 12:1-7).
11. Ibzan judged Israel for seven years (Judges 12:8, 9).
12. Elon judged Israel for ten years (Judges 12:11).
13. Abdon judged Israel for eight years (Judges 12:14).
14. Samson fought the Philistines and judged Israel for 20 years (Judges 13-16).
15. Eli the high priest judged Israel for 40 years (1 Sam. 4:18).
16. Samuel judged Israel all of the days of his life (1 Sam. 7:15-17).

17. Joel, the firstborn son of Samuel, judged Israel in Beersheba (1 Sam. 8:1, 2).
18. Abiah, the second son of Samuel, also judged Israel in Beersheba (1 Sam. 8:1, 2).

90. The Two Most Acclaimed Heroes in the Bible

1. Moses led Israel out of Egypt (Exodus).
2. Jesus died to save us from our sins (Heb. 7:22-27).

91. Nine Infamous Villains in the Bible

1. Cain committed the first murder by killing his brother, Abel (Gen. 4:8).
2. Laban made many attempts to swindle Jacob, but Jacob ultimately prospered (Gen. 29-31).
3. Saul broke many oaths of love toward David and attempted to kill him several times (1 Sam. 19-27).
4. Absolom led a revolt against his father David (2 Sam. 15).
5. Ahab, king of Israel, "did evil in the sight of the Lord above all that were before him" (1 Kings 16:30).
6. Haman plotted to have the entire Hebrew nation legally killed (Esther).
7. Herod ordered the killing of all the babies in Bethlehem two years and under, in an attempt to kill Jesus; he also authorized John the Baptist's beheading (Matt. 2:16; 14:10).
8. Judas betrayed Jesus into the hands of the Jewish leaders (Matt. 26:14, 15).
9. Pilate allowed Jesus to be crucified, though he acknowledged His innocence (John 18, 19).

92. The Best King in the Bible

King David was a man after God's own heart (1 Sam. 13:14).

93. The Wisest and Richest King in the Bible

King Solomon was wiser than all men, for God gave Solomon wisdom. God also gave Solomon riches until he exceeded all the kings of the earth in riches and in wisdom (1 Kings 10:23).

94. The Worst King in the Bible

King Ahab married Jezebel and introduced the worship of Baal into Israel (1 Kings 16:29-31).

95. The Six Hairiest Men in the Bible

1. Esau was a very hairy man (Gen. 27:11-22).
2. Samson was a Nazarite from the time he was born and never shaved or had a haircut until Delilah had his head shaved (Judges 16:17).
3. Absalom had his hair cut once a year, and the amount of hair cut off weighed two hundred shekels (2 Sam. 14:26).
4. Elijah was a hairy man (2 Kings 1:8).
5. King Nebuchadnezzar's hair grew like eagles' feathers (Dan. 4:33).
6. John the Baptist was probably a Nazarite (Luke 1:15).

96. The Bald Men in the Bible

1. Samson had his head shaved by a man that Delilah called to do the job (Judges 16:19).
2. The only naturally bald man mentioned in the Bible is Elisha (2 Kings 2:23).
3. Ezra plucked off his own hair and beard (Ezra 9:3).
4. Job shaved his head (Job 1:20).
5. Paul purified himself along with four other men who were under a vow. They shaved their heads, and Paul possibly also shaved his own head (Acts 21:23-26).

97. The Ten Most-Mentioned Men in the New Testament

1. Jesus is by far the most-mentioned man in the New Testament.
2. Paul, the writer of a large share of the books of the New Testament, is the next most-mentioned.
3. Peter was the chief apostle and is mentioned almost as many times as Paul.
4. John the Baptist is mentioned 86 times.
5. Surprisingly, Pontius Pilate, who is mentioned 56 times, claims more attention than such people as Matthew, Mark,

and Luke, who are not mentioned enough to make this list.
6. John the apostle is mentioned 35 times.
7. Here's another villain: Herod the tetrarch is mentioned 30 times.
8. Timothy's association with Paul accounts for his name being mentioned 28 times.
9. Judas Iscariot is mentioned 23 times.
10. Philip the deacon, also known as the evangelist, is mentioned 16 times.

98. The Ten Most-Mentioned Men in the Old Testament

1. King David has a clear majority with almost half again as many references as the runner-up.
2. Moses is credited with writing the first five books of the Bible and is mentioned twice as often as the third place winner.
3. Moses' brother Aaron was Israel's first high priest and was often the spokesman for Moses.
4. Jacob, as a person, is mentioned quite often. If all of the references to his new name, Israel, were taken into account, he would be the most-mentioned; however, most uses of the name Israel concern the tribes or children of Israel.
5. Saul was the first king of Israel, but didn't get as much coverage as his successor, King David. Saul has to settle for fifth place.
6. Abraham was God's friend, because he believed God. That earned him a place among the ten most famous men in the Old Testament.
7. King Solomon, the third king of Israel, was the richest and wisest king mentioned in the Bible.
8. Joseph was a dreamer and an interpreter of dreams. God used Joseph to get the tribe of Israel into Egypt. Then it took over 400 years to get Israel out of Egypt.
9. Joshua fought the battle of Jericho. He took over Moses' position.
10. Jeremiah wept much about Israel and is one of the major prophets of the Old Testament.

NOTE: The first man, Adam, is mentioned only 30 times.

99. The Ten Most-Mentioned Women in the Bible

1. Sarah, the wife of Abraham, had a child when she was 90 years old. She is mentioned 56 times in the Bible.
2. Rachel was one of Jacob's wives. Jacob loved her the most and worked 14 years for her father so that he could marry her. Rachel is mentioned 47 times in the Bible.
3. Leah was Jacob's first wife. Jacob was tricked into marrying Leah, but Leah still wins the honor of being mentioned 34 times in the Bible.
4. Rebekah was Isaac's wife and the mother of Esau and Jacob. She is mentioned 31 times.
5. The women's list also includes an infamous person. Jezebel is mentioned 23 times.
6. The Virgin Mary, the mother of Jesus, is mentioned only 19 times.
7. Abigail, the wife of Nabal, and later the wife of King David, is mentioned 15 times and is tied for seventh place.
8. Also mentioned 15 times is Miriam, the sister of Moses.
9. The last two women on this list are both mentioned 14 times. Mary Magdalene knew Jesus personally and received deliverance and forgiveness from Him.
10. Hagar was Abraham's concubine and the mother of Ishmael.

NOTE: Eve, the mother of the human race, is mentioned only four times in the whole Bible!

100. Fifteen Queens of the Bible

1. Michal, a daughter of Saul, eventually scorned her husband, King David (1 Sam. 18:20; 2 Sam. 6:16).
2. When her husband Nabal died, Abigail became a wife of David (1 Sam. 25:39).
3. Rizpah was Saul's concubine (2 Sam. 3:7).
4. Bathsheba became David's wife after he had her husband, Uriah, murdered. She became the mother of Solomon (2 Sam. 11:15, 17, 27; 12:24).
5. When the queen of Sheba heard of the fame of Solomon concerning the name of the Lord, she came to prove him with hard questions (1 Kings 10:1).
6. Tahpenes was the wife of a Pharaoh who reigned during David's and Solomon's reigns (1 Kings 11:19).

7. Jezebel married king Ahab and caused him to worship Baal (1 Kings 16:31).
8. Maacah was removed from being queen because she had made an idol in a grove (2 Chron. 15:16).
9. Athaliah attempted to destroy all the seed royal of the house of Judah (2 Chron. 22:10).
10. The queen Vashti refused to come at Ahasuerus' command to show the people and the princes her beauty (Esther 1:11, 12).
11. Ahasuerus loved Esther above all women and made her queen instead of Vashti (Esther 2:17).
12. Belshazzar's queen (unnamed) brought Daniel's prophetic gift to her husband's attention (Dan. 5:10).
13. Herodias, wife of Herod, plotted the execution of John the Baptist (Matt. 14:3-8).
14. The eunuch who received the gospel from Philip had charge of all the treasure of Candace, queen of the Ethiopians (Acts 8:27-38).
15. Though historians indicated they were not married, but were brother and sister, King Agrippa and Bernice acted as a royal couple (Acts 25:13).

101. The Antichrist

1. The antichrist will be revealed before the coming of Jesus (2 Thess. 2:3-9).
2. Little children, it is the last time: and as ye have heard that antichrist shall come, even now are there many antichrists; whereby we know it is the last time (1 John 2:18).
3. Many deceivers are entered into the world, who confess not that Jesus Christ is come in the flesh. This is a deceiver and an antichrist (2 John 7).
4. The *number* of the beast's *name* is 666 (Rev. 13:17, 18).

102. All of the Giants in the Bible

1. There were giants in the land before the great flood (Gen. 6:4).
2. Rephaim means giant; therefore it may be that the Rephaims were a race of giants. The Lord gave the land of the Rephaims to Abraham (Gen. 15:18-20).
3. Ten of the twelve spies sent to spy out the land reported that

there were giants, the sons of Anak, in the land (Num. 13:33).

4. The Emims dwelt in Ar and were tall like the Anakims "which were accounted giants" (Deut. 2:9-11).
5. In the land of the children of Ammon dwelt a people which the Ammonites called the Zamzummims. The Zamzummims were tall like the Anakims (Deut. 2:19-21).
6. Og, king of Bashan, was a giant who had a bedstead of iron which was nine cubits long and four cubits wide (Deut. 3:11).
7. Arba was possibly a giant, since he was great among the Anakims (Josh. 14:15).
8. By extension, Anak himself might have been a giant. Anak was the son of Arba (Josh. 15:13).
9. Caleb drove the three sons of Anak out of Hebron. The names of the three sons are: Sheshai, Ahiman, and Talmai. Presumably they might have been giants (Josh. 15:14).
10. The best known giant is Goliath, the one David killed with a slingshot. Goliath stood six cubits and a span in height (1 Sam. 17:4).
11. In reading the accounts given in 2 Samuel, chapter 21, and 1 Chronicles, chapter 20, it would appear that Goliath had four brothers. It would also appear that their father was a giant (2 Sam. 21:22). Assuming that the four men were Goliath's brothers, one brother's name was Saph (or Sippai), another's name was Lahmi, and the only other one named was Ishbi-benob. Although it's uncertain whether these three brothers were giants, the remaining brother had six fingers on each hand and six toes on each foot and was a man of great stature (2 Sam. 21:16-22; 1 Chron. 20:4-8).

103. Thirteen Instances of Drunkenness in the Bible

1. Noah became drunk and was naked in his tent (Gen. 9:21).
2. Lot was made drunk by his daughters in order to seduce him (Gen. 19:32).
3. God's command to Aaron that the priests not drink wine implies that Nadab and Abihu had been drunk (Lev. 10:1, 9).
4. Boaz "had drunk and his heart was merry" (Ruth 3:7).
5. Eli mistakenly thought Hannah was drunk (1 Sam. 1:13).
6. Nabal held a feast and became very drunk (1 Sam. 25:36).
7. David made Uriah drunk (2 Sam. 11:13).

8. Amnon was murdered by Absolom's servants while he was drunk (2 Sam. 13:28).
9. Elah was murdered while drunk (1 Kings 16:9).
10. Benhadad and thirty-two kings were drunk together (1 Kings 20:16).
11. Queen Vashti refused to display her beauty when king Ahasuerus was "merry with wine" (Esther 1:10).
12. Jesus was accused of being "a winebibber" (Luke 7:34).
13. At Pentecost, some mocked the disciples as being drunk (Acts 2:13).

104. Musicians of the Bible

1. Jubal was the father of all such as handle the harp and organ (Gen. 4:21).
2. Miriam took a timbrel in her hand; and all the women went out after her with timbrels and dances. And Miriam answered them, Sing ye to the Lord, for he hath triumphed gloriously; the horse and his rider hath he thrown into the sea (Ex. 15:20, 21).
3. David played the harp for Saul and thus caused the evil spirit to depart from Saul (1 Sam. 16:23).
4. The women came out of all the cities of Israel, singing and dancing, to meet King Saul, with tabrets, with joy, and with instruments of music (1 Sam. 18:6).
5. King Solomon wrote 1,005 songs (1 Kings 4:32).
6. Elisha called for a minstrel, and when the minstrel played, he prophesied, "Thus saith the Lord, Make this valley full of ditches" (2 Kings 3:15 16).
7. Additional musicians from among the Levites were used to help bring the ark back to Jerusalem. Among those not previously listed herein are: Ethan, Zechariah, Aziel, Shemiramoth, Jehiel, Unni, Eliab, Maaseiah, Elipheleh, Mikneiah, Obededom, Azariah, Shebaniah, Jehoshaphat, Nethaneel, Amasai and Eliezer (1 Chron. 15:16-24).
8. Jeiel played the psaltery and the harp (1 Chron. 16:5).
9. Asaph played the cymbals (1 Chron. 16:5).
10. Benaiah and Jahaziel played the trumpet (1 Chron. 16:6).
11. Heman played, or led the players of, the trumpet and cymbals (1 Chron. 16:42).
12. Jeduthun was one of King David's chief musicians (1 Chron. 16:42; title of Psalm 39).

13. King David had 4,000 musicians who praised the Lord with the instruments which David made (1 Chron. 23:5).
14. The number of those that David set apart to perform music in the house of the Lord was 288. Included in the 288, and not previously mentioned in this list, are Zaccur, Joseph, Nethaniah, Asarelah, Gedaliah, Zeri, Jeshaiah, Hashabiah, Mattithiah, Bukkiah, Mattaniah, Uzziel, Shebuel, Jerimoth, Hananiah, Hanani, Eliathah, Giddalti, Romamtiezer, Joshbekashah, Mallothi, Hothir, Mahazioth, Izri, Jesharelah, Shemei, Azareel, and Shubael (1 Chron. 25).
15. When Solomon dedicated the temple, there were singers, cymbal players, psaltery players, and harpists along with 120 priests who played trumpets (2 Chron. 5:11-14).
16. The priests played trumpets and the Levites, the sons of Asaph, used cymbals to praise the Lord when the foundation was laid for the rebuilding of the temple (Ezra 3:10, 11). Some of those musicians were mentioned by name in Nehemiah: Zechariah, Shemaiah, Azareel, Milalai, Gilalai, Maai, Nethaneel, Judah, and Hanani (Neh. 12:35, 36).
17. John heard "the voice of harpers harping with their harps: and they sung as it were a new song before the throne" in heaven (Rev. 14:2, 3).

105. Twenty-eight Dreamers in the Bible

1. God came to Abraham in a vision and promised him a son (Gen. 15:1).
2. Abimelech was told in a dream that he had taken Abraham's wife (Gen. 20:3).
3. Sleeping with his head on a rock, Jacob dreamed of a ladder extending from earth to heaven (Gen. 28:12).
4. Joseph (of the Old Testament) dreamed that his family bowed down to him (Gen. 37:5-8).
5. Pharaoh's butler dreamed of restoration to Pharaoh's favor (Gen. 40:9-13).
6. Pharaoh's baker dreamed of his execution (Gen. 40:16-19).
7. Pharaoh dreamed of cattle which Joseph interpreted as symbolizing years of plenty and years of famine (Gen. 41:17-32).
8. Balaam claimed he was a man who "saw the vision of the Almighty, falling into a trance, but having his eyes open" (Num. 24:4).
9. Gideon overheard a man who had dreamed that Gideon de-

feated Midian (Judges 7:13, 14).

10. In a vision, God warned Samuel about Eli's sons (1 Sam. 3:1-15)

11. God appeared to Solomon in a dream, and granted him understanding to discern judgment (1 Kings 3:5-11).

12. Some of Solomon's deeds were recorded in the visions of Iddo the seer (2 Chron. 9:29).

13. Isaiah's prophecy is called "The vision" (Isa. 1:1).

14. Ezekiel travelled to Chaldea in one of his visions (Ezek. 11:24).

15. "Nebuchadnezzar dreamed dreams, wherewith his spirit was troubled, and his sleep brake from him" (Dan. 2:1).

16. "In the first year of Belshazzar king of Babylon Daniel had a dream and visions of his head upon his bed" (Dan. 7:1).

17. The prophecy of Obadiah came in a vision (Obad. 1:1).

18. Nahum's prophecy was a recorded vision (Nahum 1:1).

19. God said to Habakkuk, "Write the vision, and make it plain upon tables, that he may run that readeth it" (Hab. 2:2).

20. Jesus' stepfather, Joseph, was reassured by an angel in a dream that Mary was pregnant by the Holy Ghost (Matt. 1:20).

21. God warned the wise men from the east not to return to Herod, in a dream (Matt. 2:12).

22. After His transfiguration, Jesus told James (also Peter and John), "Tell the vision to no man, until the Son of man be risen again from the dead" (Matt. 17:9).

23. After his vision of an angel, Zechariah remained dumb until his son John was born and named (Luke 1:22, 63, 64).

24. Ananias was told in a vision to pray for Paul, then Saul of Tarsus (Acts 9:10).

25. In a vision, Paul saw Ananias coming and praying for his sight to be restored (Acts 9:12).

26. Cornelius sent men to Peter after an angel of God spoke to him in a vision (Acts 10:3).

27. God spoke to Peter concerning unclean things in a vision (Acts 11:5).

28. John called his Revelation a vision (Rev. 9:17).

106. Lepers in the Bible

1. [Moses] put his hand into his bosom: and when he took it out, behold, his hand was leprous as snow (Ex. 4:6).

2. And the Lord spake unto Moses, saying, Command the children of Israel, that they put out of the camp every leper. . . . And the children of Israel did so, and put them out without the camp (Num. 5:1-4).

3. Behold, Miriam became leprous, white as snow (Num. 12:10).

4. Naaman, captain of the host of the king of Syria . . . was a leper (2 Kings 5:1).

5. Gehazi became a leper after lying to Elisha (2 Kings 5:27).

6. There were four leprous men at the entering in of the gate [of Samaria] (2 Kings 7:3).

7. The Lord smote [Azariah], so that he was a leper unto the day of his death (2 Kings 15:5).

8. Uzziah the king was a leper unto the day of his death (2 Chron. 26:21).

9. There came a leper and worshipped [Jesus] (Matt. 8:2).

10. Go show John again those things which ye do hear and see: . . . the lepers are cleansed (Matt. 11:5).

11. [Jesus was] in Bethany in the house of Simon the leper (Mark 14:3).

12. Many lepers were in Israel in the time of Eliseus the prophet (Luke 4:27).

13. As [Jesus] entered into a certain village, there met him ten men that were lepers, which stood afar off (Luke 17:12).

8

Sex

No matter what advocates of the "new" morality try to claim, sex was God's idea, not theirs. Since God established the marriage relationship (including sex) in the first place, should it be surprising that God's Word covers the subject? As with other gifts He gives, God has supplied us with clear instructions for using sex as He intended it.

In this chapter, you will find thirty rules of conduct concerning sex. Other lists include biblical accounts of nudity and incest, what can happen to a practicing homosexual, and some prominent harlots in the Bible.

107. Thirty Rules of Conduct Concerning Sex

1. You shall not commit adultery (Ex. 20:14).
2. You shall not covet your neighbor's wife (Ex. 20:17).
3. If you get semen on you, you are unclean regardless whether it happened during sexual intercourse or while having a wet dream. Bathe for cleansing (Lev. 15:16-18; Deut. 23:10).
4. You shall not have sexual intercourse with your mother (Lev. 18:7).
5. You shall not have sexual intercourse with your father (Lev. 18:7).
6. You shall not have sexual intercourse with your father's wife even if she's not your natural mother (Lev. 18:8).
7. You shall not have sexual intercourse with your sister even if she's only your half sister (Lev. 18:9).
8. You shall not have sexual intercourse with your granddaughter (Lev. 18:10).
9. You shall not have sexual intercourse with your aunt (Lev. 18:12, 13).
10. You shall not have sexual intercourse with your uncle (Lev. 18:14).

11. You shall not have sexual intercourse with your daughter-in-law (Lev. 18:15).
12. You shall not have sexual intercourse with your sister-in-law (Lev. 18:16).
13. You shall not have sexual intercourse with both a woman and her daughter (Lev. 18:17).
14. You shall not have sexual intercourse with both a woman and her granddaughter (Lev. 18:17).
15. You shall not have sexual intercourse with two sisters while one of the sisters is still alive (Lev 18:18).
16. You shall not have sexual intercourse with a woman while she is having her monthly period (Lev. 18:19).
17. You shall not have sexual intercourse with a person of the same sex as you are (Lev. 18:22).
18. You shall not have sexual intercourse with an animal (Lev. 18:23).
19. You shall not prostitute your daughter to cause her to become a whore (Lev. 19:29).
20. You shall not wear clothing pertaining to the opposite sex (Deut. 22:5).
21. Do not make your neighbor drunk in order to look upon his [or her] nakedness (Hab. 2:15).
22. Do not look upon a woman to lust after her (Matt. 5:28).
23. Abstain from fornication (Acts 15:29).
24. Homosexual acts are unnatural and are results of vile affections which can lead to reprobate minds (Rom. 1:26-28).
25. Fornication is a sin against your own body (1 Cor. 6:18).
26. To avoid fornication, let every man have his own wife, and let every woman have her own husband (1 Cor. 7:2).
27. The husband has power over his wife's body, and the wife has power over her husband's body. The husband or the wife should not withhold sexual favors except for short periods, by mutual consent, for purposes of fasting and prayer (1 Cor. 7:4, 5).
28. Lasciviousness and concupiscence are works of the flesh and not of the Spirit (Gal. 5:19; Col. 3:5).
29. The marriage bed is undefiled (Heb. 13:4).
30. The lust of the eyes and the lust of the flesh are of the world and not of the Father (1 John 2:16).

NOTE: For items 4 through 15, the taboo also forbids marriage; in those cases, marriage will not sanctify the sex act.

108. Thirty Results of Being a Homosexual

1. God gives homosexuals up to uncleanness (Rom. 1:24).
2. Homosexuals dishonor their own bodies between themselves (Rom. 1:24).
3. Homosexuals corrupt the Word of God by changing His truth to a lie (Rom. 1:25).
4. Homosexuals worship and serve the creature more than the Creator (Rom. 1:25).
5. God gives homosexuals up to their vile affections (Rom. 1:26, 27).
6. God gives homosexuals over to a reprobate mind (Rom. 1:28).
7. Homosexuals are filled with all unrighteousness (Rom. 1:29).
8. Homosexuals end up being motivated to do things that are not convenient (Rom. 1:28).
9. Homosexuals are filled with fornication (Rom. 1:29).
10. Homosexuals are filled with wickedness (Rom. 1:29).
11. Homosexuals are filled with covetousness (Rom. 1:29).
12. Homosexuals are filled with maliciousness (Rom. 1:29).
13. Homosexuals are filled with envy (Rom. 1:29).
14. Homosexuals are filled with murder (Rom. 1:29).
15. Homosexuals are filled with debate (Rom. 1:29).
16. Homosexuals are filled with deceit (Rom. 1:29).
17. Homosexuals are filled with malignity (Rom. 1:29).
18. Homosexuals are whisperers (Rom. 1:29).
19. Homosexuals are backbiters (Rom. 1:30).
20. Homosexuals are haters of God (Rom. 1:30).
21. Homosexuals are despiteful (Rom. 1:30).
22. Homosexuals are proud (Rom. 1:30).
23. Homosexuals are boasters (Rom. 1:30).
24. Homosexuals are inventors of evil things (Rom. 1:30).
25. Homosexuals are disobedient to parents (Rom. 1:30).
26. Homosexuals are covenant breakers (Rom. 1:31).
27. Homosexuals are without natural affection (Rom. 1:31).
28. Homosexuals are unmerciful (Rom. 1:31).
29. Homosexuals are implacable (Rom. 1:31).
30. Homosexuals are without understanding (Rom. 1:31).

109. Five Biblical Accounts of Incest

1. Lot's two daughters committed incest with their father (Gen. 19:31-36).

2. Reuben had sex with his father's concubine, Bilhah (Gen. 35:22).
3. Ammon committed incest with his sister, Tamar, by raping her (2 Sam. 13:10-14).
4. Absalom went into his father's concubines (2 Sam. 16:22).
5. A Corinthian Christian had sex with his father's wife (1 Cor. 5:1).

110. Seven Prominent Harlots in the Bible

1. Judah's daughter-in-law tired of waiting for Judah to provide her with another husband (she had already been widowed by two of Judah's sons), so she played the harlot. Her only customer, apparently, was Judah, and he made her pregnant. She gave birth to twin boys: Pharez and Zarah (Gen. 38).
2. Rahab (Rachab in New Testament) the harlot received the two spies in Jericho and hid them (Josh. 2:1-5). She later married Salmon (King David's great-great grandfather) and is listed in the genealogy of Jesus (Matt. 1:5).
3. Jephthah's mother was a harlot. Jephthah delivered Israel from the Ammonites during the time of the Judges (Judges 11:1).
4. Samson spent half the night with a harlot in Gaza and then took the gates, gateposts, and bars to the gates of the city and carried them on his shoulders to the top of the hill before Hebron (Judges 16:1-3).
5. A Levite's concubine played the part of a harlot and went home to her father (Judges 19:1, 2). This indirectly led to a situation in Gibeah where the concubine was forcibly and continuously raped until it caused her death (Judges 19:22-28). The Levite cut up the body of the concubine and sent the twelve pieces throughout the tribes of Israel. This led to a war which nearly wiped out the Benjamites and created a scarcity of wives for that tribe. This led to a slaughter of all of the inhabitants of Jabesh-gilead except for the female virgins. This provided 400 virgin wives for the Benjamites. An additional 200 virgins were required, and thus was initiated a sanctioned kidnapping of women from among the daughters of Shiloh to provide wives for the Benjamites (Judges 21).
6. Two harlots played a part in displaying the wisdom of Solomon. Each harlot had a son, but during the night one harlot

accidentally killed her baby by lying on top of it during her sleep. She switched babies during the night and claimed the living baby was her own. When Solomon heard the case, he ordered the living child to be cut in half. The real mother was willing to give up the child rather than see him killed. The other harlot was willing to have the baby killed. Thus the child's real mother was discerned (1 Kings 3:16-28).

111. Nine Cases of Public or Semi-Public Nudity in the Bible

1. Adam and Eve were naked in the garden of Eden (Gen. 2:25).
2. Practically the whole nation of Israel had a nude orgy (Ex. 32:19-25).
3. King Saul stripped off his clothes, prophesied before Samuel, and lay down naked all day and all night (1 Sam. 19:21-24).
4. Isaiah walked barefoot and naked for three years among the Hebrews in obedience to the Lord (Isa. 20:2, 3).
5. A young man (probably Mark) was with Jesus in the garden of Gethsemane when Jesus was arrested. He was wearing only a linen cloth. When some of the arresting party grabbed for him, they tore the cloth from the young man's body, and he ran away naked (Mark 14:51, 52).
6. The Gadarene demoniac ran about naked in a graveyard, until Jesus delivered him from a legion of demons (Luke 8:27).
7. The man helped by the good Samaritan was stripped of his clothes by thieves and left half dead (Luke 10:30).
8. Peter was naked in the fishing boat the last time he went fishing (John 21:7).
9. The seven sons of Sceva were stripped and wounded by a demon-possessed man when they tried to exorcise the demon (Acts 19:13-16).

9

Characteristics

When Jesus said, "By their fruits ye shall know them" (Matt. 7:20), He reflected God's concern for the visible details of our life-styles. Therefore, His word presents many characteristics which His people should or shouldn't have.

For instance, what are the works of the flesh? List 112 includes twenty works of the flesh.

What will sinners be like in the last days? See list 114.

What are the qualifications for bishops or elders, and deacons, according to the Bible? See lists 115 and 116.

What five signs will follow believers? See list 117.

What are the qualifications for discipleship? See list 118.

112. The Twenty Works of the Flesh

1. Divisions are a result of carnality (1 Cor. 3:3).
2. Adultery is a manifested work of the flesh (Gal. 5:19).
3. Fornication is a manifested work of the flesh (Gal. 5:19).
4. Uncleanness is a manifested work of the flesh (Gal. 5:19).
5. Lasciviousness is a manifested work of the flesh (Gal. 5:19).
6. Idolatry is a manifested work of the flesh (Gal. 5:20).
7. Witchcraft is a manifested work of the flesh (Gal. 5:20).
8. Hatred is a manifested work of the flesh (Gal. 5:20).
9. Variance is a manifested work of the flesh (Gal. 5:20).
10. Emulation is a manifested work of the flesh (Gal. 5:20).
11. Wrath is a manifested work of the flesh (Gal. 5:20).
12. Strife is a manifested work of the flesh (Gal. 5:20).
13. Sedition is a manifested work of the flesh (Gal. 5:20).
14. Heresy is a manifested work of the flesh (Gal. 5:20).
15. Envying is a manifested work of the flesh (Gal. 5:21).
16. Murder is a manifested work of the flesh (Gal. 5:21).

17. Drunkenness is a manifested work of the flesh (Gal. 5:21).
18. Revelling is a manifested work of the flesh (Gal. 5:21).
19. Inordinate affection is a work of the flesh (Col. 3:5).
20. Evil concupiscence is a work of the flesh (Col. 3:5).

113. Fifteen Types of People to Whom the Law Is Addressed

1. The law is for the lawless (1 Tim. 1:9).
2. The law is for the disobedient (1 Tim. 1:9).
3. The law is for the ungodly (1 Tim. 1:9).
4. The law is for the sinners (1 Tim. 1:9).
5. The law is for the unholy (1 Tim. 1:9).
6. The law is for the profane (1 Tim. 1:9).
7. The law is for the murderers of mothers (1 Tim. 1:9).
8. The law is for the murderers of fathers (1 Tim. 1:9).
9. The law is for the manslayers (1 Tim. 1:9).
10. The law is for the whoremongers (1 Tim. 1:10).
11. The law is for the homosexuals (1 Tim. 1:10).
12. The law is for the menstealers (1 Tim. 1:10).
13. The law is for the liars (1 Tim. 1:10).
14. The law is for the perjured persons (1 Tim. 1:10).
15. The law is for any other thing that is contrary to sound doctrine (1 Tim. 1:10).

114. Twenty-five Characteristics of Non-Christians in the Last Days

1. Men shall be lovers of their own selves (2 Tim. 3:2).
2. Men shall be covetous (2 Tim. 3:2).
3. Men shall be boasters (2 Tim. 3:2).
4. Men shall be proud (2 Tim. 3:2).
5. Men shall be blasphemers (2 Tim. 3:2).
6. Men shall be disobedient to parents (2 Tim. 3:2).
7. Men shall be unthankful (2 Tim. 3:2).
8. Men shall be unholy (2 Tim. 3:2).
9. Men shall be without natural affection (2 Tim. 3:3).
10. Men shall be trucebreakers (2 Tim. 3:3).
11. Men shall be false accusers (2 Tim. 3:3).
12. Men shall be incontinent (2 Tim. 3:3).
13. Men shall be fierce (2 Tim. 3:3).
14. Men shall be despisers of those who do good (2 Tim. 3:3).

15. Men shall be traitors (2 Tim. 3:4).
16. Men shall be heady (2 Tim. 3:4).
17. Men shall be highminded (2 Tim. 3:4).
18. Men shall be lovers of pleasures more than lovers of God (2 Tim. 3:4).
19. Men shall have a form of godliness, but they will deny the power thereof (2 Tim. 3:5).
20. There shall be men of the sort which creep into houses and lead captive silly, sinful women who are led away with divers lusts (2 Tim. 3:6).
21. They shall always be learning but never able to come to the knowledge of the truth (2 Tim. 3:7).
22. They shall resist the truth (2 Tim. 3:8).
23. They shall have corrupt minds (2 Tim. 3:8).
24. They shall be reprobate concerning the faith (2 Tim. 3:8).
25. They shall not progress, because their folly shall be manifested unto all men (2 Tim. 3:9).

115. Qualifications for a Bishop or Elder

1. A bishop must be blameless (1 Tim. 3:2).
2. A bishop must be the husband of one wife (1 Tim. 3:2).
3. A bishop must be vigilant (1 Tim. 3:2).
4. A bishop must be sober (1 Tim. 3:2).
5. A bishop must be of good behavior (1 Tim. 3:2).
6. A bishop must be given to hospitality (1 Tim. 3:2).
7. A bishop must be apt to teach (1 Tim. 3:2).
8. A bishop must not be given to wine (1 Tim. 3:3).
9. A bishop must not be a striker (1 Tim. 3:3).
10. A bishop must not be greedy of filthy lucre (1 Tim. 3:3).
11. A bishop must not be a brawler (1 Tim. 3:3).
12. A bishop must not be covetous (1 Tim. 3:3).
13. A bishop must be patient (1 Tim. 3:3).
14. A bishop must rule his own house well and have his children in subjection with all gravity (1 Tim. 3:4).
15. A bishop must not be a novice (1 Tim. 3:6).
16. A bishop must be of good report of them which are without (1 Tim. 3:7).
17. A bishop must not be selfwilled (Titus 1:7).
18. A bishop must not anger easily (Titus 1:7).
19. A bishop must be a lover of good men (Titus 1:8).
20. A bishop must be just (Titus 1:8).

21. A bishop must be holy (Titus 1:8).
22. A bishop must be temperate (Titus 1:8).
23. A bishop must hold fast to the faithful word as he has been taught so that with sound doctrine he may be able to exhort and convince the gainsayers (Titus 1:9).

116. Qualifications for a Deacon

1. A deacon must be of honest report (Acts 6:3).
2. A deacon must be full of the Holy Ghost (Acts 6:3).
3. A deacon must be full of wisdom (Acts 6:3).
4. A deacon must be grave (1 Tim. 3:8).
5. A deacon must not be double-tongued (1 Tim. 3:8).
6. A deacon must not be given to much wine (1 Tim. 3:8).
7. A deacon must not be greedy of filthy lucre (1 Tim. 3:8).
8. A deacon must hold the mystery of the faith in a pure conscience (1 Tim. 3:9).
9. A deacon should first be proved and then be made a deacon if he's found blameless (1 Tim. 3:10).
10. A deacon must be the husband of one wife (1 Tim. 3:12).
11. A deacon must rule his own house and children well (1 Tim. 3:12).
12. The deacon's wife must not be a slanderer but must be grave, sober, and faithful in all things (1 Tim. 3:11).

117. Five Signs That Shall Follow Believers

1. Believers shall cast out devils in Jesus' name (Mark 16:17).
2. Believers shall speak with new tongues (Mark 16:17).
3. Believers shall take up serpents (Mark 16:18).
4. If believers drink any deadly thing, it will not hurt them (Mark 16:18).
5. Believers shall lay hands on the sick, and they shall recover (Mark 16:18).

118. Qualifications for Christian Discipleship

1. You must be born again (John 3:1-8), for all have sinned, and come short of the glory of God (Rom. 3:23). The wages of sin is death, but the gift of God is eternal life through Jesus Christ our Lord (Rom. 6:23).
2. If we confess our sins, he is faithful and just to forgive us our

sins, and to cleanse us from all unrighteousness (1 John 1:9).

3. Faith cometh by hearing, and hearing by the word of God (Rom. 10:17).

4. There is no difference between the Jew and the Greek: for the same Lord over all is rich unto all that call upon him. For whosoever shall call upon the name of the Lord shall be saved (Rom. 10:12, 13).

5. If thou shalt confess with thy mouth the Lord Jesus, and shalt believe in thine heart that God hath raised him from the dead, thou shalt be saved. For with the heart man believeth unto righteousness: and with the mouth confession is made unto salvation (Rom. 10:9, 10).

6. For as many of you as have been baptized into Christ have put on Christ (Gal. 3:27).

7. Repent and be baptized every one of you for the remission of sins, and ye shall receive the gift of the Holy Ghost (Acts 2:38).

8. If ye then, being evil, know how to give good gifts unto your children; how much more shall your heavenly Father give the Holy Spirit to them that ask him? (Luke 11:13).

9. Ye shall receive power, after that the Holy Ghost is come upon you: and ye shall be witnesses unto me both in Jerusalem, and in all Judea, and in Samaria, and unto the uttermost part of the earth (Acts 1:8).

10. For we are his workmanship, created in Christ Jesus unto good works, which God hath before ordained that we should walk in them (Eph. 2:10).

11. He that taketh not his cross, and followeth after me, is not worthy of me. He that findeth his life shall lose it: and he that loseth his life for my sake shall find it (Matt. 10:38, 39).

12. Verily, verily, I say unto you, Except ye eat the flesh of the Son of man, and drink his blood, ye have no life in you (John 6:53).

13. Think not that I am come to send peace on earth: I came not to send peace, but a sword. For I am come to set a man at variance against his father, and the daughter against her mother, and the daughter-in-law against her mother-in-law. And a man's foes shall be they of his own household. He that loveth father or mother more than me is not worthy of me: and he that loveth son or daughter more than me is not worthy of me (Matt. 10:34-37).

14. If we walk in the light, as he is in the light, we have fellow-

       ship one with another, and the blood of Jesus Christ his Son cleanseth us from all sin (1 John 1:7).

15. By this shall all men know that ye are my disciples, if ye have love one to another (John 13:35).

16. If ye continue in my word, then are ye my disciples indeed; and ye shall know the truth, and the truth shall make you free (John 8:31, 32).

17. Then said Jesus unto the twelve, Will ye also go away? Then Simon Peter answered him, Lord, to whom shall we go? Thou hast the words of eternal life. And we believe and are sure that thou art the Christ, the Son of the living God (John 6:67-69).

18. If ye abide in me, and my words abide in you, ye shall ask what ye will, and it shall be done unto you. Herein is my Father glorified, that ye bear much fruit; so shall ye be my disciples (John 15:7, 8).

10

Love

Poets still write, singers still sing, philosophers still discuss the concept of love. And the definitions of love stretch all the way from warm puppies to the hot flush of sexual attraction.

Divine love, what the Greeks call "agape," is another matter. With His infinite precision, God has told us clearly what His love—real love—is, and isn't. That's what this chapter is about.

119. Who Is Love?

God is love (1 John 4:8, 16).

120. Eleven Descriptions of Love

1. Love is a commandment (John 13:34).
2. Love is shed abroad in our hearts by the Holy Ghost (Rom. 5:5).
3. Love is the fulfilling of the law (Rom. 13:10).
4. Love is the catalyst that gives meaning to speaking in tongues, to prophesying, to understanding, to faith, to charitable works, and to self-sacrifice (1 Cor. 13:1-3).
5. Love is kind (1 Cor. 13:4).
6. Love is greater than faith (1 Cor. 13:13).
7. Love is greater than hope (1 Cor. 13:13).
8. Love is the fruit of the Spirit (Gal. 5:22).
9. Love is the bond of perfectness (Col. 3:14).
10. Love is of God (1 John 4:7).
11. Love is living according to God's commandments (2 John 6).

121. Ten Things Which Cannot Separate Us from the Love of God

1. Death cannot separate us from the love of God (Rom. 8:38).
2. Life cannot separate us from the love of God (Rom. 8:38).
3. Angels cannot separate us from the love of God (Rom. 8:38).
4. Principalities cannot separate us from the love of God (Rom. 8:38).
5. Powers cannot separate us from the love of God (Rom. 8:38).
6. Things present cannot separate us from the love of God (Rom. 8:38).
7. Things to come cannot separate us from the love of God (Rom. 8:38).
8. Height cannot separate us from the love of God (Rom. 8:39).
9. Depth cannot separate us from the love of God (Rom. 8:39).
10. No other creature can separate us from the love of God (Rom. 8:39).

122. Nine Things That Love Does

1. Love suffers long (1 Cor. 13:4).
2. Love rejoices in truth (1 Cor. 13:6).
3. Love bears all things (1 Cor. 13:7).
4. Love believes all things (1 Cor. 13:7).
5. Love hopes all things (1 Cor. 13:7).
6. Love endures all things (1 Cor. 13:7).
7. Love abides now (1 Cor. 13:13).
8. Love covers a multitude of sins (1 Pet. 4:8).
9. Perfect love casts out fear (1 John 4:18).

123. Three Things That Love Is Not

1. Love is not envious (1 Cor. 13:4).
2. Love is not puffed up (1 Cor. 13:4).
3. Love is not easily provoked (1 Cor. 13:5).

124. Seven Things That Love Does Not Do

1. Love does not vaunt itself (1 Cor. 13:4).
2. Love does not behave unseemly (1 Cor. 13:5).
3. Love does not seek its own (1 Cor. 13:5).
4. Love thinks no evil (1 Cor. 13:5).

5. Love does not rejoice in iniquity (1 Cor. 13:6).
6. Love never fails (1 Cor. 13:8).
7. Love works no ill to his neighbor (Rom. 13:10).

11

God's Gifts to Men

Paul wrote in 1 Corinthians 14:1 that we should desire spiritual gifts. Many have missed out by saying, "But which gift should I seek?" Others have sold themselves short by limiting the number of spiritual gifts to nine, or twelve, or eighteen. Even this chapter does not claim to list them all, but perhaps there are enough here to expand our spiritual horizons.

Could it be that there is more available in the Lord than we seek to obtain?

125. Nine Gifts of the Spirit

1. To one is given by the Spirit the word of wisdom (1 Cor. 12:8).
2. To another is given the word of knowledge by the same Spirit (1 Cor. 12:8).
3. To another is given faith by the same Spirit (1 Cor. 12:9).
4. To another is given the gifts of healing by the same Spirit (1 Cor. 12:9).
5. To another is given the working of miracles (1 Cor. 12:10).
6. To another is given prophecy (1 Cor. 12:10).
7. To another is given the discerning of Spirits (1 Cor. 12:10).
8. To another is given divers kinds of tongues (1 Cor. 12:10).
9. To yet another is given the interpretation of tongues (1 Cor. 12:10).

126. Nine Ministries God Gave to the Church

1. Exhorters have a ministry in the church (Rom. 12:4, 8).
2. Those who give have a definite ministry in the church (Rom. 12:4, 8).

3. God gave apostles to the church (1 Cor. 12:28).
4. God gave prophets to the church (1 Cor. 12:28).
5. God gave teachers to the church (1 Cor. 12:28).
6. God gave helpers to the church (1 Cor. 12:28).
7. God gave administrators to the church (1 Cor. 12:28).
8. The Lord gave evangelists to the church to help perfect and edify the body of Christ (Eph. 4:11, 12).
9. The Lord gave pastors to the church for the work of the ministry and to help perfect and edify the body of Christ (Eph. 4:11, 12).

127. Eleven Fruits of the Spirit

1. The fruit of the Spirit is love (Gal. 5:22).
2. The fruit of the Spirit is joy (Gal. 5:22).
3. The fruit of the Spirit is peace (Gal. 5:22).
4. The fruit of the Spirit is long-suffering (Gal. 5:22).
5. The fruit of the Spirit is gentleness (Gal. 5:22).
6. The fruit of the Spirit is goodness (Gal. 5:22).
7. The fruit of the Spirit is faith (Gal. 5:22).
8. The fruit of the Spirit is meekness (Gal. 5:23).
9. The fruit of the Spirit is temperance (Gal. 5:23).
10. The fruit of the Spirit is in all righteousness (Eph. 5:9).
11. The fruit of the Spirit is in all truth (Eph. 5:9).

128. Seven Virtues

1. Give all diligence to add faith [to your other virtues] (2 Pet. 1:5).
2. Give all diligence to add knowledge (2 Pet. 1:5).
3. Give all diligence to add temperance (2 Pet. 1:6).
4. Give all diligence to add patience (2 Pet. 1:6).
5. Give all diligence to add godliness (2 Pet. 1:6).
6. Give all diligence to add brotherly kindness (2 Pet. 1:7).
7. Give all diligence to add charity (2 Pet. 1:7).

129. Armor Every Christian Should Have

1. Cast off the works of darkness, and put on the armor of light (Rom. 13:12).
2. Put on the whole armor of God, that you may be able to stand against the wiles of the devil and to withstand the evil

day. Start by having your loins girt about with truth (Eph. 6:11-14).

3. Have on the breastplate of righteousness (Eph. 6:14).

4. Have your feet shod with the preparation of the gospel of peace (Eph. 6:15).

5. Above all, take the shield of faith to quench all of the fiery darts of the wicked (Eph. 6:16).

6. Take the helmet of salvation (Eph. 6:17).

7. Take the sword of the Spirit which is the Word of God (Eph. 6:17).

12

Sin

In a book of lists with a chapter titled "Sin," you might expect to find a list of several thousand sins. This chapter, however, is not of that sort.

What is sin anyway? Paul said, "Whatsoever is not of faith is sin" (Rom. 14:23).

James wrote, "To him that knoweth to do good, and doeth it not, it is sin" (James 4:17).

John declared, "Sin is the transgression of the law" (1 John 3:4).

The list of possible sins could be very long. This chapter focuses on sin from some different points of view. Here we look at six sins that King David committed, six accounts of people whom Jesus personally forgave, and ten things that you can do about sin. For specific revelation of sin in one's life, the Holy Spirit will illuminate a person's God-given conscience (Rom. 2:15).

In this section is included some information about Satan, since he is the "father of lies" and attempts to draw mankind into sin.

130. Six Sins That King David Committed

1. He took back Michal as his wife after she was married to another man (2 Sam. 3:13-16; Deut. 24:1-4).
2. He coveted his neighbor's wife (2 Sam. 11:2, 3).
3. He committed adultery with Bathsheba (2 Sam. 11:4, 5).
4. He tried to cover up the adultery (2 Sam. 11:6-13).
5. He ordered the murder of Uriah (2 Sam. 11:14-17).
6. He numbered Israel (1 Chron. 21:1, 17).

131. Murderers in the Bible

1. "*Cain* rose up against Abel his brother, and slew him" (Gen. 4:8).
2. "*Simeon* and *Levi* . . . slew all the males" of Shalem (Gen. 34:25).
3. *Moses* "slew the Egyptian and hid him in the sand" (Ex. 2:12).
4. *Achan*, through disobedience, was responsible for the death of 36 Israelites (Josh. 7:5, 20).
5. *Abimelech* murdered his 70 half-brothers (Judges 9:5).
6. "Certain *sons of Belial*" raped the Levite's concubine until she died (Judges 19:22-28).
7. *Saul* ordered the killing of 85 priests and the people and animals of Nob because they aided David (1 Sam. 22:18, 19).
8. "*Joab* and *Abishai* his brother slew Abner" (2 Sam. 3:30).
9. The *sons of Rimmon, Rechab, and Baanah* killed Ishbosheth on his bed (2 Sam. 4:5, 6).

Cain Kills Abel

10. *David* arranged Uriah's death (2 Sam. 11:14, 15).
11. "The *servants of Absolom* [killed] Amnon as *Absolom* had commanded" (2 Sam. 13:28, 29).
12. *Joab* killed Absolom as he hung from a tree (2 Sam. 18:14).
13. *Joab* tricked Amasa, then killed him (2 Sam. 20:10).
14. *Solomon* had his brother Adonijah killed by Benaiah (1 Kings 2:23-25).
15. *Baasha* killed Nadab at Gebbethon (1 Kings 15:27).
16. Elah was killed by *Zimri*, captain of half his chariots (1 Kings 16:9, 10).
17. "*Jezebel* slew the prophets of the Lord" (1 Kings 18:13).
18. *Jezebel* plotted Naboth's death (1 Kings 21:7-14).
19. *Hazael* smothered Benhadad as he lay sick (2 Kings 8:15).
20. *Shallum* killed Zachariah and took the throne of Israel (2 Kings 15:10).
21. *Menahem* killed Shallum and reigned for a month (2 Kings 15:14).
22. *Pekah* killed Pekahiah and took the throne (2 Kings 15:25).
23. *Hoshea* murdered Pekah and succeeded him (2 Kings 15:30).
24. Sennacherib was killed by his sons, *Adramelech* and *Sharezer*, as he worshiped Nisroch (2 Kings 19:36, 37).
25. "The *servants of Amon* conspired against him, and slew the king in his own household" (2 Kings 21:23).
26. The *children of Israel* killed Hadoram with stones (2 Chron. 10:18).
27. *Joash* commanded Zechariah to be stoned (2 Chron. 24:20-22).
28. "*Herod* . . . sent forth, and slew all the children that were in Bethlehem, and in all the coasts thereof, from two years old and under" (Matt. 2:16).
29. *Herodias* requested John the Baptist's beheading (Matt. 14:8).
30. *Judas* betrayed Jesus to the hands of the Jews (Matt. 26:14, 15).
31. Jesus said the *devil* "was a murderer from the beginning" (John 8:44).
32. Peter speaks of *Barabbas* as "a murderer" (Acts 3:14).
33. Stephen was stoned by furious *Jews* (Acts 7:57-59).
34. An Egyptian "leddest out into the wilderness *four thousand men* that were murderers" (Acts 21:38).

132. Six People Jesus Forgave During His Earthly Ministry

1. The man who was let down through the ceiling was forgiven by Jesus and also healed of palsy (Matt. 9:2).
2. Mary was forgiven of her sins when she anointed Jesus' feet (Luke 7:47-50).
3. Jesus forgave those who crucified Him (Luke 23:34).
4. The thief on the cross was told by Jesus that he would be in paradise with Jesus (Luke 23:39-43).
5. The impotent man that Jesus healed at the pool of Bethesda was probably forgiven by Jesus, since Jesus told him to sin no more (John 5:14).
6. To the woman taken in adultery, Jesus said, "Neither do I condemn thee: go and sin no more" (John 8:3-11).

133. Twenty-eight Names of Satan

1. Abaddon (Rev. 9:11).
2. Accuser of our brethren (Rev. 12:10).
3. Adversary (1 Pet. 5:8).
4. Angel of the bottomless pit (Rev. 9:11).
5. Apollyon (Rev. 9:11).
6. Beelzebub (Matt. 12:24).
7. Belial (2 Cor. 6:15).
8. The devil (Matt. 4:1).
9. Enemy (Matt. 13:39).
10. Evil spirit (1 Sam. 16:14).
11. Father of lies (John 8:44).
12. God of this world (2 Cor. 4:4).
13. Great red dragon (Rev. 12:3, 9).
14. King of Tyrus (Ezek. 28:12).
15. Liar (John 8:44).
16. Lucifer (Isa. 14:12).
17. Old serpent (Rev. 12: 9).
18. Power of darkness (Col. 1:13).
19. Prince of this world (John 12:31).
20. Prince of the devils (Matt. 12:24).
21. Prince of the power of the air (Eph. 2:2).
22. Ruler of the darkness of this world (Eph. 6:12).
23. Satan (1 Chron. 21:1).
24. Serpent (Gen. 3:4).

25. Spirit that worketh in the children of disobedience (Eph. 2:2).
26. Tempter (Matt. 12:43).
27. Unclean spirit (Matt. 12:43).
28. Wicked one (Matt. 13:19, 38).

134. Twenty-one Facts About Satan

1. God said to Satan, "I will put enmity between thee and the woman, and between thy seed and her seed; it shall bruise thy head, and thou shalt bruise his heel" (Gen. 3:15).
2. How art thou fallen from heaven, O Lucifer, son of the morning! how art thou cut down to the ground, which didst weaken the nations! For thou hast said in thine heart, I will ascend into heaven, I will exalt my throne above the stars of God: I will sit also upon the mount of the congregation, in the sides of the north: I will ascend above the heights of the clouds; I will be like the most High (Isa. 14:12-14).
3. Thou hast been in Eden the garden of God; every precious stone was thy covering, the sardius, topaz, and the diamond, the beryl, the onyx, and the jasper, the sapphire, the emerald, and the carbuncle, and gold: the workmanship of thy tabrets and of thy pipes was prepared in thee in the day that thou wast created. Thou art the anointed cherub that covereth; and I have set thee so: thou wast upon the holy mountain of God; thou hast walked up and down in the midst of the stones of fire. Thou wast perfect in thy ways from the day that thou wast created, till iniquity was found in thee. Thine heart was lifted up because of thy beauty, thou hast corrupted thy wisdom by reason of thy brightness: I will cast thee to the ground, I will lay thee before kings, that they may behold thee (Ezek. 28:13-15, 17).
4. When any one heareth the word of the kingdom and understandeth it not, then cometh the wicked one, and catcheth away that which was sown in his heart (Matt. 13:19).
5. [The devil] was a murderer from the beginning, and abode not in the truth, because there is no truth in him. When he speaketh a lie, he speaketh of his own: for he is a liar, and the father of it (John 8:44).
6. The devil . . . put into the heart of Judas Iscariot, Simon's son, to betray [Jesus] (John 13:2).

7. [Jesus said], the prince of this world . . . hath nothing in me (John 14:30).
8. The prince of this world is judged (John 16:11).
9. Satan filled [Ananias'] heart to lie to the Holy Ghost, and to keep back part of the price of the land (Acts 5:3).
10. The God of peace shall bruise Satan under your feet shortly (Rom. 16:20).
11. We are not ignorant of [Satan's] devices (2 Cor. 2:11).
12. The God of this world hath blinded the minds of them which believe not, lest the light of the glorious gospel of Christ, who is the image of God, should shine unto them (2 Cor. 4:4).
13. Satan himself is transformed into an angel of light (2 Cor. 11:14).
14. Having spoiled principalities and powers, [Jesus] made a shew of them openly, triumphing over them in it (Col. 2:15).
15. Resist the devil and he will flee from you (James 4:7).
16. Your adversary the devil, as a roaring lion, walketh about, seeking whom he may devour (1 Pet. 5:8).
17. He that committeth sin is of the devil; for the devil sinneth from the beginning (1 John 3:8).
18. He that is begotten of God keepeth himself, and that wicked one toucheth him not (1 John 5:18).
19. Michael the archangel, when contending with the devil . . . durst not bring against him a railing accusation, but said, The Lord rebuke thee (Jude 9).
20. [Satan] accused them before our God day and night (Rev. 12:10).
21. The devil that deceived them was cast into the lake of fire and brimstone, where the beast and the false prophet are, and shall be tormented day and night for ever and ever (Rev. 20:10).

135. Ten Things You Can Do About Sin

1. For, if ye forgive men their trespasses, your heavenly Father will also forgive you: but if ye forgive not men their trespasses, neither will your Father forgive your trespasses (Matt. 6:14, 15).
2. Repent, and be baptized every one of you in the name of Jesus Christ for the remission of sins (Acts 2:38).
3. This I say then, Walk in the Spirit, and ye shall not fulfill the lust of the flesh (Gal. 5:16).

4. For whom the Lord loveth he chasteneth, and scourgeth every son whom he receiveth. If ye endure chastening, God dealeth with you as with sons (Heb. 12:6, 7).

5. And the prayer of faith shall save the sick, and the Lord shall raise him up; and if he have committed sins, they shall be forgiven him (James 5:15).

6. Brethren, if any of you do err from the truth, and one convert him; let him know, that he which converteth the sinner from the error of his way shall save a soul from death, and shall hide a multitude of sins (James 5:19, 20).

7. And above all things have fervent charity among yourselves: for charity shall cover the multitude of sins (1 Pet. 4:8).

8. But if we walk in the light, as he is in the light, we have fellowship one with another, and the blood of Jesus Christ his Son cleanseth us from all sin (1 John 1:7).

9. If we confess our sins, he is faithful and just to forgive us our sins, and to cleanse us from all unrighteousness (1 John 1:9).

10. If any man see his brother sin a sin which is not unto death, he shall ask, and he shall give him life for them that sin not unto death. There is a sin unto death: I do not say that he shall pray for it (1 John 5:16).

13

Lies

The Bible contains many intriguing and sometimes appalling accounts of liars and their lies. The reasons for some lies *seem* justifiable. For example, the Gibeonites lied to save their lives. The Bible is very clear, though, concerning God's view of lying: " . . . and all liars, shall have their part in the lake which burneth with fire" (Rev. 21:8).

136. The Only Animal in the Bible That Lied

Now the serpent was more subtle than any beast of the field which the Lord God had made. And he said unto the woman, Yea, hath God said, Ye shall not eat of every tree of the garden? And the woman [Eve] said unto the serpent, We may eat of the fruit of the trees of the garden: but the fruit of the tree which is in the midst of the garden, God hath said, Ye shall not eat of it, neither shall ye touch it, lest ye die. And the serpent said unto the woman, Ye shall not surely die: for God doth know that in the day ye eat thereof, then your eyes shall be opened, and ye shall be as gods, knowing good and evil (Gen. 3:1-5).

137. The First Cover-up

And Cain talked with Abel his brother: and it came to pass, when they were in the field, that Cain rose up against Abel his brother, and slew him. And the Lord said unto Cain, where is Abel thy brother? And he said, I know not: Am I my brother's keeper? (Gen. 4:8, 9).

138. Five Accounts of Lying Relatives in the Bible

1. And Rebekah spake unto Jacob her son, saying, Behold, I

heard thy father speak unto Esau thy brother, saying, Bring me venison . . . that I may eat and bless thee before the Lord before my death. Now therefore, my son [Jacob], obey my voice according to that which I command thee. . . . And Rebekah took goodly raiment of her eldest son Esau . . . and put them upon Jacob. . . . And she put the skins of . . . kids of . . . goats upon his hands and . . . his neck: and she gave the savoury meat and the bread, which she had prepared [to] Jacob. And he came unto his father, and said, My father: and he said, Here am I; who art thou my son? And Jacob said unto his father, I am Esau thy first-born; I have done according as thou badest me. . . . And Isaac said . . . How is it that thou hast found it so quickly my son? And he said, Because the Lord thy God brought it to me (Gen. 27:6-8, 15-20).

2. Laban said unto Jacob, . . . What shall thy wages be? . . . And Jacob . . . said, I will serve thee seven years for Rachel. . . . And Laban said, It is better that I give her to thee, than . . . to another man. . . . And Jacob served seven years . . . and said to Laban, Give me my wife. [But Laban tricked Jacob.] He took Leah his daughter, and brought her to him; and he went in unto her. . . . And it came to pass, that in the morning, behold it was Leah; and he said to Laban, What is this that thou hast done unto me? did I not serve with thee for Rachel? wherefore then hast thou beguiled me? (Gen. 29:15, 18, 19-21, 23, 25).

3. Laban went to shear his sheep: and Rachel had stolen the images that were her father's. And Jacob stole away unawares to Laban. . . . And it was told Laban on the third day that Jacob was fled. And he . . . pursued after him. . . . Then Laban overtook Jacob . . . and said, . . . Wherefore hast thou stolen my gods? . . . And Laban . . . entered into Rachel's tent. Now Rachel had taken the images, and put them in the camel's furniture, and sat upon them. And Laban searched all the tent, but found them not. And she said unto her father, Let it not displease my lord that I cannot rise up before thee; for the custom of women is upon me (Gen. 31:19, 20, 22, 23, 25, 30, 33, 34).

4. Joseph's brothers "sold Joseph to the Ishmeelites for twenty pieces of silver: and they brought Joseph into Egypt. . . . And they [Joseph's brothers] took Joseph's coat, and killed a kid of the goats, and dipped the coat in the blood; and they sent the coat of many colours, and they brought it to their

200

father; and said, This have we found: know now whether it be thy son's coat or no. And he knew it, and said, It is my son's coat; an evil beast hath devoured him; Joseph is without doubt rent in pieces" (Gen. 37:28, 31-33).

5. And all the people brake off the golden earrings which were in their ears, and brought them to Aaron. And he received them at their hand, and fashioned it with a graving tool, after he had made it a molten calf. . . . And Moses said unto Aaron, What did this people unto thee, that thou hast brought so great a sin upon them? And Aaron said, Let not the anger of my lord wax hot: thou knowest the people, that they are set on mischief. For they said unto me, Make us gods. . . . And I said unto them, Whosoever hath any gold, let them break it off. So they gave it me: then I cast it into the fire, and there came out this calf (Ex. 32:3, 4, 21-24).

139. Accounts of "Good" People Who Lied

1. And Isaac dwelt in Gerar: and the men of the place asked him of his wife; and he said, She is my sister: for he feared to say, She is my wife; lest, said he, the men of the place should kill me for Rebekah; because she was fair to look upon (Gen. 26:6, 7).

2. Delilah said to Samson, Tell me, I pray thee, wherein thy great strength lieth, and wherewith thou mightest be bound to afflict thee. And Samson said unto her, If they bind me with seven green withs that were never dried, then shall I be weak, and be as another man. [When this didn't prove to be true], Delilah said unto Samson, Behold, thou hast mocked me, and told me lies. . . . [He lied in a similar manner twice more before he got his head shaved.] (Judges 16:6, 7, 10).

3. David said unto Jonathan, Behold, tomorrow is the new moon, and I should not fail to sit with the king at meat: but let me go, that I may hide myself in the field unto the third day at even. If thy father at all miss me, then say, David earnestly asked leave of me that he might run to Bethlehem his city: for there is a yearly sacrifice there for all the family. (And this plan was carried out by Jonathan.) (1 Sam. 20:5, 6).

4. When David was sure that Saul meant to kill him, he fled. "Then came David to Nob to Ahimelech the priest: and Ahimelech was afraid at the meeting of David, and said unto

him, Why art thou alone, and no man with thee? And David said unto Ahimelech the priest, The king hath commanded me a business, and hath said unto me, Let no man know any thing of the business whereabout I send thee, and what I have commanded thee: and I have appointed my servants to such and such a place" (1 Sam. 21:1, 2).

5. David and his men dwelt in Ziklag in the country of the Philistines which was ruled by King Achish. "And David and his men went up, and invaded the Geshurites, and the Gezrites, and the Amalekites. . . . And David smote the land, and left neither man nor woman alive . . . and returned and came to Achish. And Achish said, Whither have ye made a road to day? And David said, Against the south of Judah, and against the south of the Jerahmeelites, and against the south of the Kenites. And David saved neither man nor woman alive, to bring tidings to Gath, saying, Lest they should tell on us. . . . And Achish believed David, saying, He hath made his people Israel to abhor him; therefore he shall be my servant for ever" (1 Sam. 27:8-12).

6. Now Peter sat without in the palace: and a damsel came unto him, saying, Thou also wast with Jesus of Galilee. But he denied before them all, saying, I know not what thou sayest. And when he was gone out into the porch, another maid saw him, and said unto them that were there, This fellow was also with Jesus of Nazareth. And again he denied with an oath, I do not know the man. And after a while came unto him they that stood by, and said to Peter, Surely thou also art one of them; for thy speech betrayeth thee. Then began he to curse and to swear, saying, I know not the man (Matt. 26:69-74).

140. The Father of Lies

Jesus said that the devil "abode not in the truth, because there is no truth in him. When he speaketh a lie, he speaketh of his own: for he is a liar, and the father of it" (John 8:44).

141. Three Lying Prophets

1. There was a prophet who prophesied against the altar at Bethel and who besought the Lord for the healing of King Jeroboam. After the king was healed, "the king said unto the

man of God, Come home with me, and refresh thyself, and I will give thee a reward. And the man of God said unto the king, . . . I will not go in with thee, . . . for . . . the Lord [said], Eat no bread, nor drink water, nor turn again by the same way that thou camest. . . . Now there dwelt an old prophet at Bethel . . . [who] went after the man of God and found him sitting under an oak: and he said unto him, . . . I am a prophet also as thou art; and an angel spake unto me by the word of the Lord, saying, Bring him back with thee into thine house, that he may eat bread and drink water. But he lied unto him. So he went back with him, and did eat bread in his house, and drink water." [Because of his disobedience, the man of God was slain by a lion.] (1 Kings 13:7, 8, 11, 14, 18, 19).

2. Pashur . . . who was . . . chief governor in the house of the Lord . . . smote Jeremiah the prophet, and put him in . . . stocks. . . . On the morrow, . . . Pashur brought forth Jeremiah out of the stocks. Then said Jeremiah unto him, . . . Thou, Pashur, and all that dwell in thine house shall go into captivity . . . and there thou shalt die, . . . thou and all thy friends, to whom thou hast prophesied lies (Jer. 20:1-3, 6).

3. Then came the word of the Lord unto Jeremiah, saying, Send to all of the captivity, saying, Thus saith the Lord concerning Shemaiah the Nehelamite; Because that Shemaiah hath prophesied unto you, and I sent him not, and he caused you to believe a lie; therefore thus saith the Lord; Behold, I will punish Shemaiah the Nehelamite, and his seed: he shall not have a man to dwell among this people: neither shall he behold the good that I will do for my people, saith the Lord; because he hath taught rebellion against the Lord (Jer. 29:30-32).

142. Lies Which Helped Destroy Two Cities

1. The sons of Jacob answered Shechem and Hamor his father deceitfully, and said, Because he [Shechem] had defiled Dinah their sister: . . . we cannot . . . give our sister to one that is uncircumcised, . . . but . . . if . . . every male of you [will] be circumcised; then will we give our daughters unto you, and we will take your daughters to us, and we will dwell with you, and we will become one people. . . . And every

male was circumcised. . . . And it came to pass on the third day, when they were sore, that . . . Simeon and Levi, Dinah's brethren . . . came upon the city boldly and slew all the males . . . and spoiled the city because they had defiled their sister (Gen. 34:13-16, 24, 25, 27).

2. Joshua . . . sent . . . two men to spy secretly. . . . And they went, and came into an harlot's house, named Rahab. . . . And it was told the king of Jericho. . . . And the king of Jericho sent unto Rahab, saying, Bring forth the men that are come to thee. . . . And the woman took the two men, and hid them, and said thus, There came men unto me, but I wist not whence they were: and it came to pass about the time of shutting of the gate, when it was dark, that the men went out: whither the men went I wot not: pursue after them quickly; for you shall overtake them (Josh. 2:1-5).

143. The Woman Who Yelled "Rape!"

Potiphar bought Joseph as a slave and made him overseer over his house. "And it came to pass after these things, that his master's wife cast her eyes upon Joseph; and she said, Lie with me. But he refused. . . . And it came to pass, as she spake to Joseph day by day, that he hearkened not unto her, to lie by her, or to be with her. And it came to pass about this time that Joseph went into the house to do his business; and there was none of the men of the house there within. And she caught him by his garment, saying, Lie with me: and he left his garment, in her hand, and fled, and got him out. . . . Then she called unto the men of her house, and spake unto them, saying, See, he hath brought in an Hebrew to mock us; he came in unto me to lie with me, and I cried with a loud voice: . . . [then] he left his garment with me, and fled. . . . And it came to pass, when his master heard the words of his wife, . . . Joseph's master . . . put him into the prison" (Gen. 39:7, 8, 10-12, 14, 15, 19, 20).

144. The Lie That Saved the Gibeonites

And when the inhabitants of Gibeon heard what Joshua had done unto Jericho and to Ai, they did work wilily, and went and made as if they had been ambassadors, and took old sacks upon their asses, and wine bottles, old and rent, and bound up; and old shoes and clouted upon their feet, and old garments upon them; and all the bread of their provision was dry and mouldy. And they went to Joshua, . . . and said unto him and to the men of Israel, we be come from a far country: now therefore make ye a league with us. . . . The men [of Israel] took of their victuals and asked not counsel at the mouth of the Lord. And Joshua made peace with them, and made a league with them, to let them live: and the princes of the congregation sware unto them. And . . . at the end of three days . . . they heard they were their neighbours . . . And the children of Israel smote them not, because the princes . . . had sworn unto them by the Lord God of Israel (Josh. 9:3-6, 14-16, 18).

145. Lies That Led to Leprosy

Gehazi, the servant of Elisha . . . said, Behold, my master hath spared Naaman . . . in not receiving . . . that which he brought: but . . . I will run after him, and take somewhat of him. . . . And when Naaman saw him running after him, he lighted down from the chariot to meet him, and said, Is all well? And he said, All is well. My master hath sent me, saying, Behold, even now there be come . . . two young . . . sons of the prophets: give them, I pray thee, a talent of silver, and two changes of garments. And Naaman said, Be content, take two talents. . . . And when he [Gehazi] came to the tower, he took them from their hand, and bestowed them in the house: and he let the men go. . . . But he went in, and stood before his master. And Elisha said unto him, Whence comest thou, Gehazi? And he said, Thy servant went no whither. And he said unto him, . . . Is it time to receive money? . . . The leprosy therefore of Naaman shall cleave unto thee, and unto thy seed for ever. And he went out from his presence, a leper as white as snow (2 Kings 5:20-27).

146. The Lie That God Seemed to Condone

Ahab said, "Micaiah, shall we go to battle, or shall we forbear? And he answered him, Go, and prosper: for the Lord shall deliver it into the hand of the king. And the king said unto him, How many times shall I adjure thee that thou tell me nothing but that which is true in the name of the Lord? And he said, I saw all Israel scattered upon the hills, as sheep that have not a shepherd: and the Lord said, These have no master: Let them return every man to his house in peace." . . . And Micaiah continued,

"Hear thou therefore the word of the Lord: I saw the Lord sitting on his throne, and all the host of heaven standing by him on his right hand and on his left. And the Lord said, Who shall persuade Ahab, that he may go up and fall at Ramoth-gilead? . . . And there came forth a spirit, and stood before the Lord, and said, I will persuade him. And the Lord said to him, Wherewith? And he said, I will go forth, and I will be a lying spirit in the mouth of all his prophets. And he said, Thou shalt persuade him, and prevail also: go forth, and do so. Now therefore, behold, the Lord hath put a lying spirit in the mouth of all these thy prophets, and the Lord hath spoken evil concerning thee." . . . So the king of Israel [Ahab] and Jehoshaphat the king of Judah went up to Ramoth-gilead [anyway] . . . And it came to pass . . . that . . . a certain man drew a bow at a venture, and smote the king of Israel . . . so the king died (1 Kings 22:15-17, 19-23, 29, 32, 34, 37).

147. Lies That Killed a Man

Ahab spake unto Naboth, saying, Give me thy vineyard, that I may have it for a garden of herbs, because it is near unto my house: and I will give thee for it a better vineyard than it; or, if it seem good to thee, I will give thee the worth of it in money. And Naboth said to Ahab, The Lord forbid me, that I should give the inheritance of my fathers unto thee. And Ahab came into his house heavy and displeased. . . . And Jezebel his wife said unto him, Dost thou now govern the kingdom of Israel? . . . I will give thee the vineyard of Naboth. . . . And she wrote letters in Ahab's name . . . and sent [them] to the nobles that were in his city. . . . She wrote . . . saying, Proclaim a fast, and set Naboth on high . . . and set two men . . . before him, to bear false witness against him, saying, Thou didst blaspheme God and the king. And then carry him out, and stone him, that he may die. And the men of his city . . . did as Jezebel had sent unto them. . . . When Jezebel heard that Naboth . . . was dead, . . . Jezebel said to Ahab, Arise, take possession of the vineyard. . . . When Ahab heard that Naboth was dead, . . . Ahab [took possession of the vineyard] (1 Kings 21:2-4, 7-11, 15, 16).

148. The Lie That Helped Destroy the Worshippers of Baal

And Jehu gathered all the people together, and said unto

them, Ahab served Baal a little; but Jehu shall serve him much. Now therefore call unto me all the prophets of Baal, all his servants and all his priests; let none be wanting: for I have a great sacrifice to do to Baal; whosoever shall be wanting, he shall not live. But Jehu did it in subtilty, to the intent that he might destroy the worshippers of Baal. And Jehu said, Proclaim a solemn assembly for Baal, and they proclaimed it. And Jehu sent through all Israel: and all the worshippers of Baal came . . . into the house of Baal. . . . And when they went in to offer sacrifices, . . . Jehu appointed fourscore men without, and said, If any of the men whom I have brought into your hands escape, he that letteth him go, his life shall be for the life of him . . . Thus Jehu destroyed Baal out of Israel (2 Kings 10:18-21, 24, 28).

149. Two People Who Falsely Reported Their Income

Ananias [and] Sapphira his wife sold a possession, and kept back part of the price . . . and brought a certain part, and laid it at the apostles' feet. But Peter said, Ananias, why hath Satan filled thine heart to lie to the Holy Ghost, and to keep back part of the price of the land? . . . And Ananias hearing these words fell down, and gave up the ghost. . . . And the young men . . . carried him out, and buried him. . . . About . . . three hours later, when his wife, not knowing what was done, came in. And Peter answered unto her, Tell me whether ye sold the land for so much? And she said, yea, for so much. Then Peter said unto her, How is it that ye have agreed together to tempt the Spirit of the Lord? . . . Then fell she down . . . and yielded up the ghost (Acts 5:1-3, 5-9).

14

Miracle Workers and Their Deeds

This chapter is about six men who accomplished marvelous things. But they didn't do it by themselves; they did it as God miraculously intervened in the affairs of men through them.

You will marvel at the variety (yet similarity), and magnitude of the miracles associated with Moses, Elijah, Elisha, Peter, Paul and, of course—the greatest miracle-worker of them all—Jesus Christ.

150. Thirty-eight Miracles Associated with Moses

1. Moses' rod turned into a serpent and then back into a rod (Ex. 4:2-4).
2. Moses' hand became leprous and then returned to normal (Ex. 4:7).
3. Aaron's rod became a serpent and swallowed up the sorcerers' serpents (Ex. 7:10-12).
4. The water in Egypt turned into blood (Ex. 7:19-25).
5. Frogs were brought forth upon the land of Egypt (Ex. 8:5-7).
6. All of the frogs were killed (Ex. 8:12, 13).
7. Dust was changed into lice (Ex. 8:16, 17).
8. Swarms of flies were produced everywhere in Egypt except in the land of Goshen (Ex. 8:20-24).
9. The flies in Egypt were made to depart (Ex. 8:29-31).
10. Murrain was brought upon the Egyptian cattle but not upon Israel's cattle. The infected cattle died (Ex. 9:1-7).
11. Ashes were changed into dust. Wherever the dust landed on Egyptians or upon their beasts, it caused boils (Ex. 9:8-12).
12. A grievous hailstorm, with fire that ran along the ground, was sent upon the Egyptians (Ex. 9:22-26).
13. The thunder and hail stopped upon command (Ex. 9:33).

Moses and Aaron Before Pharaoh

14. Then a plague of locusts was brought against the Egyptians (Ex. 10:12-15).
15. Upon request, the locusts were blown away (Ex. 10:16-20).
16. Thick darkness was brought upon Egypt for three days, but the Hebrews had light (Ex. 10:21-23).
17. All of the firstborn in Egypt were slain unless there was Passover blood on their doorposts and the people were inside (Ex. 12:21-30).
18. The Lord hid the Hebrews with a cloud (Ex. 14:19, 20).
19. The Red Sea was parted (Ex. 14:21).

20. The sea bottom was made dry land (Ex. 14:21).
21. The wheels were taken off of the Egyptian chariots when they tried to cross over the dry sea bottom (Ex. 14:23-25).
22. The waters of the Red Sea returned and drowned the Egyptian army (Ex. 14:27, 28).
23. Moses cast a tree into the bitter waters at Marah and made the water sweet (Ex. 15:23-25).
24. The Hebrews were fed with quail (Ex. 16:11-13).
25. The Hebrews were fed with manna (Ex. 16:14, 15).
26. The manna wouldn't store until morning except on the Sabbath (Ex. 16:19, 20, 23, 24).
27. Each Hebrew gathered manna per his exact needs including twice as much on the sixth day (Ex. 16:16-22).
28. Moses struck the rock in Horeb to produce water for the Hebrews (Ex. 17:1-6).
29. Fire from the Lord consumed the burnt offering (Lev. 9:22-24).
30. Miriam was made leprous and then healed (Num. 12).
31. Complaining Hebrews were burned up by fire from the Lord, until Moses intervened by prayer (Num. 11:1, 2).
32. Fire came out from the Lord and consumed 250 men who offered incense (Num. 16:16-18, 35).
33. The earth opened up and swallowed Korah and his men (Num. 16:28-33).
34. A plague that killed 14,700 was stayed by making an offering of incense (Num. 16:46-50).
35. Aaron's rod budded (Num. 17).
36. Moses struck the rock twice to bring forth water (Num. 20:1-11).
37. Moses made a brass serpent and put it on a pole. If anyone was bitten by a fiery serpent and then looked upon the brass serpent, his life was saved (Num. 21:5-9).
38. Moses appeared on the mount of transfiguration with Jesus (Luke 9:28-36).

151. Eleven Miracles Associated with Elijah

1. Elijah prayed, and it didn't rain for three and a half years (1 Kings 17:1).
2. A continuous supply of meal and oil was supplied for a widow and her son from nearly empty containers of same (1 Kings 17:13-16).

3. A widow's son was raised from the dead (1 Kings 17:17-23).
4. When Elijah prayed, a fire came down from heaven and burned up a sacrifice, the altar, and the water that was placed in a trench around the altar (1 Kings 18:17-38).
5. When Elijah prayed at the end of three and a half year drought, there was an abundance of rain (1 Kings 18:41-46).
6. Elijah was fed two miraculous meals that sustained him for 40 days (1 Kings 19:4-8).
7. Elijah was fed by ravens (1 Kings 17:2-7).
8. Fire from heaven came down at the word of Elijah to burn up two different bands of soldiers [102 men] (2 Kings 1:10-12).
9. Elijah parted the waters of the Jordan River by hitting it with his mantle. He and Elisha walked across the Jordan River on *dry* ground (2 Kings 2:8).
10. Elijah was taken into heaven by a whirlwind (2 Kings 2:11).
11. Elijah appeared atop the mount of transfiguration with Jesus and Moses (Luke 9:28-36).

152. Fifteen Miracles Associated with Elisha

1. Elisha parted the waters of the Jordan River with Elijah's mantle and walked across the riverbed on dry ground (2 Kings 2:13, 14).
2. Elisha healed a water source by throwing a cruse of salt into the water (2 Kings 2:19-22).
3. Forty-two children were torn up by two she bears when they were cursed by Elisha because they mocked him (2 Kings 2:23-25).
4. Water was supplied for the kings of Israel, Judah, and Edom, and for their armies and cattle (2 Kings 3:14-20).
5. A widow's pot of oil was made to produce large quantities of oil (2 Kings 4:1-7).
6. A Shunammite woman was healed so that she conceived and had a son as prophesied by Elisha (2 Kings 4:14-17).
7. Elisha raised the Shunammite's son from the dead (2 Kings 4:32-37).
8. Elisha counteracted the poison pottage made of wild gourds by putting meal in the pottage (2 Kings 4:38-41).
9. One hundred men were fed with 20 loaves of barley and some ears of corn (2 Kings 4:42-44).
10. Naaman was healed of leprosy by following Elisha's instructions (2 Kings 5:1-14).

11. Elisha made an iron axe head float to the top of the water by throwing a stick in the water (2 Kings 6:4-7).
12. Elisha's servant's spiritual eyes were opened, in response to Elisha's prayer, to see an angelic army (2 Kings 6:15-17).
13. The Syrian army was struck blind by the Lord when Elisha prayed (2 Kings 6:18).
14. The men in the Syrian army were healed of their blindness after Elisha led them to Samaria and prayed for their eyes to be opened (2 Kings 6:19, 20).
15. The bones of Elisha caused a man to be raised from the dead (2 Kings 13:20, 21).

153. Forty-three Miracles Which Happened During Jesus' Earthly Ministry

1. Jesus was conceived by the Holy Ghost and the Virgin Mary (Matt. 1:18-25).
2. Jesus healed a leper who worshipped Him (Matt. 8:1-4).
3. Jesus healed a centurion's servant of palsy by speaking the word only (Matt. 8:5-13).
4. Jesus healed Peter's mother-in-law of a fever by touching her hand (Matt. 8:14, 15).
5. Jesus cast out devils [demons] with His word (Matt. 8:16).
6. Jesus rebuked the wind and the raging sea and caused them to be calm (Matt. 8:23-27).
7. Jesus cast a legion of demons out of two men and let the demons go into a herd of swine (Matt. 8:28-34).
8. Jesus healed a palsied man and also forgave his sins (Matt. 9:1-8).
9. A woman with an issue of blood was healed when she touched the hem of Jesus' garment (Matt. 9:20-22).
10. Jesus raised Jairus' daughter from the dead (Matt. 9:23-25).
11. Two blind men were healed when Jesus touched their eyes (Matt. 9:27-30).
12. Jesus exorcised a dumb demoniac, and then the demoniac was able to speak (Matt. 9:32, 33).
13. Jesus healed a man who had a withered hand (Matt. 12:10-13).
14. A blind and dumb demoniac was exorcised by Jesus and was then able to speak and to see (Matt. 12:22).
15. Jesus fed 5,000 with five loaves and two fish (Matt. 14:15-21).

16. Jesus walked on the water of a raging sea (Matt. 14:25).
17. Jesus made it possible for Peter to walk on the water (Matt. 14:28-31).
18. Jesus cast a demon out of a Canaanite woman's daughter without even going to her (Matt. 15:22-28).
19. Jesus healed the lame, blind, dumb, and the maimed (Matt. 15:30, 31).
20. Jesus fed 4,000 men plus women and children with seven loaves and a few fish (Matt. 15:32-39).
21. Jesus was transfigured (Matt. 17:1-9).
22. Jesus cast a demon out of a young boy (Matt. 17:14-18).
23. Jesus sent Peter to catch a fish with money in its mouth, so that Peter could pay tribute (Matt. 17:24-27).
24. Jesus healed two blind men at the wayside by touching their eyes (Matt. 20:30-34).
25. Jesus healed the blind and the lame in the temple (Matt. 21:14).
26. Jesus cursed a fig tree and thus caused it to wither and die very quickly (Matt. 21:17-20).
27. Jesus was resurrected (Matt. 28:5-10).
28. Jesus healed a deaf and dumb man at Decapolis (Mark 7:31-35).
29. Jesus healed a blind man at Bethsaida by spitting on his eyes (Mark 8:22-26).
30. Jesus walked right through a crowd which was trying to throw Him off a cliff (Luke 4:29, 30).
31. Jesus exorcised an unclean demon from a man in a synagogue (Luke 4:33-36).
32. Jesus caused Peter to make a great catch of fish that filled two ships (Luke 5:4-11).
33. Jesus brought to life the dead son of the widow of Nain (Luke 7:11-15).
34. Jesus healed a woman who was bent over and couldn't straighten up (Luke 13:11-13).
35. Jesus healed a man of dropsy in the house of one of the chief Pharisees (Luke 14:1-4).
36. Jesus healed ten lepers at the same time (Luke 17:11-19).
37. Jesus healed the ear of Malchus after Peter chopped it off with a sword (Luke 22:50, 51).
38. Jesus turned water into wine (John 2:1-11).
39. Jesus healed a nobleman's son of a fever (John 4:46-54).
40. Jesus healed an impotent man who was sick for 38 years at

the pool of Bethesda (John 5:2-9).

41. Jesus healed a man who was born blind (John 9:1-7).
42. Jesus raised Lazarus from the dead (John 11:41-44).
43. Jesus caused the apostles to make a miraculous catch of fish after Jesus was resurrected (John 21:3-11).

154. Ten Miracles Associated with Peter

1. Peter walked on water in a stormy sea (Matt. 14:28-31).
2. The man at the Beautiful Gate of the temple was healed when Peter spoke to him (Acts 3:1-8).
3. Peter discerned the secret of Ananias and Sapphira when they agreed to withhold money from the sale of their property (Acts 5:1-11).
4. There was a multitude of healings when Peter's shadow fell upon the sick (Acts 5:15, 16).
5. The apostles were delivered from prison by the angel of the Lord (Acts 5:17-29).
6. The Holy Ghost was imparted by the laying on of Peter's hands at Samaria (Acts 8:14-17).
7. Aeneas was healed of palsy after he had been sick for eight years (Acts 9:33, 34).
8. Dorcas was raised from the dead by Peter (Acts 9:36-41).
9. The outpouring of the Holy Ghost at the house of Cornelius occurred while Peter was preaching (Acts 10:34-48).
10. Peter was delivered from prison a second time (Acts 12:1-17).

155. Eleven Miracles Associated with Paul

1. Paul had a miraculous conversion on the road to Damascus (Acts 9:1-9).
2. Paul's eyes were healed (Acts 9:10-18).
3. Elymas the sorcerer was blinded for a season at Paul's word (Acts 13:8-11).
4. A crippled man at Lystra was healed by Paul (Acts 14:8-10).
5. A girl in Philippi was exorcised by Paul (Acts 16:16-18).
6. Paul and Silas were delivered from prison by a divine earthquake (Acts 16:25-33).
7. The Holy Ghost was imparted at Ephesus by the laying on of Paul's hands (Acts 19:1-7).
8. Healings and exorcisms took place via handkerchiefs and aprons that had been placed on Paul's body (Acts 19:11, 12).

9. Eutychus was raised from the dead at Troas after he had fallen from a third-story window (Acts 20:9, 10).
10. Paul was unaffected after being bitten by a viper (Acts 28:3-6).
11. Publius' father and others were healed through Paul's ministry (Acts 28:8, 9).

15

Numbers

This section is not about the biblical book of Numbers. Rather, it is about the quality, quantity, and size of things and people referred to in the Bible. Are you curious about how many words there are in the Bible, the oddest verse in the Bible, or the two longest words in the Bible? Then this is the place to look for these and many more.

156. The Shortest Reign in the Bible

King Zimri ruled Israel for seven days and them committed suicide by burning down his palace around himself (1 Kings 16:15).

157. The Longest Reign

King Manasseh started his reign when he was 12 years old, and ruled Judah for 55 years (2 Kings 21:1).

158. The Youngest King

Joash (also known as Jehoash) was seven years old when he began to reign as king of Judah. He reigned for 40 years (2 Chron. 24:1)

159. The Largest Army Actually Assembled in the Bible

Zerah the Ethiopian had an host of one million which he brought against King Asa (2 Chron. 14:9).

160. The Largest Numbers in the Bible

1. The largest general number is "thousands of millions." Rebekah's family blessed her by saying " . . . be thou the mother of thousands of millions" (Gen. 24:60).
2. The largest specific number is the army of 200 million horsemen mentioned in Revelation (9:16).

161. The Longest Book in the Old Testament

The longest book in the Old Testament is Psalms, with 150 chapters and a total of 2,461 verses. Psalms is also the longest book in the whole Bible.

162. The Shortest Book in the Old Testament

The shortest book in the Old Testament is Obadiah, which is comprised of 21 verses with a total of only 670 words.

163. The Longest Book in the New Testament

The longest book in the New Testament is Luke, which has 1,151 verses.

164. The Shortest Book in the New Testament

The shortest book in the New Testament is 2 John, which is comprised of 13 verses with a total of only 298 words, thus making 2 John the shortest book in the Bible.

165. The Longest Chapter in the Bible

The longest chapter in the Bible is Psalm 119, which has 176 verses.

166. The Shortest Chapter in the Bible

The shortest chapter in the Bible is Psalm 117, which has only 2 verses with a total of 33 words.

167. The Two Shortest Verses in the Bible

1. Jesus wept (John 11:35).

2. Eber, Peleg, Reu (1 Chron. 1:25).

168. The Longest Verse in the Bible

The longest verse in the Bible is Esther 8:9, which contains 90 words.

169. The Total Number of Verses in the Bible

The total number of verses in the Bible is 30,442 verses (Old Testament: 22,485 verses; New Testament: 7,957 verses).

170. The Oddest Verse in the Bible

"At Parbar westward, four at the causeway, and two at Parbar" (1 Chron. 26:18).

171. The Total Number of Words in the Bible

In round numbers, the total number of words in the Bible is 845,000 (Old Testament: 647,000 words; New Testament: 198,000 words).

172. The Most-Used Words in the Bible

The word most used in the Bible is the word "the," which is used approximately 58,000 times. The most-used noun in the Bible is the word "Lord," which is used 7,736 times (non-capitalized usages counted also).

173. The Two Longest Words in the Bible

Two words tie for the honor of being the longest words in the Bible: Jonath-elem-rechokim and Maher-shalal-hash-baz. Both words have 18 letters in them. Jonath-elem-rechokim is found in the title of Psalm 56 and means "a silent dove of far off lands." Maher-shalal-hash-baz is found in Isaiah 8:1 and 8:3; it is the name of Isaiah's son, and means "spoil speedeth, prey hasteth."

174. The Shortest Prayer in the Bible

When Peter was walking on the water and became afraid, he cried out, "Lord, save me" (Matt. 14:30).

175. The Longest Prayers in the Bible

1. Since it is directed toward God, Psalm 119 may be considered the longest prayer in the Bible.
2. The longest prayer which is not a Psalm is found in Nehemiah 9:5-38. It is a prayer of praise, confession, and covenant.
3. The longest prayer in the New Testament is Jesus' high priestly prayer, found in John 17.

176. The Biggest Animal in the Bible

The biggest animal in the Bible is the whale. It is mentioned in the first chapter of the first book of the Bible (Gen. 1:21).

177. The Five Smallest Things Mentioned in the Bible

1. David said to King Saul, "After whom is the king of Israel come out? . . . after a *flea*" (1 Sam. 24:14).
2. King Solomon, said, "Go to the *ant*, thou sluggard" (Prov. 6:6).
3. Jesus said, "One jot or one *tittle* shall in no wise pass from the law" [a tittle is a small part of a Hebrew letter] (Matt. 5:18).
4. Jesus said, "Ye blind guides, which strain at a *gnat*, and swallow a camel" (Matt. 23:24).
5. Jesus said, "A grain of *mustard seed* is the smallest seed of all the seeds in the earth" (Mark 4:31).

16

Flora and Fauna

The Bible is a book about life and all of the things that affect life. As well as speaking about God and people, the Bible has much to say about plants, trees, animals, birds, insects, and reptiles.

In many cases, Bible scholars have not been able to positively identify the flora and fauna mentioned in the Bible. Therefore, in this chapter, most names given for the various animals, birds, etc., are as found in the King James Version of the Bible.

178. Plants and Trees Mentioned in the Bible

1. Noah built the ark out of *gopher wood* (Gen. 6:14).
2. Leah bought a night in bed with Jacob from Rachel with some *mandrakes* (Gen. 30:14-16).
3. Jacob used rods of green *poplar*, *hazel*, and *chestnut trees* to make his cattle bring forth offspring that were ringstraked, speckled, and spotted (Gen. 30:37-39).
4. Jacob told his sons to take some *almonds*, as part of a gift to Joseph, when they went to Egypt a second time for food (Gen. 43:11).
5. The *rie* in Egypt was not smitten by the hail because it was not grown up yet (Ex. 9:32).
6. The *bitter herbs* that were supposed to be eaten with the Passover are said to consist of *lettuce, watercress, endive, chicory, sorrel*, and *dandelion greens* (Ex. 12:8).
7. Manna looked like *coriander seed* (Ex. 16:31).
8. Spice from the *cassia tree* was used in the making of the holy anointing oil for anointing the tabernacle of the congregation (Ex. 30:24).
9. The Hebrews ate *cucumbers, melons, leeks, onions*, and *gar-*

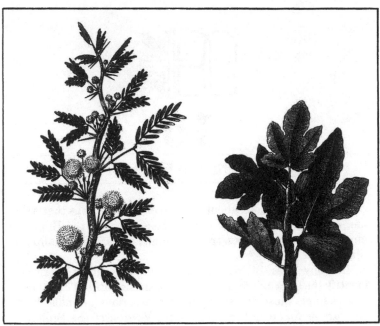

Acacia   **Fig**

lic when they were in Egypt (Num. 11:5).

10. The *vine of Sodom* is mentioned in an unfavorable light in Deuteronomy (Deut. 32:32).

11. Rahab hid the Hebrew spies on her roof under stalks of *flax* (Josh. 2:6).

12. The *brambles* mentioned in Judges are thought to be *wild blackberry bushes* (Judges 9:14, 15).

13. "The sound of a going in the tops of the *mulberry trees*" was the signal used to indicate that the Lord had begun to "smite the host of the Philistines" (2 Sam. 5:24).

14. Solomon spoke of the *cedar trees of Lebanon* and of *hyssop* (1 Kings 4:33).

15. The navy of Hiram brought *almug trees* to King Solomon (1 Kings 10:11).

16. Elijah sat under a *juniper tree* (1 Kings 19:4).

17. Bildad the Shuhite asked, "Can the *rush* grow up without mire? Can the *flag* grow up without water? (Job 8:11).

18. Job spoke of *mallows* and *nettles* (Job 30:4, 7).

19. Job spoke of *thistles, wheat, cockle,* and *barley* in one sentence (Job 31:40).

20. The Lord, speaking to Job, said that behemoth eats *grass*, lies in the covert of the *reed*, and that the *willows* of the brook compass him about (Job 40:15-22).
21. The *green bay tree* is mentioned in Psalms (Ps. 37:35).
22. "I am the *rose of Sharon*, and the *lily of the valleys*" (Song of Sol. 2:1).
23. "As the *apple tree* among the trees of the wood . . . " (Song of Sol. 2:3).
24. In the Song of Solomon, *pomegranate trees, camphire trees, spikenard plants, saffron plants, calamus plants, cinnamon trees, frankincense trees, myrrh trees*, and *aloe trees* are all mentioned (Song of Sol. 4:13, 14).
25. *Wild grapes* are mentioned in Isaiah (Isa. 5:2).
26. Isaiah spoke of a *teil tree* (Isa. 6:13).
27. Isaiah spoke of vessels made of *bulrushes* (Isa. 18:2).
28. God, speaking to Isaiah, said, "I will plant in the wilderness the *cedar*, the *shittah tree*, the *myrtle*, and the *oil tree*; I will set in the desert the *fir tree*, and the *pine*, and the *box tree* together" (Isa. 41:19).
29. The Lord accused Israel of not bringing Him *sweet cane* (Isa. 43:24).
30. Likewise the prophet Isaiah mentioned in quick order: *cedars, cypress trees, oak trees*, and *ash trees* (Isa. 44:14).
31. The Lord spoke of feeding *wormwood* to backslidden Israel (Jer. 9:15).
32. The Lord mentioned *desert heath* to Jeremiah (Jer. 17:5, 6).
33. Ezekiel was told by God to make bread of *wheat, barley, beans, lentiles, millet*, and *fitches* (Ezek. 4:9).
34. Ezekiel said that the men of Dedan brought a present of *ebony* to Tyrus (Ezek. 27:15).
35. Hosea said that the people made sacrifices on the tops of the mountains under *oaks, poplars*, and *elms* (Hosea 4:13).
36. Hosea spoke of *hemlock* springing up in the furrows of the field (Hos. 10:4).
37. The prophet Joel mentioned, in quick succession, the following trees and plants: *corn, grape vines, olive trees, wheat, barley, fig trees, palm trees*, and *apple trees* (Joel 1:10-12).
38. God prepared a *gourd vine* that grew up overnight and shaded Jonah (Jonah 4:6).
39. Jesus mentioned *tares* in a parable (Matt. 13:25).
40. Jesus spoke of the *mustard seed* in a parable about faith (Matt. 13:31).

41. Jesus said that the scribes and Pharisees paid tithes on their *mint, anise,* and *cummin* (Matt. 23:23).
42. Jesus mentioned that the scribes and Pharisees tithed *mint* and *rue* (Luke 11:42).
43. Jesus mentioned the *sycamine tree* in a lesson about faith (Luke 17:6).
44. Zacchaeus climbed up a *sycamore tree* so that he could see Jesus (Luke 19:1-4).
45. *Thyine wood* is mentioned in Revelation (Rev. 18:12).

NOTE: Though we do not know what kind of trees they were, the "tree of the knowledge of good and evil" (Gen. 2:17) and the "tree of life" (Gen. 3:22) could also be included.

179. Animals Mentioned in the Bible

1. *Whales* are the biggest animals listed in the Bible. The whale is mentioned in the first chapter of the Bible (Gen. 1:21).
2. Rebekah fooled Isaac by cooking a couple of young *goats.* He thought that he was eating venison (Gen. 27:1-10).
3. Jacob and his sons brought their *cattle* with them to Egypt (Gen. 46:6).
4. Joseph exchanged bread for *horses* during the seven year famine in Egypt (Gen. 47:17).
5. *Badger* skins were used in the making of the tabernacle in the wilderness (Ex. 25:5).
6. *Bats* were classified as unclean and not to be eaten (Lev. 11:13-19).
7. *Weasels* were also listed as being unclean (Lev. 11:29).
8. The Lord told Moses that *mice* should not be eaten, because they are unclean (Lev. 11:29).
9. The *hart* (*hind* being the female) was listed as a clean animal and therefore good to eat (Deut. 12:15).
10. A *roebuck* or a *pygarg* could also be eaten (Deut. 14:5).
11. The *wild ox* could be eaten (Deut. 14:5).
12. The *chamois* was listed as one of the eatable clean animals (Deut. 14:5).
13. *Hares* were also listed as unclean and unfit for human consumption (Deut. 14:7).
14. The *coney* was listed as an unclean animal (Deut. 14:7).
15. Samson killed a young *lion* with his bare hands (Judges 14:5, 6).
16. David was in charge of his father's *sheep* (1 Sam. 16:11-13).

Sheep, Oxen and Goats

17. David killed a *bear* and thus saved one of his *lambs* (1 Sam. 17:34, 35).
18. Goliath said to David, "Am I a *dog*, that thou comest to me with staves?" (1 Sam. 17:43).
19. King David rode a *mule* (1 Kings 1:32, 33).
20. Indirect reference is made in the Bible to *elephants*, since King Solomon had a throne made of ivory (1 Kings 10:18).
21. Elijah prophesied that the *dogs* would eat Jezebel by the wall of Jezreel (1 Kings 21:20-23), and this prophecy was fulfilled (2 Kings 9:30-37).
22. King Solomon's ships went to Tarshish and brought back *apes* (2 Chron. 9:21).
23. Job had 3,000 *camels* (Job 1:3).
24. The Lord spoke to Job about *behemoth* which eats grass like an *ox* (Job 40:15).
25. The wild *boar* is mentioned in a psalm (Ps. 80:13).
26. Solomon said, "The little *foxes* spoil the vines: for our vines have tender grapes" (Song of Sol. 2:15).
27. *Moles* were mentioned by Isaiah (Isa. 2:20).
28. Both *camels* and *dromedaries* (one-humped camels) were mentioned by Isaiah (Isa. 60:6).
29. Jeremiah asked if it was possible for a *leopard* to change his spots (Jer. 13:23).
30. Jesus warned of *wolves* in *sheeps'* clothing (Matt. 7:15).
31. Jesus allowed a legion of demons to go into a herd of *swine* (Mark 5:1-13).
32. Jesus rode into Jerusalem on an *ass* (John 12:12-15).

180. Birds of the Bible

1. The following birds are listed as being unclean: *eagle, ossifrage, ospray, vulture, kite, raven, owl, nighthawk, cuckow, hawk, little owl, cormorant, great owl, swan, pelican, gier eagle, stork, heron,* and *lapwing* (Lev. 11:13-19).
2. God sent *quails* to feed the children of Israel during their exodus from Egypt (Ex. 16:13).
3. The *glede* is also listed as being an unclean fowl (Deut. 14:13).
4. King Solomon imported *peacocks* (1 Kings 10:21, 22).

Pheasant, Dove, Peacock and Pigeons

5. The *sparrow* and the *swallow* are both mentioned in a psalm (Ps. 84:3).
6. Isaiah prophesied that the Lord would destroy Idumea and that the *cormorant, bittern, owl,* and the *raven* would live there (Isa. 34:1-11).
7. King Hezekiah, in writing about his sickness, described his situation in part by writing, "Like a *crane* or a *swallow,* so did I chatter: I did mourn as a *dove*" (Isa. 38:14).
8. Jeremiah likened his heritage unto a *speckled bird* (Jer. 12:9).
9. Thus saith the Lord, As the *partridge* sitteth on eggs and hatcheth them not; so he that getteth riches, and not by right, shall leave them in the midst of his days, and his end shall be a fool (Jer. 17:11).
10. Jesus said, O Jerusalem, Jerusalem . . . how often would I have gathered thy children together, even as a *hen* gathereth

her *chickens* under her wings, and ye would not! (Matt. 23:37).

11. Jesus accurately predicted that before the *cock* crowed, Peter would deny Him three times (Matt. 26:34).

12. Mary and Joseph made an offering of two *turtledoves* or two young *pigeons* when Jesus was circumcised (Luke 2:21-24).

181. Insects of the Bible

1. Two of the plagues that God brought upon Egypt were swarms of *flies* and an abundance of *lice* (Ex. 8:16-24).

2. God promised Israel that He would send *hornets* before them to drive out the Hivites and the Canaanites (Ex. 23:28).

3. The following insects are listed as being edible: *locusts, bald locusts, beetles,* and *grasshoppers* (Lev. 11:22).

4. Moses told the children of Israel that the Amorites chased them as *bees* do (Deut. 1:44).

5. Moses said that there were *scorpions* in the wilderness (Deut. 8:15).

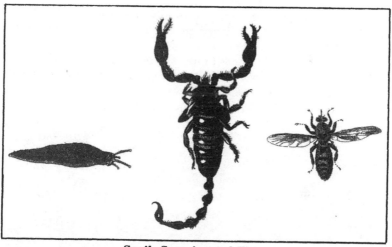

Snail, Scorpion and Fly

6. David compared himself to a *flea* when he was being chased by King Saul (1 Sam. 24:14).

7. Melting *snails* are mentioned in a psalm (Ps. 58:8).

8. *Ants* are mentioned twice in Proverbs. King Solomon thought highly of them (Prov. 6:6; 30:25).

9. The *horseleach* is mentioned in Proverbs (Prov. 30:15).
10. Agur the son of Jakeh noted that *spiders* live in kings' palaces (Prov. 30:28).
11. Isaiah had confidence that his enemies would "wax old as a garment; the *moth* shall eat them up" (Isa. 50:9).
12. The prophet Joel spoke about *palmerworms, locusts, cankerworms,* and *caterpillers* (Joel 1:4).
13. Jesus accused the scribes and Pharisees of straining at a *gnat* and swallowing a camel (Matt. 23:23, 24).
14. Herod didn't give God the glory for his fine oration; therefore, "he was eaten of *worms*, and gave up the ghost" (Acts 12:20-23).

182. Reptiles of the Bible

1. The term *serpent* covers a multitude of reptiles and is sometimes used in referring to Satan (Gen. 3:1).
2. God brought a plague of *frogs* upon Egypt (Ex. 8:2-15).
3. The *tortoise, chameleon,* and the *lizard* are listed as being unclean (Lev. 11:29, 30).
4. Moses sang of the cruel venom of *asps* (Deut. 32:33).
5. The *leviathan* mentioned in Job is actually the *crocodile* (Job 41:1).
6. The wicked are likened unto the deaf *adder* (Ps. 58:4).
7. The *cockatrice* is thought to be the great yellow viper which is poisonous (Jer. 8:17).
8. Paul was bitten by a *viper* but was unharmed (Acts 28:3-5).

Scink, Frog and Viper

17

Names

This section includes all of the men's and women's names in the Bible, the names of all of the firstborn in the Bible and thirty-nine names given to Jesus.

Spelling variations within the King James Version of the Bible are treated as separate entries. Spelling variations because of translations from the Greek in the New Testament concerning Old Testament characters may or may not be included.

In the two lists dealing with all of the names of Bible characters, the meaning of each name, when known, is given. For the firstborn, the name of the firstborn's father is given, except in a few cases where the firstborn's mother is given.

Being the firstborn was very important to these Bible characters, for the oldest's share of the father's estate was a double portion.

183. The Names of the Men in the Bible

A

Aaron—enlightened.
Abagtha—happy.
Abda—worshipper.
Abdeel—servant of God.
Abdi—servant of Jehovah.
Abdiel—servant of God.
Abdon—cloud of judgment.
Abednego—servant of light.
Abel—meadow.
Abia—Jehovah is Father.
Abiah—Jehovah is Father.
Abialbon—father of strength.
Abiasaph—remover of reproach.
Abiathar—excellent father.
Abida—father of knowledge.

Abidah—father of knowledge.
Abidan—the father judges.
Abiel—father of strength.
Abiezer—father of help.
Abihail—father of might.
Abihu—he is my father.
Abihud—father of majesty.
Abijah—Jehovah is my Father.
Abijam—father of light.
Abimael—my Father is God.
Abimelech—father of the king.
Abinadab—father of liberality.
Abinoam—father of beauty.
Abiram—father is the exalted one.
Abishai—possessor of all that is desirable.

Abishalom—father of peace.
Abishua—father of safety.
Abishur—father of oxen.
Abitub—father of goodness.
Abiud—father of honor.
Abner—father of light.
Abraham—the father of a
multitude.
Abram—father of height.
Absalom—father of peace.
Achaicus—belonging to Achaia.
Achan—trouble.
Achar—trouble.
Achaz—Jehovah sustains.
Achbor—a mouse.
Achim—Jehovah will establish.
Achish—serpent charmer.
Adaiah—Jehovah hath adorned.
Adalia—the honor of Ized.
Adam—taken out of the red
earth.
Adar—fire God.
Adbeel—languishing for God.
Addar—height.
Addi—my witness.
Ader—a flock.
Adiel—ornament of God.
Adin—delicate.
Adina—ornament.
Adino—delicate.
Adlai—weary.
Admatha—God-given.
Adna—pleasure.
Adnah—pleasure.
Adoni-bezek—Lord of lightning.
Adonijah—Jehovah is Lord.
Adonikam—my Lord has raised
me.
Adoniram—my Lord is high.
Adonizedek—Lord of justice.
Adoram—strength.
Adrammelech—Adar is king.
Adriel—flock of God.
Aeneas—praise.
Agabus—a locust.
Agag—warlike.
Agee—fugitive.
Agrippa—one who at birth
causes pain.
Agur—gatherer.

Ahab—father's brother.
Aharah—brother of Rach.
Aharhel—brother of Rachel.
Ahasai—clearsighted.
Ahasbai—shining.
Ahasuerus—mighty man.
Ahaz—Jehovah sustains.
Ahaziah—Jehovah possesses.
Ahban—brother of intelligence.
Aher—another.
Ahi—Jehovah's brother.
Ahiah—Jehovah's brother.
Ahiam—a mother's brother.
Ahian—brotherly.
Ahiezer—brother of help.
Ahihud—brother of mystery.
Ahijah—a brother in Jehovah.
Ahikam—my brother has risen.
Ahilud—a brother of one born.
Ahimaaz—a rascal.
Ahiman—brother of man.
Ahimelech—brother of the king.
Ahimoth—brother of death.
Ahinadab—brother of liberality.
Ahio—his brother.
Ahira—brother of evil.
Ahiram—exalted brother.
Ahisamach—brother of support.
Ahishahar—brother of the
dawn.
Ahishar—brother of song.
Ahithophel—brother of folly.
Ahitub—brother of benevolence.
Ahlai—Jehovah is staying.
Ahoah—a brother's need.
Aholah—a tent.
Aholiab—a tent.
Aholibah—a tent.
Aholibamah—a tent.
Ahumai—brother of water.
Ahuzam—possession.
Ahuzzath—holding fast.
Aiah—a vulture.
Ajah—bird of prey.
Akan—acute.
Akkub—cunning.
Alameth—youthful vigor.
Alemeth—covering.
Alexander—defender.
Aliah—sublimity.

Alian—sublime.
Allon—an oak.
Almodad—the agitator.
Alphaeus—transient.
Alvah—high.
Alvan—sublime.
Amal—sorrow.
Amalek—dweller in the vale.
Amariah—Jehovah has promised.
Amasa—burden-bearer.
Amasai—burdensome.
Amashai—carrying spoil.
Amasiah—Jehovah is strong.
Amaziah—Jehovah has strength.
Ami—the beginning.
Aminadab—the kinsman is generous.
Amittai—truthful.
Ammiel—kinsman of God.
Ammihud—my people are honorable.
Amminadab—my kinsman is generous.
Amminadib—my people are princely.
Ammishaddai—the Almighty is an ally.
Ammizabad—the kinsman has endowed.
Ammon—pertaining to the nation.
Amnon—tutelage.
Amok—deep.
Amon—security.
Amos—one with a burden.
Amoz—brass.
Amplias—enlarged.
Amram—inexperience.
Amraphel—powerful people.
Amzi—robust.
Anah—answering.
Anaiah—Jehovah has answered.
Anak—giant.
Anan—he covers.
Anani—covered with God.
Ananiah—Jehovah is a protector.
Ananias—Jehovah is gracious.

Anath—answer.
Anathoth—answered prayers.
Andrew—manliness.
Andronicus—conqueror.
Aner—waterfall.
Aniam—sighing of the people.
Annas—grace of Jehovah.
Antipas—likeness of his father.
Antothijah—Jehovah's answer.
Anub—strong.
Apelles—I exclude.
Aphiah—striving.
Aphses—the dispersed.
Apollos—youthful god of music.
Appaim—presence.
Aquila—eagle.
Ara—strong.
Arad—fugitive.
Arah—wayfarer.
Aram—exalted.
Aran—firmness.
Araunah—Jehovah is firm.
Arba—the croucher.
Archelaus—people's chief.
Archippus—master of the horse.
Ard—descent.
Ardon—descendant.
Areli—heroic.
Aretas—pleasing.
Argob—strong.
Aridai—the bull.
Aridatha—great birth.
Arieh—lion of Jehovah.
Ariel—lion of God.
Arioch—lion-like.
Arisai—meaning unknown.
Aristarchus—the best ruler.
Aristobulus—the best counselor.
Armoni—pertaining to the palace.
Arnan—agile.
Arod—posterity.
Arphaxad—one that releases.
Artaxerxes—possessor of an exalted kingdom.
Artemas—whole.
Arza—delight.
Asa—physician.
Asahel—God has made.

Asahiah—Jehovah has made.
Asaiah—Jehovah is a doer.
Asaph—he that removed reproach.
Asareel—God is joined.
Asarelah—upright toward God.
Ashbea—man of Baal.
Ashbel—man of Baal.
Ashchenaz—a fire that spreads.
Asher—happiness.
Ashkenaz—a fire that spreads.
Ashpenaz—horse's nose.
Ashriel—God is joined.
Ashur—freeman.
Ashvath—wrought.
Asiel—God has made.
Asnah—a dweller in the thornbush.
Asnapper—Asnap the great.
Aspatha—horse-given.
Asriel—God is joined.
Asshur—level plain.
Asshurim—mighty ones.
Assir—captive.
Assur—level plain.
Asyncritus—incomparable.
Ater—bound.
Athaiah—Jehovah is helper.
Athaliah—has afflicted.
Athlai—Jehovah is strong.
Attai—seasonable.
Augustus—sacred.
Azaliah—Jehovah is noble.
Azaniah—Jehovah is a hearer.
Azarael—God is a helper.
Azareel—God is a helper.
Azariah—Jehovah is a keeper.
Azaz—strong.
Azaziah—Jehovah is strong.
Azbuk—pardon.
Azel—noble.
Azgad—worship.
Aziel—God is might.
Aziza—strong.
Azmaveth—counsel.
Azor—helper.
Azriel—help of God.
Azrikam—my help has risen.
Azur—helper.
Azzan—sharp.
Azzur—helper.

B

Baal—controller.
Baal-hanan—the Lord is gracious.
Baalis—Lord of joy.
Baana—son of grief.
Baanah—son of grief.
Baaseiah—Jehovah is bold.
Baasha—boldness.
Bakbakkar—diligent searcher.
Bakbuk—a flagon.
Bakbukiah—wasted by Jehovah.
Balaam—Lord of the people.
Baladan—having power.
Balac—waster.
Balak—waster.
Bani—built.
Barabbas—son of return.
Barachel—God has blessed.
Barak—thunder.
Bariah—fugitive.
Bar-jesus—son of Joshua.
Barkos—partly-colored.
Barnabas—son of prophecy.
Barsabas—a son that suspends the water.
Barsabbas—a son that suspends the water.
Bartholomew—son of Tolmai.
Bartimaeus—honorable.
Baruch—blessed.
Barzillai—made of iron.
Bavai—wishes.
Bazlith—asking.
Bazluth—asking.
Bealiah—Jehovah is Lord.
Bebai—fatherly.
Becher—firstborn.
Bechorath—first birth.
Bedad—separation.
Bedan—son of judgment.
Bedeiah—servant of Jehovah.
Beeliada—the Lord knows.
Beera—a well.
Beerah—expounder.
Beeri—man of the well.
Bela—devouring.
Belah—devouring.
Belshazzar—the Lord's leader.

Belteshazzar—the Lord's leader.
Benaiah—Jehovah has built.
Ben-Ammi—son of my people.
Ben-Hadad—son of the God Hadah.
Ben-Hail—son of valiant.
Ben-Hanan—son of kind one.
Beninu—our son.
Benjamin—son of the right hand.
Beno—his son.
Benoni—son of my sorrow.
Ben-Zoheth—strong.
Boor—shepherd.
Bera—gift.
Berachah—blessing.
Berachiah—Jehovah is blessing.
Beraiah—Jehovah has created.
Berechiah—Jehovah is blessing.
Bered—seed.
Beri—expounder.
Beriah—in evil.
Berodach-baladan—bold.
Besai—treading down.
Besodeiah—familiar with Jehovah.
Beth-gader—walled place.
Bethlehem—house of bread.
Beth-rapha—place of fear.
Bethuel—dweller in God.
Beth-zur—place of rock.
Bezai—high.
Bezaleel—under God's shadow.
Bezer—strong.
Bichri—first-fruits.
Bidkar—sharp pain.
Bigtha—given by fortune.
Bigthan—gift of fortune.
Bigthana—gift of fortune.
Bigvai—happy.
Bildad—son of contention.
Bilgah—cheerful.
Bilgai—firstborn.
Bilhan—tender.
Bilshan—searcher.
Bimhal—son of circumcision.
Binea—wanderer.
Binnui—familyship.

Birsha—thick.
Birzavith—wounds.
Bishlam—peaceful.
Biztha—eunuch.
Blastus—a bud.
Boaz—strength.
Bocheru—youth.
Booz—Greek for Boaz.
Bukki—devastation sent by Jehovah.
Bukkiah—mouth of Jehovah.
Bunah—understanding.
Bunni—my understanding.
Buz—contempt.
Buzi—my contempt.

C

Caesar—one cut out.
Caiaphas—a searcher.
Cain—fabrication.
Cainan—acquisition.
Calcol—who nourishes.
Caleb—bold.
Canaan—lowland.
Carcas—severe.
Careah—bald head.
Carmi—noble.
Carpus—fruit.
Carshena—spoiler.
Cephas—rock.
Chalcol—who nourishes.
Chedorlaomer—sheaf band.
Chelluh—union.
Chelub—wicker basket.
Chelubai—binding together of the Lord.
Chenaanah—subduer.
Chenani—creator.
Chenaniah—Jehovah is firm.
Cheran—union.
Chesed—a devil.
Chileab—perfection of the father.
Chilion—wasting away.
Chimham—longing.
Chislon—trust.
Chushan-rishathaim—blackness of iniquities.
Chuza—modest.
Cis—snaring.

Claudius—lame.
Clement—kind.
Cleopas—the whole glory.
Cleophas—the whole glory.
Colhozeh—a seer.
Conaniah—Jehovah has
  established.
Coniah—God-appointed.
Cononiah—Jehovah has
  established.
Core—hard.
Cornelius—the sunbeam.
Cosam—most abundant.
Coz—nimble.
Crescens—increase.
Crispus—curled.
Cush—black.
Cushi—black.
Cyrenius—one who governs.
Cyrus—an heir.

D

Dalaiah—Jehovah is the
  deliverer.
Dalphon—dropping.
Dan—he that judges.
Daniel—God is my judge.
Dara—bearer.
Darda—a pearl of wisdom.
Darius—he that informs
  himself.
Darkon—bearer.
Dathan—belonging to law.
David—beloved.
Debir—speaker.
Dedan—low.
Dekar—lance bearer.
Delaiah—Jehovah is the
  deliverer.
Demas—ruler of people.
Demetrius—belonging to
  Demeter.
Deuel—invocation of God.
Diblaim—double embrace.
Dibri—promise of the Lord.
Didymus—a twin.
Diklah—palm grove.
Dionysius—divinely touched.
Diothephes—nourished by
  Jupiter.

Dishan—leaping.
Dishon—leaping.
Dodai—beloved of Jehovah.
Dodanim—a leader.
Dodavah—Jehovah is loving.
Dodo—loving.
Doeg—timid.
Dumah—silence.

E

Ebal—bare.
Ebed—slave.
Ebed-melech—slave of the king.
Eber—a shoot.
Ebiasaph—the father of
  gathering.
Eden—delight.
Eder—a flock.
Edom—red earth.
Eglon—circle.
Ehi—unity.
Ehud—strong.
Eker—one transplanted.
Eladah—God has adorned.
Elah—like a tree.
Elam—youth.
Elasah—God has made.
Eldaah—whom God called.
Eldad—God has loved.
Elead—God is witness.
Eleasah—God has made.
Eleazar—God is helper.
Elhanan—mercy of God.
Eli—my God.
Eliab—God is a father.
Eliada—God is knowing.
Eliadah—God is knowing.
Eliah—God is Jehovah.
Eliahba—God hides.
Eliakim—God establishes.
Eliam—God is one of the family.
Elias—Greek form of Elijah.
Eliasaph—God has added.
Eliashib—God has restored.
Eliathah—God has come.
Elidad—God is a friend.
Eliel—God is God.
Elienai—my eyes are unto God.
Eliezer—God is my help.
Elihoenai—my eyes are to
  Jehovah.

Elihoreph—God is a reward.
Elihu—he is God himself.
Elijah—God himself.
Elika—God has spewed out.
Elimelech—God is King.
Elioenai—my eyes are to Jehovah.
Eliphal—God has judged.
Eliphalet—God is escape.
Eliphaz—God is fine gold.
Elipheleh—Jehovah is distinguished.
Eliphelet—God is escape.
Eliseus—Greek form of Elisha.
Elisha—God is Savior.
Elishah—God is Savior.
Elishama—God has heard.
Elishaphat—God is judge.
Elishua—God is salvation.
Eliud—God is my praise.
Elizaphan—God is protector.
Elizur—God is a rock.
Elkanah—God is jealous.
Elmodam—the God of measure.
Elnaam—God is pleasant.
Elnathan—God has given.
Elon—strong.
Elpaal—God is a reward.
Elpalet—God is escape.
Eluzai—God is my strength.
Elymas—a sorcerer.
Elzabad—God has endowed.
Elzaphan—God has protected.
Emmor—an ass.
Enan—having eyes.
Enoch—teacher.
Enos—man is his frailty.
Enosh—man is his frailty.
Epaenetus—worthy of praise.
Epaphras—charming.
Epaphroditus—handsome.
Ephah—darkness.
Ephai—fatigued.
Epher—mule.
Ephlal—judging.
Ephod—covering.
Ephraim—doubly fruitful.
Ephron—strong.
Er—on the watch.
Eran—watchful.

Erastus—beloved.
Eri—my watcher.
Esaias—Greek for Isaiah.
Esar-haddon—victorious.
Esau—hairy.
Eshbaal—a man of Baal.
Eshban—man of understanding.
Eshcol—cluster of grapes.
Eshek—strife.
Eshtemoa—obedience.
Eshtemoh—obedience.
Eshton—rest.
Esli—God at my side.
Esrom—enclosure.
Etam—wild beasts' lair.
Ethan—perplexity.
Ethbaal—with him is Baal.
Ethnan—gift.
Ethni—my gift.
Eubulus—well-advised.
Eutychus—happy.
Evi—desire.
Evil-merodach—man of the god Merodach.
Ezar—treasure.
Ezbai—beautiful.
Ezbon—splendor.
Ezekias—Greek for Hezekiah.
Ezekiel—God is strong.
Ezer—treasure.
Ezra—help.
Ezri—God is a help.

F

Felix—prosperous.
Festus—prosperous.
Fortunatus—prosperous.

G

Gaal—rejection.
Gabbai—ingatherer.
Gad—good fortune.
Gaddi—belonging to fortune.
Gaddiel—God is fortune bringer.
Gadi—fortunate.
Gaham—blackness.
Gahar—hiding place.
Gaius—I am glad.
Galal—rolling of one's day upon the Lord.

Gallio—he that sucks.
Gamaliel—reward of God.
Gamul—matured.
Gareb—rough.
Gashmu—corporealness.
Gatam—puny.
Gazez—shearer.
Gazzam—devourer.
Geber—a hero.
Gedaliah—Jehovah is great.
Gedeon—Greek for Gideon.
Gedor—a fortress.
Gehazi—valley of vision.
Gemalli—camel owner.
Gemariah—Jehovah hath
  fulfilled.
Genubath—theft.
Gera—enmity.
Gershom—a stranger there.
Gershon—a stranger there.
Gesham—firm.
Geshem—rain.
Gether—vale of trial.
Geuel—salvation of God.
Gibbar—mighty man.
Gibea—highlander.
Giddalti—I magnify God.
Giddel—he has magnified.
Gideon—great warrior.
Gideoni—he that bruises.
Gilalai—weighty.
Gilead—mass of testimony.
Ginath—protection.
Ginnetho—great protection.
Ginnethon—great protection.
Gispa—attentive.
Gog—a mountain.
Goliath—the exile.
Gomer—completion.
Guni—protected.

H

Haahashtari—the courier.
Habaiah—Jehovah has hidden.
Habakkuk—love's embrace.
Habaziniah—God's light.
Hachaliah—Jehovah is hidden.
Hachmoni—the wise.
Hadad—mighty.
Hadadezer—mighty is the help.

Hadarezer—mighty is the help.
Hadlai—frail.
Hadoram—Hadar is high.
Hagab—a locust.
Hagaba—a locust.
Hagabah—a locust.
Haggai—festive.
Haggeri—wanderer.
Haggi—festive.
Haggiah—feast of Jehovah.
Hakkatan—the younger.
Hakkoz—the nimble.
Hakupha—curved.
Hallohesh—the enchanter.
Halohesh—the enchanter.
Ham—dark, colored, swarthy.
Haman—well disposed.
Hammath—warmth.
Hammedatha—he that
  troubleth the law.
Hammelech—the king.
Hamor—an ass.
Hammuel—warmth of God.
Hamuel—warmth of God.
Hamul—pity.
Hanameel—grace of God.
Hanamel—grace of God.
Hanan—merciful.
Hananeel—the mercy of God.
Hanani—he has shown me
  mercy.
Hananiah—Jehovah is gracious.
Haniel—grace of God.
Hanniel—grace of God.
Hanoch—dedicated.
Hanun—gracious.
Haran—enlightened.
Harbona—ass driver.
Harbonah—ass driver.
Hareph—born early.
Harhaiah—Jehovah is
  protecting.
Harhas—splendor.
Harhur—distinction.
Harim—consecrated.
Hariph—autumn rain.
Harnepher—panting.
Haroeh—the seer.
Harum—exalted.
Harumaph—flat nose.

Haruz—industrious.
Hasadiah—Jehovah is kind.
Hasenuah—the violated.
Hashabiah—Jehovah is associated.
Hashabnah—Jehovah is a friend.
Hashabniah—Jehovah is a friend.
Hashbadana—reason.
Hashem—astonished.
Hashub—thoughtful.
Hashubah—esteemed.
Hashum—wealthy.
Hashupha—nakedness.
Hasrah—splendor.
Hassenaah—the thorn hedge.
Hasshub—thoughtful.
Hasupha—nakedness.
Hatach—a gift.
Hathath—bruised.
Hatipha—captive.
Hatita—exploration.
Hattil—decaying.
Hattush—contender.
Havilah—circle.
Hazael—God sees.
Hazaiah—Jehovah is seeing.
Hazarmaveth—court of death.
Haziel—vision of God.
Hazo—vision.
Heber—fellowship.
Hebron—company.
Hegai—venerable.
Hege—venerable.
Heldai—enduring.
Heleb—endurance.
Heled—endurance.
Helek—smoothness.
Helem—manly vigor.
Helez—alertness.
Heli—ascending.
Helkai—Jehovah is a portion.
Helon—strong.
Hemam—faithful.
Heman—faithful.
Hemath—warmth.
Hemdan—desirable.
Hen—grace.
Henadad—favor.

Henoch—dedicated.
Hepher—a well.
Heresh—silence.
Hermas—interpreter.
Hermes—gain.
Hermogenes—begotten.
Herod—son of the hero.
Herodion—conqueror of heroes.
Hesed—kindness.
Heth—terrible.
Hezeki—Jehovah is strength.
Hezekiah—Jehovah is strength.
Hezion—vision.
Hezir—returning home.
Hezrai—beautiful.
Hezro—enclosed.
Hezron—dart of joy.
Hiddai—mighty.
Hiel—the life of God.
Hilkiah—Jehovah is protection
Hillel—praised greatly.
Hinnom—gratis.
Hirah—nobility.
Hiram—consecration.
Hizkiah—Jehovah is strong.
Hizkijah—Jehovah is strong.
Hobab—lover.
Hod—majesty.
Hodaiah—honorer of Jehovah.
Hodaviah—Jehovah is his praise.
Hodevah—Jehovah is honor.
Hodiah—splendor of Jehovah.
Hodijah—splendor of Jehovah.
Hoham—Jehovah protects the multitude.
Homam—destroyer.
Hophni—strong.
Horam—elevated.
Hori—free.
Hosah—refuge.
Hosea—salvation.
Hoshaiah—God has saved.
Hoshama—Jehovah has heard.
Hoshea—salvation.
Hotham—signet ring.
Hothan—signet ring.
Hothir—abundance.
Hul—circle.
Hupham—covering.

Huppah—a covering.
Huppim—coverings.
Hur—noble.
Hurai—a linen weaver.
Huram—ingenious.
Huri—linen weaver.
Hushah—passion.
Hushai—quick.
Husham—passion.
Hushim—hasting.
Huz—firm.
Hymenaeus—the god of
marriage.

I

Ibhar—God chooses.
Ibneiah—Jehovah builds.
Ibnijah—Jehovah is builder.
Ibri—passer over.
Ibzan—active.
Ichabod—the glory is not.
Idbash—honey sweet.
Iddo—affectionate.
Igal—he will vindicate.
Igdaliah—great is Jehovah.
Igeal—deliverer.
Ikkesh—subtle.
Ilai—supreme.
Imla—fulfilling.
Imlah—fulfilling.
Immer—prominent.
Imna—God restrains.
Imnah—prosperity.
Imrah—stubborn.
Imri—eloquent.
Iphedeiah—redemption of the
Lord.
Ir—watcher.
Ira—watchful.
Irad—wild ass.
Iram—watchful.
Iri—Jehovah watches.
Irijah—God sees.
Irnahash—serpent.
Iru—watch.
Isaac—laughing one.
Isaiah—salvation is of the Lord.
Ishbah—appeaser.
Ishbak—free.
Ishbi-benob—predicter.

Ishbosheth—man of shame.
Ishi—saving.
Ishiah—Jehovah forgives.
Ishijah—Jehovah is.
Ishma—elevated.
Ishmael—God hears.
Ishmaiah—Jehovah hears.
Ishmerai—God keeps.
Ishod—man of honor.
Ishpan—firm.
Ishuah—equal.
Ishuai—equality.
Ishui—equality.
Ismachiah—Jehovah supports.
Ismaiah—Jehovah hears.
Ispah—he will be eminent.
Israel—ruling with God.
Isaachar—reward.
Isshiah—Jehovah forgives.
Isuah—self-satisfied.
Isui—equality.
Ithai—existing.
Ithamar—palm tree.
Ithiel—God is with me.
Ithmah—purity.
Ithra—excellence.
Ithran—abundance.
Ithream—remnant.
Ittai—plowman.
Izehar—bright one.
Izhar—olive oil.
Izrahiah—Jehovah arises.
Izri—creative.

J

Jaakan—intelligent.
Jaakobah—to Jacob.
Jaala—doe.
Jaalah—elevation.
Jaalam—he will be hid.
Jaanai—Jehovah answers.
Jaare-oregim—foresters.
Jaasau—Jehovah makes.
Jaasiel—God is maker.
Jaazaniah—Jehovah hearkens.
Jaaziah—God determines.
Jaaziel—God is consoling.
Jabal—river.
Jabesh—dry place.
Jabez—maker of sorrow.

Jabin—God discerns.
Jachan—afflicting.
Jachin—founding.
Jacob—supplanter.
Jada—wise.
Jadau—favorite.
Jaddua—known.
Jadon—he that abides.
Jahath—revival.
Jahaziah—Jehovah reveals.
Jahaziel—God sees.
Jahdai—guide.
Jahdiel—God gladdens.
Jahdo—union.
Jahleel—God waits.
Jahmai—lusty.
Jahzeel—God distributes.
Jahzerah—Jehovah protects.
Jahziel—God distributes.
Jair—Jehovah arouses.
Jairus—he will enlighten.
Jakan—intelligent.
Jakeh—pious.
Jakim—he raises up.
Jalon—obstinate.
Jambres—opposer.
James—supplanter.
Jamin—prosperity's right hand.
Jamlech—Jehovah rules.
Janna—he will answer.
Jannes—full of pleasure.
Japheth—persuader.
Japhia—shining.
Japhlet—Jehovah causes to
  escape.
Jarah—honey.
Jareb—avenger.
Jared—descending.
Jaresiah—Jehovah gives a
  couch.
Jarha—adversary.
Jarib—striving.
Jaroah—new moon.
Jashen—sleeping.
Jashobeam—the people return
  to God.
Jashub—returning.
Jashubi-lehem—bread returns.
Jason—healing.
Jathniel—God gives gifts.

Javan—clay.
Jaziz—shining.
Jeaterai—steadfast.
Jeberechiah—Jehovah blesses.
Jecamiah—meaning unknown.
Jechonias—established of the
  Lord.
Jeconiah—preparation of the
  Lord.
Jedaiah—Jehovah knows.
Jediael—known of God.
Jedidiah—beloved of Jehovah.
Jeduthun—choir of praise.
Jeezer—help.
Jehaleleel—he praises God.
Jehalelel—he praises God.
Jehdeiah—Jehovah's union.
Jehezekel—God is strong.
Jehiah—God lives.
Jehiel—God lives.
Jehieli—he lives by mercy.
Jehizkiah—Jehovah
  strengthens.
Jehoadah—Jehovah unveils.
Jehoahaz—Jehovah upholds.
Jehoash—God supplies.
Jehohanan—Jehovah is
  gracious.
Jehoiachin—Jehovah
  establishes.
Jehoiada—knowledge of God.
Jehoiakim—Jehovah sets up.
Jehoiarib—Jehovah contends.
Jehonadab—Jehovah is liberal.
Jehonathan—Jehovah has
  given.
Jehoram—Jehovah is exalted.
Jehoshaphat—Jehovah is
  judge.
Jehoshua—Jehovah saves.
Jehoshuah—Jehovah is
  salvation.
Jehozabad—Jehovah has
  endowed.
Jehozadak—Jehovah is just.
Jehu—Jehovah is He.
Jehubbah—hidden.
Jehucal—Jehovah is able.
Jehudi—Jew.
Jehush—collector.

Jeiel—treasure of God.
Jekameam—he assembles the people.
Jekamiah—Jehovah gathers.
Jekuthiel—God is mighty.
Jemuel—God is light.
Jephthae—Greek for Jephthah.
Jephthah—he sets free.
Jephunneh—it will be prepared.
Jerah—moon.
Jerahmeel—God is merciful.
Jered—flowing.
Jeremai—Jehovah is high.
Jeremiah—exalted of God.
Jeremias—Jehovah is high.
Jeremoth—heights.
Jeremy—Greek for Jeremiah.
Jeriah—Jehovah founded.
Jeribai—contentious.
Jeriel—God's foundation.
Jerijah—Jehovah has founded.
Jerimoth—heights.
Jeroboam—enlarges.
Jeroham—loved.
Jerubbaal—let Baal defend his cause.
Jerubbesheth—idol contender.
Jesaiah—Jehovah is rich.
Jeshaiah—Jehovah is rich.
Jesharelah—upright towards God.
Jeshebeab—father's house.
Jesher—uprightness.
Jeshishai—Jehovah is ancient.
Jeshohaiah—humbled by Jehovah.
Jeshua—Jehovah is salvation.
Jeshuah—Jehovah is salvation.
Jesiah—Jehovah is.
Jesimiel—God sets up.
Jesse—Jehovah is.
Jesui—Jehovah is satisfied.
Jesus—Jehovah is salvation.
Jether—abundance.
Jetheth—subjection.
Jethro—excellence.
Jetur—defense.
Jeuel—God's treasure.
Jeush—he will gather together.
Jeuz—counselor.

Jezaniah—Jehovah determines.
Jezer—formation.
Jeziah—Jehovah unites.
Jeziel—assembly of God.
Jezliah—Jehovah unites.
Jezoar—tawny.
Jezrahiah—the Lord arises.
Jezreel—God sows.
Jibsam—sweet.
Jidlaph—distiller.
Jimna—prosperity.
Jimnah—prosperity.
Joab—Jehovah is a good Father.
Joah—Jehovah is a brother.
Joahaz—Jehovah helps.
Joanna—Jehovah has been gracious.
Joash—Jehovah hastens to help.
Joatham—the Lord is upright.
Job—he that weeps.
Jobab—howling.
Joed—Jehovah is witness.
Joel—Jehovah is God.
Joelah—God is snatching.
Joezer—Jehovah is help.
Jogli—exiled.
Joha—Jehovah lives.
Johanan—Jehovah is gracious.
John—Jehovah has been gracious.
Joiada—has known.
Joiakim—establishes.
Joiarib—Jehovah depends.
Jokim—Jehovah sets up.
Jokshan—fowler.
Joktan—little.
Jona—a dove.
Jonadab—who acts as a prince.
Jonah—a dove.
Jonan—God has been gracious.
Jonas—a dove.
Jonathan—the Lord gave.
Jorah—rain of autumn.
Joram—Jehovah is high.
Jorim—he that exalts the Lord.
Jorkoam—spreading the people.
Josabad—Jehovah has bestowed.
Josaphat—the Lord judges.

Jose—aid.
Josedech—Jehovah is righteous.
Joseph—may God add.
Joses—he that pardons.
Joshah—uprightness.
Joshaphat—Jehovah judges.
Joshaviah—sits upright.
Joshbekashah—seat of
  hardness.
Joshua—Jehovah is salvation.
Josiah—the fire of the Lord.
Josias—Greek for Josiah.
Josibiah—Jehovah causes to
  dwell.
Josiphiah—Jehovah will
  increase.
Jotham—Jehovah is upright.
Jozabad—endowed.
Jozachar—Jehovah remembers.
Jozadak—Jehovah is great.
Jubal—a trumpet.
Jucal—able.
Juda—praise of the Lord.
Judah—praise of the Lord.
Judas—praise of the Lord.
Jude—praise of the Lord.
Julius—curly headed.
Junia—belonging to Juno.
Jushab-hesed—lovingkindness
  is returned.
Justus—just.

K
Kadmiel—God is of old.
Kallai—swift.
Kareah—bald.
Kedar—powerful.
Kedemah—eastern.
Keilah—enclosed.
Kelaiah—Jehovah is light.
Kelita—poverty.
Kemuel—congregation of God.
Kenan—begotten.
Kenaz—hunting.
Keros—the reed of a weaver's
  beam.
Kirjath-jearim—city of forests.
Kish—straw.
Kishi—bow of Jehovah.
Kittim—they that bruise.

Kohath—assembly.
Kolaiah—the voice of Jehovah.
Korah—baldness.
Kore—baldness.
Koz—the thorn.
Kushaiah—bow of Jehovah.

L
Laadah—festival.
Laadan—festive-born.
Laban—glorious.
Lael—devoted to God.
Lahad—oppressed.
Lahmi—a warrior.
Laish—a lion.
Lamech—overthrower.
Lapidoth—enlightened.
Lazarus—God has helped.
Lebana—poetic designation for
  the moon.
Lebanah—poetic designation
  for the moon.
Lebbaeus—man of heart.
Lecah—addition.
Lehabim—flame.
Lemuel—devoted to God.
Letushim—oppressed.
Leummim—nations.
Levi—joined.
Libni—distinguished.
Likhi—Jehovah is doctrine.
Linus—nets.
Lo-ammi—not my people.
Lot—concealed.
Lotan—covering.
Lucas—light-giving.
Lucifer—the shining one.
Lucius—of the light.
Lud—bending.
Ludim—bending.
Luke—light-giving.
Lysanias—drives away sorrow.
Lysias—he who has the power to
  set free.

M
Maacah—oppression.
Maachah—oppression.
Maadai—wavering.
Maadiah—ornament of
  Jehovah.

Maai—Jehovah is compassionable.
Maaseiah—work of Jehovah.
Maasiai—work of Jehovah.
Maath—wiping away.
Maaz—anger.
Maaziah—consolation.
Machbanai—clothed with a cloak.
Machi—decrease.
Machir—sold.
Machnadebai—gift of the noble one.
Madai—middle.
Madmannah—heap.
Magbish—cluster of stars.
Magdiel—honor of God.
Magog—expansion.
Magor-missabib—fear.
Magpiash—cluster of stars.
Mahalah—disease.
Mahalaleel—the praise of God.
Mahali—sick.
Maharai—impetuous.
Mahath—instrument.
Mahazioth—vision of significance.
Maher-shalal-hash-baz—rush on the prey.
Mahlah—disease.
Mahli—sick.
Mahlon—sickly.
Mahol—joy.
Malachi—messenger of Jehovah.
Malcham—rule.
Malchiah—Jehovah is King.
Malchiel—God is King.
Malchijah—Jehovah is King.
Malchiram—my King is exalted.
Malchi-shua—king of help.
Malchus—king.
Maleleel—praise of God.
Mallothi—Jehovah is speaking.
Malluch—counselor.
Mamre—vigor.
Manaen—comforter.
Manahath—resting place.
Manasseh—causing forgetfulness.

Manasses—causing forgetfulness.
Manoah—rest.
Maoch—poor.
Maon—habitation.
Marcus—polite.
Mareshah—at the head.
Mark—polite.
Marsena—worthy.
Mash—drawn out.
Massa—burden.
Mathusala—when he is dead, it shall be sent.
Matri—Jehovah is watching.
Mattan—gift.
Mattaniah—gift of Jehovah.
Mattatha—gift.
Mattathah—a gift
Mattathias—gift of Jehovah.
Mattenai—gift of Jehovah.
Matthan—a gift.
Matthat—gift.
Matthew—gift of Jehovah.
Matthias—gift of God.
Mattithiah—gift of Jehovah.
Mebunnai—built up.
Medad—love.
Medan—judgment.
Mehetabeel—God blesses.
Mehetabel—God blesses.
Mehida—famous.
Mehir—dexterity.
Mehujael—God is combating.
Mehuman—faithful.
Mehunim—place of habitation.
Melatiah—Jehovah has set free.
Melchi—Jehovah is my King.
Melchiah—Jehovah is King.
Melchisedec—King of righteousness.
Melchishua—king of help.
Melchizedek—King of righteousness.
Melea—fullness.
Melech—a king.
Melicu—counselor.
Melzar—the overseer.
Memucan—impoverished.
Menahem—comforter.
Menan—consoling.

Meonothai—Jehovah's habitations.
Mephibosheth—destroying shame.
Meraiah—stubbornness.
Meraioth—rebellion.
Merari—unhappy.
Mered—rebellious.
Meremoth—strong.
Meres—worthy.
Merib-baal—contender against Baal.
Merodach-baladan—the son of death.
Mesech—drawing out.
Mesha—retreat.
Meshach—agile.
Meshech—drawing out.
Meshelemiah—Jehovah recompenses.
Meshezabeel—God sets free.
Meshillemith—recompenses.
Meshillemoth—recompenses.
Meshobab—delivered.
Meshullam—associate.
Methusael—man of God.
Methuselah—when he is dead, it shall be sent.
Meunim—place of habitation.
Mezahab—offspring.
Miamin—fortunate.
Mibhar—youth.
Mibsam—sweet odor.
Mibzar—a stronghold.
Michah—who is like Jehovah.
Micaiah—who is like Jehovah.
Micha—who is like Jehovah.
Michael—who is like God.
Michah—who is like Jehovah.
Michaiah—who is like Jehovah.
Michri—Jehovah possesses.
Midian—strife.
Mijamin—fortunate.
Mikloth—sticks.
Mikneiah—Jehovah is jealous.
Milalai—eloquent.
Miniamin—fortunate.
Mirma—deceit.
Mishael—who is what God is.
Misham—swiftness.

Mishma—fame.
Mishmannah—vigor.
Mispereth—writing.
Mithredath—animating spirit of fire.
Mizpar—writing.
Mizraim—tribulations.
Mizzah—terror.
Mnason—a diligent seeker.
Moab—desire.
Moadiah—festival of Jehovah.
Molid—begetter.
Mordecai—dedicated to Mars.
Moses—taken out of the water.
Moza—a going forth.
Muppim—obscurities.
Mushi—drawn out.

N
Naam—pleasantness.
Naaman—pleasant.
Naarai—pleasantness of Jehovah.
Naashon—one that foretells.
Naasson—enchanter.
Nabal—foolish.
Naboth—prominence.
Nachon—stroke.
Nachor—snorer.
Nadab—of one's free will.
Nagge—splendor of the sun.
Naham—solace.
Nahamani—compassionate.
Naharai—snoring.
Nahari—snoring.
Nahash—serpent.
Nahath—lowness.
Nahbi—Jehovah's protection.
Nahor—snorer.
Nahshon—ominous.
Nahum—compassionate.
Naphish—numerous.
Naphtali—obtained by wrestling.
Narcissus—flower causing lethargy.
Nathan—he has given.
Nathanael—the gift of God.
Nathan-melech—the king is giver.

Naum—comfort.
Neariah—drives away.
Nebai—projecting.
Nebaioth—husbandry.
Nebajoth—husbandry.
Nebat—cultivation.
Nebo—height.
Nebuchadnezzar—defend the
boundary.
Nebuchadrezzar—defend the
boundary.
Nebushasban—save me.
Nebuzar-adan—Nebo has an
offspring.
Necho—who was beaten.
Nedabiah—Jehovah is willing.
Nehemiah—Jehovah has
consoled.
Nehum—consolation.
Nekoda—herdsman.
Nemuel—God is spreading.
Nepheg—an offshoot.
Nephish—numerous.
Nephthalim—obtained by
wrestling.
Ner—a lamp.
Nereus—name of a sea god.
Nergal-sharezer—protect the
king.
Neri—light of the Lord.
Neriah—lamp of Jehovah.
Nethaneel—God gives.
Nethaniah—Jehovah has given.
Neziah—pure.
Nicanor—conqueror.
Nicodemus—victor over the
people.
Nicolas—conqueror of the
people.
Niger—black.
Nimrod—valiant.
Nimshi—Jehovah reveals.
Noadiah—Jehovah has met.
Noah—rest.
Nobah—barking.
Nogah—brilliance.
Nohah—rest.
Non—fish.
Nun—fish.
Nymphas—bridegroom.

O

Obadiah—worshiper of
Jehovah.
Obal—bare.
Obed—worshiper.
Obed-edom—laborer of the
earth.
Obil—one who weeps.
Ocran—troubler.
Oded—aiding.
Og—long-necked.
Ohad—powerful.
Ohel—a tent.
Olympas—heavenly.
Omar—mountaineer.
Omri—impetuous.
On—sun.
Onam—wealthy.
Onan—strong.
Onesimus—profitable.
Onesiphorus—bringing
advantage.
Ophir—fat.
Ophrah—hamlet.
Oreb—a raven.
Oren—fine tree.
Ornan—that rejoices.
Osee—salvation.
Oshea—God saves.
Othni—lion of God.
Othniel—lion of God.
Ozem—that fasts.
Ozias—strength from the Lord.
Ozni—attentive.

P

Paarai—revelation of Jehovah.
Padon—redemption.
Pagiel—God meets.
Pahath-moab—governor.
Palal—he has judged.
Pallu—wonderful.
Palti—deliverance by God.
Paltiel—deliverer of the Lord.
Parmashta—superior.
Parmenas—faithful.
Parnach—very nimble.
Parosh—a fugitive.
Parshandatha—dung of
impurity.

Paruah—increase.
Pasach—limping.
Paseah—lame.
Pashur—free.
Pathrusim—the south land.
Patrobas—pursuer of his
father's steps.
Paul—little.
Pedahel—God has saved.
Pedahzur—powerful.
Pedaiah—redemption.
Pekah—watchfulness.
Pekahiah—Jehovah has given
sight.
Pelaiah—Jehovah has made
illustrious.
Pelaliah—Jehovah judges.
Pelatiah—freedom giver.
Peleg—division.
Pelet—escape.
Peleth—swiftness.
Peniel—the face of God.
Penuel—the face of God.
Peresh—separate.
Perez—a breach.
Perida—separation.
Persis—that which divides.
Peter—a rock.
Pethahiah—Jehovah has set
free.
Pethuel—God delivers.
Peulthai—full of work.
Phalec—division.
Phallu—admirable.
Phalti—deliverance.
Phaltiel—deliverer of the Lord.
Phanuel—vision of God.
Pharaoh—the destroyer.
Pharaoh-hophra—priest of the
sun.
Pharaoh-necho—Pharaoh the
lame.
Phares—rupture.
Pharez—break forth violently.
Pharosh—a fugitive.
Phaseah—lame.
Phichol—great.
Philemon—affectionate.
Philetus—beloved.
Philip—warrior.

Philologus—word lover.
Phinehas—serpent's mouth.
Phlegon—zealous.
Phurah—fruitbearer.
Phut—extension.
Phuvah—utterance.
Phygellus—fugitive.
Pilate—one armed with a dart.
Pildash—flame of fire.
Pileha—worship.
Piltai—Jehovah causes to
escape.
Pinon—pearl.
Piram—a wild ass.
Pispah—expansion.
Pithon—gift of mouth.
Pochereth—binding.
Poratha—fruitful.
Porcius—meaning unknown.
Potiphar—who is of the sun.
Poti-pherah—belonging to the
sun.
Prochorus—leading in a chorus.
Pua—utterance.
Puah—utterance.
Publius—common.
Pudens—bashful.
Pul—strong.
Put—extension.
Putiel—God enlightens.

Q
Quartus—the fourth.

R
Raamah—trembling.
Raamiah—Jehovah causes
trembling.
Rabmag—chief of the
magicians.
Rabsaris—grand master of the
eunuchs.
Rabshakeh—head of the
cupbearers.
Raddai—Jehovah subdues.
Ragau—a friend.
Raguel—friend of God.
Raham—pity.
Rakem—friendship.
Ram—high.
Ramiah—exalted is Jehovah.

Ramoth—high places.
Rapha—fearful.
Raphah—fearful.
Raphu—feared.
Reaia—provided for.
Reaiah—provided for.
Reba—offspring.
Rechab—companionship.
Reelaiah—trembling caused by Jehovah.
Regem—a friend.
Regem-melech—friend of the king.
Rehabiah—God is my extent.
Rehob—width.
Rehoboam—freer of the people.
Rehoboth—wide spaces.
Rehum—pity.
Rei—friendly.
Rekem—friendship.
Remaliah—Jehovah increases.
Rephael—God is a healer.
Rephah—riches.
Rephaiah—Jehovah heals.
Resheph—haste.
Reu—friend.
Reuben—behold a son.
Reuel—friend of God.
Rezia—Jehovah is pleasing.
Rezin—good will.
Rezon—noble.
Rhesa—will.
Ribai—Jehovah contends.
Rimmon—a pomegranate.
Riphath—enemies.
Roboam—freer of the people.
Rohgah—alarm.
Romamti-ezer—highest help.
Rosh—prince.
Rufus—red.

S
Sabta—breaking through.
Sabtah—breaking through.
Sabtecha—surrender.
Sabtechah—surrender.
Sacar—merchandise.
Sadoc—righteous.
Sala—branch.
Salah—offshoot.

Salathiel—loan of God.
Sallai—rejected.
Salma—firmness.
Salmon—peaceable.
Salu—unfortunate.
Samgar-nebo—be gracious.
Samlah—astonishment.
Samson—strong.
Samuel—asked of God.
Sanballat—the enemy.
Saph—preserver.
Saraph—burning.
Sargon—the constituted king.
Sarsechim—chief of the eunuchs.
Saruch—branch.
Saul—demanded.
Sceva—I dispose.
Seba—old man.
Secundus—secondary.
Segub—exalted.
Seir—rough.
Seled—exultation.
Sem—Greek for Shem.
Semachiah—Jehovah supports.
Semei—obey.
Senaah—thorny.
Sennacherib—the moon-god.
Senuah—the violated.
Seorim—fear.
Seraiah—the Lord is my Prince.
Sered—fear.
Sergius Paulus—small.
Serug—firmness.
Seth—appointed.
Sethur—hidden.
Shaaph—friendship.
Shaashgaz—servant of the beautiful.
Shabbethai—sabbath born.
Shachia—captive of the Lord.
Shadrach—moon-god.
Shage—erring.
Shaharaim—double dawning.
Shallum—recompense.
Shallun—recompense.
Shalmai—Jehovah is recompenser.
Shalman—peaceable.
Shalmaneser—peace taken away.

Shama—he hath heard.
Shamed—destroyer.
Shamer—preserver.
Shamgar—cupbearer.
Shamhuth—fame.
Shamir—oppressed.
Shamma—renown.
Shammah—loss.
Shammai—celebrated.
Shammoth—renown.
Shammua—famous.
Shammuah—famous.
Shamsherai—heroic.
Shapham—vigorous.
Shaphan—shy.
Shaphat—judge.
Sharai—my son.
Sharar—firm.
Sharezer—preserve the king.
Shashai—pale.
Shashak—runner.
Shaul—asked.
Shavsha—splendor.
Sheal—request.
Shealtiel—I have asked of God.
Sheariah—Jehovah has
 esteemed.
Shear-jashub—a remnant
 returns.
Sheba—seventh.
Shebaniah—the Lord converts.
Sheber—fracture.
Shebna—youthfulness.
Shebuel—God is renown.
Shecaniah—Jehovah is a
 neighbor.
Shechaniah—Jehovah is a
 neighbor.
Shechem—shoulder.
Shedeur—all mighty.
Shehariah—Jehovah is the
 dawn.
Shelah—peace.
Shelemiah—God is my
 perfection.
Sheleph—drawn out.
Shelesh—might.
Shelomi—Jehovah is peace.
Shelomith—peacefulness.
Shelomoth—peacefulness.

Shelumiel—God's peace.
Shem—name.
Shema—fame.
Shemaah—the fame.
Shemaiah—Jehovah is fame.
Shemariah—God is my guard.
Shemember—splendor.
Shemer—guardian.
Shemida—science of the
 heavens.
Shemidah—science of the
 heavens.
Shemiramoth—fame of the
 highest.
Shomuel—heard of God.
Shenazar—light.
Shephatiah—Jehovah is judge.
Shephi—smoothness.
Shepho—unconcern.
Shephupham—an adder.
Shephuphan—an adder.
Sherebiah—Jehovah is the
 originator.
Sheresh—root.
Sherezer—protect the king.
Sheshai—noble.
Sheshan—free.
Sheshbazzar—O Sun-god
 protect the son.
Sheth—compensation.
Shethar—star.
Shetar-boznai—starry
 splendor.
Sheva—vanity.
Shilhi—armed with darts.
Shillem—retribution.
Shiloni—sent one.
Shilshah—heroism.
Shimea—splendor.
Shimeah—splendor.
Shimeam—rumor.
Shimei—Jehovah is famous.
Shimeon—hearing.
Shimhi—Jehovah is famous.
Shimi—Jehovah is famous.
Shimma—fame.
Shimon—tried.
Shimrath—watch.
Shimri—Jehovah is watching.

Shimrom—a guard.
Shimron—a guard.
Shimshai—Jehovah is splendor.
Shinab—father's tooth.
Shiphi—Jehovah is fulness.
Shiphtan—judge.
Shisha—nobility.
Shishak—meaning unknown.
Shitrai—Jehovah is deciding.
Shiza—vehement love.
Shobab—restored.
Shobach—expansion.
Shobai—Jehovah is glorious.
Shobal—wandering.
Shobek—free.
Shobi—Jehovah is glorious.
Shoham—onyx.
Shomer—watchman.
Shophach—extension.
Shua—wealth.
Shuah—prosperity.
Shual—a fox.
Shubael—meaning unknown.
Shuham—depression.
Shuni—calm.
Shupham—serpent.
Shuppim—serpent.
Shuthelah—a plant.
Sia—congregation.
Siaha—congregation.
Sibbecai—Jehovah is
   intervening.
Sibbechai—Jehovah is
   intervening.
Sichem—shoulder.
Sidon—fortified.
Sihon—great.
Silas—lover of words.
Silvanus—lover of words.
Simeon—hears and obeys.
Simon—hearing.
Simri—Jehovah is watching.
Sippai—Jehovah is the
   preserver.
Sisamai—Jehovah is
   distinguished.
Sisera—meditation.
So—lifted up.
Socho—fortification.
Sodi—my secret.
Solomon—peace.

Sopater—father defender.
Sophereth—learning.
Sosipater—father defender.
Sosthenes—of sound strength.
Sotai—deviator.
Stachys—yoke.
Stephanas—crowned.
Stephen—wreath.
Suah—riches.
Susi—Jehovah is swift.
Sychar—shoulder.
Sychem—shoulder.

T

Tabbaoth—spots.
Tabeal—God is good.
Tabeel—God is good.
Tabrimon—rimmon is god.
Tahan—preciousness.
Tahath—humility.
Tahrea—flight.
Talmai—spirited.
Talmon—violent.
Tamah—laughter.
Tanhumeth—consolation.
Tappuah—apple.
Tarah—wild goat.
Tarea—adroitness.
Tarshish—hard.
Tartan—great increase.
Tatnai—overseer of gifts.
Tebah—thick.
Tebaliah—Jehovah has
   purified.
Tehinnah—supplication.
Tekoa—firm.
Telah—vigor.
Telem—lamb.
Tema—admiration.
Teman—perfect.
Temani—perfect.
Temeni—fortunate.
Terah—wandering.
Teresh—reverence.
Tertius—the third.
Tertullus—liar.
Thaddaeus—breast.
Thahash—reddish.
Thamah—combat.
Thara—turning.
Tharshish—hard.

Theophilus—lover of God.
Theudas—false teacher.
Thomas—twin.
Tiberius—son of Tiber.
Tibni—straw.
Tidal—renown.
Tiglath-pileser—binds.
Tikvah—strength.
Tikvath—expectation.
Tilgath-pilneser—hinders.
Tilon—scorn.
Timaeus—highly prized.
Timna—restraining.
Timnah—restraining.
Timon—deemed worthy.
Timotheus—honored of God.
Timothy—honored of God.
Tiras—desire of parents.
Tirhakah—exalted.
Tirhanah—kindness.
Tiria—foundation.
Tirshatha—reverence.
Titus—honorable.
Toah—humility.
Tob-adonijah—good is my Lord
  Jehovah.
Tobiah—Jehovah is good.
Tobijah—Jehovah is good.
Togarmah—strong.
Tohu—humility.
Toi—wandering.
Tola—scarlet.
Tou—wandering.
Trophimus—well educated.
Tubal—worldly.
Tubal-cain—flowing forth of
  Cain.
Tychicus—fortunate.
Tyrannus—absolute.

U

Ucal—power.
Uel—will of God.
Ulam—solitary.
Ulla—burden.
Unni—poor.
Ur—light.
Urbane—polite.
Uri—light of Jehovah.
Uriah—Jehovah is light.

Urias—Jehovah is light.
Uriel—a light.
Urijah—Jehovah is light.
Uthai—Jehovah is help.
Uz—firmness.
Uzai—hoped for.
Uzal—a wanderer.
Uzza—strength.
Uzzah—strength.
Uzzi—the might of Jehovah.
Uzzia—might of Jehovah.
Uzziah—strength of the Lord.
Uzziel—God is strong.

V

Vajezatha—strong as the wind.
Vaniah—God is praise.
Vashni—God is strong.
Vophsi—fragrant.

Z

Zaavan—causing fear.
Zavan—causing fear.
Zabad—a gift.
Zabbai—humming.
Zabbud—well remembered.
Zabdi—the gift of Jehovah.
Zabdiel—my gift is God.
Zabud—giver.
Zaccai—pure.
Zacchaeus—pure.
Zacchur—well remembered.
Zaccur—well remembered.
Zachariah—Jehovah is
  renowned.
Zacharias—Jehovah is
  renowned.
Zacher—fame.
Zadok—righteous.
Zaham—loathing.
Zalaph—purification.
Zalmon—shady.
Zalmunna—shelter is denied.
Zanoah—broken district.
Zaphnath-paaneah—giver of
  the nourishment of life.
Zaphon—dark.
Zara—brightness.
Zarah—brightness.
Zatthu—lovely.
Zattu—lovely.

248

Zaza—projection.
Zebadiah—the Lord is my portion.
Zebah—victim.
Zebedee—the gift of God.
Zebina—one who is bought.
Zebul—an habitation.
Zebulun—dwelling.
Zechariah—Jehovah remembers.
Zecher—Jehovah remembers.
Zedekiah—Jehovah is righteous.
Zeeb—wolf.
Zelek—a shadow.
Zelophehad—the firstborn.
Zelotes—full of zeal.
Zemira—a melody.
Zenas—the gift of Zeus.
Zephaniah—God hides.
Zephi—watch.
Zepho—watch.
Zephon—dark.
Zerah—springing up of light.
Zerahiah—the Lord is risen.
Zereth—brightness.
Zeri—balm.
Zeror—a bundle.
Zerubbabel—an offspring of Babel.
Zetham—place of olives.
Zethan—place of olives.
Zethar—sacrifice.

Zia—terror.
Ziba—plantation.
Zibeon—wild robber.
Zibia—strength.
Zichri—renowned.
Zidkijah—Jehovah is might.
Zidon—fortress.
Ziha—sunniness.
Zilthai—shadow of the Lord.
Zimmah—counsel.
Zimran—the singer.
Zimri—celebrated.
Zina—borrowed.
Ziph—refining place.
Ziphah—lent.
Ziphion—serpent.
Zippor—a sparrow.
Zithri—overturn.
Ziza—fertility.
Zizah—fertility.
Zohar—distinction.
Zoheth—corpulent.
Zophah—watch.
Zophai—watcher.
Zophar—hairy.
Zorobabel—an offspring of Babel.
Zuar—little.
Zuph—honeycomb.
Zur—rock.
Zuriel—God is a rock.
Zurishaddai—the Almighty is a rock.

184. The Names of the Women of the Bible

A
Abi—God's will.
Abia—God is Father.
Abiah—God is Father.
Abigail—cause of joy.
Abihail—cause of strength.
Abijah—God's will.
Abishag—my father wanders.
Achsa—adorned.
Achsah—adorned.
Agar—fugitive.

Ahinoam—brother of pleasantries.
Ahlai—O would that!
Aholibaham—tent of the high places.
Anah—meaning unknown.
Anna—grace.
Apphia—fruitful.
Asenath—belongs to Neit.
Atarah—crown.
Athaliah—Jehovah has afflicted.

Azubah—desolation.

B

Baara—the burning one.
Bashemath—perfumed.
Basmath—perfumed.
Bathsheba—seventh daughter.
Bernice—victorious.
Bilhah—timid.
Bithiah—Jehovah's daughter.

C

Candace—queen.
Chloe—green herb.
Claudia—lame.
Cozbi—deceiver.

D

Damaris—a heifer.
Deborah—bee.
Delilah—delicate.
Dinah—justice.
Dorcas—a gazelle.
Drusilla—watered by the dew.

E

Eglah—chariot.
Elisabeth—a worshipper of God.
Elisheba—God is her oath.
Elizabeth—worshipper of God.
Ephah—darkness.
Ephrath—fruitland.
Esther—a star.
Eunice—conquering well.
Euodias—prosperous journey.
Eve—life.

G

Gomer—completion.

H

Hadassah—Jewish name for Esther.
Hagar—fugitive.
Haggith—dancer.
Hammoleketh—the queen.
Hamutal—kinsman of the dew.
Hannah—gracious.
Hazelelponi—deliverance of the God who regards me.

Helah—sick.
Hephzibah—my delight is in her.
Herodias—heroic.
Hodesh—new moon.
Hodiah—the splendor of Jehovah.
Hoglah—a partridge.
Huldah—weasel.
Hushim—hasten.

I

Iscah—she will look out.

J

Jael—gazelle.
Jecholiah—powerful.
Jecoliah—powerful.
Jedidah—Jehovah's darling.
Jehoaddan—her ornament is Jehovah.
Jehoshabeath—Jehovah is her oath.
Jehosheba—Jehovah is her oath.
Jehudijah—Jehovah's splendor.
Jemima—little dove.
Jerioth—tent curtains.
Jerusha—married.
Jerushah—married.
Jezebel—chaste.
Joanna—the Lord is grace.
Jochebed—Jehovah's glory.
Judith—the praised one.
Julia—curly headed.

K

Keren-happuch—beautifier.
Keturah—incense.
Kezia—cassia.

L

Leah—wearied.
Lois—desirable.
Lo-ruhamah—not pitied.
Lydia—bending.

M

Maachah—depression.
Mahalah—sickness.

Mahlah—sickness.
Mara—bitter.
Martha—mistress of the house.
Mary—bitterness.
Mary Magdalene—bitterness.
Matred—thrusting forward.
Mehetabel—benefited of God.
Merab—increase.
Meshullemeth—retribution.
Michaiah—who is like Jehovah?
Michal—who is like Jehovah?
Milcah—counsel.
Miriam—bitterness.

N
Naamah—sweetness.
Narah—child of the Lord.
Naomi—my joy.
Nehushta—piece of brass.
Noadiah—one to whom the Lord revealed himself.
Noah—comfort.

O
Orpah—a fawn.

P
Peninnah—coral.
Persis—one who takes by storm.
Phanuel—vision of God.
Phebe—pure.
Prisca—worthy.
Priscilla—worthy.
Puah—child bearing.

R
Rachel—ewe.
Rahab—broad.
Rebecca—captivating.
Rebekah—captivating.
Reumah—exalted.
Rhoda—rose.
Rizpah—baking stone.
Ruth—something worth seeing.

S
Salome—peace.
Sapphira—sapphire.
Sara—queen.
Sarah—queen.

Sarai—princess.
Serah—abundance.
Shelomith—peaceful.
Sherah—a female relation by blood.
Shimeath—fame.
Shimrith—keeper.
Shiphrah—prolific.
Shomer—keeper.
Shua—rich.
Susanna—a white lily.
Syntyche—fortunate.

T
Tabitha—gazelle.
Tahpenes—the head of the age.
Tamar—a palm tree.
Taphath—a drop of myrrh.
Thamar—palm tree.
Timna—restraint.
Tirzah—pleasantness.
Tryphena—dainty one.
Tryphosa—dainty one.

V
Vashti—beautiful woman.

Z
Zebudah—a gift.
Zeresh—gold.
Zeruah—leprous.
Zeruiah—balsam from Jehovah.
Zibiah—female gazelle.
Zillah—protection.
Zilpah—meaning unknown.
Zipporah—little bird.

185. Names of Firstborn in the Bible

Abdon—firstborn of Jehiel.
Abiram—firstborn of Hiel.
Amnon—firstborn of David.
Arphaxad—firstborn of Shem.
Asaiah—firstborn of an unknown Shilonite.
Bela—firstborn of Benjamin.
Cain—firstborn of Adam.
Cainan—firstborn of Enos.
Dan—firstborn of Bilhah.
Eber—firstborn of Salah.
Eliab—firstborn of Jesse.
Eliphaz—firstborn of Esau.
Enoch—firstborn of Cain.
Enoch—firstborn of Jared.
Enos—firstborn of Seth.
Ephraim—the Lord said, I am a father to Israel, and Ephraim is my firstborn (Jer. 31:9).
Er—firstborn of Judah.
Esau—firstborn of Isaac.
Gad—firstborn of Zilpah.
Gershom—firstborn of Moses.
Hur—firstborn of Ephratah.
Huz—firstborn of Nahor.
Irad—firstborn of Enoch.
Isaac—firstborn of Sarah.
Ishmael—firstborn of Abram.
Israel—God said that Israel was His firstborn son (Ex. 4:22).
Isshiah—firstborn of Rehabiah.
Jared—firstborn of Mahalaleel.
Jehoram—firstborn of Jehoshaphat.
Jerahmeel—firstborn of Hezron.
Jeriah—firstborn of Hebron.
Jesus—firstborn of Mary. First begotten of the Father.
Jether—firstborn of Gideon.
Jezreel—firstborn of Hosea.
Joel—firstborn of Samuel.
Johanan—firstborn of Josiah.

John—firstborn of Zechariah.
Joseph—firstborn of Rachel.
Lamech—firstborn of Methuselah.
Leah—firstborn of Laban.
Machir—firstborn of Manasseh.
Mahalaleel—firstborn of Cainan.
Manasseh—firstborn of Joseph.
Mattithiah—firstborn of Shallum.
Mehujael—firstborn of Irad.
Merab—firstborn daughter of Saul.
Mesha—firstborn of Caleb.
Methsael—firstborn of Mehujael.
Methuselah—firstborn of Enoch.
Micah—firstborn of Uzziel.
Miriam—firstborn of Amram.
Nadab—firstborn of Aaron.
Nahor—firstborn of Serug.
Nebajoth—firstborn of Ishmael.
Noah—firstborn of Lamech.
Peleg—firstborn of Eber.
Ram—firstborn of Jerahmeel.
Reu—firstborn of Peleg.
Reuben—firstborn of Jacob.
Salah—firstborn of Arphaxad.
Samson—firstborn of Manoah.
Samuel—firstborn of Hannah.
Serug—firstborn of Reu.
Shem—firstborn of Noah.
Shemaiah—firstborn of Obededom.
Sidon—firstborn of Canaan.
Terah—firstborn of Nahor.
Ulam—firstborn of Eshek.
Vashni—firstborn of Samuel.
Zechariah—firstborn of Meshelemiah.
Zidon—firstborn of Canaan.

186. Thirty-nine Names of Jesus

1. Anointed (Ps. 2:2).

2. Alpha and Omega (Rev. 1:11).

3. Branch (Zech. 6:12).
4. Bright and Morning Star (Rev. 22:16).
5. Christ (Matt. 1:16).
6. Dayspring (Luke 1:78).
7. Daystar (2 Pet. 1:19).
8. Door (John 10:9).
9. Everlasting Father (Isa. 9:6).
10. Good Shepherd (John 10:14).
11. Holy One of God (Mark 1:24).
12. I Am (John 8:58).
13. Immanuel (Isa. 7:14).
14. Jesus (Luke 2:21).
15. Jesus of Nazareth (Matt. 26:71).
16. Judge (Acts 10:42).
17. Just (Acts 3:14).
18. King of Kings (Rev. 19:16).
19. Lamb of God (John 1:29).
20. Lion of Judah (Rev. 5:5).
21. Lord (Matt. 7:21).
22. Lord God Almighty (Rev. 4:8).
23. Lord of Lords (Rev. 19:16).
24. Master (John 1:38).
25. Mighty God (Isa. 9:6).
26. Nazarene (Matt. 2:23).
27. Prince of Life (Acts 3:15).
28. Prince of Peace (Isa. 9:6).
29. Potentate (1 Tim. 6:15).
30. Root of David (Rev. 5:5).
31. Root of Jesse (Isa. 11:10).
32. Son of David (Matt. 15:22).
33. Son of God (Matt. 4:3).
34. Son of Joseph (John 1:45).
35. Son of Man (Dan. 7:13).
36. Son of Mary (Mark 6:3).
37. True Vine (John 15:1).
38. Wonderful Counselor (Isa. 9:6).
39. Word (John 1:1).

18

Bible Treasures

What did people use for money during Bible times? What kind of metals did they use? What kind of gemstones did they consider precious? All of these questions are answered by the lists in this chapter. It is also interesting to note that metals of all kinds were precious commodities, especially during Old Testament times.

187. Money Used in the Bible

1. The only actual coin mentioned in the Old Testament is the gold *dram*. "And some of the chief of the fathers, when they came to the house of the Lord which is at Jerusalem, offered freely for the house of God to set it up in his place: they gave after their ability unto the treasure of the work threescore and one thousand *drams* of gold" (Ezra 2:68, 69).
2. Silver and gold were measured in units of weights called shekels, talents, and pounds in Old Testament times. "And Abraham hearkened unto Ephron; and Abraham *weighed* to Ephron the silver, which he had named in the audience of the sons of Heth, four hundred shekels of silver, current money with the merchant" (Gen. 23:16).
3. In the New Testament, several coins are mentioned. The Jews made their own silver shekel coins for the first time about A.D. 66. In the meantime, Roman and Greek coinage was used. The smallest coin in value was the *mite* that Jesus saw the widow give into the temple treasury (Luke 21:2).
4. Jesus said, "Agree with thine adversary quickly, whiles thou art in the way with him; lest at any time the adversary deliver thee to the judge, and the judge deliver thee to the officer, and thou be cast into prison. Verily I say unto thee,

Thou shalt by no means come out thence, till thou hast paid the uttermost *farthing*" (Matt. 5:25, 26).

5. For the kingdom of heaven is like unto a man that is an householder, which went out early in the morning to hire labourers into his vineyard. And when he had agreed with the labourers for a *penny* a day, he sent them into his vineyard (Matt. 20:1, 2).

6. By New Testament times, there was a monetary unit known as the pound. "A certain nobleman went into a far country to receive for himself a kingdom, and to return. And he called his ten servants, and delivered them ten *pounds*" (Luke 19:12, 13).

7. There was also a monetary unit in New Testament times known as the talent. It is mentioned in a parable which is the same as the one mentioned above in Luke. "For the kingdom of heaven is as a man travelling into a far country, who called his own servants, and delivered unto them his goods. And unto one he gave five *talents*, to another two, and to another one" (Matt. 25:14, 15).

188. Eight Metals Mentioned in the Bible

1. Gold is the first metal mentioned in the Bible: " . . . the whole land of Havilah, where there is *gold*; and the *gold* of that land is good" (Gen. 2:11, 12).

2. Tubal-cain [was] an instructer of every artificer of *brass* and *iron* (Gen. 4:22).

3. Abram was very rich in cattle, in *silver*, and in *gold* (Gen. 13:2).

4. And Eleazar the priest said unto the men of war which went to the battle, This is the ordinance of the law which the Lord commanded Moses; only the *gold*, and the *silver*, the *brass*, the *iron*, the *tin*, and the *lead*, everything that may abide the fire, ye shall make it go through the fire, and it shall be clean (Num. 31:21-23).

5. King David sang a psalm which included this sentence, "He teacheth my hands to war; so that a bow of *steel* is broken by mine arms" (2 Sam. 22:35).

6. Ezra inventoried "two vessels of fine *copper*, precious as *gold*" (Ezra 8:27).

189. Precious Stones Mentioned in the Bible

1. The breastplate of the high priest contained "even four rows of stones: the first row shall be a *sardius*, a *topaz*, and a *carbuncle* . . . the second row shall be an *emerald*, a *sapphire*, and a *diamond*. And the third row a *ligure*, an *agate*, and an *amethyst*. And the fourth row a *beryl*, and an *onyx*, and a *jasper*: they shall be set in gold in their inclosings" (Ex. 28:17-20).

2. Job said of wisdom that "the gold and *crystal* cannot equal it: the exchange of it shall not be for jewels of fine gold. No mention shall be made of *coral*, or of *pearls*: for the price of wisdom is above *rubies*" (Job 28:17, 18).

3. The twelve foundations of the wall of the New Jerusalem "were garnished with all manner of precious stones. The first foundation was *jasper*; the second, *sapphire*; the third, a *chalcedony*; the fourth, an *emerald*; the fifth, *sardonyx*; the sixth, *sardius*; the seventh, *chrysolyte*; the eighth, *beryl*; the ninth, a *topaz*; the tenth, a *chrysoprasus*; the eleventh, a *jacinth*; the twelfth, an *amethyst*" (Rev. 21:19, 20).

19

Ships and Other Floating Objects

Ever since Noah built the Ark, men have been going down to sea in ships. The first mention of ships in the Bible is in Genesis and the last mention is in Revelation. There have been many strange tales of things that have happened at sea. This chapter highlights the accounts of the normal, strange, and wonderful accounts of floating things in the Bible.

190. The Only Ferry Boat in the Bible

And Shimei . . . came down with the men of Judah to meet king David . . . and they went over Jordan before the king. And there went over a ferry boat to carry over the king's household (2 Sam. 19:16-18).

191. A Lifeboat That Was Discarded the Night Before It Was Needed

And as the shipmen were about to flee out of the ship, when they had let down the boat into the sea, under colour as though they would have cast anchors out of the foreship, Paul said to the centurion and to the soldiers, Except these abide in the ship, ye cannot be saved. Then the soldiers cut off the ropes of the boat, and let her fall off. And when it was day, (the ship ran aground, and) the hinder part was broken with the violence of the waves. . . . They which could swim . . . cast themselves . . . into the sea and (got) to land: and the rest, some on boards, and some on broken pieces of the ship. And so it came to pass, that they escaped all safe to land (Acts 27:30, 31, 32, 39, 41, 43, 44).

192. The Only Ship Designed by God and Built by a Man

And God said unto Noah, . . . Make thee an ark of gopher wood; rooms shalt thou make in the ark, and shalt pitch it within and without with pitch. And this is the fashion which thou shalt make it of: The length of the ark shall be three hundred cubits, the breadth of it fifty cubits, and the height of it thirty cubits. A window shalt thou make to the ark, and in a cubit shalt thou finish it above; and the door of the ark shalt thou set in the side thereof; with lower, second, and third stories shalt thou make it. Thus did Noah; according to all that God commanded him, so did he (Gen. 6:13-16, 22).

193. A Cradle Built Purposely to Float

When the mother of the baby Moses could no longer hide him from the Egyptians, "she took for him an ark of bulrushes, and daubed it with slime and with pitch, and put the child therein; and she laid it in the flags by the river's brink." When the daughter of Pharaoh "saw the ark among the flags, she sent her maid to fetch it." Pharaoh's daughter paid Moses' mother to nurse Moses. And when "the child grew, . . . she brought him unto Pharaoh's daughter, and he became her son. And she called his name Moses: and she said, Because I drew him out of the water" (Ex. 2:3, 5, 9, 10).

194. The Navy That Was Destroyed

Jehoshaphat king of Judah (joined) himself with Ahaziah king of Israel, who did very wickedly: and he joined himself with him to make ships to go to Tarshish: and they made the ships in Eziongeber. Then Eliezer the son of Dodavah of Mareshah prophesied against Jehoshaphat, saying, Because thou hast joined thyself with Ahaziah, the Lord hath broken thy works. And the ships were broken, that they were not able to go to Tarshish (2 Chron. 20:35-37).

195. The Ship That Was Saved by Throwing a Man Overboard

Then they said unto [Jonah], What shall we do unto thee,

that the sea may be calm unto us? for the sea wrought, and was tempestuous. And he said unto them, Take me up, and cast me forth into the sea; so shall the sea be calm unto you: for I know that for my sake this great tempest is upon you. . . . So they took up Jonah, and cast him forth into the sea: and the sea ceased from her raging. Then the men feared the Lord exceedingly, and offered a sacrifice unto the Lord, and made vows (Jonah 1:11, 12, 15, 16).

196. The King Who Had Two Navies

1. King Solomon made a navy of ships in Eziongeber, which is beside Eloth, on the shore of the Red sea, in the land of Edom. And Hiram sent in the navy his servants, shipmen that had knowledge of the sea, with the servants of Solomon. And they came to Ophir, and fetched from thence gold, four hundred and twenty talents, and brought it to king Solomon (1 Kings 9:26-28).
2. King Solomon "had at sea a navy of Tharshish with the navy of Hiram: once in three years came the navy of Tharshish, bringing gold, and silver, ivory, and apes, and peacocks" (1 Kings 10:22).

197. The Most Elaborate Description of Shipbuilding in the Bible

The ships of Tyrus were made "of fir trees of Senir: they have taken cedars from Lebanon to make masts for thee. Of the oaks of Bashan have they made thine oars: the company of the Ashurites have made thy benches of ivory, brought out of the isles of Chittim. Fine linen with broidered work from Egypt was that which thou spreadest forth to be thy sail; blue and purple from the isles of Elishah was that which covered thee. The inhabitants of Zidon and Arvad were thy mariners: thy wise men, O Tyrus, that were in thee, were thy pilots. The ancients of Gebal and the wise men thereof were in thee thy calkers: all the ships of the sea with their mariners were in thee to occupy thy merchandise" (Ezek. 27:5-9).

198. A Trip on a Slow Boat to a Desert Place

And they departed into a desert place by ship privately. And the people saw them [Jesus and His disciples] departing, and many knew him, and ran afoot thither out of all cities, and outwent them, and came together unto him (Mark 6:32, 33).

199. Two Ships That Jesus Saved from Storms

1. And straightway Jesus constrained his disciples to get into a ship, and to go before him unto the other side, while he sent the multitudes away. And when he had sent the multitudes away, he went up into a mountain apart to pray: and when the evening was come, he was there alone. But the ship was now in the midst of the sea, tossed with waves: for the wind was contrary. [Jesus then walked out to the ship on the water. And when Jesus got] into the ship, the wind ceased (Matt. 14:22-24, 32).
2. Now it came to pass on a certain day, that he [Jesus] went into a ship with his disciples: and he said unto them, Let us go over unto the other side of the lake. And they launched forth. But as they sailed, he fell asleep: and there came down a storm of wind on the lake; and they were filled with water, and were in jeopardy. And they came to him, and awoke him, saying, Master, Master, we perish. Then he arose, and rebuked the wind and the raging of the water: and they ceased, and there was a calm (Luke 8:22-24).

200. The Only Ship in the Bible Called by Name

After being on Melita for three months, Paul "departed in a ship of Alexandria which had wintered in the isle, whose sign was Castor and Pollux" (Acts 28:11).

201. The Signal That Shall Sound the Destruction for One-third of the Ships at Sea

And the second angel sounded [his trumpet], and as it were a great mountain burning with fire was cast into the sea . . . and the third part of the ships were destroyed (Rev. 8:8, 9).

202. The Oddest Boat Construction Material in the Bible

Woe to the land shadowing with wings, which is beyond the

rivers of Ethiopia: that sendeth ambassadors by the sea, even in vessels of bulrushes upon the waters (Isa. 18:1, 2).

Jesus Preaching at the Sea of Galilee

203. The Ship That Was Used for a Pulpit

Jesus "entered into one of the ships, which was Simon's, and prayed him that he would thrust out a little from the land. And he sat down, and taught the people out of the ship" (Luke 5:3).

204. Five Facts Gleaned from a Shipwreck

1. *The ship's origin*: At Myra, a city of Lycia, "the centurion found a ship of Alexandria sailing into Italy; and he put us [Paul and Luke] therein" (Acts 27:5, 6).
2. *The ship's motive force*: And when the ship was caught, and could not bear up into the wind, we let her drive. And running under a certain island which is called Clauda, we had much work to come by the boat: which when they had taken up, they used helps, undergirding the ship; and fearing lest they should fall into the quicksands, strake sail, and so were driven (Acts 27:15-17).
3. *The number of passengers*: And we were in all in the ship two hundred threescore and sixteen souls (Acts 27:37).
4. *The non-human cargo*: And when they had eaten enough, they lightened the ship, and cast out the wheat into the sea (Acts 27:38).
5. *The location of the shipwreck*: And when they had escaped [from the shipwreck], then they knew that the island was called Melita (Acts 28:1).

205. Ships of War

1. Balaam the son of Beor prophesied, "Ships shall come from the coast of Chittim, and shall afflict Asshur, and shall afflict Eber, and he shall perish forever" (Num. 24:24).
2. A vile person in the last days "shall come in peaceably, and obtain the kingdom by flatteries. . . . The ships of Chittim shall come against him: therefore he shall be grieved. . . . And at the time of the end shall the king of the south push at him: and the king of the north shall come against him like a whirlwind, with chariots, and with horsemen, and with many ships" (Dan. 11:21, 30, 40).

206. A Fishing Fleet

Jesus "said unto Simon, Launch out into the deep, and let down your nets for a draught. And Simon answering said unto him, Master, we have toiled all the night, and have taken nothing: nevertheless at thy word I will let down the net. And when they had this done, they inclosed a great multitude of fishes: and their net brake. And they beckoned unto their partners, which were in the other ship, that they should come and help them. And they came, and filled both the ships, so that they began to sink. . . . James and John the sons of Zebedee . . . were partners with Simon" (Luke 5:4-7, 10).

207. Timber Also Floats

Hiram sent to Solomon, saying, I have considered the things which thou sentest to me for: and I will do all thy desire concerning timber of cedar, and concerning timber of fir. My servants shall bring them down from Lebanon unto the sea: and I will convey them by sea in floats unto the place that thou shalt appoint me (1 Kings 5:8, 9).

208. Two Final Thoughts About Ships

1. In Zion, "the glorious Lord will be unto us a place of broad rivers and streams; wherein shall go no galley with oars, neither shall gallant ship pass by" (Isa. 33:21).
2. Behold also the ships, which though they be so great, and are driven of fierce winds, yet are they turned about with a very small helm, withersoever the governor listeth (James 3:4).

20

Other Things

"What else is listed in the Bible?" you may be asking.

I can't list them all, but here are some examples: Eighteen Descriptions of the Kingdom of Heaven, The Twenty-eight Seasons, Eight Things That Are Worthy to Think Upon, Four Things That Are Never Satisfied, Four Things That Are Too Wonderful, Four Things the Earth Cannot Bear, Four Creatures Which Are Exceedingly Wise, Four Things Which Are Comely in Moving About, Forty-three Things That God Hates, Musical Instruments Mentioned in the Bible, Tools of Bible People, and Bible Foods.

209. Eighteen Descriptions of the Kingdom of Heaven

1. The kingdom of heaven is like a field sown with good seed and bad (Matt. 13:24-30).
2. The kingdom of heaven is like a grain of mustard seed (Matt. 13:31).
3. The kingdom of heaven is like leaven hid in meal until the whole is leavened (Matt. 13:33).
4. The kingdom of heaven is like a treasure hid in a field (Matt. 13:44).
5. The kingdom of heaven is like a merchant, seeking goodly pearls (Matt. 13:45, 46).
6. The kingdom of heaven is like a fishnet that gathers of every kind (Matt. 13:47-50).
7. Whosoever will humble himself as this little child, the same is greatest in the kingdom of heaven (Matt. 18:4).
8. The kingdom of heaven is like a king who would take account of his servants (Matt. 18:23-35).
9. A rich man shall hardly enter into the kingdom of heaven (Matt. 19:23-26).

10. The kingdom of heaven is like a householder who hired laborers for his vineyard and then paid each a day's wages even if they didn't work a full day (Matt. 20:1-16).
11. The kingdom of heaven is like a king who made a wedding feast for his son, and sent forth his servants to call them that were bidden to the wedding: and they would not come (Matt. 22:1-14).
12. The kingdom of heaven shall be likened unto ten virgins, which took their lamps, and went forth to meet the bridegroom. And five of them were wise, and five were foolish (Matt. 25:1-13).
13. The kingdom of heaven is as a man travelling into a far country, who called his own servants, and delivered unto them his goods (Matt. 25:14-30).
14. So is the kingdom of God, as if a man should cast seed into the ground; and should sleep, and rise night and day, and the seed should spring and grow up (Mark 4:26-29).
15. The kingdom of God cometh not with observation; . . . the kingdom of God is within you (Luke 17:20, 21).
16. The kingdom of God is not meat and drink; but is righteousness, peace, and joy in the Holy Ghost (Rom. 14:17).
17. The kingdom of God is not in word but in power (1 Cor. 4:20).
18. The kingdom of our Lord is everlasting (2 Pet. 1:11).

210. The Twenty-eight Seasons

1. To everything there is a season. There is a time to be born (Eccles. 3:1, 2).
2. There is a time to die (Eccles. 3:2).
3. There is a time to plant (Eccles. 3:2).
4. There is a time to pluck up that which has been planted (Eccles. 3:2).
5. There is a time to kill (Eccles. 3:3).
6. There is a time to heal (Eccles. 3:3).
7. There is a time to break down (Eccles. 3:3).
8. There is a time to build up (Eccles. 3:3).
9. There is a time to weep (Eccles. 3:4).
10. There is a time to laugh (Eccles. 3:4).
11. There is a time to mourn (Eccles. 3:4).
12. There is a time to dance (Eccles. 3:4).
13. There is a time to cast away stones (Eccles. 3:5).

14. There is a time to gather stones together (Eccles. 3:5).
15. There is a time to embrace (Eccles. 3:5).
16. There is a time to refrain from embracing (Eccles. 3:5).
17. There is a time to get (Eccles. 3:6).
18. There is a time to lose (Eccles. 3:6).
19. There is a time to keep (Eccles. 3:6).
20. There is a time to cast away (Eccles. 3:6).
21. There is a time to rend (Eccles. 3:7).
22. There is a time to sew (Eccles. 3:7).
23. There is a time to keep silence (Eccles. 3:7).
24. There is a time to speak (Eccles. 3:7).
25. There is a time to love (Eccles. 3:8).
26. There is a time to hate (Eccles. 3:8).
27. There is a time of war (Eccles. 3:8).
28. There is a time of peace (Eccles. 3:8).

211. Eight Things That Are Worthy to Think Upon

1. Think on whatsoever things that are true (Phil. 4:8).
2. Think on whatsoever things that are honest (Phil. 4:8).
3. Think on whatsoever things that are just (Phil. 4:8).
4. Think on whatsoever things that are pure (Phil. 4:8).
5. Think on whatsoever things that are lovely (Phil. 4:8).
6. Think on whatsoever things that are of good report (Phil. 4:8).
7. Think on virtue (Phil. 4:8).
8. Think on praise (Phil. 4:8).

212. Four Things That Are Never Satisfied

1. The grave never says, "It is enough" (Prov. 30:15, 16).
2. The barren womb never says, "It is enough" (Prov. 30:15, 16).
3. The earth that is not filled with water never says, "It is enough" (Prov. 30:15, 16).
4. The fire never says, "It is enough" (Prov. 30:15, 16).

213. Four Things That Are Too Wonderful

1. "The way of an eagle in the air is too wonderful to me," said Agur the son of Jakeh (Prov. 31:1, 18, 19).

2. The way of a serpent upon a rock is too wonderful and hard to know (Prov. 30:18, 19).
3. The way of a ship in the midst of the sea is too wonderful and hard to know (Prov. 30:18, 19).
4. The way of a man with a maid is too wonderful and hard to know (Prov. 30:18, 19).

214. Four Things the Earth Cannot Bear

1. The earth cannot bear when a servant reigns (Prov. 30:21, 22).
2. The earth cannot bear a fool when he is filled with meat (Prov. 30:21, 22).
3. The earth cannot bear an odious woman when she is married (Prov. 30:21, 23).
4. The earth cannot bear a handmaid that is heir to her mistress (Prov. 30:21, 23).

215. Four Little Creatures Which Are Exceedingly Wise

1. Ants prepare their food in the summer (Prov. 30:24, 25).
2. Conies make their houses in the rocks (Prov. 30:24, 26).
3. Locusts go forth in bands although they have no leader (Prov. 30:24, 27).
4. Spiders work with their hands and live in kings' palaces (Prov. 30:24, 28).

216. Four Things Which Are Comely in Moving About

1. A lion turns not away for any (Prov. 30:29, 30).
2. A greyhound is comely in going (Prov. 30:29, 31).
3. A he goat is comely in going (Prov. 30:29, 31).
4. A king, against whom there is no rising up, is comely in going (Prov. 30:29, 31).

217. Successful and Attempted Stonings in the Bible

1. And all the congregation brought [the man that gathered sticks upon the sabbath] without the camp, and stoned him

with stones, and he died (Num. 15:36).

2. And all Israel stoned [Achan and his family and possessions] with stones, and burned them with fire (Josh. 7:24, 25).

3. The Lord cast down great stones from heaven upon them. . . . They were more which died with hailstones than they whom the children of Israel slew with the sword (Josh. 10:11).

4. And David put his hand in his bag, and took thence a stone, and slang it, and smote the Philistine in his forehead, that the stone sunk into his forehead; and he fell upon his face to the earth (1 Sam. 17:49).

5. David was greatly distressed; for the people spake of stoning him (1 Sam. 30:6).

6. [Shimei] cast stones at David, and at all the servants of king David (2 Sam. 16:5, 6).

7. All Israel stoned [Adoram] with stones, that he died (1 Kings 12:18).

8. They carried [Naboth] forth out of the city, and stoned him with stones, that he died (1 Kings 21:13).

9. And they conspired against [Zechariah], and stoned him with stones at the commandment of the king in the court of the house of the Lord (2 Chron. 24:20-22).

10. And the husbandmen took [the householder's] servants, and beat one, and killed another, and stoned another (Matt. 21:35).

11. The scribes and Pharisees intended to stone the woman caught in adultery (John 8:3-11).

12. They took up stones to cast at him: but Jesus hid himself, and went out of the temple, going through the midst of them, and so passed by (John 8:59).

13. The Jews took up stones again to stone [Jesus]. But he escaped out of their hand (John 10:31, 39).

14. They stoned Stephen, calling upon God, and saying, Lord Jesus, receive my spirit (Acts 7:59).

15. When there was an assault made both of the Gentiles, and also of the Jews with their rulers, to use [Paul and Barnabas] despitefully, and to stone them, they were aware of it and fled into Lystra and Derbe (Acts 14:5, 6).

16. There came thither certain Jews from Antioch and Iconium, who persuaded the people, and, having stoned Paul, drew him out of the city, supposing him to be dead (Acts 14:19).

268

218. Forty-three Things That God Hates

1. God hates homosexual acts (Lev. 18:22).
2. God hates sexual acts between humans and animals (Lev. 18:23).
3. God hates idols and even the precious metals and other materials which have been used in making idols (Deut. 7:25).
4. God hates blemished sacrifices (Deut. 17:1).
5. God hates the worship of the sun, moon, or stars (Deut. 17:3, 4).
6. God hates divination (Deut. 18:10).
7. God hates astrology (Deut. 18:10).
8. God hates enchanters (Deut. 18:10).
9. God hates witches (Deut. 18:10).
10. God hates charmers (Deut. 18:11).
11. God hates wizards (Deut. 18:11).
12. God hates necromancers (Deut. 18:11).
13. God hates the wearing of clothing of the opposite sex (Deut. 22:5).
14. God hates and will not accept as an offering the hire of a whore (Deut. 23:18).
15. God hates remarriage to a former wife after she has been married to another man (Deut. 24:4).
16. God hates scales that are falsely calibrated to cheat the customer (Deut. 25:13-16).
17. God hates the workers of iniquity (Ps. 5:5).
18. God hates the wicked (Ps. 11:5).
19. God hates those who love violence (Ps. 11:5).
20. God hates the froward (Prov. 3:32).
21. God hates a proud look (Prov. 6:16, 17).
22. God hates a lying tongue (Prov. 6:17).
23. God hates hands that shed innocent blood (Prov. 6:17).
24. God hates a heart that devises wicked imaginations (Prov. 6:18).
25. God hates feet that are swift in running to mischief (Prov. 6:18).
26. God hates a false witness who speaks lies (Prov. 6:19).
27. God hates anyone who sows discord among brethren (Prov. 6:19).
28. God hates lying lips (Prov. 12:22).
29. God hates the sacrifices of the wicked (Prov. 15:8).
30. God hates the ways of the wicked (Prov. 15:9).

31. God hates the thoughts of the wicked (Prov. 15:26).
32. God hates the proud in heart (Prov. 16:5).
33. God hates those who justify the wicked (Prov. 17:15).
34. God hates those who condemn the just (Prov. 17:15).
35. God hates vain sacrifices (Isa. 1:13).
36. God hated the feasts of the new moon celebrated by the Hebrews during the days of Isaiah (Isa. 1:14).
37. God hates robbery for burnt offering (Isa. 61:8).
38. God hates idolatry (Jer. 44:2-4).
39. God hates evil plans against neighbors (Zech. 8:17).
40. God hates false oaths (Zech. 8:17).
41. God hated Esau (Mal. 1:1-3; Rom. 9:13).
42. God hates divorce (Mal. 2:14-16).
43. God hates the deeds of the Nicolaitanes (Rev. 2:6).

219. Important Doors and Gates in the Bible

1. God shut the door of Noah's ark (Gen. 7:16).
2. The two angels at Lot's house blinded the mob, "so that they wearied themselves to find the door" (Gen. 19:11).
3. At the first Passover, the Israelites were to apply lamb's blood on the side posts and the upper door posts of their houses (Ex. 12:7).
4. Aaron and his sons were to be washed at the door of the tabernacle (Ex. 29:4).
5. The burnt offering was to be at the door of the tabernacle (Ex. 29:42).
6. God's words were to be written "upon the door posts of thine house, and upon thy gates" (Deut. 11:20).
7. Samson removed the doors from the gate of Gaza to a hill at Hebrom (Judges 16:3).
8. Uriah slept at the door of the king's house, rather than go to his wife (2 Sam. 11:9).
9. A lord of the king of Samaria, as prophesied by Elisha, was trampled in the gate of the city (2 Kings 7:17).
10. Hezekiah removed the gold from the doors of the temple and gave it to the king of Assyria (2 Kings 18:16).
11. The sheep gate was the gate of Jerusalem rebuilt under Nehemiah's leadership (Neh. 3:1).
12. Mordecai sat in the king's gate (Esther 2:19).
13. God spoke to Job of the gates of death (Job 38:17).

14. David wrote of everlasting doors (Ps. 24:7).
15. God opened the doors of heaven (Ps. 78:23).
16. David wrote, "The Lord loveth the gate of Zion" (Ps. 87:2).
17. David asked God to open the gates of righteousness (Ps. 118:19).
18. David said the righteous enter the gate of the Lord (Ps. 118:20).
19. David desired God to keep the "door of my lips" (Ps. 141:3).
20. We are warned to stay away from the door of the house of the strange woman (Prov. 5:8).
21. Wisdom "crieth at the gates" (Prov. 8:3).
22. Zion's gates shall be called Praise (Isa. 60:18).
23. Jeremiah said the gates of Zion had sunk into the ground (Lam. 2:9).
24. Ezekiel measured the doors and gates of the house of Israel and the temple (Ezek. 40, 41).
25. The angel of the Lord rolled back the stone from the door of Jesus' tomb (Matt. 28:2).
26. Enter ye in at the strait gate: for wide is the gate, and broad is the way, that leadeth to destruction, and many there be which go in thereat: because strait is the gate, and narrow is the way, which leadeth unto life, and few there be that find it (Matt. 7:13, 14).
27. Upon this rock will I [Jesus] build my church; and the gates of hell shall not prevail against it (Matt. 16:18).
28. Jesus said, "I am the door: by me if any man enter in, he shall be saved" (John 10:9).
29. Peter and John healed a lame man at the gate Beautiful of the temple (Acts 3:2-7).
30. An angel opened the prison doors and released the apostles (Acts 5:19).
31. The iron gate "opened to them of his own accord" as the angel led Peter out of prison (Acts 12:10).
32. Paul recounted how God had "opened the door of faith to the Gentiles" (Acts 14:27).
33. All the prison doors were opened in the earthquake in Philippi (Acts 16:26).
34. Jesus suffered "without the gate" (Heb. 13:12).
35. Jesus said to the church in Philadelphia, "I have set before thee an open door, and no man can shut it" (Rev. 3:8).
36. Jesus said to the Laodiceans, "Behold, I stand at the door and knock: if any man hear my voice, and open the door, I

will come in to him . . . " (Rev. 3:20).

37. John "looked, and behold, a door was opened in heaven" (Rev. 4:1).
38. The new Jerusalem had 12 gates, each a pearl, with twelve angels. Each gate bore the name of a tribe of Israel, and was never shut (Rev. 21:12, 21, 25).
39. Blessed are they that do his commandments, that they may have right to the tree of life, and may enter in through the gates into the city (Rev. 22:14).

Jephtha Met by His Daughter

220. Musical Instruments Mentioned in the Bible

1. The organ was among the first musical instruments invented by Jubal (Gen. 4:21).

2. Rams' horns were blown by seven priests when they marched around Jericho (Josh. 6:4).
3. The women came out of all of the cities of Israel to meet David and King Saul with singing, dancing, tabrets, and other musical instruments (1 Sam. 18:5, 6).
4. Asaph played the cymbals when King David brought the ark to Jerusalem (1 Chron. 16:1-5).
5. Benaiah and Jahaziel the priests played trumpets while the ark was being brought to Jerusalem (1 Chron. 16:6).
6. Job spoke of the timbrel, harp, and organ (Job 21:12).
7. The word neginoth means stringed instruments. Many of the psalms had instructions in their titles to play the psalm on neginoth or stringed instruments (Psalm 4 title).
8. The signal to worship King Nebuchadnezzar's golden image was the playing of the cornet, flute, harp, sackbut, psaltery, and the dulcimer (Dan. 3:1-7).
9. Amos complained about those who were "at ease in Zion" . . . who "chant to the sound of the viol" (Amos 6:1, 5).
10. Pipers are mentioned in Revelation (Rev. 18:22).

221. Tools of Bible People

1. Zipporah took a *sharp stone*, and cut off the foreskin of her son (Ex. 4:25).
2. The Hebrew women used *kneading troughs* to knead their bread (Ex. 12:34).
3. If a slave preferred to remain with his master rather than be freed, "his master shall bore his ear through with an *awl*" (Ex. 21:6).
4. Moses was instructed to make *ash pans*, *shovels*, *fleshhooks*, and *firepans* to be used with the altar in the tabernacle (Ex. 27:3).
5. Aaron fashioned the golden calf with a *graving tool* (Ex. 32:4).
6. *Snuffers* were made as accessories to the lamps in the tabernacle (Ex. 37:23).
7. The Israelites went down to the Philistines, to sharpen every man his *share*, and his *coulter*, and his *ax*, and his *mattock*. Yet they had a *file* for the *mattocks*, and for the *coulters*, and for the *forks*, and for the *axes*, and to sharpen the *goads* (1 Sam. 13:20, 21).

8. Joab fought against the city Rabbah. The prisoners taken in this battle were forced to work with *iron harrows* (2 Sam. 12:26, 31).
9. The stones in Solomon's house were "sawed with *saws*, within and without" (1 Kings 7:8, 9).
10. The prophets of Baal cut themselves with *knives* and *lancets* till the blood gushed out upon them (1 Kings 18:28).
11. Job said, "My days are swifter than a *weaver's shuttle*" (Job 7:6).
12. The Lord asked Job if he could fill leviathan's head with *fish spears* (Job 41:7).
13. One of the shepherd's main tools was his *staff* (Ps. 23:4).
14. As the *fining pot* for silver, and the *furnace* for gold; so is a man to his praise (Prov. 27:21).
15. Solomon wrote, "Though thou shouldest bray a fool in a *mortar* among wheat with a *pestle*, yet will not his foolishness depart from him" (Prov. 27:22).
16. The carpenter encouraged the goldsmith, and he that smootheth with the *hammer* him that smote the *anvil*, saying, It is ready for the sodering (Isa. 41:7).
17. The Lord said that He would make Israel to be "a new *sharp threshing instrument having teeth*" (Isa. 41:14, 15).
18. The smith with the *tongs* both worketh in the coals, and fashioneth it with *hammers* (Isa. 44:12).
19. The carpenter stretcheth out his *rule*; he marketh it out with a *line*; he fitteth it with *planes*, and he marketh it out with the *compass* (Isa. 44:13).
20. The *balance* was used to weigh gold and silver (Isa. 46:6).
21. *Millstones* were used to grind meal (Isa. 47:2).
22. The *yoke* was used for carrying things (Isa. 47:6).
23. Jeremiah "went down to the potter's house, and, behold, he wrought a work on the *wheels*" (Jer. 18:3).
24. God told Ezekiel to shave his head and beard with a *barber's razor* (Ezek. 5:1).
25. Ezekiel had a vision wherein he saw an angel measure the temple with a *measuring reed* (Ezek. 40:1-5).
26. Joel prophesied and said, "Beat your *plowshares* into swords, and your *pruning hooks* into spears" (Joel 3:10).
27. Joel also said, "Put ye in the *sickle*, for the harvest is ripe" (Joel 3:13).
28. The prophet Amos spoke of *hooks* and *fishhooks* (Amos 4:2).

29. Amos saw a vision of the Lord with a *plumbline* in His hand (Amos 7:7).
30. A *fan* was used in threshing wheat (Matt. 3:12).
31. Jesus said, "It is easier for a camel to go through a *needle's* eye, than for a rich man to enter the kingdom of God" (Luke 18:25).

222. Bible Foods

1. Jacob traded bread and pottage of lentiles to Esau for Esau's birthright (Gen. 25:29-34).
2. Isaac liked venison, and Rebekah cooked him some young goats (Gen. 27:1-10).
3. Pharaoh had a baker who baked pastries (bakemeats) for him (Gen. 40:16, 17).
4. The Passover meal was comprised of a cooked lamb, bitter herbs, and unleavened bread (Ex. 12:3-10).
5. Gideon fixed a meal for an angel. The meal included a pot of broth (Judges 6:19).
6. Abigail supplied David and his men with two hundred loaves, two bottles of wine, five ready dressed sheep, five measures of parched corn, a hundred clusters of raisins, and two hundred cakes of figs (1 Sam. 25:18-20).
7. During the time that Eli was high priest, the Israelites boiled their meat (1 Sam. 2:12-17).
8. When King David fled from Absalom, various people "brought . . . wheat, and barley, and flour, and parched corn, and beans, and lentiles, and parched pulse, and honey, and butter, and sheep, and cheese of kine, for David, and for the people that were with him, to eat" (2 Sam. 17:27-29).
9. Daniel, Hananiah, Mishael, and Azariah preferred to eat pulse and drink water rather than eat the king's meat and drink his wine (Dan. 1:3-16).
10. Jesus fed the multitude with fish and barley bread (John 6:9-14).

NOTE: For additional edible plants and animals, see the lists of trees and plants, and animals of the Bible.

223. Trials Before the Courts and Councils

1. Moses sat to judge the people: and the people stood by Moses from the morning unto the evening. And when Moses' father

in law saw all that he did to the people, he said, What is this thing that thou doest to the people? ... And Moses said, ... The people come unto me to enquire of God ... and I judge between one and another, and I do make them know the statutes of God and his laws. And Moses' father in law said, ... Thou wilt surely wear away, both thou, and this people that is with thee: for this thing is too heavy for thee; thou are not able to perform it ... alone. Hearken now unto my voice. ... Be thou for the people to Godward, that thou mayest bring the causes to God: and ... provide out of all the people able men ... and place ... them to be rulers of thousands, and rulers of hundreds, rulers of fifties, and rulers of tens. And let them judge the people at all seasons: and it shall be, that every great matter they shall bring unto thee, but every small matter they shall judge. ... So Moses hearkened to the voice of his father in law, and did all that he had said (Ex. 18:13-19, 20-22, 24).

2. The son of an Israelitish woman, whose father was an Egyptian, went out among the children of Israel: and ... [he] and a man of Israel strove together in the camp; and the Israelitish woman's son blasphemed the name of the Lord, and cursed. And they brought him to Moses: ... And they put him in ward, that the mind of the Lord might be shewed them. And the Lord spoke unto Moses, saying, Bring forth him that hath cursed without the camp; and let all that heard him lay their hands upon his head, and let all the congregation stone him. ... And Moses spake to the children of Israel, ... and the children of Moses did as the Lord commanded Moses (Lev. 24:10-14, 23).

3. These be ... words which Moses spake unto all Israel. ... I charged your judges ... saying, Hear the causes between your brethren, and judge righteously between every man and his brother, and the stranger that is with him. Ye shall not respect persons in judgment; but ye shall hear the small as well as the great; ye shall not be afraid of the face of man; for the judgment is God's: and the cause that is too hard for you, bring it unto me, and I will hear it (Deut. 1:1, 16, 17).

4. At the mouth of two witnesses, or three witnesses, shall he that is worthy of death be put to death; but at the mouth of one witness he shall not be put to death (Deut. 17:6).

5. Jesus said, "Behold, I send you forth as sheep in the midst of wolves: be ye therefore wise as serpents, and harmless as

doves. But beware of men: for they will deliver you up to the councils, and they will scourge you in their synagogues; and ye shall be brought before governors and kings for my sake, for a testimony against them and the Gentiles. But when they deliver you up, take no thought how or what ye shall speak: for it shall be given you in that same hour what ye shall speak. For it is not ye that speak, but the Spirit of your Father which speaketh in you" (Matt. 10:16-20).

6. And they that had laid hold on Jesus led him away to Caiaphas the high priest, where the scribes and the elders were assembled. . . . Now the chief priests, and elders, and all the council, sought false witness against Jesus, to put him to death; but found none: yea, though many false witnesses came, yet found they none. At last came two false witnesses, and said, This fellow said, I am able to destroy the temple of God, and to build it in three days. And the high priest arose, and said unto him, Answerest thou nothing? what is it which these witness against Thee? But Jesus held his peace. And the high priest . . . said unto him, I adjure thee by the living God, that thou tell us whether thou be the Christ, the Son of God. Jesus saith unto him, Thou hast said: nevertheless I say unto you, Hereafter shall ye see the Son of man sitting on the right hand of power, and coming in the clouds of heaven. Then the high priest rent his clothes, saying, He hath spoken blasphemy: what further need have we of witnesses? behold, now ye have hard his blasphemy. What think ye? They answered and said, He is guilty of death (Matt. 26:57, 59-66).

7. And the whole multitude of them arose, and led him unto Pilate. And they began to accuse him, saying, We found this fellow perverting the nation, and forbidding to give tribute to Caesar, saying that he himself is Christ a King. And Pilate asked Him, saying, Art thou the King of the Jews? And he answered him and said, Thou sayest it. Then said Pilate to the chief priests and to the people, I find no fault in this man. And they were the more fierce, saying, He stirreth up the people, teaching throughout all Jewry, beginning from Galilee to this place. When Pilate heard of Galilee, he asked whether the man were a Galilean. And as soon as he knew that he belonged unto Herod's jurisdiction, he sent him to Herod, who himself also was at Jerusalem at that time. And . . . Herod . . . . questioned [Jesus] in many words; but he answered him nothing. And the chief priests and scribes

stood and vehemently accused him. And Herod with his men of war set him at nought, and mocked him and arrayed him in a gorgeous robe, and sent him again to Pilate (Luke 23:1-7, 9-11).

8. Pilate therefore went forth again, and saith unto them, Behold, I bring him forth to you, that ye may know that I find no fault in him. Then came Jesus forth, wearing the crown of thorns, and the purple robe. And Pilate saith unto them, Behold the man! When the chief priests therefore and officers saw him, they cried out, saying, Crucify him, crucify him. Pilate saith unto them, Take ye him, and crucify him: for I find no fault in him. The Jews answered him, We have a law, and by our law he ought to die, because he made himself the Son of God. When Pilate therefore heard that saying, he was the more afraid; and went again into the judgment hall, and saith unto Jesus, Whence art thou? But Jesus gave him no answer. Then saith Pilate unto him, Speakest thou not unto me? knowest thou not that I have power to crucify thee, and have power to release thee? Jesus answered, Thou couldest have no power at all against me, except it were given thee from above: therefore he that delivered me unto thee hath the greater sin. And from thenceforth Pilate sought to release him: but the Jews cried out, saying, If thou let this man go, thou art not Caesar's friend: whosoever maketh himself a king speaketh against Caesar. When Pilate therefore heard that saying, he brought Jesus forth, and sat down in the judgment seat in a place that is called the Pavement, but in the Hebrew, Gabbatha. And it was the preparation of the passover, and about the sixth hour: and he saith unto the Jews, Behold your King! But they cried out, Away with him, away with him, crucify him. Pilate saith unto them, Shall I crucify your King? The chief priests answered, We have no king but Caesar. Then delivered he him therefore unto them to be crucified. And they took Jesus, and led him away. And he bearing his cross went forth into a place called the place of a skull, which is called in the Hebrew Golgotha: where they crucified him (John 19:4-16).

9. As Peter and John talked to the people in the temple in Solomon's porch after the healing of the lame man, "the priests, and the captain of the temple, and the Sadducees, came upon them, being grieved that they taught the people, and preached through Jesus the resurrection from the dead. And

they laid hands on them, and put them in hold unto the next day: for it was now eventide. . . . And it came to pass on the morrow, that their rulers, and elders, and scribes, and Annas the high priest, and Caiaphas, and John, and Alexander, and as many as were of the kindred of the high priest, were gathered together at Jerusalem. And when they had set them in the midst, they asked, By what power, or by what name, have ye done this? Then Peter, filled with the Holy Ghost, said unto them, Ye rulers of the people, and elders of Israel, If we this day be examined of the good deed done to the impotent man, by what means he was made whole; be it known unto you all, and to all the people of Israel, that by the name of Jesus Christ of Nazareth, whom ye crucified, whom God raised from the dead, even by him doth this man stand before you whole. . . . Neither is there salvation in any other: for there is none other name under heaven given among men, whereby we must be saved. Now when they saw the boldness of Peter and John, and perceived that they were unlearned and ignorant men, they marvelled; and they took knowledge of them, that they had been with Jesus. And beholding the man which was healed standing with them, they could say nothing against it. But when they had commanded them to go aside out of the council, they conferred among themselves, saying, What shall we do to these men? for that indeed a notable miracle hath been done by them is manifest to all them that dwell in Jerusalem; and we cannot deny it. . . . And they called them, and commanded them not to speak at all nor teach in the name of Jesus. But Peter and John answered and said unto them, Whether it be right in the sight of God to hearken unto you more than unto God, judge ye. For we cannot but speak the things which we have seen and heard. So when they had further threatened them, they let them go, finding nothing how they might punish them, because of the people: for all men glorified God for that which was done. (Acts 4:1-3, 5-10, 12-16, 18-21).

10. The high priest . . . and all they that were with him, [which is the sect of the Sadducees] . . . laid their hands on the apostles and put them in the common prison. But the angel of the Lord by night opened the prison doors, and . . . said, Go, stand, and speak in the temple to the people all the words of this life. . . . [Then] the officers came and found them not in the prison. . . . Then came one and told them,

saying, Behold, the men whom ye put in prison are standing in the temple, and teaching the people. Then went the captain with the officers, and brought them without violence. . . . and . . . they sat them before the council: and the high priest asked them, saying, Did not we straitly command you that ye should not teach in this name? and, behold ye have filled Jerusalem with your doctrine. . . . Then Peter and the other apostles answered and said, We ought to obey God rather than men. The God of our fathers raised up Jesus, whom ye slew and hanged on a tree. Him hath God exalted . . . to be a Prince and a Saviour . . . to Israel. . . . And we are witnesses of these things: and so also is the Holy Ghost, whom God hath given to them that obey him. When they heard that, they were cut to the heart, and took counsel to slay them. Then . . . Gamaliel . . . commanded to put the apostles forth a little space; and said unto them, Ye men of Israel, take heed to yourselves what ye intend to do as touching these men. . . . Refrain from these men, and let them alone: for if this counsel or this work be of men, it will come to nought: but if it be of God, ye cannot overthrow it; lest haply ye be found even to fight against God. And to him they agreed: and when they had called the apostles, and beaten them, they commanded that they should not speak in the name of Jesus, and let them go (Acts 5;17-20, 22, 25-35, 38-40).

11. There arose certain of the synagogue, disputing with Stephen. And they were not able to resist the wisdom and the spirit by which he spake. Then they suborned men, which said, We have heard him speak blasphemous words against Moses, and against God. And they stirred up the people, and the elders, and the scribes, . . . and caught him and brought him to the council, and set up false witnesses, which said, . . . We have heard him say, that Jesus of Nazareth shall destroy this place, and shall change the customs which Moses delivered us. . . . Then said the high priest, Are these things so? [Then Stephen made a long speech about the patriarchs and about Moses, David, and Solomon. He ended by saying,] Ye stiffnecked and uncircumcised in heart and ears, ye do always resist the Holy Ghost: as your fathers did, so do ye. Which of the prophets have not your fathers persecuted? and they have slain them which shewed before the coming of the Just One; of whom ye have been now the

betrayers and murderers: who have received the law by the disposition of angels, and have not kept it. When they heard these things, they were cut to the heart, and they gnashed on him with their teeth. But he, being full of the Holy Ghost, looked up stedfastly into heaven . . . and said, Behold, I see the heavens opened, and the Son of man standing on the right hand of God. Then they cried out with a loud voice, . . . and ran upon him with one accord, and cast him out of the city, and stoned him . . . and he kneeled down, and cried with a loud voice, Lord, lay not this sin to their charge. And when he had said this, he fell asleep. And Saul was consenting unto his death (Acts 6:9-14; 7:1, 51-58, 60).

12. A certain damsel possessed with a spirit of divination . . . which brought her masters much gain by soothsaying . . . followed Paul and us, and cried, saying, These men are the servants of the most high God, which shew unto us the way of salvation. And this she did many days. But Paul, being grieved, turned and said to the spirit, I command thee in the name of Jesus Christ to come out of her. And he came out the same hour. And when her masters saw that the hope of their gains was gone, they caught Paul and Silas, and drew them into the marketplace unto the rulers, and brought them to the magistrates, saying, These men, being Jews, do exceedingly trouble our city, and teach customs, which are not lawful for us to receive, neither to observe, being Romans. And the multitude rose up together against them: and the magistrates rent off their clothes, and commanded to beat them. And when they had laid many stripes upon them, they cast them into prison, charging the jailor to keep them safely: who, having received such a charge, thrust them into the inner prison, and made their feet fast in the stocks (Acts 16:16-24).

13. After Paul was mobbed in the temple and rescued by the chief Roman captain, Paul was brought before "the chief priests and all their council. . . . And Paul, earnestly beholding the council, said, Men and brethren, I have lived in all good conscience before God until this day. And the high priest Ananias commanded them that stood by him to smite him on the mouth. Then said Paul unto him, God shall smite thee, thou whited wall: for sittest thou to judge me after the law, and commandest me to be smitten contrary to the law?

And they that stood by said, Revilest thou God's high priest? Then said Paul, I wist not, brethren, that he was the high priest: for it is written, Thou shalt not speak evil of the ruler of thy people. But when Paul perceived that the one part were Sadducees, and the other Pharisees, he cried out in the council, Men and brethren, I am a Pharisee, the son of a Pharisee: of the hope and resurrection of the dead I am called in question. And when he had so said, there arose a dissension between the Pharisees and the Sadducees: and the multitude was divided. For the Sadducees say that there is no resurrection, neither angel, nor spirit: but the Pharisees confess both. And there arose a great cry: and the scribes that were of the Pharisees' part arose, and strove, saying, We find no evil in this man: but if a spirit or an angel hath spoken to him, let us not fight against God. And when there arose a great dissension, the chief captain, fearing lest Paul should have been pulled in pieces of them, commanded the soldiers to go down, and to take him by force from among them, and to bring him into the castle" (Acts 22:30; 23:1-10).

14. After Paul was taken from Jerusalem [to escape a conspiracy to kill him] to Caesarea, he was kept in Herod's judgment hall. "And after five days Ananias the high priest descended with the elders, and with a certain orator named Tertullus, who informed the governor against Paul . . . saying, . . . Most noble Felix . . . I pray thee that thou wouldest hear us of thy clemency a few words. For we have found this man a pestilent fellow and a mover of sedition among all the Jews . . . who also hath gone about to profane the temple. . . . And the Jews also assented, saying that these things were so. Then Paul, after that the governor had beckoned unto him to speak, answered, Forasmuch as I know that thou hast been of many years a judge unto this nation, I do the more cheerfully answer for myself: . . . I went up to Jerusalem for to worship. And they neither found me in the temple disputing with any man, neither . . . can they prove the things whereof they now accuse me. But this I confess unto thee, that after the way which they call heresy, so worship I the God of my fathers, believing all things which are written in the law and in the prophets: and have hope toward God . . . that there shall be a resurrection of the dead, both of the just and unjust. . . . And when Felix heard these

things, having more perfect knowledge of that way, he deferred them, and said, When Lysias the chief captain shall come down, I will know the uttermost of your matter. And he commanded a centurion to keep Paul, and to let him have liberty, and that he should forbid none of his acquaintance to minister or to come to him" (Acts 24:1-6, 9, 10-15, 22, 23).

15. When Festus was come into the province, . . . the high priest and the chief of the Jews informed him against Paul . . . and desired . . . that he would send for him to Jerusalem, laying in wait . . . to kill him. But Festus answered, that Paul should be kept at Caesarea. . . . Let them therefore, said he, which among you are able, go down with me, and accuse this man. . . . [After] ten days, he went down unto Caesarea, and the next day sitting on the judgment seat commanded Paul to be brought. And when he was come, the Jews . . . laid many and grievous complaints against Paul, which they could not prove. While he answered for himself, Neither against the law of the Jews, neither against the temple, nor yet against Caesar, have I offended any thing at all. But Festus . . . said, Wilt thou go up to Jerusalem, and there be judged of these things before me? Then said Paul, I stand at Caesar's judgment seat, where I ought to be judged. . . . I appeal to Caesar. Then Festus, when he had conferred with the council, answered, Hast thou appealed unto Caesar? unto Caesar shalt thou go (Acts 25:1-12).

16. And after certain days king Agrippa and Bernice came unto Caesarea to salute Festus. And when they had been there many days, Festus declared Paul's cause to the king. . . . Then Agrippa said unto Festus, I would also hear the man myself. . . . Agrippa said unto Paul, Thou art permitted to speak for thyself. [Then Paul told Agrippa the story of his life, including his persecution of the Christians and his own conversion. He ended by saying,] King Agrippa, believest thou the prophets? I know that thou believest. Then Agrippa said unto Paul, Almost thou persuadest me to be a Christian. And Paul said, I would to God, that not only thou, but also all that hear me this day, were both almost, and altogether such as I am, except these bonds. And when he had thus spoken, the king rose up, and the governor, and Bernice, and they that sat with them: and when they were gone aside, they talked among themselves, saying, This man doeth nothing worthy of death or of bonds. Then said Agrippa unto Festus,

This man might have been set at liberty, if he had not appealed unto Caesar (Acts 25:13, 14, 22; 26:1, 27-32).

17. When the Son of man shall come in his glory, and all the holy angels with him, then shall he sit upon the throne of his glory: and before him shall be gathered all nations; and he shall separate them one from another, as a shepherd divideth his sheep from the goats: and he shall set the sheep on his right hand, but the goats on the left. Then shall the King say unto them on his right hand, Come, ye blessed of my Father, inherit the kingdom prepared for you from the foundation of the world: For I was an hungred, and ye gave me meat: I was thirsty, and ye gave me drink: I was a stranger, and ye took me in: naked, and ye clothed me: I was sick, and ye visited me: I was in prison, and ye came unto me. Then shall the righteous answer him, saying, Lord, when saw we thee an hungred, and fed thee? or thirsty, and gave thee drink? When saw we thee a stranger, and took thee in? or naked, and clothed thee? Or when saw we thee sick, or in prison, and came unto thee? And the King shall answer and say unto them, Verily I say unto you, Inasmuch as ye have done it unto one of the least of these my brethren, ye have done it unto me. Then shall he say also unto them on the left hand, Depart from me, ye cursed, into everlasting fire, prepared for the devil and his angels: for I was an hungred, and ye gave me no meat: I . . . was a stranger, and ye took me not in: naked and ye clothed me not: sick, and in prison, and ye visited me not. Then shall they also answer him, saying, Lord, when saw we thee an hungred, or athirst, or a stranger, or naked, or sick, or in prison, and did not minister unto thee? Then shall he answer them, saying, Verily I say unto you, Inasmuch as ye did it not to one of the least of these, ye did it not to me. And these shall go away into everlasting punishment: but the righteous into life eternal (Matt. 25:31-46).

Abbreviations Used in Meredith's Book of Bible Lists

1 Chron. ....1 Chronicles	Josh. ....Joshua
2 Chron. ....2 Chronicles	Lev. ....Leviticus
Col. ....Colossians	Matt. ......Matthew
Cont'd .....Continued	Neh. ....Nehemiah
1 Cor. ......1 Corinthians	Num. ....Numbers
2 Cor. ......2 Corinthians	1 Pet. ......1 Peter
Dan. ....Daniel	2 Pet. ......2 Peter
Deut. ......Deuteronomy	Phil. ....Philippians
Eccles. .....Ecclesiastes	Prov. ....Proverbs
Eph. ....Ephesians	Ps. ....Psalms
Ex. ....Exodus	Rev. ......Revelation
Ezek. ......Ezekiel	Rom. ......Romans
Gal. ....Galatians	1 Sam. .....1 Samuel
Gen. ....Genesis	2 Sam. .....2 Samuel
Hab. ....Habakkuk	1 Thess. ....1 Thessalonians
Hag. ....Haggai	2 Thess. ....2 Thessalonians
Heb. ....Hebrews	1 Tim. .....1 Timothy
Hos. ....Hosea	2 Tim. .....2 Timothy
Isa. ....Isaiah	Zech. ......Zechariah
Jer. ....Jeremiah	Zeph. .....Zephaniah

Bibliography

A Harmony of the Gospels
  by A. T. Robertson
  Published by Harper & Row
  Copyright 1950
Aids to Understanding the Holy Bible—Appendix to *Family Bible*
  General Editor John Rea
  Published by The World Publishing Co.
  Copyright 1968
All the Kings and Queens of the Bible
  Herbert Lockyer
  Zondervan. G.R., 1961
All the Men of the Bible
  by Herbert Lockyer
  Published by Zondervan Publishing House
  Copyright 1958, 26th printing, January 1979
All the Women of the Bible
  by Herbert Lockyer
  Published by Zondervan Publishing House
  Copyright 1967, 18th printing, April 1979
Bible Dictionary—Concordance to Holy Bible, Appendix to King James Version
  Published by A. J. Holman Co.
  Copyright 1942
For Today and Everyday—Appendix to Holy Bible, King James Version
  Published by A. J. Holman Co.
  Copyright 1947 & 1949
Jesus Person Pocket Promise Book, The
  by David Wilkerson
  Published by Regal Book Division of G/L Publications
  Copyright 1972, 18th printing, 1979
Nave's Topical Bible,
  Orville J. Nave
  Moody, Chicago, 1921
New Bible Dictionary, The
  J. O. Douglas, ed.
  Wm. B. Eerdmans, G.R., 1962

Reese Chronological Bible, The
Edward Reese, ed.
Bethany House Publishers
Copyright 1977, 1980 edition
Strong's Exhaustive Concordance of the Bible
    by James Strong
    Published by Abingdon Press
    Copyright 1890, 25th printing, 1963
Universal Bible Dictionary, The
    Edited by A. R. Buckland & Assisted by A. Lukyn Williams
    Published by Fleming H. Revell Co.
    No copyright, 1951 edition
Wycliffe Bible Commentary, The
    Edited by Charles F. Pfeiffer (O.T.) & Everett F. Harrison
    (N.T.)
    Published by Moody Press
    Copyright 1962, 7th printing, 1972

MEREDITH'S SECOND BOOK OF BIBLE LISTS

More Stimulating, Informative
and Often Surprising
Bible Facts in List Form

Dedication

This book is dedicated to my mother, Barbara O'Keeffe.

Acknowledgments

I wish to pay tribute to the following people for their invaluable help in the preparation and publication of this book.

To my wife, Lorraine, I owe much thanks for her long hours of typing and proofreading. I owe her even more thanks perhaps for her encouragement and her continuous support both as a wife and as a prayer warrior. Her many suggestions for lists were also very helpful.

I want to especially thank the editorial staff at Bethany House for all the work that they have done on this book and on my previous book. They also provided me with many ideas for lists, and they were so kind and patient with me.

I also want to thank the numerous people who wrote to me with suggestions for new lists.

I met a man in Dallas, Texas, who told me that he had given *Meredith's Book of Bible Lists* to his son; it turned his son's life around. That sort of thing makes it all worthwhile!

Table of Contents

Abbreviations Used in this Book

1 Chron.	1 Chronicles	Mal.	Malachi
2 Chron.	2 Chronicles	Matt.	Matthew
Col.	Colossians	Mic.	Micah
1 Cor.	1 Corinthians	Neh.	Nehemiah
2 Cor.	2 Corinthians	Num.	Numbers
Dan.	Daniel	1 Pet.	1 Peter
Deut.	Deuteronomy	2 Pet.	2 Peter
Eccles.	Ecclesiastes	Phil.	Philippians
Eph.	Ephesians	Prov.	Proverbs
Ex.	Exodus	Ps.	Psalms
Ezek.	Ezekiel	Rev.	Revelation
Gal.	Galatians	Rom.	Romans
Gen.	Genesis	1 Sam.	1 Samuel
Hab.	Habakkuk	2 Sam.	2 Samuel
Hag.	Haggai	Song of Sol.	Song of Solomon
Heb.	Hebrews	1 Thess.	1 Thessalonians
Hos.	Hosea	2 Thess.	2 Thessalonians
Isa.	Isaiah	1 Tim.	1 Timothy
Jer.	Jeremiah	2 Tim.	2 Timothy
Josh.	Joshua	Zech.	Zechariah
Lam.	Lamentations	Zeph.	Zephaniah
Lev.	Leviticus		

1

Family Affairs

Though the Bible holds a wide variety of themes, the central theme of the Bible is the redemptive role of Jesus Christ. From the fall of Adam and Eve in the garden, God's plan of redemption through the seed of the woman (Gen. 3:15) has been the focal point. It is little wonder that from Genesis 12 onwards, we see the narrowing of God's attention to the family of Abraham and his descendants. From this family Jesus Christ would be born nearly 1900 years later.

Zeroing in on this family necessarily meant zeroing in on the families that came from Abraham. Thus, the Bible is very much a family book, and many of the joys and the frustrations of family life are depicted. Looking over the lists, we find that we have much in common with the families of the Bible: preparations for weddings, the rearing of large families, miraculous pregnancies, twins being born, the devastation of divorce, and death during childbirth. Few of us will have as large a family as some of these people did, however. You'd need a hotel to house them and a farm to feed them.

1. Five Dowries

1. Jacob served Laban for fourteen years so he could marry Rachel (Gen. 29:16-30).
2. "Leah said, God hath endued me with a good dowry; now will my husband dwell with me, because I have born him six sons" (Gen. 30:20).
3. When Shechem the Hivite sought to marry Dinah, her brothers responded, "In this will we consent unto you: If ye will

be as we be, that every male of you be circumcised; then we will give our daughters unto you" (Gen. 34:1-16).

4. Boaz obtained Ruth as his wife by purchasing Naomi's property (Ruth 3-4).

5. Saul said, "Thus shall ye say to David, The king desireth not any dowry, but an hundred foreskins of the Philistines, to be avenged of the king's enemies. Wherefore David arose and went, he and his men, and slew of the Philistines two hundred men; and David brought their foreskins, and they gave them in full tale to the king, that he might be the king's son in law" (1 Sam. 18:25, 27).

The wedding at Cana

2. Seven Weddings

1. God gave the bride (Eve) away in mankind's first wedding (Gen. 2:22-24)!
2. Laban made a public wedding feast before deceitfully giving his daughter Leah to Jacob in marriage (Gen. 29:22-25).
3. Samson made a seven-day feast and was given thirty attendants for his wedding. However, the festivities were cut short by Samson's fit of anger, and he never did actually marry the woman (Judges 14:10-20).
4. Jesus told a parable of a king who made a wedding feast for his son. The king invited guests and required that each wear a wedding garment provided for him (Matt. 22:1-14).
5. In another parable, Jesus told of ten virgins who waited at night to accompany the bride and bridegroom to their marriage feast (Matt. 25:1-13).
6. Jesus accepted an invitation to a wedding at Cana. There Jesus performed His first miracle—He changed water into wine for the marriage feast (John 2:1-11).
7. John described the future union of Christ and His Church as a marriage. The Church, Christ's bride, wore fine, white linen (typifying its righteousness). People were invited to the marriage feast (Rev. 19:7-9).

3. Five Divorces

1. Abraham sent away Hagar, who gave birth to Ishmael, at Sarah's urging and God's approval (Gen. 21:9-14).
2. The post-exilic Jews, at Ezra's prompting, divorced their foreign wives (Ezra 10).
3. King Ahasuerus may have divorced Queen Vashti for her disobedience (Esther 1:9-22).
4. God "divorced" the Northern Kingdom for their idolatry (Jer. 3:8).
5. Herod and Herodias both divorced their spouses in order to marry each other (Josephus; cf. Matt. 14:3-4).

4. The Five Men With the Most Wives

1. Solomon had 700 wives and 300 concubines (1 Kings 11:3).
2. King Rehoboam had 18 wives and 60 concubines (2 Chron. 11:21).

3. David likely had over 17 wives, counting his concubines (2 Sam. 3:2-5; 5:13; 20:3).
4. King Abijah had 14 wives (2 Chron. 13:21).
5. Gideon had many wives and 70 sons (Judges 8:30).

5. Ten Miraculous Pregnancies

1. God closed all the wombs of Abimelech's household because Abimelech had taken Sarah for himself. After Sarah was restored to Abraham, Abraham prayed and the women bore children (Gen. 20:17-18).
2. Although Sarah was old, and unable to bear children before, she gave birth to Isaac when she was 90 years old, as the Lord fulfilled His promise. Abraham was 100 years old when Isaac was born (Gen. 21:1-5).
3. After Sarah's death (at which time Abraham was 137 years old), Abraham remarried and fathered more children (Gen. 25:1-6).
4. Rebekah was barren until her husband Isaac prayed for her. Then she conceived and gave birth to twins: Jacob and Esau (Gen. 25:21-26).
5. God opened the womb of barren Rachel, and she gave birth to Joseph and Benjamin (Gen. 30:22-24; 35:18).
6. The angel of the Lord appeared to Manoah's barren wife, foretelling that she would bear a son (Samson) who would begin to deliver Israel from the Philistines (Judges 13:3, 5).
7. The Lord had shut up Hannah's womb, so that she was childless. But then, in answer to Hannah's intense prayer, she gave birth to Samuel (1 Sam. 1:1-20).
8. Although her husband was "too old," the Shunammite woman bore a son, fulfilling Elisha's word (2 Kings 4:13-17).
9. Barren Elisabeth gave birth to John (the Baptist), fulfilling Gabriel's message to her husband, Zacharias. Both Elisabeth and Zacharias were "well stricken in years" (Luke 1:7-9, 13, 18, 57).
10. Jesus was conceived by the Holy Spirit in the Virgin Mary (Matt. 1:18-20; Luke 1:31, 35).

6. Four Sets of Twins

1. The wording in Gen. 4:1-2 suggests that perhaps Cain and Abel were twins.

2. Jacob and Esau (Gen. 25:23-26).
3. Pharez and Zerah (Gen. 38:29-30).
4. The apostle Thomas was called Didymus, which means "a twin" (John 11:16).

7. Women Who Died in Childbirth

1. Rachel died in giving birth to Benjamin (Gen. 35:16-18).
2. Phinehas' wife died right after giving birth to a son. The stress of her delivery was aggravated by her grief at much tragic news—the ark of God was captured, her husband and father-in-law had died, and Israel was defeated in battle by the Philistines (1 Sam. 4:19-22).

8. Youngest Sons

1. Seth was the youngest mentioned son of Adam. Seth's two older brothers were Cain and Abel (Gen. 4).
2. Ham was the youngest of Noah's three sons (Gen. 9:18-24).
3. Jacob was Esau's younger brother (Gen. 25:25, 26).
4. Benjamin was youngest of twelve brothers, all of them sons of Jacob (Gen. 35:16-18; 43:29).
5. Ephraim was the youngest son of Joseph. Ephraim's older brother was Manasseh (Gen. 41:51, 52).
6. Moses was three years younger than his brother Aaron (Ex. 7:7).
7. Kenaz was Caleb's younger brother (Judges 1:13).
8. Jotham was the youngest of the seventy sons of Jerubbaal (Gideon) (Judges 9:5).
9. David was the youngest of eight brothers (1 Sam. 17:12-14).
10. Segub was the youngest son of Hiel. Segub's older brother was Abiram (1 Kings 16:34).
11. Jehoahaz (Ahaziah) was Jehoram's youngest son (2 Chron. 21:16, 17).
12. The prodigal son was the younger of two brothers (Luke 15:11-32).

9. Ten Families with the Most Children

1. Rehoboam had 28 sons and 60 daughters (2 Chron. 11:21).
2. Gideon had 70 sons (Judges 8:30).
3. Ahab had 70 sons (2 Kings 10:1).

The sons of Gideon murdered by Abimelech

4. Ibzan had 30 sons and 30 daughters (Judges 12:8, 9).
5. Abdon had 40 sons and 30 nephews (Judges 12:13, 14).
6. Abijah had 22 sons and 16 daughters (2 Chron. 13:21).
7. Jair had 30 sons (Judges 10:3, 4).
8. Shimei had 16 sons and 6 daughters (1 Chron. 4:27).
9. David had 19 sons and 1 daughter plus an unknown additional number of children by his concubines (1 Chron. 3:1-9).
10. Heman had 14 sons and 3 daughters (1 Chron. 25:5).

Note: It is not known how many children Solomon had.

2

Dwellings

From the Eskimo igloos of the North to the bamboo huts of the Asian tropics, we see a vast array of human dwellings. For some people, a house means barely having a roof over their heads. For others, it means living in a palace of extraordinary beauty and vigilant guards. The contrast in dwelling places are found wherever one goes.

Time has not changed the contrasts in dwelling places. In the Bible we find great men like Elijah and David residing temporarily in caves. We find the glory of the king's palaces in Babylon and the lowliness of tents (such as those of Noah, Abraham, Isaac, and Jacob). Lifeless gods dwelt in temples of grandeur, while powerful men of God, such as John the Baptist, and even the Son of God, had no home of their own.

In this chapter you will learn many interesting facts about Bible dwellings.

10. Eight Important Caves

1. After the destruction of Sodom and Gomorrah, Lot lived in a cave with his two daughters (Gen. 19:30).
2. Joshua trapped five kings of southern Canaan in the cave in which they were hiding. Later they were brought out, killed, and entombed in the same cave (Josh. 10:16-27).
3. The Israelites fled to live in mountain caves and dens to escape the Midianite oppression (Judges 6:2).
4. In Saul's time, Israel again fled to caves and other hiding places to escape the Philistine army (1 Sam. 13:5-7).

5. David used caves as his hideouts and headquarters while Saul sought to kill him (1 Sam. 22:1-2; 23:14, 29).
6. "When Jezebel cut off the prophets of the Lord, ... Obadiah took an hundred prophets, and hid them by fifty in a cave, and fed them with bread and water" (1 Kings 18:4).
7. When Elijah fled from Jezebel, "he came ... unto a cave, and lodged there; and, behold, the word of the Lord came to him, and he said unto him, What doest thou here, Elijah?" (1 Kings 19:9).
8. Lazarus was buried in a cave (John 11:38).

11. Five Buildings That Collapsed

1. Gideon "beat down the tower of Penuel, and slew the men of the city" (Judges 8:17).
2. Samson pushed on the two main pillars of a large building and caused it to fall, resulting in the deaths of thousands of Philistines and of Samson himself (Judges 16:23-30).
3. While Job's sons and daughters were feasting in their oldest brother's house, a great wind struck the house, causing it to collapse and kill them (Job 1:18-19).
4. In Jesus' parable, the foolish man's house, built on sand, collapsed when battered by rain, floods, and wind (Matt. 7:26-27).
5. Eighteen people died when the tower of Siloam fell on them (Luke 13:4).

12. Nine Rooftops

1. Rahab the harlot brought the two Israelite spies "up to the roof of the house, and hid them with the stalks of flax, which she had laid in order upon the roof" (Josh. 2:6).
2. "There were upon the roof [of the building that Samson pulled down] about three thousand men and women, that beheld while Samson made sport" (Judges 16:27).
3. Samuel talked with Saul on Samuel's roof (1 Sam. 9:25-26).
4. While walking on his palace roof one evening, David saw Bathsheba bathing, and lusted after her (2 Sam. 11:2-4).
5. "They spread Absalom a tent upon the top of the house; and Absalom went in unto his father's concubines in the sight of all Israel" (2 Sam. 16:22).
6. Some Jews of Ezra's day built booths on their roofs to observe the Feast of Tabernacles (Neh. 8:14-16).

7. Jeremiah prophesied judgment on the houses of Jerusalem because the people were burning incense and offering drink offerings to idols on their roofs (Jer. 19:13).
8. Four men in Capernaum carried a paralytic to the house where Jesus was, seeking his healing. Being otherwise unable to get close to Jesus because of the crowd, they removed a section of the roof and lowered the man on his stretcher to Jesus (Mark 2:3-4).
9. While praying on a housetop, Peter had a vision which led to the first Gentile evangelization (Acts 10:9-16).

13. Fifteen References to Important Tents

1. Jabal "was the father of such as dwell in tents" (Gen. 4:20).
2. Noah lived in a tent (Gen. 9:21).
3. Abraham, Isaac, and Jacob lived in tents as they sojourned in Canaan (Heb. 11:9).
4. Isaac took Rebekah into his mother Sarah's tent on their wedding night (Gen. 24:67).
5. When Jacob finally left Laban, each of the following people had his own tent: Jacob, Laban, Laban's brethren, Leah, Bilhah, Zilpah, and Rachel (Gen. 31:25, 33).
6. The tabernacle in the wilderness was a tent made according to God's specifications. God's presence was there in a special way (Ex. 26:1-4; 2 Sam. 7:6).
7. While the children of Israel were in the wilderness of Sin, they lived in tents (Ex. 33:10).
8. Phineas killed Zimri and Cozbi in Zimri's tent because of their immorality (Num. 25:6-8).
9. Achan took some of the spoils from the battle of Jericho and buried them inside his tent (Josh. 7:21).
10. When Sisera fled from Israel in battle, Jael invited him into her tent to hide. Then, as he slept, Jael drove a tent peg through his temples, killing him (Judges 4:17-21).
11. A Midianite soldier dreamed that a loaf of barley bread had tumbled into the Midianite camp, striking and flattening a tent. His friend interpreted this to mean that God would give Midian over to Gideon (Judges 7:13-14).
12. After killing the giant, David stored Goliath's armor in his own tent (1 Sam. 17:54).
13. After God caused the Syrian army to flee from their camp, four Samaritan lepers, and then all the Samaritans, plundered their tents (2 Kings 7:3-16).

14. David pitched a tent in Jerusalem to house the Ark of God (1 Chron. 15:1).
15. Jonadab commanded his descendants to always live in tents (Jer. 35:6-10).

14. Sixteen Temples

1. About one thousand men and women of Shechem entered the house (temple) of the god Berith for protection from Abimelech. However, Abimelech and his men set fire to the building, killing them all (Judges 9:46-49).
2. During Samuel's earlier years, the Philistines captured the Ark of the Covenant and set it by their idol Dagon in his temple. Twice Dagon fell face down before the Ark (1 Sam. 5:2-4).
3. After Saul was slain, the Philistines "put his armour in the house [temple] of Ashtaroth" (1 Sam. 31:10).
4. Solomon built the temple of the Lord to replace the portable tabernacle-tent (1 Kings 6).
5. Ahab "reared up an altar for Baal in the house [temple] of Baal, which he had built in Samaria" (1 Kings 16:32).
6. When his master worshiped in the house [temple] of Rimnon, Naaman bowed down with him (2 Kings 5:18).
7. Sennacherib was assassinated by his two sons "as he was worshipping in the house [temple] of Nisroch his god" (2 Kings 19:37).
8. The Philistines "fastened [Saul's] head in the temple of Dagon" (1 Chron. 10:10).
9. Nebuchadnezzar carried some of "the vessels of the house of the Lord to Babylon, and put them in his temple at Babylon" (2 Chron. 36:7).
10. After returning from exile in Babylon, the Jews rebuilt the temple, but on a smaller scale than Solomon's temple (Ezra 6:3-15).
11. While in Exile in Babylon, Ezekiel received a very detailed vision of a temple in Israel. He recorded dimensions of pillars, halls, and rooms (Ezek. 40-42).
12. Jesus said, "Destroy this temple, and in three days I will raise it up. Then said the Jews, Forty and six years was this temple in building, and wilt thou rear it up in three days? But he spake of the temple of his body" (John 2:19-21).
13. There was a temple of the goddess Diana at Ephesus (Acts 19:27, 28).

The feast in Belshazzar's palace

14. Believers are called the temple of God, both individually (1 Cor. 6:19) and corporately (2 Cor. 6:16).
15. In John's vision, he was told to measure the temple in Jerusalem (Rev. 11:1-2).

310

16. "I [John] saw no temple [in the new Jerusalem] therein: for the Lord God Almighty and the Lamb are the temple of it" (Rev. 21:22).

15. Eleven Kings' Palaces

1. "Hiram king of Tyre sent messengers to David, and cedar trees, and carpenters, and masons: and they built David an house" (2 Sam. 5:11).
2. David referred to the temple which Solomon was to build as a "palace . . . for the Lord God" (1 Chron. 29:1, 19).
3. It took Solomon thirteen years to build his large, lavish palace (1 Kings 7:1-12).
4. When Zimri's coup failed, he burned Israel's royal palace over himself and died in the flames (1 Kings 16:15-18).
5. Israel's King Ahab coveted Naboth's vineyard because it was close to his palace. When Naboth refused to sell it, Queen Jezebel had him killed (1 Kings 21:1-19).
6. King Pekahiah of Israel was assassinated in his palace in a coup led by Pekah (2 Kings 15:25).
7. When ambassadors from Babylon came to King Hezekiah, the king showed them the wealth in his palace. Then Isaiah prophesied to Hezekiah that his palace would be plundered by Babylon and his sons would serve in the Babylonian palace (2 Kings 20:16-18).
8. Nehemiah served as cupbearer to the king in Persia's royal palace before going to Jerusalem to rebuild the city wall (Neh. 1:1; 2:1).
9. Persia's palace had beds of gold and silver and marble pillars and pavement in the garden court (Esther 1:5-6).
10. King Nebuchadnezzar went insane while walking in his palace (Dan. 4:28-33).
11. The "handwriting on the wall," foretelling the end of the Babylonian empire, appeared on a wall in the Babylonian palace during King Belshazzar's feast (Dan. 5:5).

3

Just for Looks

When was the last time you saw a true hippie—long, greasy hair, tangled moustache and beard, hip-length fringed leather coat, and patched blue jeans? It's been a while. The patched jeans have been replaced by Jordache and Vanderbilt; the leather coat has been succeeded by Izod; the tangled hair has given way to a succession of short, precise styles.

Westerners place great importance upon conforming to the latest styles. Conformity to the style of the day generally guarantees acceptance by others, especially one's peers. Eastern cultures, however, seldom change their styles, but conformity to the style is still important.

Styles may not have been a major issue in Bible times, but any deviation from that style indicated something of real importance. To shave one's head meant one thing, as did pulling out hair. To wear sackcloth was an indication of grief, as was also the use of ashes. One did not tear his garments in public unless he was declaring something. Chains or ropes were another important "apparel" that one might be unfortunate enough to wear.

But to those seeking after God, there is no style or designer label that can match God's custom-designed "garments of righteousness."

16. Haircuts

1. Part of the ceremony for a leper who recovered involved shaving all his hair twice, six days apart (Lev. 14:8-9).
2. The Jews were forbidden to "round the corners of [their] heads," referring to a certain hairstyle (Lev. 19:27).

3. When an Israelite took a Nazarite vow, he was not to cut his hair. When this time of separation was completed, he shaved his head and burned the hair (Num. 6:5, 13, 18).
4. The Levites shaved their whole bodies as part of the ceremony consecrating them to the Lord (Num. 8:5-7).
5. If an Israelite took a woman from among the captives in war to be his wife, she first had to shave her head (Deut. 21:10-12).
6. When Samson's head was shaved, his strength left him (Judges 16:19).

Absalom caught by his hair in the oak tree

7. Absalom cut his hair once a year because it got too heavy (2 Sam. 14:25,26).

8. When Ezra heard that the Jews were intermarrying with the Canaanites and other nationalities, he was so upset that he pulled hair from his head and beard (Ezra 9:1-3).

9. In another occurrence of wrong intermarriage, Nehemiah pulled out the hair of some men of Judah as he charged them not to intermarry (Neh. 13:23-27).

10. After losing his children and wealth, Job shaved his head in his grief (Job 1:20).

11. The people of Jerusalem were told to cut off their hair in response to the Lord's rejection of them (Jer. 7:29).

12. God told Ezekiel to shave his head and beard, and then use the hair to symbolize Israel (Ezek. 5:1-4).

13. Haircuts were prescribed for the priests. They were not to shave their heads or let their hair grow long (Ezek. 44:20).

14. Paul shaved his head at Cenchrea, in connection with a vow (Acts 18:18).

15. Shaving one's head in relation to a vow is also seen in Acts 21:23-26.

17. Rings

1. When Pharaoh promoted Joseph, he put his own ring on Joseph's finger (Gen. 41:42).

2. Some Israelites gave a freewill offering for the tabernacle and its furnishings from their rings and other gold jewelry (Ex. 35:22).

3. King Ahasuerus of Persia gave his signet ring to Haman. The ring was then used to seal copies of an edict ordering the destruction of all Jews (Esther 3:10-13).

4. After Haman was hanged, Ahasuerus gave his royal signet ring to Mordecai. The ring was then used to seal copies of Mordecai's edict, which reversed Haman's decree and allowed the Jews to take vengeance on their enemies (Esther 8:2-13).

5. When Daniel was thrown into the lions' den, they laid a stone upon the mouth of the den, and the king sealed it with his *signet*. This signet may have been a ring (Dan. 6:17).

6. When the father welcomed back his prodigal son, he ordered that a ring be put on the son's finger (Luke 15:22).

18. Perfume and Cosmetics

1. The holy oil used for anointing Israel's priests was perfumed with aromatic spices (Ex. 30:23-33).
2. Jezebel "painted her face" before meeting with Jehu (2 Kings 9:30).
3. Women in King Ahasuerus' harem were "purified" with perfumes (Esther 2:12).
4. The adulteress of Proverbs 7 perfumed her bed with myrrh, aloes, and cinnamon (7:17).
5. "Ointment and perfume rejoice the heart" (Prov. 27:9).
6. The lovers of the Song of Solomon lavishly used valuable perfumes:
   a. Solomon used myrrh, frankincense, and other spices (1:3; 3:6; 4:6).
   b. His wife used spikenard, camphire, saffron, calamus, cinnamon, frankincense, myrrh and aloes, among others (1:12; 4:10-14; 5:1,5).
7. Jer. 4:30 and Ezek. 23:40 mention fictitious women painting their eyes.
8. Daniel used no anointing oils during his three weeks of mourning (Dan. 10:3).
9. Frankincense and myrrh were given to Jesus by the wise men (Matt. 2:11).
10. A sinful woman anointed Jesus' feet with ointment (perfume) (Luke 7:37-38).
11. Mary (Lazarus' sister) anointed Jesus' feet with expensive spikenard. The odor of the ointment filled the house (John 12:3).
12. On yet another occasion, a woman came to Jesus and poured "very precious ointment" on his head (Matt. 26:7).

19. Chains, Ropes, and Threads

1. When Tamar gave birth, one of her twins "put out his hand: and the midwife took and bound upon his hand a scarlet thread, saying, This came out first" (Gen. 38:28).
2. Pharaoh "put a gold chain about [Joseph's] neck" (Gen. 41:42).
3. Aaron's ephod included gold chains of wreathen work (Ex. 28:14).
4. Rahab dropped a scarlet cord from her window to aid the

spies to leave the city and then she used it later to show them where she lived (Josh. 2:15-19).

5. Gideon claimed for himself the gold chains that were about the necks of the Midianites' camels (Judges 8:26).

6. The Philistines bound Samson with seven fresh cords, but he broke them as soon as the Philistines came to get him (Judges 16:6-9).

7. Samson said, "If they bind me fast with new ropes that never were occupied, then shall I be weak, and be as another man . . . and he brake them from off his arms like a thread" (Judges 16:11-12).

8. Ben-hadad's servants put sackcloth on their loins and ropes on their heads to beg for mercy from King Ahab (1 Kings 20:31).

9. Solomon made chains strung with pomegranates to decorate the temple (2 Chron. 3:16).

10. Nebuchadrezzar "put out Zedekiah's eyes, and bound him with chains, to carry him to Babylon" (Jer. 39:7).

11. Jeremiah was "bound in chains among all that were carried away captive of Jerusalem and Judah" (Jer. 40:1).

12. Belshazzar "clothed Daniel with scarlet, and put a chain of gold about his neck" (Dan. 5:29).

13. The Gadarene demoniac had been bound, but "the chains had been plucked asunder by him, and the fetters broken in pieces" (Mark 5:3,4).

Samson after his capture

14. When the angel woke Peter up in prison, Peter's chains fell off and he was set free (Acts 12:6,7).
15. "The chief captain came near, and took [Paul], and commanded him to be bound with two chains; and demanded who he was and what he had done" (Acts 21:33).
16. The soldiers on Paul's ship cut the ropes holding the lifeboat so that the crew could not escape (Acts 27:30-32).
17. When Paul arrived in Rome, he was bound with a chain (Acts 28:20).
18. John "saw an angel come down from heaven, having the key of the bottomless pit and a great chain in his hand. And he laid hold on the dragon, that old serpent, which is the Devil, and Satan, and bound him a thousand years" (Rev. 20:1,2).

20. Fourteen Colors in the Bible

1. In middle of the fiery cloud in Ezekiel's vision was "as the colour of *amber*" (Ezek. 1:4).
2. "In the fourth chariot [were] grisled and *bay* horses" (Zech. 6:3).
3. "His locks are bushy, and *black* as a raven" (Song of Sol. 5:11).
4. When the Israelite camp moved, various utensils in the tabernacle would be covered with *blue* cloths before being carried (Num. 4:5-12).
5. The "man" that came to Daniel in Daniel 10 had arms and feet "like in colour to polished *brass*" (10:6).
6. "And he [Jacob] removed ... all the *brown* among the sheep" (Gen. 30:35).
7. "What be these two olive branches which through the two *golden* pipes empty the *golden* oil out of themselves?" (Zech. 4:12).
8. "Then shall ye bring down my *gray* hairs with sorrow to the grave" (Gen. 42:38).
9. "He maketh me to lie down in *green* pastures" (Ps. 23:2).
10. "They put on [Jesus] a *purple* robe" (John 19:2).
11. "It will be fair weather: for the sky is *red*" (Matt. 16:2).
12. "I saw a woman sit upon a *scarlet* coloured beast" (Rev. 17:3).
13. "And I saw a great *white* throne" (Rev. 20:11).
14. "She saw ... the images of the Chaldeans portrayed with *vermilion*" (Ezek. 23:14).

21. Seven Types of Fabrics

1. "John had his raiment of *camel's hair*" (Matt. 3:4).
2. "And thou shalt make curtains of *goat's hair* to be a covering upon the tabernacle" (Ex. 26:7).
3. "He wrapped [the body of Jesus] in a clean *linen* cloth" (Matt. 27:59).
4. Lydia was "a seller of *purple*" (Acts 16:14).
5. "The sun became black as *sackcloth of hair*" (Rev. 6:12).
6. *Silk* was one of the items which the merchants of the earth sold to Babylon (Rev. 18:11-12).
7. "Your sins . . . shall be as *wool*" (Isa. 1:18).

22. Sackcloth

1. Jacob put on sackcloth when he heard that Joseph had perished (Gen. 37:34).
2. Ben-hadad's servants wore sackcloth before Ahab (1 Kings 20:31,32).
3. Job wore sackcloth (Job 16:15).
4. Jeremiah prophesied that the people of Zion should put on sackcloth in view of the coming destroyer (Jer. 4:8).
5. The elders of the daughters of Zion wore sackcloth (Lam. 2:10).
6. Daniel sought the Lord in sackcloth (Dan. 9:3).
7. Prophecy was given in order that a nation might lament in sackcloth (Joel 1:8).
8. A pagan city wore sackcloth in repentance before the Lord (Jonah 3:8).

23. Uses of Ashes

1. Used as a symbol of mourning (2 Sam. 13:19; Esther 4:1,3).
2. Used as a symbol of repenting (Job 42:6; Dan. 9:3; Jonah 3:6; Matt. 11:21; Luke 10:13).
3. Used as a means of a disguise (1 Kings 20:38,41).
4. Used to sit in (Job 2:8; Isa. 58:5; Jer. 6:26).

24. Twenty-one Instances of Rending of Garments

1. Both Reuben and Jacob rent their clothes when they heard that Joseph had been killed (Gen. 37:29,34).

2. Joseph's brothers rent their clothes upon finding the silver cup in Benjamin's sack (Gen. 44:13).

3. Joshua and Caleb rent their clothes when the people murmured against the Lord about going into the Promised Land (Num. 14:6).

4. Jephthah rent his clothes when his hasty words came back to torment him (Judges 11:35).

5. David and all the men with him rent their clothes when they heard that King Saul was dead (2 Sam. 1:11).

6. David commanded Joab and the people with him to rend their clothes upon the death of Abner (2 Sam. 3:31).

7. Tamar rent her clothing after being raped by Amnon (2 Sam. 13:19).

8. David rent his clothes when he heard that Absalom had taken his revenge upon Amnon (2 Sam. 13:31).

9. Hushai the Archite came to meet David with rent clothes (2 Sam. 15:32).

10. Elisha rent his clothes when Elijah was taken up to heaven (2 Kings 2:12).

11. The king of Israel rent his clothes when Naaman came to him to be healed of leprosy (2 Kings 5:7).

12. The king of Israel rent his clothes when he heard a woman quarreling about eating another woman's son (2 Kings 6:30).

13. Athaliah rent her clothes when Jehoiada the priest put her out of power (2 Kings 11:14).

14. King Hezekiah rent his clothes when Rabshakeh denounced the Lord before the people of Israel (2 Kings 19:1).

15. Josiah rent his clothes when the book of the law was read in his presence for the first time (2 Kings 22:11, 19).

16. Ezra rent his clothing when he heard about the mixture of marriages between God's people and the nations around them (Ezra 9:3,5).

17. Job rent his clothes when he heard the evil report (Job 1:20).

18. Job's three friends rent their clothes when they saw Job (Job 2:12).

19. Eighty men came to the house of the Lord with rent clothes (Jer. 41:5).

20. The high priest rent his clothes when Jesus spoke of His being seated at the right hand of God's power (Matt. 26:65).

21. Barnabas and Paul rent their clothes when those who witnessed the miracle at Lystra began to worship them as gods (Acts 14:14).

4

Eat and Drink

There was a time when sitting down for a meal was both enjoyable and relaxing. It was a time to enjoy the family being together and to discuss the expectations and the experiences of the day. People weren't in such a hurry that they had to gulp their meals down. Neither were they so concerned about whether the food was absolutely the most nutritious. Somehow, we have lost some of the benefit of God's purpose for eating and drinking—fellowship and enjoyment.

Eating and drinking form a central role in the activities of people in the Bible. The following sixteen lists show many aspects of this role in their lives. Menus may have changed since then, but the vital role it had in life has not changed. Do these sound familiar: family meals, banquets, meals with friends, marriage feasts, community picnics, discussions about wine and its purposes, times of fasting, times of severe shortage, breads, water, soups, "miraculous" meals you didn't know were coming, strange foods, poisonous foods, and horrible foods? Most of them are familiar to us.

25. Twenty-seven Important Meals

1. The original sin occurred when Adam and Eve ate the fruit of the forbidden tree (Gen. 3:6).
2. When the Lord and two angels came to Abraham in human form, Abraham served a meal to them (Gen. 18:1-8).
3. After leaving Abraham, the two angels went to Sodom. Lot welcomed them into his house and made them a feast (Gen. 19:1-3).

4. Esau sold his birthright for a meal of bread and pottage of lentils (Gen. 25:29-34).

5. Jacob obtained his father's blessing by bringing him a meal and pretending he was Esau (Gen. 27:1-29).

6. When Joseph's brothers went down to Egypt the second time, Joseph (still hiding his identity) invited them to eat with him (Gen. 43:16-34).

7. In the first Passover observance, each Jewish household killed a lamb, applied its blood to the doorposts, roasted the meat, and ate it. God commanded that the Passover meal, plus seven days of eating unleavened bread, be observed annually from then on, in remembrance of Israel's deliverance from Egypt (Ex. 12:1-20).

8. When David's daughter Tamar served some food to her half brother Amnon (who was pretending to be sick), he raped her (2 Sam. 13:1-14).

9. Ravens brought Elijah bread and meat while he hid by the brook Cherith (1 Kings 17:3-6).

10. Later, a widow of Zarephath fed Elijah. Her supply of meal and oil was miraculously replenished during the famine (1 Kings 17:8-16).

11. When Elijah called Elisha to be a prophet, Elisha killed and boiled his yoke of oxen and gave a feast before following Elijah (1 Kings 19:19-21).

12. Queen Vashti was deposed during a seven-day banquet King Ahasuerus gave for people of Shushan (Esther 1:5-21).

13. At the second of two banquets which Queen Esther gave for the king and Haman, she revealed Haman's plot to have all the Jews killed. As a result, Haman was hanged and the Jews were saved (Esther 7).

14. The Jews feasted to celebrate their victory over Haman and their other enemies. Mordecai and Esther made this feast (called Purim) an annual event (Esther 9:17-32).

15. As Job's sons and daughters were feasting in their eldest brother's house, the house collapsed, killing them all (Job 1:18-19).

16. Daniel and his friends chose to eat vegetables rather than defile themselves with the king's food (Dan. 1:5-16).

17. As Belshazzar gave a great feast in his palace, the "handwriting on the wall" announced the end of his kingdom (Dan. 5).

18. The Pharisees criticized the disciples for plucking grain on the Sabbath (Matt. 12:1-8).

19. John the Baptist was beheaded at Herodias' daughter's request after she danced at Herod's birthday supper (Mark 6:21-28).
20. Jesus miraculously fed five thousand men with five loaves and two fish (John 6:5-14). Later He fed four thousand in similar fashion (Matt. 15:32-38).
21. Martha and Mary invited Jesus to their home for a meal. Martha occupied herself with preparation for the meal, but Mary sat at Jesus' feet (Luke 10:38-42).
22. Jesus told a parable of a man who made a great banquet and invited many people. They all turned him down, so he had others brought in from the streets so that his house would be filled (Luke 14:16-24).
23. The father made a joyful feast when his prodigal son returned home (Luke 15:20-25).
24. Mary anointed Jesus' feet with precious ointment while He was their supper guest (John 12:1-3). Jesus was also anointed by women at two other mealtimes during His lifetime (Luke 7:36-50; Matt. 26:6-13).
25. Jesus' "Last Supper" was the Passover meal that He ate with the twelve disciples in the Upper Room (Matt. 26:1-30).
26. Jesus ate three meals with His disciples after His resurrection: He broke bread in Emmaus (Luke 24:30), ate fish at Jerusalem to prove that He was not a ghost (Luke 24:38-43), and ate fish and bread by the Sea of Galilee (John 21:12-14).
27. John witnessed the marriage feast of the Lamb in heaven (Rev. 19:9).

26. Three Forty-Day Fasts

1. Moses neither ate nor drank while he talked with God for forty days on Mount Sinai (Ex. 34:27, 28).
2. The angel of the Lord fed Elijah two meals which gave him strength for the next forty days (1 Kings 19:5-8).
3. Jesus fasted for forty days in the wilderness after His baptism (Matt. 4:1,2).

27. Twenty-four Shorter Fasts

1. The Israelites fasted for the rest of the day after the Benjamites had defeated them in two successive battles (Judges 20:26).

322

2. The children of Israel repented of their idolatry and fasted with Samuel at Mizpah for a day (1 Sam. 7:3-6).
3. Saul ordered a fast for his soldiers while pursuing the Philistines. His son Jonathan had not heard about it, so he ate some wild honey that day (1 Sam. 14:24-27).
4. When Saul was unsuccessfully inquiring of the Lord, he fasted all day and night (1 Sam. 28:20).
5. The inhabitants of Jabesh-gilead fasted for seven days (1 Sam. 31:11-13) and David and his men fasted the rest of the day when they heard about the deaths of Saul and his sons (2 Sam. 1:11,12).
6. "The Lord struck the child that Uriah's wife bore unto David and it was very sick. David therefore besought God for the child; and David fasted" (2 Sam. 12:15,16).
7. Because her husband Ahab wanted Naboth's vineyard, Queen Jezebel proclaimed a day of fasting as part of a scheme to get it (1 Kings 21:8-10).
8. King Ahab humbled himself and fasted when Elijah accused him of Naboth's murder (1 Kings 21:27).
9. King Jehoshaphat sought the Lord and proclaimed a fast in Judah when the Moabites attacked (2 Chron. 20:1-4).
10. Before leaving Babylonia for Jerusalem, Ezra and his troop sought the Lord and fasted (Ezra 8:21-23).
11. Nehemiah fasted when asking the Lord for favor before the king of Persia (Neh. 1:1-4).
12. The inhabitants of Jerusalem separated themselves from the people of the land and fasted (Neh. 9:1-3).
13. Mordecai and the rest of the Jews in Media-Persia fasted after the king declared that they were all to be killed (Esther 4:1-3,15,16).
14. The people of Judah came to Jerusalem for a fast, and Baruch read them the prophecy of Jeremiah (Jer. 36:9,10).
15. After Daniel had been thrown into the lions' den, King Darius spent the night fasting (Dan. 6:18).
16. Daniel fasted as he sought the Lord for the liberation of his people from Media-Persia (Dan. 9:3,4).
17. Jonah's warning of God's wrath drove the people of Nineveh to repentance, and the king declared a fast until God's wrath was turned away (Jonah 3:4-10).
18. Jesus told the disciples that they should have prayed and fasted in order to gain power over a demon that they had not been able to cast out (Matt. 17:21).

19. Saul fasted for three days in Damascus while he waited for Ananias (Acts 9:9).
20. Cornelius was fasting and praying when an angel appeared to him and told him to send for Peter (Acts 10:1-3).
21. The elders at Antioch fasted and prayed and laid hands on Paul and Barnabas before sending them out as missionaries (Acts 13:1-3).
22. Paul and Barnabas fasted and prayed as they chose elders for each new church (Acts 14:23).
23. Forty men bound themselves by oath neither to eat nor drink until they had killed Paul (Acts 23:20,21).
24. The 275 passengers on the storm-tossed ship with Paul had fasted for fourteen days (Acts 27:33).

28. Winepresses

1. Gideon threshed wheat by the winepress to hide it from the Midianites (Judges 6:11).
2. Gideon's army slew Zeeb the Midianite at the winepress of Zeeb (Judges 7:25).
3. Isaiah spoke of Judah as a vineyard and of God putting them into His winepress of wrath (Isa. 5:1,2; 63:1-4).
4. Jesus told a parable about a householder who planted a vineyard, dug a winepress, and rented it out to tenants (Matt. 21:33-41).

29. Jesus and Wine

1. Jesus turned the water into wine at the wedding in Cana (John 2:1-10).
2. "No man putteth new wine into old [wineskins]; else the new wine will burst the [wineskins], and be spilled, and the [wineskins] shall perish. But new wine must be put into new [wineskins]; and both are preserved" (Luke 5:37,38).
3. "The Son of man came eating and drinking, and they say, Behold a man gluttonous, and a winebibber, a friend of publicans and sinners" (Matt. 11:19; Luke 7:34).
4. "No man also having drunk old wine straightway desireth new: for he saith, The old is better" (Luke 5:39).
5. "And he took the cup, and gave thanks, and gave it to them, saying, Drink ye all of it; for this is my blood of the new testament, which is shed for many for the remission of sins.

An ancient winepress

But I say unto you, I will not drink henceforth of this fruit
of the vine, until that day when I drink it new with you in
my Father's kingdom" (Matt. 26:27-29).

6. "And they gave him to drink wine mingled with myrrh: but
he received it not" (Mark 15:23).

30. Nine Old Testament Admonitions About Wine

1. "The Lord spoke unto Aaron, saying, Do not drink wine nor
strong drink, thou, nor thy sons with thee, when ye go into
the tabernacle of the congregation, lest ye die" (Lev. 10:8,9).

2. "When either man or woman shall separate themselves to
vow a vow of a Nazarite, to separate themselves unto the
Lord: he shall separate himself from wine and strong drink,
and shall drink no vinegar of wine, or vinegar of strong

drink, neither shall he drink any liquor of grapes, nor eat moist grapes, or dried" (Num. 6:2,3).

3. "It is not for kings, O Lemuel, it is not for kings to drink wine; nor for princes strong drink: lest they drink, and forget the law, and pervert the judgment of any of the afflicted" (Prov. 31:4,5).

4. "Wine is a mocker, strong drink is raging: and whosoever is deceived thereby is not wise" (Prov. 20:1).

5. "He that loveth wine and oil shall not be rich" (Prov. 21:17).

6. "Who hath woe? who hath sorrow? who hath contentions? who hath babbling? who hath wounds without cause? who hath redness of eyes? They that tarry long at the wine; they that go to seek mixed wine" (Prov. 23:29,30).

7. "Look not thou upon wine when it is red, when it giveth his colour in the cup, when it moveth itself aright. At the last it biteth like a serpent, and stingeth like an adder" (Prov. 23:31,32).

8. "Give strong drink unto him that is ready to perish, and wine unto those that be of heavy hearts. Let him drink, and forget his poverty, and remember his misery no more" (Prov. 31:6,7).

9. "Woe unto them that rise up early in the morning, that they may follow strong drink; that continue until night, till wine inflame them!" (Isa. 5:11).

31. Four New Testament Admonitions About Wine

1. "It is good neither to eat flesh, nor to drink wine, nor any thing whereby thy brother stumbleth, or is offended, or is made weak" (Rom. 14:21).

2. "Be not drunk with wine, wherein is excess; but be filled with the Spirit" (Eph. 5:18).

3. Paul wrote to Timothy, "Drink no longer water, but use a little wine for thy stomach's sake and thine often infirmities" (1 Tim. 5:23).

4. "A bishop must be blameless ... not given to wine" (1 Tim. 3:2,3; Titus 1:7).

32. Fourteen Famines

1. "There was a famine in the land: and Abram went down into Egypt to sojourn there; for the famine was grievous in the land" (Gen. 12:10).

2. "There was a famine in the land, beside the first famine that was in the days of Abraham. And Isaac went unto Abimelech king of the Philistines unto Gerar" (Gen. 26:1).

3. Pharaoh made Joseph the food-storage supervisor in preparation for the impending famine which eventually covered all the earth (Gen. 41).

4. God sent a dense swarm of locusts to destroy all the plants that remained in Egypt after the plague of hail had destroyed most of the crops (Ex. 10:14,15).

5. The Midianites would swoop through the land of Israel during Gideon's time, plundering and destroying all the crops and livestock they found (Judges 6:3-6).

6. Elimelech and his wife Naomi moved to Moab to escape the famine in Bethlehem (Ruth 1:1,2).

7. "There was a famine in the days of David three years . . . because [Saul] slew the Gibeonites (2 Sam. 21:1).

8. Elijah prophesied a draught and Samaria suffered three years of famine until he told King Ahab that it would rain again (1 Kings 17:1; 18:2,41-45).

9. God sent a seven-year famine upon Israel during Elisha's ministry (2 Kings 8:1,2).

10. "Nebuchadnezzar king of Babylon came, he, and all his host, against Jerusalem, and pitched against it; and they built forts against it round about. And . . . the famine prevailed in the city and there was no bread for the people of the land" (2 Kings 25:1-3).

11. The Chaldeans laid siege against Jerusalem, and God allowed famine and pestilence upon the people to judge them (Jer. 32:24,36; 52:6).

12. The penniless prodigal son found himself in the midst of a great famine (Luke 15:14).

13. "And there stood up one of them named Agabus, and signified by the Spirit that there should be great dearth throughout all the world; which came to pass in the days of Claudius Caesar" (Acts 11:28).

14. The rider of the pale horse spreads famine and pestilence over the earth (Rev. 6:8).

33. Seven Miraculous Meals

1. God fed Israel with heaven-sent manna in the wilderness (Ex. 16:11-15).

2. "Ravens brought [Elijah] bread and flesh in the morning, and bread and flesh in the evening" (1 Kings 17:6).
3. The widow of Zarephath made Elijah a cake of bread and, as promised, her cruse of oil never ran dry, nor did her barrel of meal go empty (1 Kings 17:12-16).
4. An angel prepared a meal for Elijah that gave him strength for forty days and nights (1 Kings 19:5-8).
5. Elisha fed one hundred men with twenty barley biscuits. They all ate and still had leftovers (2 Kings 4:42-44).
6. Jesus fed about five thousand men (not including the women and children with them) with only five small loaves of bread and two fish. Everyone ate enough, and leftovers filled twelve baskets (Matt. 14:15-21).
7. Jesus also fed four thousand men (plus the women and children with them) with seven loaves and a few small fish. There were seven basketfuls of food left over (Matt. 15:32-38).

34. Three Soups

1. Jacob traded bread and pottage of lentils for Esau's birthright (Gen. 25:29-34).
2. Gideon fixed a meal for an angel. The meal included a pot of broth (Judges 6:19).
3. Elijah fed the sons of the prophets with a pot of pottage (2 Kings 4:38).

35. Loaves of Bread

1. Twelve loaves of bread were to be left upon the table of shewbread in the tabernacle (Lev. 24:5-7).
2. Three men confirmed Samuel's words to Saul by giving him two loaves of bread as had been prophesied (1 Sam. 10:3,4).
3. David and his men took the twelve loaves of the Bread of the Presence from the tabernacle while Saul was chasing David to kill him (1 Sam. 21:1-6).
4. The widow of Zarephath prepared a loaf of bread for Elijah out of her last bit of meal (1 Kings 17:11-16).
5. Jesus took 5 loaves and fed 5,000 men (Matt. 14:15-21) and later took 7 loaves and fed 4,000 (Matt. 15:32-38).
6. "Jesus took the bread, and blessed it, and brake it, and gave

it to his disciples, and said, Take, eat: this is my body"
(Matt. 26:26).

7. The men at Emmaus did not recognize Jesus until He took
the bread, blessed it, and broke it (Luke 24:30,31).

8. The Gibeonites fooled Joshua by showing him moldy loaves
of bread and telling him that the loaves had been freshly
baked for their journey (Josh. 9:12).

36. Sweet and Sour: Flavors in the Bible

1. God commanded Israel to keep the Passover meal by eating
a lamb with unleavened bread and bitter herbs (Ex. 12:8).

2. Moses was to make a special anointing oil with olive oil and
cinnamon (Ex. 30:23-25).

3. Garlic, onions, and leeks were some of the pleasures of Egypt
for which the Israelites longed (Num. 11:5).

4. The Psalmist said, "My meditation of him shall be sweet:
I will be glad in the Lord" (Ps. 104:34).

5. "Stolen waters are sweet, and bread eaten in secret is pleasant" (Prov. 9:17).

6. "Bread of deceit is sweet to a man; but afterwards his mouth
shall be filled with gravel" (Prov. 20:17).

7. "My son, eat thou honey, because it is good; and the honeycomb, which is sweet to thy taste" (Prov. 24:13).

8. "The full soul loatheth an honeycomb; but to the hungry
soul every bitter thing is sweet" (Prov. 27:7).

9. God asks the people why they bother making sacrifices when
"your burnt offerings are not acceptable, nor your sacrifices
sweet unto me" (Jer. 6:20).

10. "The fathers have eaten a sour grape, and the children's
teeth are set on edge" (Jer. 31:29).

11. "Behold, the days come, saith the Lord, that the plowman
shall overtake the reaper, and the treader of grapes him that
soweth seed; and the mountains shall drop sweet wine, and
all the hills shall melt" (Amos 9:13).

12. "Does a fountain send forth at the same place sweet water
and bitter?" (James 3:11).

13. Ezekiel ate a book and declared that it was as sweet as
honey in his mouth (Ezek. 2:9-3:3).

14. John also ate a book but wrote, "It was in my mouth sweet
as honey; and as soon as I had eaten it, my belly was bitter"
(Rev. 10:9,10).

37. Five Poisons

1. "The Lord sent fiery serpents among the people, and they bit the people; and much people of Israel died" (Num. 21:6).
2. Elisha "healed" a poisonous spring of water (2 Kings 2:19-22).
3. The sons of the prophets made pottage but accidentally threw in some poisonous gourds. Elisha made it fit to eat again (2 Kings 4:41).
4. James said that the tongue is "an unruly evil, full of deadly poison" (James 3:8).
5. Christ promised, "These things shall follow them that believe; ... if they drink any deadly thing, it shall not hurt them" (Mark 16:17,18).

38. Instances of Cannibalism

1. A woman in Samaria boiled her son and ate him with her neighbor and then cried to the king when her neighbor would not boil her son (2 Kings 6:24-29).
2. Women boiled and ate their children during the Babylonian siege on Jerusalem (Lam. 4:10).

39. Strange Foods

1. Moses took the *golden calf* "which they had made, and burnt it in the fire, and ground it to powder, and strawed it upon the water, and made the children of Israel drink of it" (Ex. 32:20).
2. God sent *manna* for the children of Israel to eat while they wandered in the wilderness. "Manna" means "what is it?" (Ex. 16:15).
3. Samson ate *honey* from out of a dead lion (Judges 14:8,9).
4. John the Baptist ate *locusts* and *wild honey* (Matt. 3:4).

40. The Biggest Meals in the Bible

1. The Lord fed the entire nation of Israel for forty years on manna (Deut. 8:16).
2. The people complained about the manna, so God sent then quail for an entire month (Num. 11:19,31).
3. "Solomon's provision for one day was thirty measures of

330

Jesus feeds the 5,000

fine flour, and threescore measures of meal, ten fat oxen,
and twenty oxen out of the pasture, and an hundred sheep,
besides harts, and roebucks, and fallowdeer, and fatted fowl"
(1 Kings 4:22,23).

4. Jesus fed 5,000 men with 5 loaves and 2 fishes and 4,000
men with 7 loaves and a few fish (Matt. 14:19-21; 15:32-38).

5

Water

Rarely does a week go by but that the evening news reports about another city whose wells have been discovered to be contaminated. Life for those depending upon this water sometimes becomes chaotic and frustrating. Though we usually take it for granted, good water is absolutely essential for our survival.

In Bible times water was not taken for granted. The task of drawing water was a daily chore for each family. The following seven lists show this vital role of water in the lives of Bible people. We see the importance of the local wells and their prominent place in the life of the community, miracles that occurred related to water, important rivers and lakes, the use of water in baptisms, and the need for swimming lessons.

41. Fourteen Water Miracles

1. "Moses and Aaron did so, as the Lord commanded; and he lifted up the rod, and smote the waters that were in the river ... and all the waters that were in the river were turned to blood" (Ex. 7:20).
2. While the Egyptian army pursued the children of Israel, the Lord opened a dry path across the Red Sea for the Israelites. The Egyptians followed closely behind the fleeing Hebrews but were drowned when the walls of water collapsed and filled the walkway (Ex. 14:21-29).
3. "When [the children of Israel] came to Marah, they could not drink of the waters of Marah, for they were bitter ... and the people murmured against Moses, saying, What shall we drink? And he cried unto the Lord; and the Lord showed

him a tree, which when he had cast into the waters, the waters were made sweet" (Ex. 15:23-25).

4. In the desert the Israelites twice complained about having no water. Both times the Lord caused water to come out of a rock (Ex. 17:1-6; 20:1-11).

5. The waters of the Jordan rose up in a heap far upstream when the priests carrying the Ark of the Covenant dipped the soles of their feet into the water. The Israelites crossed the river on dry ground (Josh. 3:7-17).

6. Gideon wrung out a bowlful of water from the fleece in answer to prayer (Judges 6:38).

7. Elijah struck the waters of the Jordan with his mantle and he walked across on dry ground with Elisha. Elisha returned later with the same mantle and struck the waters. He crossed again on dry ground (2 Kings 2:8-14).

8. Elisha "healed" Jericho's water supply by throwing salt into it (2 Kings 2:19-22).

9. God gave water to the thirsty army of Israel by commanding them to dig trenches and then He filled them during the night without making it rain (2 Kings 3:14-22).

10. Naaman, commander of the Syrian army, was healed after dipping seven times in the Jordan River (2 Kings 5:14).

11. "As one was felling a beam, the axe head fell into the water: and he cried, and said, Alas, master! for it was borrowed. And [Elisha] said, Where fell it? And he showed him the place. And he cut down a stick, and cast it in thither; and the iron did swim . . . and he put out his hand and took it" (2 Kings 6:5-7).

12. Jesus walked on the Sea of Galilee to meet His disciples in their ship. Peter crawled over the side to join Him, and he also walked on the water (Matt. 14:25-31).

13. Jesus spoke to the sea and calmed it (Mark 4:39).

14. Jesus turned the water into wine at the wedding feast in Cana (John 2:1-10).

42. Eight Important Water Containers

1. "[Abraham's] servant ran to meet her [Rebekah], and said, Let me, I pray thee, drink a little water of thy *pitcher*. And she said, Drink, my lord: and . . . when she had done giving him drink, she said, I will draw water for thy camels also" (Gen. 24:17-19).

David's men at the well of Bethlehem

2. "The Lord spake unto Moses, saying, Thou shalt also make a *laver* of brass, and his foot also of brass, to wash withal: and thou shalt put it between the tabernacle of the congregation and the altar, and thou shalt put water therein. For Aaron and his sons shall wash their hands and their feet thereat" (Ex. 30:17-19).

3. Gideon set out a fleece of wool on the threshing floor. In the morning, though the ground around it was dry, he wrung a *bowl* of water from the fleece (Judges 6:36-38).

4. David sneaked into Saul's camp and took Saul's spear and *cruse* of water (1 Sam. 26:7-11).

5. After the priests of Baal failed to call down fire upon their sacrifice, Elijah built his altar to the Lord and had four *barrels* of water poured over the sacrifice three times (2 Kings 18:31-38).

6. "[Jesus'] disciples said unto him, Where wilt thou that we go and prepare that thou mayest eat the passover? And he sendeth forth two of his disciples, and saith unto them, Go

ye into the city, and there shall meet you a man bearing a *pitcher* of water: follow him" (Mark 14:12,13).

7. Jesus turned the water in six *waterpots* of stone into wine at Cana (John 2:6).
8. Jesus filled a *basin* with water and washed the disciples' feet (John 13:3-5).

43. Twelve Important Wells

1. The angel of the Lord spoke to Hagar at the well called Beer-lahai-roi between Kadesh and Bered (Gen. 16:7-14).
2. Abimelech's servants attempted to take a well called Beer-sheba away from Abraham. They settled their differences by making a covenant with one another (Gen. 21:22-32).
3. Abraham's servant found a wife for Isaac by the well at the city of Nahor (Gen. 24:10-67).
4. Isaac's servants dug two wells that he gave up to other herdsmen rather than fighting over them. He called them Esek and Sitnah. They then dug two more wells that he kept without trouble. He called them Rehoboth and Beer-sheba (Gen. 26:17-33).
5. Jacob met Rachel when she came to water her sheep at a well which was covered by a stone (Gen. 29:1-12).
6. Moses met his wife Zipporah when he helped her and her sisters water their flock at a well in the land of Midian (Ex. 2:15-21).
7. It was at the well of Harod that God whittled Gideon's troops down to the courageous three hundred (Judges 7:1-7).
8. After Samson slew a thousand men with the jawbone of an ass, he was extremely thirsty. God opened the ground and water came out. Samson called the well En-hakkore (Judges 15:18-20).
9. Abner was at the well of Sirah when he was summoned to his death by Joab's vigilantes (2 Sam. 3:26,27).
10. Jonathan and Ahimaaz escaped Absalom's men by hiding in a well in Bahurim (2 Sam. 17:17-21).
11. David longed for a drink from the well at Bethlehem, so three mighty men broke through the Philistine defenses and drew water for him. He poured it out as a sacrifice to the Lord (2 Sam. 23:14-17).
12. Jesus talked with the woman of Samaria at Jacob's well (John 4:5-15).

Pharaoh's army being drowned in the Red Sea

44. Thirteen Important Rivers, Brooks, Lakes, and Seas

1. A great river flowed into the Garden of Eden and divided into the *Pison*, the *Gihon*, the *Hiddekel*, and the *Euphrates* (Gen. 2:10-14).
2. The whole earth was covered by one huge sea during the Flood (Gen. 7:17-24).
3. The *Dead Sea* is called the *Salt Sea* in Gen. 14:3.
4. "The Lord made a covenant with Abram, saying, Unto thy seed have I given this land, from the *river of Egypt* unto the great river, the river *Euphrates*" (Gen. 15:18).
5. The first plague that God sent upon the Egyptians turned the waters of the *Nile River* to blood (Ex. 7:17-25).
6. Pharaoh and his men were drowned in the *Red Sea* after the Israelites had crossed over it on dry ground (Ex. 15:4).
7. The Promised Land bordered on the *great sea* (Num. 34:6),

also called the *sea of the Philistines* (Ex. 23:31), the *sea of Joppa* (Ezra 3:7), and the *sea of Cilicia* (Acts 27:5). We know it today as the *Mediterranean Sea.*

8. The Israelites crossed the *Jordan River* when they entered the Promised Land (Josh. 1:1,2).
9. David fled across the *brook Kidron* in his escape from Absalom (2 Sam. 15:13-23).
10. Elijah lived by the *brook Cherith* during the years of drought (1 Kings 17:1-4).
11. Ezra proclaimed a fast at the river *Ahava* (Ezra 8:21).
12. Jesus taught by the *lake of Gennesaret*—or *Galilee,* as we know it today (Luke 5:1-3).
13. John saw the *pure river of water of life* (Rev. 22:1).

45. Famous Swimmers

1. An iron axhead swam (2 Kings 6:5,6).
2. Peter swam to shore to meet Jesus (John 21:7-11).
3. Paul and 275 other people swam to shore or floated safely on broken pieces of their damaged ship (Acts 27:43,44).

46. Eleven Famous Baptisms

1. "Then cometh Jesus from Galilee to Jordan unto John, to be baptized of him" (Matt. 3:13).
2. Peter and the other disciples baptized about 3,000 people on the day of Pentecost (Acts 2:41).
3. Simon the sorcerer and others from Samaria were baptized by Philip (Acts 8:12,13).
4. "[The Ethiopian eunuch] commanded the chariot to stand still: and they went down both into the water, both Philip and the eunuch; and he baptized him" (Acts 8:38).
5. Paul was baptized by Ananias in Damascus (Acts 9:18).
6. Peter baptized Cornelius and his friends (Acts 10:23-48).
7. Lydia and her household were baptized by Paul and Silas (Acts 16:14,15).
8. The Philippian jailor took Paul and Silas to his home where they baptized him and his household (Acts 16:26-33).
9. "Crispus, the chief ruler of the synagogue, believed on the Lord with all his house; and many of the Corinthians hearing believed, and were baptized" (Acts 18:8).
10. Paul baptized about twelve Ephesian believers who had known only John's baptism (Acts 19:1-7).

11. "Moreover, brethren, I would not that ye should be ignorant, how that all our fathers were under the cloud, and all passed through the sea; and were all baptized unto Moses in the cloud and in the sea" (1 Cor. 10:1,2).

47. Three Drownings

1. "Fifteen cubits upward did the waters prevail; and the mountains were covered. And all flesh died that moved upon the earth, both of fowl, and of cattle, and of beast, and of every creeping thing that creepeth upon the earth, and every man: all in whose nostrils was the breath of life, of all that was in the dry land, died . . . and Noah only remained alive, and they that were with him in the ark" (Gen. 7:20-23).
2. "The Lord is a man of war: the Lord is his name. Pharoah's chariots and his host hath he cast into the sea: his chosen captains also are drowned in the Red sea" (Ex. 15:3,4).
3. "And the unclean spirits went out, and entered into the swine: and the herd ran violently down a steep place into the sea, (they were about two thousand;) and were choked in the sea" (Mark 5:13).

6

Questions

"Why, Daddy?" "Mommy, how do I do this?" "What is that?" "Why, how and what" seem to be the only words that a two-year-old knows. Even the most patient parent is tested by this incessant bombardment. Yet, by asking questions the child learns about life and its many facets.

Macaulay wrote: "Knowledge advances by steps and not by leaps." As we mature, we may ask fewer questions, but the three-word vocabulary remains very central. If we are going to continue learning about life, we will have to continue asking questions. Questions are stepping-stones to obtain knowledge.

God asks people questions and people ask God questions. Throughout the next seven lists, we find people wanting answers from God, and God questioning people to make them face the truth about their lives. God, of course, already knows the answer, but the person may be trying to cover the truth. In these lists you may find some questions you'd like to ask God; then again, you may find God asking you some questions.

48. Twenty-four Questions the Disciples Asked Jesus

1. "The disciples came and said unto [Jesus], Why speakest thou unto [the multitudes] in parables?" (Matt. 13:10).
2. Jesus "said unto them, Hear, and understand: not that which goeth into the mouth defileth a man; but that which cometh out of the mouth, this defileth a man. Then came [Jesus'] disciples, and said unto him, knowest thou that the Phari-

sees were offended, after they heard this saying?" (Matt. 15:10-12).

3. "Jesus called his disciples unto him, and said, I have compassion on the multitude.... And his disciples say unto him, Whence should we have so much bread in the wilderness, as to fill so great a multitude?" (Matt. 15:32,33).
4. Jesus' disciples asked Him, "Why then say the scribes that Elias must first come?" (Matt. 17:10).
5. "Jesus rebuked the devil; and he departed out of him: and the child was cured from that very hour. Then came the disciples to Jesus apart, and said, Why could not we cast him out?" (Matt. 17:14-19).
6. "The disciples [came] unto Jesus, saying, Who is the greatest in the kingdom of heaven?" (Matt. 18:1).
7. Peter came to Jesus, "and said, Lord, how oft shall my brother sin against me, and I forgive him? till seven times?" (Matt. 18:21)
8. "Then said Jesus unto his disciples, ... It is easier for a camel to go through the eye of a needle, than for a rich man to enter into the kingdom of God. When his disciples heard it, they were exceedingly amazed, saying, Who then can be saved?" (Matt. 19:23-25).
9. Peter asked Jesus, "Behold, we have forsaken all, and followed thee; what shall we have therefore?" (Matt. 19:27).
10. The disciples came to Jesus privately and asked, "When shall these things be? and what shall be the sign of thy coming, and of the end of the world?" (Matt. 24:3).
11. "Now the first day of the feast of unleavened bread the disciples came to Jesus, saying unto him, Where wilt thou that we prepare for thee to eat the passover?" (Matt. 26:6-9).
12. Jesus said, "Verily I say unto you, that one of you shall betray me. And they were exceedingly sorrowful, and began every one of them to say unto him, Lord, is it I?" (Matt. 26:21,22).
13. Jesus' disciples asked Him, "What might this parable [of the sower] be?" (Luke 8:9).
14. When James and John saw that the Samaritans did not receive Jesus, "they said, Lord, wilt thou that we command fire to come down from heaven, and consume them, even as Elias did?" (Luke 9:53,54).
15. Jesus said, "Be ye therefore ready also: for the Son of man

cometh at an hour when ye think not. Then Peter said unto him, Lord, speakest thou this parable unto us, or even to all?" (Luke 12:39-41).

16. Jesus said to the disciples, "Two men shall be in the field; the one shall be taken, and the other left. And they answered and said unto him, Where Lord?" (Luke 17:34-37).
17. Many of Jesus' disciples, when they heard about eating Jesus' flesh and drinking His blood said, "This is a hard saying; who can hear it?" (John 6:60).
18. "As Jesus passed by, he saw a man which was blind from his birth. And his disciples asked him, saying, Master, who did sin, this man, or his parents, that he was born blind?" (John 9:1,2).
19. Jesus said to His disciples, "Let us go into Judaea again. His disciples say unto him, Master, the Jews of late sought to stone thee; and goest thou thither again?" (John 11:7,8).
20. Jesus began to wash His disciples' feet. When He came to Peter, "Peter saith unto him, Lord, dost thou wash my feet?" (John 13:3-6).
21. Jesus said, "Whither I go, ye cannot come; ... Simon Peter said unto him, Lord, whither goest thou?" (John 13:33,36).
22. Peter asked Jesus, "Lord, why cannot I follow thee now?" (John 13:37).
23. Thomas asked Jesus, "Lord, we know not whither thou goest; and how can we know the way?" (John 14:1-5).
24. "Judas saith unto [Jesus], not Iscariot, Lord, how is it that thou wilt manifest thyself unto us, and not unto the world?" (John 14:22).

49. Eighteen Questions the Religious Leaders Asked Jesus

1. "And they asked [Jesus], saying, Is it lawful to heal on the sabbath days?" (Matt. 12:10).
2. "Then came to Jesus scribes and Pharisees, which were of Jerusalem, saying, Why do thy disciples transgress the tradition of the elders? for they wash not their hands when they eat bread" (Matt. 15:1,2).
3. "The Pharisees also came unto Jesus, tempting him, and saying unto him, Is it lawful for a man to put away his wife for every cause?" (Matt. 19:3).
4. The Pharisees asked Jesus, "Why did Moses then command

to give a writing of divorcement, and to put her away?" (Matt. 19:7).

5. "When the chief priests and scribes saw the wonderful things that Jesus did, and the children crying in the temple, and saying, Hosanna to the son of David; they were sore displeased, and said unto him, Hearest what these say?" (Matt. 21:15,16).

6. While Jesus was in the temple teaching, the chief priests and the elders came to him and asked, "By what authority doest thou these things: and who gave thee this authority?" (Matt. 21:23).

7. The Pharisees sent men to Jesus to gather evidence against Him and they asked, "What thinkest thou? Is it lawful to give tribute to Caesar, or not?" (Matt. 22:15-17).

8. The Sadducees asked Jesus, "Now there were with us seven brethren: and the first, when he had married a wife, deceased, and, having no issue, left his wife unto his brother: likewise the second also, and the third, unto the seventh. And last of all the woman died also. Therefore in the resurrection whose wife shall she be of the seven? for they all had her" (Matt. 22:23-28).

9. A lawyer asked Jesus, "Master, which is the great commandment in the law?" (Matt. 22:35-36).

10. Jesus' disciples walked through a grain field on the Sabbath and plucked some heads of grain. The Pharisees asked Jesus, "Behold, why do they on the sabbath that which is not lawful?" (Mark 2:23,24).

11. "A certain lawyer stood up, and tempted [Jesus], saying, Master, what shall I do to inherit eternal life?" (Luke 10:25).

12. Jesus told a lawyer that he must love his neighbor as himself. "But he, willing to justify himself, said unto Jesus, And who is my neighbour?" (Luke 10:29).

13. After Jesus had chased the moneychangers out of the temple, the Jews asked Him, "What sign shewest thou unto us, seeing that thou doest these things?" (John 2:13-18).

14. "Nicodemus saith unto him, How can a man be born when he is old? can he enter the second time into his mother's womb and be born?" (John 3:3,4).

15. The scribes and Pharisees brought a woman caught in adultery to Jesus and they asked Him, "Now Moses in the law commanded us, that such should be stoned: but what sayest thou? This they said tempting him, that they might have to accuse him" (John 8:3-6).

16. Jesus said that the Father bore witness of Him. The Pharisees asked, "Where is thy Father?" (John 8:17-19).
17. The Pharisees asked Jesus, "Who art thou?" (John 8:25).
18. "Jesus said, For judgment I am come into this world, that they which see not might see; and that they which see might be made blind. And some of the Pharisees which were with him heard these words, and said unto him, Are we blind also?" (John 9:39,40).

50. Seven Questions Which Received No Answer

1. "Elijah asked the people of Israel, "How long halt ye between two opinions? If the Lord be God, follow him: but if Baal, then follow him. And the people answered him not a word" (1 Kings 18:21).
2. The King of Assyria sent his ambassador to King Hezekiah and asked him, "Who are [the gods of Samaria] among all the gods of these lands, that have delivered their land [into] my hand, that the Lord should deliver Jerusalem out of my hand? But they held their peace, and answered him not a word" (2 Kings 18:35,36).
3. The bride asked the city watchman, "Have you seen him whom my soul loves?" (Song of Sol. 3:3).
4. "Pilate asked Jesus again, saying, Answerest thou nothing? behold how many things they witness against thee. But Jesus answered nothing" (Mark 15:4,5).
5. "Jesus cried with a loud voice, saying, . . . My God, my God, why hast thou forsaken me?" (Mark 15:34).
6. "Then [Herod] questioned with him in many words; but he answered him nothing" (Luke 23:9).
7. "Pilate sayeth unto [Jesus], What is truth?" (John 18:38).

51. Twenty-five Questions People Asked God

1. Cain asked God, "Am I my brother's keeper?" (Gen. 4:9).
2. "Abram said, Lord God, what wilt thou give me, seeing I go childless, and the steward of my house is this Eliezer of Damascus?" (Gen. 15:2).
3. God said to Abram, "I am the Lord that brought thee out of Ur of the Chaldees, to give thee this land to inherit it. And he said, Lord God, whereby shall I know that I shall inherit it?" (Gen. 15:7,8).

4. Abraham questioned God about the destruction of Sodom without separating the righteous from the wicked and asked, "Shall not the Judge of all the earth do right?" (Gen. 18:25).

5. Abimelech had taken Sarah as his wife, but God showed him that she was actually Abraham's wife. He prayed for mercy and said, "Lord, wilt thou slay also a righteous nation?" (Gen. 20:4).

6. God called Moses to go to Pharaoh and release the Israelites, but Moses said, "Who am I, that I should go unto Pharaoh, and that I should bring forth the children of Israel out of Egypt?" (Ex. 3:10,11).

7. "Moses said unto God, Behold, when I come unto the children of Israel, and shall say unto them, The God of your fathers hath sent me unto you; and they shall say to me, What is his name? what shall I say unto them?" (Ex. 3:13).

8. After Moses' first failure to convince Pharaoh to let Israel go, "Moses returned unto the Lord, and said, Lord, wherefore hast thou so evil entreated this people? why is it that thou hast sent me?" (Ex. 5:22).

9. God commanded Moses to go back to Pharaoh, but Moses balked and said, "Behold, the children of Israel have not hearkened unto me; how then shall Pharaoh hear me, who am of uncircumcised lips?" (Ex. 6:12).

10. The people murmured against Moses "and Moses cried unto the Lord, saying, What shall I do unto this people? they be almost ready to stone me" (Ex. 17:3,4).

11. Moses pleaded with God not to destroy the Israelites, praying, "Wherefore should the Egyptians speak, and say, For mischief did he bring them out, to slay them in the mountains, and to consume them from the face of the earth?" (Ex. 32:12).

12. Moses asked God, "Wherein shall it be known here that I and thy people have found grace in thy sight? is it not that thou goest with us?" (Ex. 33:16).

13. The Israelites cried to Moses for meat, "and Moses said unto the Lord, Wherefore hast thou afflicted thy servant? and wherefore have I not found favour in thy sight, that thou layest the burden of all this people upon me?" (Num. 11:11).

14. Korah had rebelled against the authority of Moses, and God was about to destroy him. Moses and Aaron, fearing for the rest of the people, cried, "O God, the God of the spirits of

all flesh, shall one man sin, and wilt thou be wroth with all the congregation?" (Num 16:22).

15. After Israel lost their first battle against Ai, "Joshua said, Alas O Lord God, wherefore hast thou at all brought this people over Jordan, to deliver us into the hand of the Amorites, to destroy us?" (Josh. 7:7).

16. "Now after the death of Joshua it came to pass, that the children of Israel asked the Lord, saying, Who shall go up for us against the Canaanites first, to fight against them?" (Judges 1:1).

17. After nearly exterminating the tribe of Benjamin, the Israelites prayed, "O Lord God of Israel, why is this come to pass in Israel, that there should be today one tribe lacking in Israel?" (Judges 21:2,3).

18. The Philistines were plundering Keilah. "Therefore David inquired of the Lord, saying, Shall I go and smite these Philistines?" (1 Sam. 23:1,2).

19. After the Amalekites had taken Ziklag and had carried away the inhabitants, "David inquired at the Lord, saying, Shall I pursue after this troop? shall I overtake them?" (1 Sam. 30:3-8).

20. Solomon prayed, "Give therefore thy servant an understanding heart to judge thy people, that I may discern between good and bad: for who is able to judge this thy so great a people?" (1 Kings 3:5-9).

21. Elijah cried to the Lord, "and said, O Lord my God, hast thou also brought evil upon the widow with whom I sojourn, by slaying her son?" (1 Kings 17:20).

22. Job answered the Lord in response to a long list of hard questions "and said, Behold, I am vile; what shall I answer thee?" (Job 40:3,4).

23. Jeremiah cried to God, "Why is my pain perpetual, and my wound incurable, which refuseth to be healed? wilt thou be altogether unto me as a liar, and as waters that fail?" (Jer. 15:18).

24. Ezekiel fell on his face, "and cried with a loud voice, and said, Ah Lord God! wilt thou make a full end of the remnant of Israel?" (Ezek. 11:13).

25. "The burden which Habakkuk the prophet did see. O Lord, how long shall I cry, and thou wilt not hear! . . . Why dost thou shew me iniquity, and cause me to behold grievance?" (Hab. 1:1-3).

52. Forty-five Questions God Asked People

1. When Adam and Eve had sinned, they hid from the presence of God "and the Lord God called unto Adam, and said unto him, Where art thou?" (Gen. 3:6-9).

2. The Lord asked Adam, "Who told thee that thou wast naked? Hast thou eaten of the tree, whereof I commanded thee that thou shouldest not eat?" (Gen. 3:11).

3. "And the Lord God said unto the woman, What is this that thou hast done?" (Gen. 3:13).

4. After Cain's offering was rejected by God, "Cain was very wroth, and his countenance fell. And the Lord said unto Cain, Why art thou wroth? and why is thy countenance fallen? If thou doest well, shalt thou not be accepted?" (Gen. 4:6-7).

5. "Cain rose up against Abel his brother, and slew him. And the Lord said unto Cain, Where is Abel thy brother?... What hast thou done?" (Gen 4:8-10).

6. "The Lord said unto Abraham, Wherefore did Sarah laugh, saying, Shall I of a surety bear a child, which am old? Is anything too hard for the Lord?" (Gen. 18:13).

7. "The Lord said unto [Moses], What is that in thine hand?" (Ex. 4:2).

8. "Moses said unto the Lord, O my Lord, I am not eloquent, ... And the Lord said unto him, Who hath made man's mouth?" (Ex. 4:10,11).

9. As Pharaoh's army approached, the people cried to Moses, "and the Lord said unto Moses, Wherefore criest thou unto me?" (Ex. 14:15).

10. The Israelites questioned God's provision of manna for the Sabbath. "And the Lord said unto Moses, How long refuse ye to keep my commandments and my laws?" (Ex. 16:27,28).

11. Moses asked the Lord how he was to get the meat that the people demanded, and "the Lord said unto Moses, Is the Lord's hand waxed short? thou shalt see whether my word shall come to pass or not" (Num. 11:23).

12. Aaron and Miriam criticized Moses, and God said, "With him will I speak mouth to mouth, ... wherefore then were ye not afraid to speak against my servant Moses?" (Num. 12:8).

13. Moses asked the Lord to lift the judgment of leprosy from Miriam "and the Lord said unto Moses, If her father had

Cain after Abel's murder

but spit in her face, should she not be ashamed seven days?"
(Num. 12:13,14).

14. When the children of Israel refused to go into the Promised
Land, "the Lord said unto Moses, How long will this people
provoke me?" (Num. 14:11).

15. After Moses had died, God asked Joshua, "Have not I commanded thee? Be strong and of good courage; be not afraid,
neither be thou dismayed" (Josh. 1:1,9).

16. "The Lord said unto Samuel, How long wilt thou mourn for
Saul, seeing I have rejected him from reigning over Israel?"
(1 Sam. 16:1).

17. "The word of the Lord came unto Nathan, saying, Go and
tell my servant David, Thus saith the Lord, Shalt thou build
me an house for me to dwell in?" (2 Sam. 7:4,5).

18. After David had engineered the death of Uriah, God spoke to him through Nathan and said, "Wherefore hast thou despised the commandment of the Lord, to do evil in his sight?" (2 Sam. 12:9).

19. After David had sinned by numbering Israel and Judah, God offered him a choice of judgments, asking, "Shall seven years of famine come unto thee in thy land? or wilt thou flee three months before thine enemies, while they pursue thee? or that there be three days' pestilence in thy land?" (2 Sam. 24:13).

20. After Elijah ran away from Jezebel, he came to a cave, and "behold, the word of the Lord came to him, and he said unto him, What doest thou here, Elijah?" (1 Kings 19:9).

21. When Ahab had taken Naboth's vineyard, God sent Elijah, "saying, Thus saith the Lord, Hast thou killed, and also taken possession?" (1 Kings 21:19).

22. After Elijah had rebuked Ahab, God asked Elijah, "Seest thou how Ahab humbleth himself before me?" (1 Kings 21:29).

23. Isaiah "heard the voice of the Lord, saying, Whom shall I send, and who will go for us?" (Isa. 6:8).

24. "Is there a God beside me?" (Isa. 44:8).

25. The Lord asked Cyrus, "Shall the clay say to him that fashioneth it, What makest thou?" (Isa. 45:1-9).

26. "Is my hand shortened at all, that it cannot redeem? or have I no power to deliver?" (Isa. 50:2).

27. Jeremiah cried out in the temple, "Is this house, which is called by my name, become a den of robbers in your eyes? Behold, even I have seen it, saith the Lord" (Jer. 7:11).

28. The Lord asked, "Why is this people of Jerusalem slidden back by a perpetual backsliding?" (Jer. 8:4-12).

29. "Am I a God at hand, saith the Lord, and not a God afar off? Can any hide himself in secret places that I shall not see him? saith the Lord. Do not I fill heaven and earth? saith the Lord" (Jer. 23:23,24).

30. "Then came the word of the Lord unto Jeremiah, saying, Behold, I am the Lord, the God of all flesh: is there anything too hard for me?" (Jer. 32:26,27).

31. "Thus saith the Lord, the God of Israel, unto thee, O Baruch; . . . Seekest thou great things for thyself? seek them not" (Jer. 45:2,5).

32. Ezekiel prophesied against the false prophets of Israel

saying, "Have ye not seen a vain vision, and have ye not spoken a lying divination, whereas ye say, The Lord saith it; albeit I have not spoken?" (Ezek. 13:7).

33. Several Elders of Israel came to Ezekiel and God said, "Son of man, these men have set up their idols in their heart, and put the stumbling-block of their iniquity before their face: should I be inquired of at all by them?" (Ezek. 14:1-3).

34. "Have I any pleasure at all that the wicked should die? saith the Lord God: and not that he should return from his ways, and live?" (Ezek. 18:23).

35. The Lord asked Israel, "Can thine heart endure, or can thine hands be strong, in the days that I shall deal with thee?" (Ezek. 22:14).

36. Ezekiel prophesied against Israel, "Thus saith the Lord God; Ye eat with the blood, and lift up your eyes toward your idols, and shed blood: and shall ye possess the land?" (Ezek. 33:25).

37. God showed Ezekiel a valley of dry bones and asked him, "Son of man, can these bones live?" (Ezek. 37:3).

38. The Lord asked Israel, "Shall a trumpet be blown in the city, and the people not be afraid? shall there be evil in a city, and the Lord hath not done it?" (Amos 3:6).

39. Jonah was angry about his gourd that had died. "Then said the Lord, Doest thou well to be angry?" (Jonah 4:9).

40. The Lord asked Jonah, "Should not I spare Nineveh, that great city, wherein are more than sixscore thousand persons that cannot discern between their right hand and their left hand; and also much cattle?" (Jonah 4:11).

41. "Thus saith the Lord of hosts; Ask now the priests concerning the law, saying, If one bear holy flesh in the skirt of his garment, and with his skirt do touch bread, or pottage, or wine, or oil, or any meat, shall it be holy?" (Hag. 2:11,12).

42. Zechariah prophesied to the people and the priests, saying, "When ye fasted and mourned in the fifth and seventh month, even those seventy years, did ye at all fast unto me?" (Zech. 7:4-6).

43. "A son honoureth his father, and a servant his master: if then I be a father, where is mine honour? and if I be a master where is my fear? saith the Lord of hosts unto you, O priests, that despise my name" (Mal. 1:6).

44. Malachi spoke forth the word of the Lord, asking, "If ye offer the blind sacrifice, is it not evil? and if ye offer the

lame and sick, is it not evil? offer it now unto thy governor; will he be pleased with thee, or accept thy person?" (Mal. 1:8).

45. God pleaded for Israel to tithe, asking, "Will a man rob God?" (Mal. 3:8).

53. Thirty-four Questions God Asked Job

1. "Who is this that darkeneth counsel by words without knowledge?" (Job 38:2).
2. "Gird up now thy loins like a man; for I will demand of thee, and answer thou me. Where wast thou when I laid the foundations of the earth?" (Job 38:3,4).
3. "Who shut up the sea with doors, when it brake forth, as if it had issued out of the womb?" (Job 38:8).
4. "Hast thou commanded the morning since thy days; and caused the day-spring to know his place; that it might take hold of the ends of the earth, that the wicked might be shaken out of it?" (Job 38:12,13).
5. "Hast thou entered into the springs of the sea? or hast thou walked in the search of the depth?" (Job 38:16).
6. "Have the gates of death been opened unto thee? or hast thou seen the doors of the shadow of death?" (Job 38:17).
7. "Hast thou perceived the breadth of the earth?" (Job 38:18).
8. "Where is the way where light dwelleth? and as for darkness, where is the place thereof, that thou shouldest take it to the bound thereof, and that thou shouldest know the paths to the house thereof?" (Job 38:19,20).
9. "Hast thou entered into the treasures of the snow? or hast thou seen the treasures of the hail, which I have reserved against the time of trouble, against the day of battle and war?" (Job 38:22,23).
10. "By what way is the light parted, which scattereth the east wind upon the earth?" (Job 38:24).
11. "Who hath divided a watercourse for the overflowing of waters, or a way for the lightning of thunder; to cause it to rain on the earth, where no man is; on the wilderness, wherein there is no man; to satisfy the desolate and waste ground; and to cause the bud of the tender herb to spring forth?" (Job 38:25-27).
12. "Hath the rain a father? or who hath begotten the drops of dew?" (Job 38:28).

13. "Out of whose womb came the ice? and the hoary frost of heaven, who hath gendered it?" (Job 38:29).

14. "Canst thou bind the sweet influences of Pleiades, or loose the bands of Orion? Canst thou bring forth Mazzaroth in his season? or canst thou guide Arcturus with his sons?" (Job 38:31,32).

15. "Knowest thou the ordinances of heaven? canst thou set the dominion thereof in the earth?" (Job 38:33).

16. "Canst thou lift up thy voice to the clouds, that abundance of waters may cover thee?" (Job 38:34).

17. "Canst thou send lightnings, that they may go, and say unto thee, Here we are?" (Job 38:35).

18. "Who hath put wisdom in the inward parts? or who hath given understanding to the heart?" (Job 38:36).

19. "Who can number the clouds in wisdom? or who can stay the bottles of heaven, when the dust groweth into hardness, and the clods cleave fast together?" (Job 38:37,38).

20. "Wilt thou hunt the prey for the lion? or fill the appetite of the young lions, when they couch in their dens, and abide in the covert to lie in wait?" (Job 38:39,40).

21. "Who provideth for the raven his food?" (Job 38:41).

22. "Knowest thou the time when the wild goats of the rock bring forth? or canst thou mark when the hinds do calve?" (Job 39:1).

23. "Who hath sent out the wild ass free? or who hath loosed the bands of the wild ass?" (Job 39:5).

24. "Canst thou bind the unicorn with his band in the furrow? or will he harrow the valleys after thee? Wilt thou trust him, because his strength is great?" (Job 39:10,11).

25. "Gavest thou the goodly wings unto the peacocks? or wings and feathers unto the ostrich?" (Job 39:13).

26. "Hast thou given the horse strength? hast thou clothed his neck with thunder? Canst thou make him afraid as a grasshopper?" (Job 39:19,20).

27. "Doth the hawk fly by thy wisdom, and stretch her wings toward the south?" (Job 39:26).

28. "Doth the eagle mount up at thy command, and make her nest on high?" (Job 39:27).

29. "Moreover the Lord answered Job, and said, Shall he that contendeth with the Almighty instruct him? he that reproveth God, let him answer it" (Job 40:1,2).

30. "Wilt thou also disannul my judgment? wilt thou condemn me, that thou mayest be righteous?" (Job 40:8).

31. "Hast thou an arm like God? or canst thou thunder with a voice like him?" (Job 40:9).
32. "Canst thou draw out leviathan with an hook? or his tongue with a cord which thou lettest down? Canst thou put an hook into his nose?" (Job 41:1,2).
33. "None is so fierce that dare stir [leviathan] up: who then is able to stand before me?" (Job 41:10).
34. "Who hath prevented me, that I should repay him? whatsoever is under the whole heaven is mine" (Job 41:11).

54. Forty-six Questions Jesus Asked People

1. Clarifying our need for a single heart: "If therefore the light that is in thee be darkness, how great is the darkness!" (Matt. 6:23).
2. When speaking about God's ability to provide, Jesus asked His disciples, "Why take ye thought for raiment . . . shall he not much more clothe you, O ye of little faith?" (Matt. 6:28-30).
3. "Why beholdest thou the mote that is in thy brother's eye, but considerest not the beam that is in thine own eye?" (Matt. 7:3).
4. "How much more shall your Father which is in heaven give good things to them that ask him?" (Matt. 7:11).
5. When the disciples were afraid the storm would sink their boat, Jesus asked, "Why are ye fearful, O ye of little faith?" (Matt. 8:26).
6. Jesus began to say unto the multitudes concerning John, "What went ye out into the wilderness to see?" (Matt. 11:7-10).
7. When Jesus spoke about removing a sheep from a pit on the Sabbath, He asked, "How much then is a man better than a sheep?" (Matt. 12:12).
8. To the Pharisees and scribes: "O generation of vipers, how can ye, being evil, speak good things?" (Matt. 12:34).
9. When confronted with feeding the multitude, Jesus asked the disciples, "How many loaves have ye?" (Matt. 15:34).
10. To a forgetful band of disciples: "Do ye not yet understand, neither remember the five loaves of the five thousand, and how many baskets ye took up?" (Matt. 16:9).
11. When speaking about discipleship, Jesus asked, "For what is a man profited, if he shall gain the whole world, and lose

his own soul? or what shall a man give in exchange for his soul?" (Matt. 16:26).

12. When the disciples were unable to deliver the boy possessed by the devil, Jesus asked, "O faithless and perverse generation, how long shall I be with you? how long shall I suffer you?" (Matt. 17:17).

13. "What thinkest thou, Simon? Of whom do the kings of the earth take custom or tribute? of their children, or of strangers?" (Matt. 17:25).

14. To the person who labeled Jesus good: "Why callest thou me good?" (Matt. 19:17).

15. When the mother of James and John desired her sons to be in a prominent role, Jesus asked her, "What wilt thou?" (Matt. 20:21).

16. Jesus to the two blind men: "What will ye that I shall do unto you?" (Matt. 20:32).

17. When challenged as to the source of his authority, Jesus countered the chief priests by asking, "The baptism of John, whence was it? from heaven, or of men?" (Matt. 21:25).

18. When beginning a parable, Jesus asked, "But what think ye?" (Matt. 21:28).

19. When questioned by the Pharisees, Jesus unmasked their request by asking, "Why tempt ye me, ye hypocrites?" (Matt. 22:18).

20. Jesus took the offensive and asked the Pharisees, "What think ye of Christ? whose son is he?" (Matt. 22:42).

21. Jesus asked the scribes and Pharisees, "Ye serpents, ye generation of vipers, how can ye escape the damnation of hell?" (Matt. 23:33).

22. When His disciples questioned the woman about wasting the ointment on Jesus, He asked them, "Why trouble ye the woman?" (Matt. 26:10).

23. When the disciples fell asleep before Jesus was betrayed, He asked them, "What, could ye not watch with me one hour?" (Matt. 26:40).

24. To the scribes, who questioned Jesus' ability to forgive sins, He asked, "Why reason ye these things in your hearts?" (Mark 2:8).

25. To those who claimed that Jesus' power over demons came from Satan, He questioned, "How can Satan cast out Satan?" (Mark 3:23).

26. To the demoniac, "What is thy name?" (Mark 5:9).

27. To those who mourned the death of the ruler of the syno-gogue's daughter, "Why make ye this ado, and weep?" (Mark 5:39).

28. Deeply disturbed by the Pharisees tempting Him, Jesus asked, "Why doth this generation seek after a sign?" (Mark 8:12).

29. To the father whose son was demon possessed: "How long is it ago since this came unto him?" (Mark 9:21).

30. To the disciples who were discussing which of them was the greatest: "What was it that ye disputed among yourselves by the way?" (Mark 9:33).

31. To the Pharisees who were trying to find fault with Jesus' teaching: "What did Moses command you?" (Mark 10:3).

32. "My God, my God, why hast thou forsaken me?" (Mark 15:34).

33. "Why call ye me, Lord, Lord, and do not the things which I say?" (Luke 6:46).

34. "Ye hypocrites, ye can discern the face of the sky and of the earth; but how is it that ye do not discern this time?" (Luke 12:56).

35. To the inquiring of Nicodemus: "If I have told you earthly things, and ye believe not, how shall ye believe, if I tell you of heavenly things?" (John 3:12).

36. To the Jews whose trust was not rooted in God: "How can ye believe, which receive honour one of another and seek not the honour that cometh from God only?" (John 5:44).

37. When His disciples could not handle Jesus' teaching, Jesus asked them, "Doth this offend you?" (John 6:61).

38. Before a crowd of skeptical Jews He asked, "Did not Moses give you the law, and yet none of you keepeth the law? Why go ye about to kill me?" (John 7:19).

39. In challenging the Jewish belief that their heritage made them God's people: "Which of you convinceth me of sin? And if I say the truth, why do ye not believe me?" (John 8:46).

40. To His Father in heaven: "Now is my soul troubled; and what shall I say?" (John 12:27).

41. After washing the disciples' feet, "Know ye what I have done to you?" (John 13:12).

42. "Have I been so long time with you, and yet hast thou not known me, Philip?" (John 14:9).

43. To the officer who defended the high priest: "Why smitest thou me?" (John 18:23).

44. To Mary after His resurrection: "Woman, why weepest thou? whom seekest thou?" (John 20:15).
45. To a troubled, searching disciple: "Simon, son of Jonas, lovest thou me?" (John 21:17).
46. To a prostrating hater of the Church: "Saul, Saul, why persecutest thou me?" (Acts 9:4).

7

Decisions

Every day our lives are filled with decisions. Many decisions are routine (should I have juice for breakfast? etc.) and will not have a particularly profound effect. Others will have varying degrees of importance and impact upon us.

There is one decision, though, that ranks far above every other decision an individual faces: Am I going to obey God or not? Even our everyday decisions reflect whether we seek to glorify God or serve our own interests.

The following three lists demonstrate the impact of decisions in the lives of people in the Bible.

55. Ten Decisions to Follow God

1. Noah
   "Noah was a just man and perfect in his generations, and Noah walked with God.... And God said unto Noah,... Make thee an ark of gopher wood;... Thus did Noah; according to all that God commanded him, so did he" (Gen. 6:9,13,14,22).

2. Abraham
   "Now the Lord had said unto Abram, Get thee out of thy country, and from thy kindred, and from thy father's house, unto a land that I will shew thee ... so Abram departed, as the Lord had spoken unto him" (Gen. 12:1,4).

3. Moses
   "And the Lord said unto Moses in Midian, Go, return into Egypt: for all the men are dead which sought thy life. And Moses took his wife and sons, and set them upon an ass, and

he returned to the land of Egypt: and Moses took the rod of God in his hand" (Ex. 4:19,20).

4. Israel

"[Joshua commanded] Choose you this day whom ye will serve; whether the gods which your fathers served that were on the other side of the flood, or the gods of the Amorites, in whose land ye dwell: but as for me and my house, we well serve the Lord. And the people answered and said, God forbid that we should forsake the Lord, to serve other gods ... we will serve the Lord" (Josh. 24:15,16,21).

5. King Josiah

"When the king had heard the words of the book of the law, he rent his clothes ... and made a covenant before the Lord to walk after the Lord, and to keep his commandments" (2 Kings 22:11; 23:3).

6. Daniel

"But Daniel purposed in his heart that he would not defile himself with the portion of the king's meat, nor with the wine which he drank" (Dan. 1:8).

7. Nebuchadnezzar

"And at the end of the days I Nebuchadnezzar lifted up mine eyes unto heaven, and mine understanding returned unto me, and I blessed the most High, and I praised and honoured him that liveth for ever, whose dominion is an everlasting dominion.... At the same time my reason returned to me.... Now I Nebuchadnezzar praise and extol and honour the King of heaven" (Dan. 4:34-37).

8. The king and the people of Nineveh

"So the people of Nineveh believed God, and proclaimed a fast, and put on sackcloth, from the greatest of them even to the least of them. For word came unto the king of Nineveh, and he arose from his throne, and he laid his robe from him, and covered him with sackcloth, and sat in ashes" (Jonah 3:5,6).

9. Peter and Andrew

"Jesus, walking by the sea of Galilee, saw two brethren, Simon called Peter, and Andrew his brother, casting a net into the sea: for they were fishers. And he saith unto them, Follow me, and I will make you fishers of men. And they straightway left their nets, and followed him" (Matt. 4:18-20).

10. The Philippian jailor

"The jailor fell down before Paul and Silas, and brought them out, and said, Sirs, what must I do to be saved? . . . When he had brought them into his house, he set meat before them, and rejoiced, believing in God with all his house" (Acts 16:29,30,34).

56. Ten Decisions to Serve the Devil

1. Eve

"When the woman saw that the tree was good for food, and that it was pleasant to the eyes, and a tree to be desired to make one wise, she took of the fruit thereof, and did eat, and gave also unto her husband with her and he did eat" (Gen. 3:6).

Jesus calls Simon and Andrew

2. Lot's wife
"But his wife looked back from behind him, and she became a pillar of salt" (Gen. 19:26).

3. Aaron and the people of Israel
"When the people saw that Moses delayed to come down out of the mount, the people gathered themselves together unto Aaron, and said unto him, Up, make us gods, which shall go before us ..." and Aaron did so (Ex. 32:1).

4. Solomon
"It came to pass, when Solomon was old, that his wives turned away his heart after other gods: and his heart was not perfect with the Lord his God, as was the heart of David his father" (1 Kings 11:4).

5. Jeroboam
"The king took counsel, and made two calves of gold, and said unto [Israel], It is too much for you to go up to Jerusalem: behold thy gods, O Israel, which brought thee up out of the land of Egypt" (1 Kings 12:28).

6. Ahab
"And it came to pass, as if it had been a light thing for [Ahab] to walk in the sins of Jeroboam the son of Nebat, that he took to wife Jezebel the daughter of Ethbaal king of the Zidonians, and went and served Baal, and worshipped him" (1 Kings 16:31).

7. Judas Iscariot
"Then entered Satan into Judas. . . . And he promised, and sought opportunity to betray [Jesus] unto them in the absence of the multitude" (Luke 22:3,6).

8. Ananias
"A certain man named Ananias, with Sapphira his wife, sold a possession, and kept back part of the price, his wife also being privy to it, and brought a certain part and laid it at the apostles' feet. But Peter said, Ananias, why hath Satan filled thine heart to lie to the Holy Ghost, and to keep back part of the price of the land?" (Acts 5:1-3).

9. Elymas
"Elymas the sorcerer ... withstood [Barnabas and Saul], seeking to turn away the deputy [Sergius Paulus] from the faith" (Acts 13:8).

10. Demas
"Demas hath forsaken me, having loved this present world" (2 Tim. 4:10).

57. Decisions and the Heart

1. "O that there were such an heart in them, that they would fear me, and keep all my commandments always" (Deut. 5:29).
2. "To prove thee, to know what was in thine heart, whether thou wouldst keep his commandments" (Deut. 8:2).
3. "Only fear the Lord, and serve him in truth with all your heart" (1 Sam. 12:24).
4. "The Lord was angry with Solomon, because his heart turned away from the Lord God of Israel" (1 Kings 11:9).
5. "I have walked before thee in truth and with perfect heart, and have done that which is good in thy sight" (2 Kings 20:3).
6. "Solomon my son, know thou the God of thy father, and serve him with a perfect heart and with a willing mind" (1 Chron. 28:9).
7. "The people rejoiced, for that they offered willingly, because with perfect heart they offered willingly to the Lord" (1 Chron. 29:9).
8. "Keep thy heart with all diligence; for out of it are the issues of life" (Prov. 4:23).
9. "The heart is deceitful above all things. . . . I the Lord search the heart, I try the reins, even to give every man according to his ways" (Jer. 17:9,10).
10. "Cast away from you all your transgressions, whereby ye have transgressed; and make you a new heart and a new spirit: for why will ye die?" (Ezek. 18:31).
11. "But Daniel purposed in his heart that he would not defile himself" (Dan. 1:8).
12. "For where your treasure is, there will your heart be also" (Matt. 6:21).
13. "A good man out of the good treasure of the heart bringeth forth good things" (Matt. 12:35).
14. "For from within, out of the heart of men, proceed evil thoughts, adulteries. . . . These evil things come from within, and defile the man" (Mark 7:21,23).
15. "That which fell on the good ground are they, which in an honest and good heart, having heard the word, keep it, and bring forth fruit with patience" (Luke 8:15).
16. To Simon the sorcerer: "Thou hast neither part nor lot in this matter: for thy heart is not right in the sight of God" (Acts 8:21).

17. "Ye have obeyed from the heart that form of doctrine which was delivered you" (Rom. 6:17).
18. "Harden not your hearts. . . . Take heed, brethren, lest there be in any of you an evil heart of unbelief, in departing from the living God" (Heb. 3:8,12).
19. "I am he which searcheth the reins and hearts: and I will give unto every one of you according to your works" (Rev. 2:23).

8

God's Personality

Devout Orientals speak of God as the all-pervading "Force" in the universe. On every continent there are people who think God is the sovereign "bogeyman" in every tree, rock and river. And in our culture, many people see God as an aloof old man who set the cosmos in motion, then retired to some deserted asteroid.

Happily, none of the above ideas is correct. In fact, *God is the most fascinating person in the universe.* And what makes God's personality most interesting is that *we* are similar to Him in many respects. We are able to reason, to create, to choose, to feel emotion, even as God is able to do these things. We must realize, of course, that He does all these perfectly, unlike our *human* attempts.

Because we are created in the image of God and because of his concern for us, we can speak to Him, listen to Him, and become more like Him in character. As you read the following lists, you may be surprised to learn what God is really like. And, hopefully, you will be aroused to study and better understand His personality.

58. *Six Times God Expressed Contentment*

1. God expresses His intense desire to find people to whom He can entrust himself: "For the eyes of the Lord run to and fro throughout the whole earth, to show himself strong in the behalf of them whose heart is perfect toward him" (2 Chron. 16:9).
2. God expresses His happiness in extending forgiveness: "He retaineth not his anger for ever, because he delighteth in

mercy. He will turn again, he will have compassion upon us" (Mic. 7:18-19).

3. God expresses His heart of joy over an obedient people: "The Lord thy God in the midst of thee is mighty; he will save, he will rejoice over thee with joy; he will rest in his love, he will joy over thee with singing" (Zeph. 3:17).

4. Jesus compared His Father's compassion and anger to a human lord: "The lord of that servant was moved with compassion, and loosed him, and forgave him the debt. . . . His lord was wroth. . . . So likewise shall my heavenly father do . . ." (Matt. 18:27,34,35).

5. The happiness of heaven can only be a reflection of the heart of God: "There is joy in the presence of the angels of God over one sinner that repenteth" (Luke 15:7,10).

6. An amazing revelation of God's desire for us: "For the Father seeketh such to worship him" (John 4:23).

59. Six Times God Expressed Disappointment

1. When sin ran rampant throughout mankind after the fall: "It repented the Lord that he had made man on earth, and it grieved him at his heart" (Gen. 6:5,6).

2. A historical view of the children of Israel: "For they provoked him to anger with their high places, and moved him to jealousy with their graven images. When God heard this, he was wroth, and greatly abhorred Israel" (Ps. 78:58,59).

3. The heart of God as He was so long-suffering with a disobedient people: "Forty years long was I grieved with this generation . . . unto whom I sware in my wrath that they should not enter my rest" (Ps. 95:10,11).

4. "Thou wast angry with me, thine anger is turned away, and thou comfortedst me" (Isa. 12:1).

5. "Because I am broken with their whorish heart" (Ezek. 6:9).

6. "I am jealous for Jerusalem and for Zion with a great jealousy. And I am very sore displeased with the heathen that are at ease: for I was but a little displeased, and they helped toward the affliction" (Zech. 1:14,15).

60. Thirteen Times God Revealed New Choices

1. "God said, Let us make man in our image, after our likeness" (Gen. 1:26).

2. "Therefore, the Lord sent him forth from the garden of Eden" (Gen. 3:23).
3. "It repented the Lord that he had made man on the earth" (Gen. 6:6).
4. God chose to destroy all mankind, except Noah and his family, because they were utterly corrupted (Gen. 6:12-13).
5. "I will establish my covenant with you; neither shall all flesh be cut off any more by the waters of a flood" (Gen. 9:11,12).
6. The Lord chose to withhold his anger and not destroy the rebellious children of Israel (Ex. 32:7-14,30-33).
7. King Hezekiah's seeking the Lord resulted in God's changing His decision and extending Hezekiah's life fifteen years (2 Kings 20:5,6).
8. "Even so the Son quickeneth whom he will" (John 5:21).
9. "I have power to lay it down, and I have power to take it again" (John 10:18).
10. "It is not for you to know the times or the seasons, which the Father hath put in his own power" (Acts 1:7).
11. "All these worketh that one and the self-same Spirit, dividing to every man severally as he will" (1 Cor. 12:11).
12. "Of his own will begat he us with the word of truth" (James 1:18).
13. "The Father sent the Son to be the Saviour of the world" (1 John 4:14).

61. Eight Times God Revealed His Thoughts

1. Moses by reasoning with the Lord staved off the wrath of God when Israel worshipped the golden calf (Ex. 32:7-14).
2. "I will raise up a faithful priest, that shall do according to that which is in mine heart and in my mind" (1 Sam. 2:35).
3. "Come now, and let us reason together, saith the Lord" (Isa. 1:18).
4. "Produce your cause, saith the Lord; bring forth your strong reasons, saith the King of Jacob" (Isa. 41:21).
5. "For my thoughts are not your thoughts. . . . As the heavens are higher than the earth, so are . . . my thoughts than your thoughts" (Isa. 55:8,9).
6. "For I know the thoughts that I think toward you, saith the Lord, thoughts of peace, and not of evil, to give you an expected end" (Jer. 29:11).
7. "Wherefore I will yet plead with you, saith the Lord, and with your children's children will I plead" (Jer. 2:1-13).

8. "For the Lord hath a controversy with his people, and he will plead with Israel. O my people, what have I done unto thee? and wherein have I wearied thee? testify against me" (Mic. 6:1-3).

62. Sixteen Times God Showed Flexibility in Dealing with Mankind

1. God regretted that man had been created. Here we find an aroused state of grief and disappointment over man's persistent rebellion (Gen. 6:3,5-7).
2. Here we have the amazing statement from God concerning the implications of Abraham's obedience: "For now I know that thou fearest God." A ram was provided in Isaac's place (Gen. 22:12).

The Ninevites repent

3. Here Moses' intercessions changed the mind of God to not destroy the nation of Israel (Ex. 32:7-14).

4. God was waiting to see Israel's reaction of humility after the golden-calf incident before determining His judgment upon them (Ex. 33:5).

5. Another of God's judgments was stayed by the humility and prayer of Moses (Num. 11:1,2).

6. God was using the forty years of wandering in the wilderness to discover Israel's true heart toward His rule (Deut. 8:2).

7. God decided not to drive out some of the nations in Palestine because of Israel's sin. They would be His instrument to test and prove Israel's faithfulness (Judges 2:20-22).

8. When Saul disobeyed God's directions, God was grieved and determined a new plan of direction. God had reluctantly given Saul to be king over His people in response to their demands (1 Sam. 8:6-7; see also 1 Sam. 15:10,11,23,35).

9. God changed His mind and decided to add fifteen years to King Hezekiah's reign. This was in response to humble prayer (2 Kings 20:1-7).

10. God gave David three options of punishment for sin. David chose the direct hand of God, banking upon the mercy of God. God did choose to extend mercy and stayed the angel's hand from further judgment (1 Chron. 21:11-15).

11. When King Rehoboam and his leaders humbled themselves, God changed His threatened judgment and granted them "some deliverance" (2 Chron. 12:5-8).

12. God declared that He will change His purpose of judgment and blessing in accordance with man's reactions (Jer. 18:5-10).

13. Jeremiah proclaimed the possibility of God changing His purpose of judgment if Israel would respond in repentance (Jer. 26:2-7,12-13).

14. God might be induced to change His judgment if Israel would turn to God with sincere repentance (Joel 2:12-14).

15. God's judgment upon Nineveh was averted by one of the greatest examples of mass repentance ever recorded (Jonah 3).

16. Names can be blotted out of the Book of Life (Rev. 3:5).

9

Good Guys/Bad Guys

Luke Skywalker versus Darth Vader; Superman versus sinister Lex Luthor; the Lone Ranger versus outlaws; Snow White versus the witch envious of her beauty. Whether in fiction or real life the conflict is ever the same: good guys versus bad guys. The bad guys are almost always in the majority, while the good guys are seemingly the underdogs. At the movies, most of us cheer for the good guys to triumph and we are rarely disappointed. (These days, however, it's often hard to discern who really are the good guys.)

The next thirteen lists explore these two categories. As usual, the bad guys eclipse the good guys in number. But in the end, guess who wins?

63. Twenty Instances of Exile

1. God drove *Adam* and *Eve* out of the Garden of Eden (Gen. 3:24).
2. The Lord exiled *Cain* to the land of Nod (Gen. 4:13-16).
3. *Noah, Shem, Ham, Japheth,* and their wives were exiled from their homes forever by the flood (Gen. 7:23).
4. In obedience to God, *Abram* exiled himself and his family from their home in Ur (Gen. 12:1-5).
5. Abraham banished *Hagar* and *Ishmael* (Gen. 21:14).
6. *Jacob* chose exile rather than constant contention with Esau (Gen. 27:41-45).
7. "*Joseph* was brought down to Egypt; and Potiphar . . . bought him" (Gen. 39:1).

8. The *children of Israel* were exiles in Egypt for 430 years (Ex. 12:40).
9. "*Moses* fled from the face of Pharaoh, and dwelt in the land of Midian" (Ex. 2:15).
10. "The *children of Israel* walked forty years in the wilderness" (Josh. 5:6).
11. "*Jephthah* fled from his brethren and dwelt in the land of Tob" (Judges 11:3).
12. *David* lived in exile when he was fleeing from Saul (1 Sam. 27:1-7).
13. After he had had Amnon killed, "*Absalom* fled, and went to Talmai ... and was there three years" (2 Sam. 13:37,38).
14. "Solomon sought therefore to kill Jeroboam. And *Jeroboam* arose, and fled into Egypt ... until the death of Solomon" (1 Kings 11:40).
15. Assyria carried *Israel* into exile (2 Kings 17:6).
16. Nebuchadnezzar carried all in *Jerusalem* to Babylon (2 Kings 24:14,15).
17. The remnant of *Judah*, including *Jeremiah*, was exiled to Egypt (Jer. 43:5-7).
18. *Joseph* and *Mary* fled with *Jesus* into Egypt until Herod died (Matt. 2:13-15).
19. "There was a great persecution against *the church* which was at Jerusalem; and they were all scattered abroad throughout the regions of Judaea and Samaria" (Acts 8:1).
20. *John* was exiled to Patmos (Rev. 1:9).

64. Prisons and Prisoners

1. *Joseph* was thrown into prison, where he met *Pharaoh's butler and baker* (Gen. 39:20-40:3).
2. As governor of Egypt, Joseph put *his brothers* in prison for three days and left *Simeon* there until his brothers returned with Benjamin (Gen. 42:17-24).
3. Joshua had the *five Amorite kings* sealed inside a cave, and then posted a guard until he could return for them (Josh. 10:16-18).
4. The Philistines put out *Samson's* eyes and made him grind in the prison (Judges 16:21).
5. Ahab threw the prophet *Micaiah* into prison because he did not like Micaiah's prophecy (1 Kings 22:26,27).
6. The king of Assyria bound *King Hoshea* of Israel in prison (2 Kings 17:4).

7. *Jehoiachin,* king of Judah, was imprisoned in Babylon (2 Kings 25:27,28).
8. King Asa threw *Hanani* into prison for delivering an unfavorable word from the Lord (2 Chron. 16:10).
9. The king had *Jeremiah* put into prison and finally into a miry dungeon (Jer. 32:2; 37:16; 38:6).
10. The king of Babylon put out the eyes of *Zedekiah* and bound him in chains (Jer. 52:11).
11. Herod put *John the Baptist* into prison for speaking against Herod's adulterous marriage (Matt. 14:3,4).
12. *Jesus* was taken prisoner (John 18:12) and the convict *Barabbas* was released in His place (Matt. 27:26).
13. *Peter* and *John* spent a night in prison for preaching (Acts 4:3).
14. *The apostles* were imprisoned, but the angel of the Lord led them out at night (Acts 5:17,19).
15. Herod put *Peter* into prison, but an angel released him (Acts 12:4,6).
16. *Paul* was imprisoned with *Silas* at Philippi (Acts 16:22-24) and alone in Jerusalem (Acts 22:24,25), in Caesarea (Acts 23:33-35), and in Rome (Acts 28:16).

65. Fourteen Great Escapes

1. *Lot* and his *two daughters* escaped the destruction of Sodom after being warned by two angels (Gen. 19:15-26).
2. The ten plagues allowed the *600,000 Israelite men* (plus women and children) to escape from Egypt (Ex. 12:37).
3. The *two spies* that went to Jericho escaped because Rahab hid them on her roof, sent their pursuers off on a wild-goose chase, and let the spies down the wall with a rope that hung from her window (Josh. 2:1-22).
4. *Samson* escaped the Philistines by breaking new ropes that bound him. He then found the jawbone of an ass and killed 1,000 men before running away (Judges 15:11-15).
5. *Samson* escaped again by removing the doors from the gates of the city of Gaza and carrying them to the top of a nearby hill (Judges 16:1-3).
6. While *David* was fleeing from Saul, his wife let him down through a window and put an idol in his bed to fool Saul's messengers (1 Sam. 19:12-16).
7. *David* escaped the king of Gath by pretending to be a madman (1 Sam. 21:10-22:1).

8. *Jonathan* and *Ahimaaz* escaped from Absalom's men by hiding in a well that a woman covered to look like a pile of grain (2 Sam. 17:15-21).
9. *Jonah* tried to "flee unto Tarshish from the presence of the Lord." It didn't work (Jonah 1:3).
10. The people of the synagogue in Nazareth were going to

Paul escapes from Damascus

stone *Jesus,* "but he passing through the midst of them went his way" (Luke 4:29,30).

11. "[The Jews] sought again to take [*Jesus*]: but he escaped out of their hand" (John 10:39).

12. *The apostles,* and later *Peter* alone, were released from prison by angels (Acts 5:18,19; 12:6-10).

13. *Paul* escaped Jewish assassins in Damascus by leaving the city in a basket let down the side of the wall through a window (Acts 9:23-25).

14. *Paul* and *Silas* were released from prison in Philippi by an earthquake and then led out by the jailor (Acts 16:25-30).

66. Arsonists

1. *The children of Israel* burned the cities of Jericho (Josh. 6:24), Ai (Josh. 8:19), Hazor (Josh. 11:11), and all the cities of the Midianites (Num. 31:9,10).

2. *Israel* stoned Achan and then burned him and all his belongings (Josh. 7:24,25).

3. *Judah* fought the Canaanites at Jerusalem and burned the city (Judges 1:8).

4. *Abimelech and his men* burned down the tower of Shechem, killing about a thousand men and women (Judges 9:49).

5. *Samson* tied torches to foxes' tails and "let them go into the standing [grain] of the Philistines and burnt up both the shocks and also the standing [grain]" (Judges 15:4,5).

6. *Men of Dan* burned down the Canaanite city of Laish (Judges 18:26,27).

7. *"The men of Israel* turned again upon the children of Benjamin, and smote them with the edge of the sword. . . . Also they set on fire all the cities that they came to" (Judges 20:48).

8. *The Amalekites* burned David's city of Ziklag (1 Sam. 30:1).

9. *Absalom* burned Joab's barley field just to get his attention (2 Sam. 14:28-33).

10. *"Pharaoh* king of Egypt had gone up, and taken Gezer, and burnt it with fire" (1 Kings 9:16).

11. *King Zimri* committed suicide by burning down his house while he was in it (1 Kings 16:18).

12. *Nebuchadnezzar* burned Jerusalem (2 Kings 25:9).

13. *Ephesian converts* burned magic books worth 50,000 pieces of silver (Acts 19:19).

67. Thieves and Robbers

1. "*Rachel* had stolen the images that were her father's" (Gen. 31:19).
2. *Achan* took a beautiful Babylonian garment, a bar of silver, and a bar of gold during the battle at Ai (Josh. 7:11-21).
3. "The *men of Shechem* set liers in wait for Abimelech in the top of the mountains, and they robbed all that came along that way by them" (Judges 9:25).
4. *Micah* stole 1,100 shekels of silver from his mother (Judges 17:2).
5. Six hundred *Danites* stopped at Micah's house and stole his carved image, ephod, teraphim, and molten image (Judges 18:16-18).
6. The *people of Judah* were robbing the Lord of His rightful tithes (Mal. 3:8).
7. "Then were there *two thieves* crucified with Jesus, one on the right hand, and another on the left" (Matt. 27:38).
8. *Judas Iscariot* stole from the disciples' treasury (John 12:4-6).
9. "Now *Barabbas* was a robber" (John 18:40).

68. Impersonators

1. *Sarai* posed as Abram's sister in Egypt (Gen. 12:10-20).
2. *Rebekah* posed as Isaac's sister in Gerar (Gen. 26:6-11).
3. *Jacob* disguised himself as Esau so well that his father Isaac believed it (Gen. 27:1-29).
4. *Leah* posed as her sister Rachel when Jacob married her (Gen. 29:21-25).
5. *The Gibeonites* fooled Joshua by impersonating ambassadors from a distant country (Josh. 9:4-16).
6. *David* escaped from King Achish by pretending to be a madman (1 Sam. 21:12-22:1).
7. "*Saul* disguised himself, and put on other raiment, and he went" out to see the medium at Endor (1 Sam. 28:8).
8. Joab convinced *the wise woman of Tekoah* to pretend to be a mourning widow and to ask for King David's help (2 Sam. 14:1-24).
9. *Jeroboam's wife* disguised herself and went to the prophet Ahijah to find out what the future held, but the Lord told him who she was (1 Kings 14:1-6).

10. *A prophet* disguised himself as a wounded soldier in order to get a point across to King Ahab (1 Kings 20:35-43).
11. *King Ahab* disguised himself when fighting the Syrians, but a fatal arrow found him anyway (1 Kings 22:30-40).
12. *King Josiah* also disguised himself for battle against King Necho of Egypt. He too was fatally wounded (2 Chron. 35:20-24).
13. The chief priests and scribes sent *spies,* pretending to be sincere followers, to Jesus to try to trap him (Luke 20:19,20).

69. Four Kidnappers

1. Joseph was kidnapped and sold into slavery by *his brothers* (Gen. 37:17-28).
2. *The men of Benjamin* grabbed wives for themselves from the women of Shiloh during a festal dance (Judges 21:16-23).
3. Solomon had to judge a case in which two harlots had borne boys. One baby had died, and his *mother* had secretly traded the corpse for the other mother's son (1 Kings 3:16-21).
4. Prince Joash was kidnapped by his aunt *Jehosheba* to protect him from his murderous grandmother Athaliah (2 Kings 11:1-3).

70. Seven Good Kings—All from Judah

1. *David* was "a man after [God's] own heart" (1 Sam 13:14; Acts 13:22).
2. *Asa's* "heart was perfect with the Lord all his days" (1 Kings 15:11,14).
3. *Jehoshaphat* "turned not aside from ... doing what was right in the eyes of the Lord" (1 Kings 22:42,43).
4. *Uzziah* (also known as Azariah) "did that which was right in the eyes of the Lord" (2 Kings 15:1-3).
5. *Jotham* "did that which was right in the sight of the Lord" (2 Kings 15:32-34).
6. *Hezekiah* "did that which was right in the sight of the Lord" (2 Kings 18:1-3).
7. *Josiah* was like no other king in turning "to the Lord with all his heart, and with all his soul, and with all his might" (2 Kings 22:1,2; 23:25).

71. Thirty Bad Kings

1. *Jeroboam* the son of Nebat made two golden calves and appointed priests for the high places (1 Kings 12:28; 13:33,34).
2. *Rehoboam* (Judah) "did evil, because he prepared not his heart to seek the Lord" (2 Chron. 12:14).
3. *Abijam* (Judah) "walked in all the sins of his father" (1 Kings 15:1-3).
4. *Nadab* "made Israel to sin" (1 Kings 15:25,26).
5. *Baasha* "walked in the way of Jeroboam" (1 Kings 15:33,34).
6. *Elah* provoked the Lord to anger with his idols (1 Kings 16:8-14).
7. *Zimri* killed Elah to obtain the throne for a seven-day reign (1 Kings 16:9-20).
8. *Omri* "did worse than all that were before him" (1 Kings 16:25).
9. *Ahab* "did sell himself to work wickedness" like none other before him (1 Kings 16:30; 21:25).
10. *Ahaziah* son of Ahab "served Baal, and worshipped him" (1 Kings 22:51-53).
11. *Jehoram* son of Ahab "cleaved unto the sins of Jeroboam" (2 Kings 3:1-3).
12. *Jehoram* (Judah) son of Jehoshaphat "walked in the way of the kings of Israel" (2 Kings 8:16-18).
13. *Ahaziah* (Judah) son of Jehoram "did evil in the sight of the Lord" (2 Kings 8:25-27).
14. *"Jehu* took no heed to walk in the law of the Lord God of Israel" (2 Kings 10:29-31).
15. *Jehoahaz* the son of Jehu "followed the sins of Jeroboam" (2 Kings 13:1,2).
16. *Jehoash* the son of Jehoahaz "did that which was evil in the sight of the Lord" (2 Kings 13:10,11).
17. *Jeroboam* the son of Joash "did that which was evil in the sight of the Lord" (2 Kings 14:23,24).
18. *Zachariah* did "as his fathers had done" (2 Kings 15:8,9).
19. *Shallum* slew Zachariah to gain his throne (2 Kings 15:10).
20. *Menahem* "departed not all his days from the sins of Jeroboam" (2 Kings 15:17,18).
21. *Pekahiah* "did that which was evil in the sight of the Lord" (2 Kings 15:23,24).
22. *Pekah* killed Pekahiah to gain the throne (2 Kings 15:27,28).
23. *Ahaz* (Judah) sacrificed his son to idols (2 Kings 16:2-4).

24. *Hoshea* did evil and was finally carried away to exile in Assyria (Kings 17:1,2).
25. *Manasseh* (Judah) "built up again the high places which Hezekiah his father had destroyed" (2 Kings 21:1-7).
26. *Amon* (Judah) "forsook the Lord God of his fathers" (2 Kings 21:19-22).
27. *Jehoahaz* (Judah) the son of Josiah "did that which was evil in the sight of the Lord" (2 Kings 23:31,32).
28. *Jehoiakim* (Judah) did "according to all that his fathers had done" (2 Kings 23:36,37).
29. *Jehoiachin* (Judah) "did that which was evil in the sight of the Lord" (2 Kings 24:8,9).
30. *Zedekiah* (Judah) "did that which was evil in the sight of the Lord" (2 Kings 24:18,19).

72. Four Good Kings Who Became Bad

1. *Saul* was given a new heart by God, but he chose to disobey God continually (1 Sam. 10:9; 13:13,14).
2. *Solomon* loved the Lord, but in his old age, he was turned to evil by his heathen wives (1 Kings 3:3; 11:4).
3. *Jehoash* (also known as Joash) the son of Ahaziah "did that which was right in the sight of the Lord," but he later forsook the Lord (2 Kings 12:1,2; 2 Chron. 24:20-22).
4. *Amaziah* "did that which was right in the sight of the Lord," but he later turned away from following the Lord (2 Kings 14:1-3; 2 Chron. 25:1,2,27).

73. Four Adulterers

1. "*Reuben* went and lay with Bilhah his father's concubine" (Gen. 35:22).
2. *David* lay with Uriah's wife Bathsheba (2 Sam. 11:3,4).
3. "*Absalom* went in unto his father's concubines in the sight of all Israel" (2 Sam. 16:22).
4. The scribes and Pharisees caught *a woman* committing adultery and brought her to Jesus (John 8:3).

74. Four Swindlers

1. *Jacob* cheated Esau out of his birthright and his blessing (Gen. 27:36).

2. *Laban* cheated Jacob by giving him Leah instead of Rachel. He also changed Jacob's wages ten times (Gen. 29:21-25; 31:7).
3. The *Gibeonites* swindled a treaty from Joshua by telling him lies (Josh. 9:4-16).
4. *Ziba* tried to swindle his master Miphibosheth by lying to David (2 Sam. 16:1-4; 19:24-30).

75. Eighteen Traitors

1. *Absalom* conspired with Ahithophel to take over the kingdom of David (2 Sam. 15:31).
2. *Sheba* conspired against David, and all the men of Israel except the tribe of Judah followed Sheba (2 Sam. 20:1,2).
3. *Baasha* conspired against King Nadab and killed him (1 Kings 15:27).
4. King Elah's servant *Zimri*, who was captain of half his chariots, conspired against him and killed him (1 Kings 16:8-10).
5. *Hazael* murdered King Ben-hadad and reigned in his stead (2 Kings 8:7-15).
6. *Jehu* conspired against King Joram and killed him and all of the house of Ahab; and Jehu reigned over Israel (2 Kings 9:14-10:36).
7. "When *Athaliah* the mother of Ahaziah saw that her son was dead, she arose and destroyed all the seed royal ... and Athaliah did reign over the land" (2 Kings 11:1,3).
8. Queen Athaliah accused *Jehoiada* the priest of treason for restoring the throne to Joash, the rightful ruler of Judah (2 Kings 11:14-16).
9. *Jozachar* and *Jehozabad* conspired against their master, King Joash, and slew him (2 Kings 12:20,21).
10. The *people of Jerusalem* conspired against King Amaziah, "and he fled to Lachish; but they sent after him to Lachish, and slew him there" (2 Kings 14:17-19).
11. "*Shallum* the son of Jabesh conspired against [King Zachariah], and smote him before the people, and slew him, and reigned in his stead" (2 Kings 15:10).
12. "*Menahem* the son of Gadi went up from Tirzah, and came to Samaria, and smote Shallum the son of Jabesh in Samaria, and slew him, and reigned in his stead" (2 Kings 15:14).
13. *Pekah* the son of Remaliah, a captain of [King Pekahiah],

Judas betrays Jesus with a kiss

conspired against him, and smote him in Samaria, in the
palace of the king's house" (2 Kings 15:25).

14. "*Hoshea* the son of Elah made conspiracy against Pekah
the son of Remaliah, and smote him, and slew him, and
reigned in his stead" (2 Kings 15:30).

15. "The king of Assyria found conspiracy in *Hoshea*: for he had sent messengers to So king of Egypt, and brought no present to the king of Assyria" (2 Kings 17:4).

16. *Adrammelech* and *Sharezer,* sons of King Sennacherib of Assyria, killed him while he worshiped his god Nisroch (2 Kings 19:37).

17. "The *servants of Amon* conspired against him, and slew the king in his own house" (2 Kings 21:23).

18. *Judas Iscariot* was the traitor who betrayed Jesus (Luke 6:16; 22:48).

10

The Spirit World

Many people deny that there is anything but a material world. Some acknowledge that there is a spiritual world, but that it consists of only good powers. Others say there are good powers and evil powers—some of these people would have you believe there is an evil power behind every problem and object in life. Still others claim that they not only believe in evil powers, but that they make contact with these powers and can exercise evil power any time they desire.

The rebirth of the popularity of occult practices in recent years can hardly escape our notice. A few years ago, a major section of an issue of *Time* magazine focused on the renaissance of the occult. In recent years an east coast university has been offering a degree in parapsychology—the study of occult phenomenon. The recent involvement of Kathryn Kübler Ross in several facets of the occult is a striking example of the direction many are taking today.

The Bible is not a textbook on occult phenomenon. However, it does mention many activities of spirit beings, including angels, demons, and Satan. The following nine lists show us what to watch out for as we face this growing movement.

76. Names of Angels in the Bible

1. When the angel of the Lord met with Manoah and his wife, he told them that his name was a secret (Judges 13:17,18).
2. Gabriel spoke with Daniel, Zacharias, and Mary (Dan. 8:15-17; Luke 1:19, 26,27).
3. Jude 9 tells about Michael the archangel.

77. Eleven Titles and Categories of Angels

1. Angel of light (2 Cor. 11:14).
2. Angel of the Lord (Gen. 16:7).
3. Angels of the churches (Rev. 1:20).
4. Archangel (Jude 9).
5. Cherubim (Gen. 3:24).
6. Chief prince (Dan. 10:13).
7. Devil's angels (Matt. 25:41).
8. Evil angels (Ps. 78:49).
9. "Guardian angels" (Matt. 18:10).
10. Seraphim (Isa. 6:1-6).
11. Watchers (Dan. 4:13,17,23).

78. Ten Statements by Satan and Demons

1. In opposition to God, Satan told Eve that she would not die for eating of the tree of the knowledge of good and evil. He said that Adam and Eve would "be as gods, knowing good and evil" (Gen. 3:1-5).
2. A spirit told God that he would be a lying spirit in the mouths of Ahab's prophets, thus bringing about Ahab's death on the battlefield (1 Kings 22:19-22).
3. Satan told the Lord that Job would curse God if everything Job had was taken away (Job 1:9-11).
4. After Job passed the first test, Satan told God that Job would curse the Lord if his body was afflicted (Job 2:1-5).
5. Lucifer's aspirations to be "like the most High" are recorded in Isa. 14:13,14.
6. The devil spoke to Jesus in the wilderness and tempted Him by quoting scripture out of context (Matt. 4:1-11).
7. When Jesus confronted demons who were inhabiting people, they acknowledged that Jesus was "the Holy One of God" (Luke 4:34) and "the Son of God" (Luke 4:41).
8. When Jesus confronted the Gadarene demoniac, the demons begged not to be tormented or sent into the deep. They identified themselves as "Legion" and asked to be sent into a herd of swine (Luke 8:26-32).
9. A demon-possessed soothsayer followed Paul and his companions, shouting that they were servants of God proclaiming the way of salvation (Acts 16:16-18).
10. When the seven sons of Sceva attempted to cast out an evil

The Gadarene demoniac

spirit, it answered them, "Jesus I know, and Paul I know; but who are ye?" (Acts 19:13-15).

79. Forty-three Past Activities of Angels

1. Cherubim guarded the tree of life in the Garden of Eden (Gen. 3:24).
2. The angel of the Lord found Hagar in the wilderness, prophesied to her, and sent her home (Gen. 16:7-12).

3. Two angels ate with Lot, blinded the Sodomites, and brought Lot and his family out of Sodom (Gen. 19:1-22).

4. The angel of God spoke to Hagar out of heaven and encouraged her (Gen. 21:17,18).

5. The angel of the Lord called to Abraham from heaven, stopped him from sacrificing Isaac, and told him that God would multiply his descendants (Gen. 22:11-18).

6. The angel of God spoke to Jacob in a dream and showed him how to get Laban's cattle (Gen. 31:11,12).

7. The angel of the Lord appeared to Moses in the burning bush and told him to go to Pharaoh and to bring the children of Israel out of Egypt (Ex. 3:1 22; 4:1 17).

8. The angel of God provided the pillar of fire and the pillar of cloud which went with the children of Israel as they traveled toward the Promised Land (Ex. 14:19,20).

9. The angel of the Lord withstood Balaam and his ass—first in a invisible form and then in a visible form. The angel warned Balaam to follow his orders (Num. 22:21-35).

10. The captain of the Lord's host appeared unto Joshua before the battle of Jericho (Josh. 5:13-15).

11. The angel of the Lord rebuked the children of Israel because they didn't stay separated from the people around them (Judges 2:1-4).

12. The angel of the Lord appeared to Gideon and told him that he was to deliver Israel from the Midianites (Judges 6:11-21).

13. The angel of the Lord appeared to Samson's parents and told them of Samson's impending birth (Judges 13:2-20).

14. An angel smote Israel with a pestilence that killed 70,000 men because David had taken a census (2 Sam. 24:15,16).

15. The angel of the Lord fed Elijah two meals (1 Kings 19:5-8).

16. The angel of the Lord gave Elijah a message for Israel's King Ahaziah, condemning his idolatry and foretelling his death (2 Kings 1:3,4).

17. "The angel of the Lord went out, and smote in the camp of the Assyrians an hundred fourscore and five thousand: and when they arose early in the morning, behold, they were all dead corpses" (2 Kings 19:35).

18. Isaiah saw and heard the seraphim praise and worship God (Isa. 6:1-3).

19. A seraph touched Isaiah's lips with a live coal and declared God's forgiveness to him (Isa. 6:5-7).

20. Nebuchadnezzar attributed the preservation of Shadrach, Meshech, and Abednego in the fiery furnace to God's angel (Dan. 3:28).

21. Daniel said, "My God hath sent his angel, and hath shut the lions' mouths, that they have not hurt me" (Dan. 6:22).

22. Twice Gabriel came to Daniel to give him understanding of future events (Dan. 8:15-26; 9:21-27).

23. Dan. 10:13-20 may refer to battles between good and evil angels.

24. The angel of the Lord prophesied and explained visions to Zechariah (Zech. 1:9-21; 2:3-5; 4:1-6).

25. The angel of the Lord appeared unto Joseph in a dream, told him that the Virgin Mary's pregnancy was of the Holy Spirit, and told him not to fear taking Mary to be his wife (Matt. 1:20).

26. The angel of the Lord again appeared to Joseph in a dream and told him to flee with Mary and Jesus to Egypt (Matt. 2:13).

27. After Herod had died, an angel again appeared to Joseph in a dream and told him that it was safe to return to Israel (Matt. 2:19,20).

28. Angels ministered to Jesus after His temptation by the devil (Matt. 4:11).

29. The angel of the Lord opened Jesus' tomb and gave the news of His resurrection to Mary Magdalene and the other Mary (Matt. 28:1-7).

30. The angel Gabriel foretold the birth of John the Baptist to his father-to-be, Zacharias (Luke 1:11-19).

31. Gabriel also announced to Mary that she would have a son, but that it would be a supernatural conception (Luke 1:26-38).

32. The angel of the Lord announced the birth of Jesus to the shepherds (Luke 2:8-14).

33. An angel told Mary to name her baby Jesus (Luke 2:21).

34. "The beggar [Lazarus] died, and was carried by the angels into Abraham's bosom" (Luke 16:22).

35. An angel from heaven appeared to Jesus in the garden of Gethsemane and strengthened him (Luke 22:43).

36. An angel of the Lord effected the apostles' escape from a Jerusalem prison. He told them to go and preach in the temple (Acts 5:19-20).

37. An angel told Philip to go south to a certain road. Philip met the Ethiopian eunuch along that road (Acts 8:26).

The angel Gabriel appears to Zacharias

38. An angel of God appeared to Cornelius in a vision and told him to send for the apostle Peter (Acts 10:3-6).
39. An angel woke Peter and freed him from prison in Jerusalem (Acts 12:6-10).
40. Because Herod did not give glory to God, an angel smote him (Acts 12:23).
41. As Paul was caught in a storm at sea, an angel assured him that all on board would live and that Paul would be brought before Caesar (Acts 27:23,24).
42. All the angels of God worshiped Jesus (Heb. 1:6).
43. Angels watched over churches (Rev. 1:20).

80. Eight Present Activities of Angels

1. "The angel of the Lord encampeth round about them that fear him, and delivereth them" (Ps. 34:7).
2. "He shall give his angels charge over thee, to keep thee in all thy ways. They shall bear thee up in their hands, lest thou dash thy foot against a stone" (Ps. 91:11,12).
3. It seems that children have "guardian angels" (Matt. 18:10).

4. "There is joy in the presence of the angels of God over one sinner that repenteth" (Luke 15:10).
5. Angels are "ministering spirits, sent forth to minister for them who shall be heirs of salvation" (Heb. 1:14).
6. Angels desire to look into the things of salvation (1 Pet. 1:12).
7. Angels watch over the churches (Rev. 1:20).
8. "I Jesus have sent mine angel to testify unto you these things in the churches" (Rev. 22:16).

81. Thirteen Future Activities of Angels

1. "In the end of this world, the Son of man shall send forth his angels, and they shall gather out of his kingdom all things that offend" (Matt. 13:40,41).
2. "The Son of man shall come in the glory of his Father with his angels; and then he shall reward every man according to his works" (Matt. 16:27).
3. The Son of man "shall send his angels with a great sound of a trumpet, and they shall gather together his elect from the four winds, from one end of heaven to the other" (Matt. 24:30,31).
4. Jesus said, "Hereafter ye shall see heaven open, and the angels of God ascending and descending upon the Son of man" (John 1:51).
5. Evil angels will be judged (2 Pet. 2:4).
6. Angels will watch over the churches (Rev. 1:20).
7. John "saw four angels standing on the four corners of the earth, holding the four winds of the earth, that the wind should not blow on the earth" (Rev. 7:1).
8. An angel will offer the prayers of the saints on the altar before God's throne (Rev. 8:3-5).
9. The angels will sound the seven trumpets of judgment (Rev. 8:7-10:7).
10. Michael and his angels will fight against the dragon and his angels (Rev. 12:7-10).
11. Seven angels will pour out vials of judgment upon the earth (Rev. 16:1-21).
12. An angel will cast Satan into the bottomless pit and bind him there (Rev. 20:1-3).
13. There will be an angel at each of the twelve gates of the New Jerusalem (Rev. 21:12).

82. Twenty-seven Past Activities of Satan and Demons

1. The serpent beguiled Eve and she ate of the forbidden fruit (Gen. 3:13).
2. Mediums were put to death in the Old Testament for dealing with familiar spirits (Lev. 20:27).
3. "God sent an evil spirit between Abimelech and the men of Shechem; and the men of Shechem dealt treacherously with Abimelech" (Judges 9:23).
4. An evil spirit bothered Saul and prophesied through him (1 Sam. 16:14-23; 18:10,11).
5. A lying spirit working through false prophets convinced Ahab to go into battle (1 Kings 22:20-22).
6. "Satan stood up against Israel, and provoked David to number Israel" (1 Chron. 21:1).
7. Satan took away Job's wealth, children, and health (Job 1:6-2:8).
8. Lucifer fell from heaven and weakened nations in his ambition to be like the Most High (Isa. 14:12-14).
9. "The Lord hath mingled a perverse spirit in the midst thereof: and they have caused Egypt to err in every work thereof" (Isa. 19:14).
10. The prince of the kingdom of Persia withstood an angel and kept him from going to Daniel for 21 days (Dan. 10:13).
11. Satan tempted Jesus (Matt. 4:1-11).
12. "They brought unto [Jesus] one possessed with a devil, blind, and dumb: and he healed him, insomuch that the blind and dumb both spake and saw" (Matt. 12:22).
13. A demon often sought to kill the boy it inhabited by casting him into fire or water. It would also throw him to the ground and cause him to grind his teeth and foam at the mouth (Mark 9:17-29).
14. An unclean spirit which recognized Jesus convulsed his victim before being cast out of him by Jesus (Mark 1:23-36).
15. "Legion" gave his victim insanity, great strength, and an inclination to harm himself (Mark 5:1-20).
16. Satan kept a woman bound for eighteen years by a spirit of infirmity so that she could not straighten herself (Luke 13:11-16).
17. Satan entered "into Judas surnamed Iscariot, . . . and

386

[Judas] went his way, and communed with the chief priests and captains, how he might betray [Jesus] unto them" (Luke 22:3,4).

18. Jesus said to Peter, "Simon, Simon, behold, Satan hath desired to have you, that he may sift you as wheat" (Luke 22:31).

19. The devil "was a murderer from the beginning, and abode not in the truth, because there is no truth in him. When he speaketh a lie, he speaketh of his own: for he is a liar, and the father of it" (John 8:44).

20. "Satan filled [Ananias'] heart to lie to the Holy Ghost, and to keep back part of the price of the land" (Acts 5:3).

21. "A certain damsel possessed with a spirit of divination ... brought her masters much gain by soothsaying" (Acts 16:16).

22. The seven sons of Sceva were overcome by an evil spirit that they were trying to cast out of a man (Acts 19:16).

23. Satan hindered Paul from going to the Thessalonians (1 Thess. 2:18).

24. The devil has taken people captive at his will (2 Tim. 2:26).

25. The devil had the power of death (Heb. 2:14).

26. "The devil sinneth from the beginning" (1 John 3:8).

27. The devil disputed with Michael the archangel about the body of Moses (Jude 9).

83. Seven Present Activities of Satan and Demons

1. Demons may leave and later return to a person (Matt. 12:43-45).

2. Satan may take away the word that has been sown in people's hearts if they don't understand it (Matt. 13:19).

3. "The god of this world hath blinded the minds of them which believe not, lest the light of the glorious gospel of Christ, who is the image of God, should shine unto them" (2 Cor. 4:4).

4. Satan disguises himself as an angel of light (2 Cor. 11:14).

5. The powers of darkness fight against the saints (Eph. 6:12).

6. The devils believe in God and tremble (James 2:19).

7. The devil accuses us before our God day and night (Rev. 12:10).

84. Six Future Activities of Satan and Demons

1. Lucifer shall "be brought down to hell, to the sides of the pit" (Isa. 14:15).
2. "In the latter times some shall depart from the faith, giving heed to seducing spirits, and doctrines of devils" (1 Tim. 4:1).
3. Satan and his angels will battle Michael and his angels. Satan and his angels will be defeated and cast out of heaven to the earth (Rev. 12:7-10).
4. Spirits of devils will perform miracles to bring the nations to war (Rev. 16:13,14).
5. Satan will be cast into the bottomless pit for 1,000 years (Rev. 20:1-3).
6. Satan will be released upon the earth after the 1,000 years, but he will finally be cast into the lake of fire (Rev. 20:7-10).

11

Heathen Practices

Most people, when first confronting the scene of fifteen or twenty devout Hare Krishna members in a local park, bowing before a picture of an Indian deity, are awestruck. To think that such a practice could take place in our American communities is shocking to most of us. It's heathen; it's something foreign; it's strange and we don't like it. Even though we may not like it, there is little in the legal realm we can do about it.

The Bible records many pagan deities and practices that God had forbidden Israel to involve itself with. These pagan gods were an abomination to Him, and the practices associated with them were heinous. Worship of some of these gods went so far as human sacrifice. Recorded in the next lists are names of these gods, practicing sorcerers and witches, and different sacrifices made to those idols.

A pagan deity is, according to Arthur Wallis, "any person or thing that has usurped in the heart the place of preeminence that belongs to Jesus Christ." Though few around us bow with shaven head to an Eastern deity, many bow before Western values of prosperity, success, and prominence. Such "gods" may not look so strange, but the effect of worshiping them will be the same as that of worshiping idols.

85. Thirty-one Pagan Gods in the Bible

1. The Sepharites burned their children to *Adrammelech* (2 Kings 17:31).
2. The Sepharites also worshiped *Anammelech* (2 Kings 17:31).
3. The men of Hamath made *Ashima* (2 Kings 17:30).

4. Solomon worshiped *Ashtoreth* the goddess of the Zidonians (1 Kings 11:5) also known as the *queen of heaven* (Jer. 44:17).
5. King Ahab and Queen Jezebel served *Baal* (1 Kings 16:31,32).
6. After Gideon died, Israel turned to *Baal-berith* (Judges 8:33).
7. Israel served *Baal-peor*, the god of Moab (Num. 25:1-3).
8. *Baal-zebub* was the god of Ekron (2 Kings 1:2).
9. *Bel* was a Babylonian god (Jer. 51:44).
10. Aaron made the children of Israel a *molten calf* to worship (Ex. 32:1-5), and King Jeroboam made *golden calves* (1 Kings 12:26-30).
11. *Castor* was a Greek god (Acts 28:11).
12. Solomon built a high place for *Chemosh*, the abomination of Moab (1 Kings 11:7).
13. Amos chastised Israel for serving *Chiun* (Amos 5:26).
14. The Philistines had a temple for *Dagon* (1 Sam 5:1-5).
15. The great temple of the goddess *Diana* was in Ephesus (Acts 19:35).
16. The Lycaonians worshiped *Jupiter* (Acts 14:11-13).
17. The Roman god *Mercury* was also worshiped by the Lycaonians (Acts 14:11-13).
18. Solomon worshiped *Milcom*, the abomination of the Ammonites (1 Kings 11:5).
19. Solomon built a high place for *Molech*, the god of Ammon (1 Kings 11:7).
20. Isaiah said that the people served *Nebo* (Isa. 46:1).
21. Israel saved the brass serpent that Moses made and worshiped it. They called it *Nehushtan* (2 Kings 18:4).
22. The men of Cuth worshiped *Nergal* (2 Kings 17:30).
23. The Avites worshiped *Nibhaz* (2 Kings 17:31).
24. Sennacherib, king of Assyria, was killed while worshiping *Nisroch* (2 Kings 19:36,37).
25. *Pollux* was a Greek god (Acts 28:11).
26. Israel worshiped images of *Remphan* (Acts 7:43).
27. *Rimmon* was the god of the Syrians (2 Kings 5:17, 18).
28. The Babylonians worshiped *Succoth-benoth* (2 Kings 17:30).
29. Ezekiel saw a woman weeping for the god *Tammuz* (Ezek. 8:14).
30. The Avites worshiped *Tartak* (2 Kings 17:31).
31. Micah built a shrine for his *teraphim*, or household gods (Judges 17:5).

Sennacherib is murdered while worshiping Nisroch

86. Witches and Sorcerers

1. Pharaoh called on his *sorcerers* and *magicians* to duplicate the miracles that Moses performed (Ex. 7:11,12).
2. The witch of Endor was a *medium* (1 Sam. 28:7-25).
3. Jezebel practiced *witchcraft* (2 Kings 9:22).
4. Edom, Moab, Ammon, Tyre, and Aidon all had *enchanters, sorcerers,* and *diviners* (Jer. 27:3-10).
5. Nebuchadnezzar's *magicians, astrologers, soothsayers,* and *sorcerers* could neither tell him his dream nor interpret it (Dan. 2:10).
6. Nahum called Nineveh the mistress of *witchcrafts* (Nah. 3:4).
7. Simon amazed the people of Samaria with his *sorcery* (Acts 8:9).
8. Elymas was a *sorcerer* on the island of Paphos (Acts 13:6-8).
9. Many of those who repented and believed at Ephesus had practiced *curious arts* (Acts 19:19).

87. Sacrifices Made to Idols

1. The children of Israel "offered burnt offerings, and brought peace offerings" to the molten calf which Aaron made (Ex. 32:6).
2. Jeroboam offered sacrifices and burned incense to the two golden calves that he had made (1 Kings 12:32-33).
3. Elijah challenged the prophets of Baal to a contest in which they offered a bullock to their god (1 Kings 18:25).
4. The king of Moab despaired in the face of battle and offered his oldest son, the heir to the throne, as a burnt offering to his god (2 Kings 3:26,27).
5. "The Sepharvites burnt their children in fire to Adrammelech and Anammelech, the gods of Sepharvaim" (2 Kings 17:31).

Saul and the witch at Endor

6. The children of Israel burned incense to the brazen serpent which Moses had made (2 Kings 18:4).
7. Idolatrous priests burned incense to Baal (2 Kings 23:5).
8. The Israelites offered up their children in the fire of Molech (2 Kings 23:10).
9. Ahaz burned incense and offered his children to Molech. He also sacrificed and burned incense to Asherah and the gods of Damascus (2 Chron. 28:1-4,23).
10. The people of Judah burned incense, sacrificed cakes, and poured out drink offerings to the queen of heaven (Jer. 44:19).
11. The people of Jerusalem offered meat, fine flour, oil, honey, and even their sons and daughters to idols (Ezek. 16:17-20).

12

What's My Line?

A recent advertisement in major national magazines quoted Christopher Morley's maxim, "There is only one success ... to be able to spend your life in your own way." In the background a man sat alone, fishing in a setting of idyllic beauty. The American dream has developed to the point where we are made to feel that the only satisfying thing in life is doing what *I* want whenever *I* want. Work is now viewed as a necessary evil, for sustaining the leisure that one finds satisfying. Work is seldom looked upon as a satisfying part of one's life.

The Bible lists that follow show many of the vocations of those who lived in Bible times. They may not have had computers and copying machines to speed up their work, but the vocations that most of them pursued are quite similar to the vocations that many of us have. Yet, we find little discontentment among them concerning their jobs—as if they sensed God's purpose for their life while working.

Dorothy L. Sayers said, "I ask that work should be looked upon, not as a necessary drudgery to be undergone for the purpose of making money, but as a way of life in which the nature of man should find its proper exercise and delight and so fulfill itself to the glory of God."

88. Spies

1. The Lord commanded Moses to send twelve men into Canaan to spy out the land (Num. 13:1-16).
2. "Joshua the son of Nun sent out of Shittim two men to spy secretly, saying, Go view the land, even Jericho" (Josh. 2:1).

394

3. Spies found the entrance to the Canaanite city of Bethel
   before the army of Ephraim came in to destroy it (Judges
   1:23-25).
4. The Danites sent five men to spy out the rest of their inheritance (Judges 18:2-28).
5. David sent spies out to see if Saul had followed him to the
   Wilderness of Ziph. He had (1 Sam. 26:3,4).
6. "Absalom sent spies throughout all the tribes of Israel, saying, As soon as ye hear the sound of the trumpet, then ye
   shall say, Absalom reigneth in Hebron" (2 Sam. 15:10).
7. Hushai, the counselor of Absalom, was actually a spy for
   David (2 Sam. 15:32-37).
8. The chief priests and scribes sent spies to watch Jesus (Luke
   20:20).
9. Paul wrote with concern about "false brethren unawares
   brought in, who came in privily to spy out our liberty which
   we have in Christ Jesus, that they might bring us into bondage" of the law (Gal. 2:4).

89. Godly Officials in Heathen Governments

1. Pharaoh appointed *Joseph* to be governor over Egypt (Gen.
   41:39-41).
2. *Nehemiah* was Artaxerxes' cupbearer (Neh. 1:11-2:1).
3. *Esther* became queen to Ahasuerus (Esther 2:17).
4. "*Mordecai* the Jew was next unto King Ahasuerus, and
   great among the Jews" (Esther 10:3).
5. "King Nebuchadnezzar made *Daniel* a great man, and gave
   him many gifts, and made him ruler over the whole province
   of Babylon, and chief of the governors over all the wise men
   of Babylon" (Dan. 2:48).
6. *Shadrach, Meshach,* and *Abednego* were appointed administrators over the province of Babylon by King Nebuchadnezzar (Dan. 2:49).
7. A godly *Roman centurion* asked Jesus to heal his servant
   (Luke 7:2-10).
8. The *Ethiopian eunuch* was a man "of great authority under
   Candace queen of the Ethiopians, who had the charge of all
   her treasure, and had come to Jerusalem for to worship"
   (Acts 8:27).
9. *Cornelius,* a Roman centurion in Caesarea, was "a devout
   man, and one that feared God with all his house, which gave

Esther becomes queen

much alms to the people, and prayed to God alway" (Acts 10:1,2).

10. *Sergius Paulus,* the proconsul of Cyprus, became a believer (Acts 13:7-12).

11. Paul greeted the Philippian church from the saints "that are of *Caesar's household*" (Phil. 4:22).

90. Artists and Craftsmen

1. Jubal was the inventor of the harp and the pipe (Gen. 4:21).
2. Tubal-cain was "an instructor of every artificer in brass and iron" (Gen. 4:22).
3. Noah built the ark of gopher wood (Gen. 6:13-22).
4. Bezaleel worked in gold, silver, brass, stone, and wood (Ex. 31:1-6).

5. Aaron made a molten calf of gold and fashioned it with a graving tool (Ex. 32:4).
6. Moses hewed two tables of stone to replace the ones he broke (Ex. 34:1,4).
7. Aholiab was an engraver and an embroiderer (Ex. 38:23).
8. "Moses made a serpent of brass" (Num. 21:9).
9. Hiram was "cunning to work all works in brass" (1 Kings 7:13,14).
10. Harhaiah was a goldsmith (Neh. 3:8).
11. Joseph was a carpenter (Matt. 13:55).
12. Jesus was a carpenter (Mark 6:3).
13. Paul, Aquila, and Priscilla were tentmakers (Acts 18:1-3).
14. Demetrius was a silversmith in Ephesus (Acts 19:24).
15. Alexander was a coppersmith (2 Tim. 4:14).

91. Physicians

1. "Joseph commanded his servants the physicians to embalm his father: and the physicians embalmed Israel" (Gen. 50:2).
2. King Asa was diseased in his feet and he sought the physicians but not the Lord (2 Chron. 16:12,13).
3. Luke, the beloved physician, sent greetings to the saints at Colosse (Col. 4:14).

92. Teachers

1. The Lord taught Moses what to say and what to do (Ex. 4:12,15).
2. Moses taught the children of Israel "ordinances and laws, and . . . the way wherein they must walk, and the work that they must do" (Ex. 18:20).
3. The Lord appointed Bezaleel and Aholiab to teach those who would construct the tabernacle (Ex. 35:30-35).
4. The Lord told Aaron to "teach the children of Israel all the statutes which the Lord hath spoken unto them by the hand of Moses" (Lev. 10:11).
5. The priests were to teach the children of Israel how to recognize and to deal with leprosy (Deut. 24:8).
6. The king of Assyria sent one of the exiled priests back to Samaria to teach the Gentile inhabitants how they should fear God (2 Kings 17:28).
7. King Jehoshaphat sent his princes throughout Judah to teach the law of the Lord to all the people (2 Chron. 17:7-9).

8. King Artaxerxes commissioned Ezra to teach the laws of God to Israel (Ezra 7:25).
9. Jesus taught the people (Matt. 11:1).
10. Jesus told His apostles, "Go ye therefore, and teach all nations, ... to observe all things whatsoever I have commanded you" (Matt. 28:19,20).
11. Jesus said, "The Comforter, ... shall teach you all things, and bring all things to your remembrance" (John 14:26).
12. "Paul and Barnabas continued in Antioch, teaching and preaching the word of the Lord, with many others also" (Acts 15:35).
13. Apollos taught in the synagogue at Ephesus, but Aquilla and Priscilla instructed him in the ways of God (Acts 18:24-26).
14. Paul disputed daily in the school of Tyrannus (Acts 19:9).
15. Paul was "brought up ... at the feet of Gamaliel, and taught according to the perfect manner of the law of the fathers" (Acts 22:3).

93. Shepherds

1. Abel was a keeper of sheep (Gen. 4:2).
2. Abram had sheep (Gen. 12:16).
3. Rachel was a shepherdess (Gen. 29:9).
4. Laban had sheep (Gen. 29:9).
5. Jacob had sheep (Gen. 32:14).
6. Jacob's sons tended his flocks (Gen. 37:13).
7. Judah had sheep (Gen. 38:12,13).
8. Moses' wife Zipporah and her sisters tended their father's sheep (Ex. 2:16,17).
9. Moses became a shepherd for his father-in-law's flock (Ex. 3:1).
10. Achan kept sheep (Josh. 7:24).
11. David was a shepherd (1 Sam. 16:11-13).
12. Nabal had three thousand sheep (1 Sam. 25:2,3).
13. Job had fourteen thousand sheep (Job 42:12).
14. David said, "The Lord is my shepherd" (Ps. 23:1).
15. Jesus said, "I am the good shepherd: the good shepherd giveth his life for the sheep" (John 10:11).
16. Jesus commanded Peter to shepherd the church (John 21:15-17).

94. Beggars

1. "Blind Bartimaeus, the son of Timaeus, sat by the highway side begging" (Mark 10:46).
2. Jesus spoke about a beggar named Lazarus who died and

Boaz sees Ruth gleaning in his field

was carried by the angels into Abraham's bosom (Luke 16:20-22).

3. Jesus healed a blind beggar by putting mud on his eyes and sending him to wash in the pool of Siloam (John 9:1-8).
4. Peter and John healed a lame beggar who had been asking for alms at the temple gate (Acts 3:2-7).

95. Thirteen Famous Farmers

1. "The Lord God planted a garden eastward in Eden" (Gen. 2:8).
2. "Cain was a tiller of the ground" (Gen. 4:2).
3. "Noah began to be an husbandman, and he planted a vineyard" (Gen. 9:20).
4. "Isaac sowed in [Gerar], and received in the same year an hundredfold" (Gen. 26:12).
5. Gideon raised wheat (Judges 6:11).
6. Boaz had a barley field (Ruth 1:22-2:3).
7. David commanded Ziba to till the land for Mephibosheth, Saul's grandson (2 Sam. 9:9,10).
8. Joab had a barley field (2 Sam. 14:30).
9. Elisha was plowing when Elijah threw his mantle upon him (1 Kings 19:19).
10. Naboth had a vineyard on which Ahab wanted to raise herbs (1 Kings 21:1,2).
11. King Uzziah loved husbandry (2 Chron. 26:9,10).
12. Job was a farmer (Job 1:14).
13. Solomon planted vineyards, gardens, and orchards (Eccles. 2:4, 5).

96. One Hundred and Ninety-eight Vocations in the Bible

1. Apostle (Acts 6:1-6).
2. Apothecary (perfumer) (Neh. 3:8).
3. Archer (Gen. 21:20).
4. Armorbearer (1 Sam. 14:12).
5. Astrologer (Dan. 1:20).
6. Baker (Gen. 40:1).
7. Barber (Ezek. 5:1).
8. Beggar (Acts 3:2).
9. Binder of sheaves (Ps. 129:7).

10. Bishop (or elder) (1 Tim. 3:1).
11. Brickmaker (Ex. 5:7).
12. Builder (1 Kings 5:18).
13. Butler (Gen. 40:1).
14. Calker (shipwright) (Ezek. 27:27).
15. Camel driver (Gen. 32:13-16; 33:13).
16. Candlestick maker (Ex. 25:31).
17. Carpenter (Mark 6:3).
18. Cattleman (Gen. 46:34).
19. Centurion (Matt. 8:5).
20. Chamberlain (Acts 12:20).
21. Chancellor (Ezra 4:8).
22. Chapman (trader) (2 Chron. 9:14).
23. Chariot driver (1 Kings 22:34).
24. Charmer (Ps. 58:5).
25. Clothes maker (Acts 9:39).
26. Confectionary (perfumer) (1 Sam. 8:13).
27. Cook (1 Sam. 8:13).
28. Coppersmith (2 Tim. 4:14).
29. Council (Sanhedrin) member (Acts 22:30).
30. Counsellor (1 Chron. 27:33).
31. Cupbearer (Neh. 1:11).
32. Daysman (mediator) (Job 9:33).
33. Deacon (Acts 6:3-5; 1 Tim. 3:8).
34. Deputy (governor) (Acts 13:7).
35. Ditchdigger (Isa. 22:11).
36. Diviner (1 Sam. 6:2).
37. Doorkeeper (1 Chron. 15:23).
38. Drawer of Water (Josh. 9:21).
39. Embroiderer (Ex. 38:23).
40. Enchanter (Jer. 27:9).
41. Engraver (Ex. 38:23).
42. Evangelist (Acts 21:8).
43. Exchanger (banker) (Matt. 25:27).
44. Executioner (Mark 6:27).
45. Exorcist (Acts 19:13).
46. Fanner (winnower) (Jer. 51:2).
47. Farmer (Matt. 22:5; Gen. 9:20 [husbandman]).
48. Feller (lumberjack) (Isa. 14:8).
49. Fisherman (Luke 5:2).
50. Footman (1 Sam. 22:17).
51. Forestkeeper (Neh. 2:8).

52. Fowler (Ps. 124:7).
53. Fruit gatherer (Amos 7:14).
54. Fuller (Mark 9:3).
55. Furniture maker (Ex. 31:6-9).
56. Gardener (John 20:15).
57. Garment maker (Ex. 31:6,10).
58. Goatherder (Gen. 32:14,16).
59. Goldsmith (Isa. 40:19).
60. Governor (Gen. 42:6).
61. Grapegatherer (Jer. 6:9).
62. Guard (Gen. 40:4).
63. Harlot (Josh. 6:17).
64. Harper (Rev. 14:2).
65. Herald (Dan. 3:4).
66. Hewer of timber (2 Chron. 2:10).
67. Hewer of wood (Josh. 9:21).
68. Horseman (2 Kings 9:17).
69. Hunter (Gen. 25:27).
70. Innkeeper (Luke 10:34,35).
71. Interpreter (Gen. 42:23).
72. Jailor (Acts 16:23).
73. Judge (2 Sam. 15:4).
74. King (Acts 25:13).
75. Lamp maker (Ex. 25:37).
76. Lawyer (Titus 3:13).
77. Lieutenant (Esther 9:3).
78. Locksmith (Neh. 3:3).
79. Magician (Dan. 2:2).
80. Magistrate (Acts 16:35).
81. Maid (Esther 4:4; Gen 16:1 [handmaid]).
82. Maidservant (Ex. 20:10).
83. Manservant (Ex. 20:10).
84. Mariner (Ezek. 27:27).
85. Mason (2 Kings 12:12).
86. Masterbuilder (1 Cor. 3:10).
87. Merchant (Rev. 18:11-13).
88. Messenger (1 Sam. 23:27).
89. Midwife (Gen. 35:17).
90. Miller (Matt. 24:41).
91. Miner (Job 28:1, 2).
92. Minister (Jer. 33:21).
93. Minstrel (2 Kings 3:15).

94. Moneychanger (Matt. 21:12).
95. Mourner (Eccles. 12:5).
96. Mover (Num. 4:1-15).
97. Musician (Ps. 4, title).
98. Necromancer (Deut. 18:11).
99. Night watchman (Isa. 21:11).
100. Nurse for children (Ex. 2:7-9).
101. Officer (Luke 12:58).
102. Orator (Acts 24:1).
103. Overseer (2 Chron. 34:12).
104. Pastor (Eph. 4:11).
105. Philosopher (Acts 17:18).
106. Physician (Col. 4:14).
107. Pilot (ship) (Ezek. 27:27).
108. Planter (Jer. 31:5).
109. Plowman (Amos 9:13).
110. Poet (Acts 17:28).
111. Porter (gatekeeper) (2 Kings 7:10).
112. Post (postman) (Esther 3:13).
113. Potter (Jer. 18:4).
114. Preacher (1 Tim. 2:7).
115. Presbyter (1 Tim. 4:14).
116. President (Dan. 6:2).
117. Priest (Hebrew) (Lev. 1:7).
118. Priest (pagan) (1 Sam. 6:2).
119. Prince (1 Chron. 5:6).
120. Prognosticator (Isa. 47:13).
121. Prophet (1 Sam. 3:20).
122. Prophetess (Judges 4:4).
123. Prostitute (see Harlot).
124. Publican (Luke 5:27).
125. Queen (1 Kings 10:1).
126. Rabbi (John 1:38).
127. Reaper (Amos 9:13; Isa. 17:5 [harvestman]).
128. Recorder (2 Sam. 8:16).
129. Refiner (Mal. 3:3).
130. Robber (Job 5:5).
131. Rower (Ezek. 27:26).
132. Runner (2 Sam. 15:1).
133. Sailor (Rev. 18:17).
134. Sawyers (2 Sam. 12:31).
135. Schoolmaster (Gal. 3:25).

136. Scientist (Dan. 1:4).
137. Scribe (2 Sam. 8:17).
138. Seamstress (Acts 9:39).
139. Seer (1 Sam. 9:9).
140. Seller (James 4:13).
141. Senator (Ps. 105:22).
142. Sergeant (Acts 16:35).
143. Servant (Gen. 24:2).
144. Sheepmaster (2 Kings 3:4).
145. Sheepshearer (Gen. 38:12).
146. Shepherd (Gen. 46:32; Amos 7:14 [herdman]).
147. Sheriff (Dan. 3:2).
148. Shipbuilder (1 Kings 22:48).
149. Shipmaster (Jonah 1:6).
150. Shipmen (1 Kings 9:27).
151. Silversmith (Acts 19:24; Judges 17:4 [founder]).
152. Singer (1 Chron. 9:33).
153. Slave (Rev. 18:13).
154. Slinger (2 Kings 3:25).
155. Smith (1 Sam. 13:19).
156. Snake charmer (Ps. 58:4, 5).
157. Soldier (Acts 27:31).
158. Soothsayer (Josh. 13:22).
159. Sorcerer (Ex. 7:11).
160. Sorceress (Isa. 57:3).
161. Sower (Isa. 55:10).
162. Spearman (Acts 23:23).
163. Spice merchant (1 Kings 10:15).
164. Spy (Josh. 2:1).
165. Stargazer (Isa. 47:13).
166. Steward (Gen. 15:2).
167. Stone cutter (1 Kings 5:18).
168. Swineherder (Mark 5:14).
169. Swordsman (Song of Sol. 3:8).
170. Tailor (Ex. 39:22).
171. Tanner (Acts 9:43).
172. Taskmaster (Ex. 1:11).
173. Tax collector (see Publican).
174. Teacher (1 Chron. 25:8).
175. Temple servants (Ezra 8:20).
176. Tentmaker (Acts 18:3).
177. Tetrarch (Matt. 14:1).

178. Thief (Joel 2:9).
179. Tormentor (Matt. 18:34).
180. Townclerk (Acts 19:35).
181. Treader of grapes (Amos 9:13).
182. Treasurer (Ezra 1:8).
183. Trumpeter (2 Kings 11:14).
184. Tutor (Gal. 4:2).
185. Usurer (Ex. 22:25).
186. Vinedresser (2 Kings 25:12).
187. Waiter (Acts 6:2).
188. Wardrobe keeper (2 Kings 22:14).
189. Watcher (Jer. 4:16).
190. Watchman (2 Kings 9:17).
191. Water drawer (Josh. 9:21).
192. Weapons maker (1 Sam. 8:12).
193. Weaver (Ex. 35:35).
194. Whore (Lev. 21:7).
195. Witch (Ex. 22:18).
196. Wizard (Lev. 20:27).
197. Woodcarver (Ex. 35:33).
198. Worker in brass (1 Kings 7:13, 14).

13

Money

"Federal Income Taxes Will Rise Thirteen Percent"—so reads the morning's headline. What's new? Year after year, it seems that government revenues fall short, so more is demanded. The IRS is busy making sure that we have paid all that is required of us. In hard economic times the burden of taxes becomes heavier and the percentage of poor people increases. Pressures to maintain our standard of living have even pushed many into illegal means of gaining money—extortion and bribery.

What is so true today was also true in the Bible times: taxes, government tax collectors, the poor becoming poorer, extortion, and bribery. Governments back then were well known to spend money lavishly on those in power and squeeze the little people for all they could get. Maybe we don't have it as bad as we think!

You may also want to reconsider the possible benefits of not being rich. The first lists show poor people and it is interesting how many of them received God's *direct* care because of their distressing situation. Had they not had such need, they might not have encountered God as they did. It's something to think about.

97. Poor People

1. Naomi and Ruth were poor when they came to the land of Israel from Moab (Ruth 1:21).
2. David was poor in his early days (1 Sam. 18:23).
3. A poor widow came to Elisha because a creditor wanted payment. It seems that the only assets she had to pay him with were a pot of oil and her two sons (2 Kings 4:1-2).
4. The widow of Zarephath was very poor and might have

starved to death if the Lord had not sent Elijah to her (1 Kings 17:8-16).

5. When the king of Babylon carried the people of Jerusalem away into captivity, he left only "the poorest sort of the people in the land" (2 Kings 24:10-14).

6. Blind Bartimaeus was a beggar before Jesus healed him (Mark 10:46).

7. Jesus commended a poor widow to His disciples, for putting all she had into the temple treasury (Mark 12:41-44).

8. When Lazarus the beggar died, angels carried him to Abraham's bosom (Luke 16:20-22).

9. Jesus healed another beggar who was blind from birth (John 9:1-8).

10. Peter and John healed a beggar lame from birth as they were going to the temple to pray (Acts 3:1-8).

11. Christians in Macedonia and Achaia made a contribution for the poor among the Jerusalem saints (Rom. 15:25-27).

The Macedonian believers contribute to the poor in Jerusalem

12. "Ye know the grace of our Lord Jesus Christ, that, though he was rich, yet for your sakes he became poor, that ye through his poverty might be rich" (2 Cor. 8:9).

98. Taxes

1. At Joseph's advice, the Egyptians were taxed 20 percent of their produce for the seven plenteous years before the famine. This tax remained even after the famine (Gen. 41:34; 47:26).
2. All Israelites twenty years old or older were required to pay a half shekel when the census was taken. The money was used for the service of the tabernacle (Ex. 30:12-16).
3. When Israel asked for a king, Samuel warned the people that he would tax them and take their children and property. Nevertheless, the people held to their request (1 Sam. 8).
4. Solomon's "heavy yoke" upon Israel probably included taxes (1 Kings 12:1-14).
5. The kingdoms Solomon reigned over brought "presents," or tribute, to his government (1 Kings 4:21).
6. Menahem, king of Israel, taxed the rich men of his kingdom fifty shekels of silver apiece to pay Pul, king of Assyria (2 Kings 15:19-20).
7. King Hoshea of Israel paid tribute to King Shalmaneser of Assyria. When it was discovered that he had ceased payments, Shalmaneser imprisoned him (2 Kings 17:3-4).
8. King Jehoiakim of Judah taxed his subjects in order to give Pharaoh Necho the tribute he demanded (2 Kings 23:33-35).
9. "Some of the Philistines brought Jehoshaphat [king of Judah] presents, and tribute silver" (2 Chron. 17:11).
10. The Jews were paying "toll, tribute, and custom" to Persia during Artaxerxes' reign (Ezra 4:13).
11. Later, King Artaxerxes exempted the priests, Levites, and other temple personnel from taxation (Ezra 7:24).
12. King Ahasuerus laid a tribute upon the land, and upon the isles of the sea [i.e., upon the whole empire]" (Esther 10:1).
13. Jesus sent Peter fishing to pay their taxes. In the fish's mouth was a coin sufficient for the tax (Matt. 17: 24-27).
14. Caesar imposed tribute on his subjects in Jerusalem in Jesus' day (Matt. 22:17-22).

15. Joseph and Mary had to go to Bethlehem to be registered before being taxed. Thus Jesus was born there (Luke 2:1-7).

99. Tax Collectors

1. Matthew (Levi) left his tax collecting to follow Jesus (Matt. 9:9).
2. Matthew then made a feast for Jesus, which many tax collectors (publicans) attended (Luke 5:29-32).
3. Zacchaeus, a rich chief tax collector, climbed a sycamore tree to see Jesus. When Jesus saw Zacchaeus and called him, he joyfully received Jesus into his home and was saved (Luke 19:1-10).
4. In one of Jesus' parables, a publican humbly prayed for mercy and was justified, whereas the self-exalting Pharisee was not (Luke 18:9-14).
5. Tax collectors came to John to be baptized; he charged them not to collect more than they were supposed to (Luke 3:12,13).

The widow's mite

100. Important Coins

1. The only coin mentioned in the Old Testament is the *dram* or *daric,* a gold Persian coin (Ezra 2:69; 8:27).
   Note: The coins mentioned in the New Testament were issued by three governments: Greek, Roman, and Jewish (Maccabaean). For the sake of clarity, it is necessary to refer to the names of the coins as given in the Greek text.
2. Sparrows were sold two for an *assarion* (farthing in KJV), a Greek coin (Matt. 10:29; cf. Luke 12:6).
3. The woman's lost coin was a *drachma,* a greek coin worth a day's wages (Luke 15:8).
4. *Tribute money* was a half shekel per person, and the *piece of money* that Peter found in the fish's mouth, a Greek *stater,* would have payed for two people (Matt. 17:24-27).
5. The man who owned the vineyard in Jesus' parable gave each laborer a *denarius* (penny in KJV), a Roman coin worth about one day's wages (Matt. 20:1,2).
6. The widow's mite was a Jewish *lepton* (mite in KJV). It was worth half a *kodrantes* (farthing in KJV) and could be used in the temple because it did not picture a pagan deity (Mark 12:42).

101. Three Cases of Extortion

1. Jacob would not feed Esau until he could extract a promise from Esau to give up his birthright (Gen. 25:29-34).
2. Samson's wedding guests threatened his wife, saying, "Entice thy husband, that he may declare unto us the riddle, lest we burn thee and thy father's house with fire" (Judges 14:15).
3. The sons of Eli threatened to take the uncooked sacrificial meat by force unless those who brought it gave it to them (1 Sam. 2:12-17).

102. Five Bribes

1. The lords of the Philistines each offered Delilah eleven hundred pieces of silver if she would find the secret of Samson's strength and tell them (Judges 16:5).
2. "When Samuel was old, . . . his sons walked not in his ways, but turned aside after lucre, and took bribes, and perverted judgment" (1 Sam. 8:1-3).

3. Judas Iscariot was given thirty pieces of silver to betray Jesus (Matt. 26:14-16).
4. The chief priests bribed the guards of Jesus' tomb to say that the disciples had stolen the body (Matt. 28:11-15).
5. Felix kept Paul in prison, hoping that Paul would bribe him for release (Acts 24:26).

14

People to People

Almost every community has a recluse; surely you must remember at least one. The old man who lived by himself back in the woods in an old dingy house, and only came to town when he was in need of food. The old lady who lived down the street in the foreboding dark house and was only seen when peering out from behind the curtains. Like Howard Hughes, at some time in life they decided to shut themselves off from others and try to find happiness by themselves. Unfortunately, the recluse's life becomes one marked by eccentricity and extreme unhappiness.

Life will not be fulfilling if we try to avoid the reality of people around us. It is necessary and good that we interact with each other. It is the way of growth and maturity. Interaction with others will create difficult situations. Just as love is the fruit of interacting with others, so are anger and people who are difficult to be with. These are all a part of maturing. The following lists include some of the interpersonal relationships we will find ourselves in: times of hugs and kisses, times of people being angry, getting to know the mothers-in-law, competition with each other, and the drawing of contracts in business relationships.

103. Thirteen Contracts

1. Abimelech swore to Abraham that the well dug by Abraham would not be bothered by his men. Abraham gave him seven ewe lambs as a witness of the deal (Gen. 21:25-32).
2. Abraham purchased a burial plot for Sarah from Ephron the Hittite. He had to pay 400 shekels of silver for the deed (Gen. 23:10-20).

3. Jacob forced the starving Esau to swear over his birthright before Jacob would feed him any pottage (Gen. 25:29-34).

4. Jacob negotiated a work contract with Laban. He would take no wages, but only the striped, spotted, and speckled sheep from Laban's flocks. The Lord blessed Laban with many striped, spotted, and speckled lambs (Gen. 30:29-43).

5. Laban and Jacob later set up a stone pillar to witness a contract of peace between them (Gen. 31:44-53).

6. Joseph's brothers sold him to slave traders for twenty shekels of silver (Gen. 37:28).

7. The lords of the Philistines each offered Delilah eleven hundred pieces of silver if she would find out the secret of Samson's strength for them (Judges 16:4,5).

8. Micah hired a Levite to be a priest in his shrine for an annual salary of ten shekels and a suit of clothing (Judges 17:10).

9. Ruth's closest relative gave Boaz the right to buy Naomi's property and to marry Ruth and then confirmed the agreement by removing his shoe (Ruth 4:1-10).

10. David pledged kindness to Jonathan and his family with an oath. He later fulfilled his oath by caring for Jonathan's son Mephibosheth (1 Sam. 20:12-17; 2 Sam. 9:6-7).

11. Solomon contracted with Hiram for the use of his servants. Hiram's men would cut cedar for the temple and Solomon would pay their wages (1 Kings 5:2-12).

12. King Ben-hadad of Syria promised King Ahab the return of all the Samarian cities taken by his father in return for his safe release (1 Kings 20:34).

13. Jeremiah bought a field from Hananeel his cousin for seventeen shekels of silver. The payment and signing of the deed was all done before witnesses (Jer. 32:6-12).

104. Fourteen Censuses

1. The population of the Garden of Eden was one until God doubled it (Gen. 2:8,22).

2. The post-Flood census showed only eight survivors (1 Pet. 3:20).

3. The Israelites numbered seventy-five when they went into the land of Egypt (Acts 7:14).

4. Six-hundred thousand men (plus women and children) left Egypt on foot in the Exodus (Ex. 12:37).

Joseph is sold to Midianite traders

5. God commanded Moses to number his army by recording every male twenty years old or older (Num. 1:1-46). The results were:
The tribe of Reuben—46,500
The tribe of Simeon—59,300
The tribe of Gad—45,650

The tribe of Judah—74,600
The tribe of Issachar—54,400
The tribe of Zebulun—57,400
The half tribe of Ephraim—40,500
The half tribe of Manasseh—32,200
The tribe of Benjamin—35,400
The tribe of Dan—62,700
The tribe of Asher—41,500
The tribe of Naphtali—53,400
Total number of Israelite fighting men—603,550

6. God also commanded that a census be taken of the Levites. Moses found 22,000 Levites more than one month old (Num. 3:39).

7. After 24,000 had died in a plague of judgment, God again commanded Moses to number the army. Moses found 601,730 men over twenty years of age (Num. 26:1-51).

8. The armies of Israel came against the tribe of Benjamin in judgment. A numbering of the armies showed 26,000 Benjamite soldiers and 400,000 from Israel. After the battle, only 600 Benjamite men remained (Judges 20:14-48).

9. Saul numbered the army that had gathered to fight the Ammonites and he counted 330,000 men (1 Sam. 11:8).

10. David brought God's wrath upon Israel by numbering the kingdom. He counted 1,300,000 "valiant men that drew the sword." God sent a plague that killed 70,000 of those men in one day (2 Sam. 24:1-15).

11. Under King David "the Levites were numbered from the age of thirty years and upward: and their number by their polls, man by man was 38,000" (1 Chron. 23:3).

12. "And Solomon numbered all the [aliens] in the land of Israel ... and they were found 153,600" (2 Chron. 2:17).

13. Ezra brought 42,360 people and 7,337 of their servants back to Jerusalem from Babylon (Ezra 2:64,65).

14. "And it came to pass in those days, that there went out a decree from Caesar Augustus, that all the world should be [enrolled]" (Luke 2:1).

105. Seventeen Hugs and Kisses

1. Isaac kissed Jacob thinking that he was Esau (Gen. 27:27).
2. Jacob kissed Rachel almost as soon as he met her. These kissing cousins were later wed (Gen. 29:11).

3. Laban embraced Jacob, kissed him, and brought him into his house (Gen. 29:13).
4. When Jacob and Laban parted company, Laban kissed his "sons and daughters and blessed them" (Gen. 31:55).
5. "Esau ran to meet [Jacob], and embraced him, and fell on his neck, and kissed him: and they wept" (Gen. 33:4).
6. Joseph kissed all his brothers and wept when they were reunited (Gen. 45:15).
7. Israel kissed, embraced, and blessed Ephraim and Manasseh, Joseph's sons (Gen. 48:10,20).
8. When Jacob died, "Joseph fell upon his father's face, and wept upon him, and kissed him" (Gen. 50:1).
9. Aaron "met Moses in the mount of God, and kissed him" (Ex. 4:27).
10. "Jethro, Moses' father-in-law, came . . . unto Moses into the wilderness, . . . and Moses went out to meet his father-in-law, and did obeisance, and kissed him" (Ex. 18:5,7).
11. Naomi kissed Orpah and Ruth, her daughters-in-law, as she left them to return to her own country (Ruth 1:9).

Naomi kisses her daughters-in-law good-bye

12. "Samuel took a vial of oil, and poured it upon [Saul's] head, and kissed him, and said, Is it not because the Lord hath anointed thee to be captain over his inheritance?" (1 Sam. 10:1).
13. David and Jonathan kissed one another and wept when David began his flight from Saul (1 Sam. 20:41).
14. After Absalom's two years in exile, he returned to his father and King David kissed him (2 Sam. 14:33).
15. "When any man came nigh to Absalom to do him obeisance, he put forth his hand, and took him, and kissed him. . . . So Absalom stole the hearts of the men of Israel" (2 Sam. 15:5,6).
16. When David returned to Jerusalem from fighting Absalom, he met and kissed Barzillai, an old man who had provided supplies for David's army (2 Sam. 19:39).
17. "Joab took Amasa by the beard with the right hand to kiss him. But Amasa took no heed to the sword that was in Joab's hand: so [Joab] smote him therewith ... and he died" (2 Sam. 20:9,10).

106. Late Night Visitors

1. Jacob was met by *a man* whom he wrestled all night. He later realized that the "man" was actually God (Gen. 32:22-31).
2. The *angel of death* came through Egypt at midnight (Ex. 12:29-31).
3. *Gideon* and his *three hundred men* attacked the Midianite camp at night (Judges 7:19).
4. *The Lord* came to Samuel at night (1 Sam. 4:1-14).
5. *David* and *Abishai* visited Saul's camp at night and took Saul's spear and a jug of water (1 Sam. 26:7-12).
6. *King Saul* visited the witch of Endor at night (1 Sam. 28:8).
7. The *shepherds* in Bethlehem were visited by a host of angels while they watched their flocks at night. After the news of the Messiah's birth had been revealed, *they* went to visit Joseph, Mary, and Jesus (Luke 2:8-16).
8. "About the fourth watch of the night [Jesus] cometh unto them, walking upon the sea" (Mark 6:48).
9. "There was a man of the Pharisees named *Nicodemus,* a ruler of the Jews: the same came to Jesus at night" (John 3:1,2).

Jacob wrestles with God

10. "*Judas* then, having received a band of men and officers from the chief priests and Pharisees, cometh thither with lanterns and torches and weapons. . . . Then the band and the captain and officers of the Jews took Jesus, and bound him" (John 18:3,12).

11. An *angel* came to Peter late at night and released him from

prison, and then *Peter* went to visit a prayer meeting at the home of John Mark's mother (Acts 12:6-17).

12. Paul was visited by an *angel* one night who assured him that all on board the storm-tossed boat would be safe (Acts 27:23,24).

107. Angry Brothers

1. "Cain rose up against Abel his brother, and slew him" (Gen. 4:8).
2. "Esau hated Jacob because of the blessing wherewith his father blessed him: and Esau said, . . . I will slay my brother Jacob" (Gen. 27:41).
3. The sons of Jacob were very angry when they heard that Shechem had raped their sister Dinah (Gen. 34:7).
4. "And when [Joseph's] brethren saw that their father loved him more than all his brethren, they hated him, and could not speak peaceably unto him" (Gen. 37:4).
5. Moses came down the mountain and saw the golden calf that Aaron his brother had made. He angrily rebuked Aaron for causing the people to sin (Ex. 32:19-22).
6. Abimelech, the son of Gideon, killed all seventy of his brothers at once (Judges 9:1-5).
7. Jephthah was thrown out of the house by his brothers because he was an illegitimate son of their father (Judges 11:1,2).
8. Eliab, David's oldest brother, was angered by David's concern over Goliath's challenge. He said that David had come out just to see the fighting (1 Sam. 17:28-30).
9. "Absalom hated his [brother] Ammon, because he had forced his sister Tamar" (2 Sam. 13:22).
10. The prodigal son's older brother was angry and would not go in to the prodigal's welcome-home party (Luke 15:28).

108. Eight Important Mothers-in-law

1. Sarah was Rebekah's mother-in-law (Gen. 21:3; 24:67).
2. Rebekah was Leah and Rachel's mother-in-law (Gen. 27:46; 29:21-28).
3. Moses' mother Jochebed was Zipporah's mother-in-law (Ex. 2:21; Num. 26:59).
4. Naomi was Ruth and Orpah's mother-in-law (Ruth 1:14).

5. King Saul's wife Ahinoam was David's mother-in-law (1 Sam. 14:50; 18:27).
6. Queen Jezebel was the mother-in-law of King Jehoram (1 Kings 21:4,5; 2 Kings 8:16-18).
7. Queen Athaliah was the mother-in-law of Ahaziah's wife Zibiah (2 Chron. 22:10-12; 24:1).
8. Peter's mother-in-law was healed of a fever by Jesus (Matt. 8:14,15).

109. Six Important Contests

1. Rachel and Leah competed for Jacob's love. They sought to have children to earn his favor (Gen. 30:1).
2. Moses and the magicians of Egypt competed in doing miracles. They all turned their rods into snakes, but Moses' ate up the other snakes (Ex. 7:10-12).
3. Korah questioned Moses' authority so Moses had Aaron and Korah take censers of incense before the Lord to see whom God would accept. Korah lost by default. A fiery crevice opened and swallowed Korah and his men before the contest could be completed (Num. 16:16-35).
4. God commanded each tribe to bring a rod and set it before him in the tabernacle overnight. Aaron's rod blossomed and thus proved that Aaron was God's chosen high priest (Num. 17:1-13).
5. Elijah challenged the priests of Baal to a contest to prove who the true God really was. Jehovah sent fire down from heaven to consume Elijah's sacrifice, including the altar (1 Kings 18:25-39).
6. The soldiers cast lots for Jesus' garments (Matt. 27:35).

15

The Animal World

"Look over there—it's a deer!" Such exclamations remind us of the wonder of the zoological kingdom. Other phrases like, "Beware of the dogs," remind us that though the animal world is wondrous, we still need to be careful. The stories of tourists being attacked by bears in Yellowstone National Park, or of a local farmer being gored by his prize bull, keep us wary.

The Bible recounts the creation of animals and is saturated with stories about, or including, animals. Many of the accounts include the enchantment that the animal world provides; other accounts include the danger that exists. Both elements are found in these lists. The lists also hold interest for those avid fishermen seeking new techniques for larger catches. There is even a section for those interested in the study of worms.

110. Five Animals That Attacked People

1. Two she *bears* attacked a group of children (2 Kings 2:24).
2. God sent *hornets* before Israel to drive away the Amorites (Josh. 24:12).
3. A young *lion* attacked Samson (Judges 14:5).
4. Jonah was swallowed by a *whale* (Matt. 12:40).
5. Paul was bitten by a *viper* on the island of Melita (Acts 28:3).

111. Monsters

1. "Behold now *behemoth* which I made with thee; he eateth grass as an ox" (Job 40:15).
2. "In the habitation of *dragons*, where each lay, shall be grass with reeds and rushes" (Isa. 35:7).
3. "The Lord with his sore and great and strong sword shall punish *leviathan* the piercing serpent" (Isa. 27:1).
4. "Even the *sea monsters* . . . give suck to their young ones" (Lam. 4:3).
5. The Lord "hath as it were the strength of an *unicorn*" (Num. 23:22).

112. Three Catches of Fish

1. Jesus told Peter to take the first fish that he caught and open its mouth. He would find a coin there to pay tribute for both Jesus and himself (Matt. 17:24-27).
2. When Jesus commanded Peter to launch out into the deep and drop his nets, Peter reminded Him of the poor fishing the previous night. Nevertheless, Peter obeyed and caught enough fish to fill two boats (Luke 5:1-7).
3. Peter was again fishing unsuccessfully when Jesus yelled out from the shore, telling him to cast his net on the other side of the boat. Peter did that and caught 153 large fish (John 21:2-11).

113. Worms

1. "Some of them left [the manna] until the morning, and it bred *worms*, and stank" (Ex. 16:20).
2. "That which the *palmerworm* hath left hath the locust eaten; and that which the locust hath left hath the *cankerworm* eaten; and that which the cankerworm hath left hath the *caterpillar* eaten" (Joel 1:4).
3. Job said, "My flesh is clothed with *worms* and clods of dust" (Job 7:5).
4. "The Lord God prepared a gourd, and made it to come up over Jonah. . . . But God prepared a *worm* when the morning rose the next day, and it smote the gourd that it withered" (Jonah 4:6,7).

422

An artist's concept of leviathan

5. "The nations shall see and be confounded. . . . They shall lick the dust like a serpent, they shall move out of their holes like *worms* of the earth" (Mic. 7:16,17).
6. Jesus said that hell is a place where the "*worm* dieth not" (Mark 9:43,44).

7. 'The angel of the Lord smote [Herod], because he gave not God the glory and he was eaten of *worms*, and gave up the ghost" (Acts 12:23).

114. Snakes

1. "And the Lord God said unto the serpent, Because thou hast done this [beguiled Eve to eat the forbidden fruit], . . . upon thy belly shalt thou go" (Gen. 3:14,15).
2. In blessing his sons, Jacob said, "Dan shall be a serpent by the way, an adder in the path, that biteth the horse heels, so that his rider shall fall backward" (Gen. 49:17).
3. Moses' rod became a serpent when he cast it on the ground (Ex. 4:2-4).
4. "The people spake against God, and against Moses. . . . And the Lord sent fiery serpents among the people, and they bit the people; and much of Israel died" (Num. 21:5,6).
5. "The day of the Lord is darkness, and not light. As if a man did flee from a lion, and a bear met him; or went into the house, and leaned his hand on the wall, and a serpent bit him" (Amos 5:18,19).
6. Jesus said to His disciples, "Behold, I give unto you power to tread on serpents and scorpions, and over all the power of the enemy: and nothing shall by any means hurt you" (Luke 10:19).
7. "When Paul had gathered a bundle of sticks, and laid them on the fire, there came a viper out of the heat, and fastened on his hand" (Acts 28:3).

115. Important Donkeys

1. An ass carried the wood upon which Abraham was planning to sacrifice Isaac (Gen. 22:1-3).
2. Jacob gave Esau twenty she asses and ten foals to appease him (Gen. 32:13-18).
3. "Moses took his wife and his sons, and set them upon an ass, and returned to the land of Egypt" (Ex. 4:20).
4. Balaam's ass verbally rebuked him for harsh treatment (Num. 22:21-33).
5. Saul was looking for his father's lost asses when he met Samuel (1 Sam. 9:1-6).
6. Abigail rode an ass to plead with David for her husband's life (1 Sam. 25:20).

7. "Absalom rode upon a mule, and the mule went under the thick boughs of a great oak, and his head caught hold of the oak" (2 Sam. 18:9).
8. The Shunammite sent her servant on an ass to Elisha to tell him that her son had died (2 Kings 4:18-32).
9. Jesus rode into Jerusalem on an ass (Matt. 21:1-9).

16

Transportation

The Bible lists that follow explore some of the transportation methods used in ancient days. The standard cart and chariots were no match for today's freeway traffic, but they certainly were economical. There are at least three methods of transportation in the lists that may be well worth our exploring as an alternative to the "gas hog" we may be driving. Check the economy rating on the following modes of travel: the chariot of fire that transported Elijah to heaven, the chariots that Zechariah saw being driven by angels, and the speedy trip that Philip made after baptizing the Ethiopian eunuch. If you could only get somebody to duplicate these, you'd be a millionaire.

116. Important Carts and Chariots

1. "Pharaoh said unto Joseph, See, I have set thee over all the land of Egypt. . . . And he made him to ride in the second chariot which he had" (Gen. 41:41,43).
2. Joseph sent wagons to Canaan to carry back his father and his brothers' families (Gen. 45:17-21).
3. "The Egyptians pursued after [the Israelites with] all the horses and chariots of Pharaoh" (Ex. 14:9).
4. The Levites were given six covered wagons in which to haul the tabernacle and its furnishings (Num. 7:1-9).
5. The Philistines sent the Ark of the Covenant back to the Israelites on a cart pulled by a cow (1 Sam. 6:7-14).
6. "Solomon . . . had a thousand and four hundred chariots" (1 Kings 10:26).

7. King Rehoboam's tax gatherer was stoned, so Rehoboam sped away to the safety of Jerusalem in his chariot (1 Kings 12:18).

8. King Ahab rode into battle in a chariot but was fatally hit by an Assyrian arrow (1 Kings 22:34-38).

9. "There appeared a chariot of fire, and horses of fire . . . and Elijah went up by a whirlwind into heaven" (2 Kings 2:11).

10. "Naaman came with his horses and with his chariot, and stood at the door of the house of Elisha" waiting to be healed of his leprosy (2 Kings 5:9).

11. The Lord sent many horses and chariots of fire to guard the Israelites against the invading Syrians (2 Kings 6:14-17).

12. Jehu rode in a chariot and chased the chariots of King Ahaziah and King Joram and killed them both (2 Kings 9:16-28).

13. While wiping out idolatry in the land, King Josiah burned the chariots of the sun (2 Kings 23:11).

14. King Josiah was wounded while fighting the Egyptians, so his servants took him from his own chariot "and put him in the second chariot that he had; and they brought him to Jerusalem, and he died" (2 Chron. 35:23,24).

A king on his chariot

15. Zechariah saw four chariots driven by angels (Zech. 6:1-8).
16. The Ethiopian eunuch was riding back to Ethiopia in a chariot when Philip came upon him (Acts 8:27,28).

117. The Longest Journeys in the Bible

1. Abraham moved his entire household from Haran to Canaan (Gen. 12:1-5).
2. Israel wandered through the wilderness for forty years after they had left Egypt to go to the Promised Land (Deut. 29:5).
3. Jesus' longest journey, made when He was a baby, was from Bethlehem to Egypt (Matt. 2:14).
4. Jesus' longest journey during His ministry was from Capernaum to Jerusalem (Matt. 17:24; 20:17).
5. The Ethiopian eunuch rode by chariot from Ethiopia to Jerusalem and back (Acts 8:27).

118. The Fastest Travelers in the Bible

1. Elijah raced Ahab's chariot on foot between Mount Carmel and Samaria and won (1 Kings 18:44-46).
2. The Spirit caught Philip away from the eunuch and took him to Azotus (Acts 8:39,40).

17

Forces of Nature

Through the advances of meteorology, we are able to watch the development of weather patterns every evening on the local TV news. It's fascinating to be able to watch the satellite pictures of the cloud cover and the radar images of rain and wind fronts. Somehow one gets the sense that we actually understand what is happening in nature. We can easily forget that, though we may now understand more about what is happening in nature, we still have no say about what happens. We still find ourselves extremely vulnerable to the powers of the wind, rain, snow, floods, etc.

The following lists show that the people in the Bible were also very vulnerable to nature's forces. In these lists, we see not only the powerful weather patterns that the writers observed, but the ways in which God was often very active in using these patterns for His purposes. Recorded are many instances when God intervened via strong winds, hail, floods, lightning, thunder, and rain. He used these methods to speak to people then, and we shouldn't be surprised if He uses them to speak to us today.

119. Thunder and Lightning

1. Thunder and lightning accompanied the veil of clouds that hung around Mount Sinai when God gave Moses the law (Ex. 19:16).
2. "The Philistines drew near to do battle against Israel: but the Lord thundered with a great thunder on that day upon the Philistines, and discomfited them" (1 Sam. 7:10).
3. "Samuel called unto the Lord; and the Lord sent thunder

and rain that day: and all the people greatly feared the Lord and Samuel" (1 Sam. 12:18).

4. John saw thunder and lightning before the Lord poured out His wrath upon the earth (Rev. 11:19).

120. Three Tornadoes (Whirlwinds)

1. "Elijah went up by a whirlwind into heaven" (2 Kings 2:11).
2. "The Lord answered Job out of the whirlwind" (Job 38:1).
3. Ezekiel "looked, and behold, a whirlwind came out of the north, a great cloud, and a fire infolding itself" (Ezek. 1:4).

121. Three Important Rainstorms

1. "The rain was upon the earth forty days and nights" while Noah was in the ark (Gen. 7:12).
2. "Samuel called unto the Lord; and the Lord sent thunder and rain that day" (1 Sam. 12:18).
3. After three-and-a-half years of devastating drought in Israel, Elijah prayed for rain and it came again (1 Kings 18:45).

122. Weather Miracles

1. The Lord sent fire and hail upon the Egyptians, but He spared the land of Goshen where the Israelites lived (Ex. 9:22-33).
2. "The Lord turned a mighty strong wind, which took away the locusts, and cast them into the Red sea" (Ex. 10:19).
3. As the Amorites fled before Israel, "the Lord cast down great stones from heaven upon them unto Azekah, and they died" (Josh. 10:11).
4. "Samuel called unto the Lord; and the Lord sent thunder and rain that day" (1 Sam. 12:18).
5. Elijah "prayed earnestly that it might not rain: and it rained not on the earth by the space of three years and six months. And he prayed again, and the heaven gave rain" (James 5:17,18).
6. Jonah's ship was hit by a mighty tempest that died down as soon as he was thrown overboard (Jonah 1:3-16).
7. The disciples were out on the Sea of Galilee in a storm when Jesus came to them walking on the water. When He got into the boat, the wind stopped (Matt. 14:24,33).

Jonah is thrown overboard to quell the storm

8. Jesus "rebuked the wind, and said unto the sea, Peace, be still. And the wind ceased, and there was a great calm" (Mark 4:39).

123. Earthquakes

1. As the Israelites waited before Mount Sinai, the Lord descended and the whole mountain quaked (Ex. 19:18).
2. Jonathan came against a Philistine garrison, and an earthquake accompanied his attack (1 Sam. 14:14-15).
3. The Lord passed by Elijah and an earthquake followed (1 Kings 19:11,12).
4. "Jesus, when he had cried again with a loud voice, yielded up the ghost. And . . . the earth did quake" (Matt. 27:50,51).

5. "There was a great earthquake: for the angel of the Lord descended from heaven, and came and rolled back the stone from the door" (Matt. 28:2).
6. Paul and Silas were in prison in Philippi when "suddenly there was a great earthquake, so that the foundations of the prison were shaken" (Acts 16:26).
7. Jesus declared that earthquakes in "divers places" would come before the end of the world (Matt. 24:7).

18

Violence

Leo Tolstoy wrote concerning mankind, "A good portion of the evils that afflict mankind is due to the erroneous belief that life can be made secure by violence." Ever since the day that Cain slew Abel, violence as a means to gain something has been a way of life. Today we live in a generation when nothing seems to shock us. On the evening news, we watch bank robbers shooting their hostages; we watch the daily bloodshed of warfare from some part of the world; we watch the riots and looting in foreign cities. We are being conditioned to violence.

The human race has not changed much over the last 2,000 years. The following lists show some of the acts of violence which took place during Bible times. Remember Coue's glowing statement from the late nineteenth century, "Every day in every way, I am getting better and better." It became a symbol of where mankind thought they were heading. I wonder what he would say today.

124. Five Riots

1. The people of Nazareth "rose up, and thrust Jesus out of the city, and led him unto the brow of the hill whereon their city was built, that they might cast him down headlong" (Luke 4:29).
2. Pilate bowed to the wishes of the crowd and allowed Jesus to be crucified because the mob had become uncontrollable (Matt. 27:23,24).
3. The unbelieving Thessalonian Jews "took unto them certain lewd fellows of the baser sort, and gathered a company,

and set all the city on an uproar, and assaulted the house of Jason, and sought to bring them out [Paul and Silas] to the people" (Acts 17:5).

4. The Ephesians "were full of wrath, and cried out, saying, Great is Diana of the Ephesians. And the whole city was filled with confusion: . . . they rushed with one accord into the theatre" (Acts 19:28,29).

5. All Jerusalem "was moved, and the people ran together: and they took Paul, and drew him out of the temple. . . . He was borne of the soldiers for the violence of the people" (Acts 21:30-35).

125. Three Ambushes

1. Joshua drew the army of Ai out of the city while another group ambushed and destroyed the city (Josh. 8:12-22).

2. The armies of Israel drew the Benjamites out of the city of Gibeah by retreating before them. But more Israelites were lurking behind the city and they ambushed Gibeah (Judges 20:29-43).

3. More than forty men were waiting in ambush for Paul, but the Roman soldiers moved him secretly out of Jerusalem at night (Acts 23:21-23).

126. Defensive Weapons

1. Goliath "had an *helmet of brass* upon his head, and he was armed with a *coat of mail*; and the weight of the coat was five thousand shekels of brass. And he had *greaves of brass* upon his legs, and a *target of brass* between his shoulders" (1 Sam. 17:4-6).

2. "Uzziah prepared for them throughout all the host *shields,* and spears, and *helmets,* and *habergeons,* and bows, and slings to cast stones. And he made in Jerusalem *engines,* invented by cunning men to be on the towers and upon the bulwarks, to shoot arrows and great stones withal" (2 Chron. 26:14,15).

3. "Order ye the *buckler* and *shield,* and draw near to battle. Harness the horses; and get up, ye horsemen, and stand forth with your *helmets*; furbish the spears, and put on the *brigandines*" (Jer. 46:3,4).

127. Offensive Weapons

1. David "took his *staff* in his hand, and chose him five smooth *stones* out of the brook, and put them in a shepherd's bag which he had, even in a scrip; and his *sling* was in his hand" (1 Sam. 17:40).
2. "'And Saul cast the *javelin*; for he said, I will smite David even to the wall with it" (1 Sam. 18:11).
3. David's men "were armed with *bows*, and could use both the right hand and the left in hurling *stones* and shooting *arrows* out of a *bow*" (1 Chron. 12:2).
4. Hezekiah "strengthened himself, . . . and made *darts* and shields in abundance" (2 Chron. 32:5).
5. "A man that beareth false witness against his neighbour is a *maul*, and a *sword*, and a sharp *arrow*" (Prov. 25:18).
6. Ezekiel was commanded to make a model of Jerusalem and "set *battering rams* against it round about" (Ezek. 4:1,2).
7. "One of the soldiers with a *spear* pierced his side" (John 19:34).

128. Murder Weapons and Devices

1. Ehud killed King Eglon of Moab with a two-edged *dagger* (Judges 3:16-21).
2. Joab "took three *darts* in his hand, and thrust them through the heart of Absalom" (2 Sam. 18:14).
3. Hazel "took a *thick cloth*, and dipped it in water, and spread it on [Ben-hadad's] face, so that he died" (2 Kings 8:15).
4. Adrammelech and Sharezer killed their father Sennácherib with a *sword* (2 Kings 19:37).
5. "King Rehoboam sent Hadoram that was over the tribute; and the children of Israel stoned him with *stones* that he died" (2 Chron. 10:18).

129. Unusual Weapons

1. "Shamgar . . . slew of the Philistines six hundred men with an *ox goad*" (Judges 3:31).
2. "Jael Heber's wife took a *nail of the tent*, and took an *hammer* in her hand, and went softly unto [Sisera], and smote the nail into his temple, and fastened it into the ground" (Judges 4:17-21).

3. Samson "found a new *jawbone of an ass,* and put forth his hand, and took it, and slew a thousand men therewith" (Judges 15:15).
4. "The staff of [Goliath's] spear was like a weaver's beam; and his spear's head weighed six hundred shekels of iron" (1 Sam. 17:7).

The death of Sisera

19

Death and Funerals

Shakespeare devoted much thought, in writing his plays, to the theme of death. In the play *King Henry VI,* he wrote these words: "Why, what is pomp, rule, reign, but earth and dust? And live we how we can, yet die we must." His characters are often made to face the issue of death, and many of them die tragically. In contrast, our Western society provides little in the way of preparation for death. It is an issue that most of us would rather not think or talk about. Shakespeare is correct, though—"yet die we must."

The following Bible lists show deaths and funerals of the people of that time. Some of the deaths recorded followed lives filled with corruption and wrongdoing. Some followed lives lived for the glory of God. In either case the sadness of the loss of a loved one was always there, but in the case of a righteous life there was always the great anticipation of the resurrection from the dead. Paul's words are always timely: "For me to live is Christ, to die is gain." He saw death as a mere stepping into eternal life with Christ.

How we view death will profoundly affect how we live. Death in the Bible is never seen as the end of life, but rather, as an entrance into eternity. As Catherine Booth declared on her deathbed, "The waters are rising but I am not sinking."

130. Nineteen Graves and Graveyards

1. "But Deborah Rebekah's nurse died, and she was buried beneath Beth-el under an oak: and the name of it was called Allon-bachuth" (Gen. 35:8).

2. "Rachel died, and was buried in the way to Ephrath, which is Bethlehem. And Jacob set a pillar upon her grave" (Gen. 35:19,20).
3. Abraham, Sarah, Isaac, Rebekah, Jacob, and Leah were all buried in the cave of the field of Machpelah before Mamre (Gen. 49:30,31; 50:13).
4. The Lord buried Moses "in a valley in the land of Moab, over against Beth-peor: but no man knoweth of his sepulchre unto this day" (Deut. 34:6).
5. A heap of stones was raised over the bodies of Achan and his family after they were stoned in the valley of Achor (Josh. 7:25,26).
6. The Israelites took the body of the king of Ai "and cast it at the entering of the gate of the city, and [raised] thereon a great heap of stones" (Josh. 8:29).
7. Israel buried Joshua "in the border of his inheritance in Timnath-serah" (Josh. 24:30).
8. "The bones of Joseph, which the children of Israel brought up out of Egypt, buried they in Shechem" (Josh. 24:32).
9. "Gideon the son of Joash died in a good old age, and was buried in the sepulchre of Joash his father" (Judges 8:32).
10. Samson was buried "between Zorah and Eshtaol in the burying place of Manoah his father" (Judges 16:31).
11. The men of Jabesh-gilead "took the body of Saul and the bodies of his sons from the wall of Beth-shan, and came to Jabesh, and burnt them there. And they took their bones, and buried them under a tree at Jabesh" (1 Sam. 31:12,13).
12. "Samuel died; and all the Israelites were gathered together, and lamented him, and buried him in his house at Ramah" (1 Sam. 25:1).
13. Joab "took Absalom, and cast him into a great pit in the wood, and laid a very great heap of stones upon him" (2 Sam. 18:17).
14. King Jehoram was killed by Jehu, and his body was cast into Naboth's field (2 Kings 9:25).
15. Ahaziah's servants "buried him in his sepulchre with his fathers in the city of David" (2 Kings 9:28).
16. "Manasseh slept with his fathers, and was buried in the garden of his own house, in the garden of Uzza" (2 Kings 21:18).
17. Amon "was buried in his sepulchre in the garden of Uzza" (2 Kings 21:26).

438

18. "Uzziah slept with his fathers, and they buried him with his fathers in the field of the burial which belonged to the kings; for they said, He is a leper" (2 Chron. 26:23).

19. "And the chief priests took the silver pieces. . . . And they took counsel, and bought with them the potter's field, to bury strangers" (Matt. 27:6,7).

131. Executions

1. The Roman soldiers crucified Jesus along with two common criminals at the demand of the Jews (Matt. 27:33-50).

Samuel executes Agag

2. Pharaoh "hanged the chief baker" (Gen. 40:22).
3. The Levites executed 3,000 men for worshiping the golden calf (Ex. 32:26-28).
4. Joshua hung the king of Ai (Josh. 8:28,20).
5. Joshua executed Adoni-zedec, king of Jerusalem; Hoham, king of Hebron; Piram, king of Jarmuth; Japhia, king of Lachish; and Debir, king of Eglon (Josh. 10:1-26).
6. "Samuel hewed Agag [the king of the Amalekites] in pieces before the Lord in Gilgal" (1 Sam. 15:33).
7. King Saul ordered Doeg to execute eighty-five priests of the Lord (1 Sam. 22:17,18).
8. David executed a young Amalekite for claiming that he had killed King Saul (2 Sam. 1:6-15).
9. David ordered his men to kill Rechab and Baanah because they had murdered Ishbosheth, Saul's son (2 Sam. 4:9-12).
10. The Gibeonites hung seven of Saul's grandsons in retribution for one of Saul's bloody actions against them (2 Sam. 21:1-9).
11. At King Solomon's command, Benaiah executed Adonijah, Joab, and Shimei (1 Kings 2:25,34,46).
12. King Ahasuerus hung his chamberlains, Bigthan and Teresh (Esther 2:21,23).
13. King Ahasuerus also hung Haman on Haman's own gallows (Esther 7:5-10).
14. Haman's ten sons were hung at Esther's request (Esther 9:13,14).
15. King Jehoiakim executed the prophet Uriah for giving unfavorable prophecies (Jer. 26:20-23).
16. See list number 217—Successful and Attempted Stonings in *Meredith's Book of Bible Lists*, page 266.

132. Unusual Funeral Processions

1. The longest funeral procession was for Joseph. The Israelites carried his body for over forty years through the wilderness from Egypt to Canaan (Josh. 24:32).
2. The shortest funeral procession never made it to the cemetery. The young man of Nain was raised from his funeral bier by Jesus as the procession left the city (Luke 7:11-16).

133. Laws of Purification After Death

1. "He that toucheth the dead body of any man shall be unclean seven days. He shall purify himself with [the ashes of a red heifer] on the third day, then the seventh day he shall ... be clean (Num. 19:11,12).

2. "This is the law, when a man dieth in a tent: all that come into the tent, and all that is in the tent, shall be unclean seven days. ... And a clean person shall take hyssop and dip it in the water, and sprinkle it upon the tent, and upon all the vessels, and upon the persons that were there" (Num. 19:14-18).

134. People Killed by Animals

1. "The Lord sent fiery serpents among the people, and they bit the people; and much people of Israel died" (Num. 21:6).

2. A disobedient prophet was killed by a lion along the path on which he was traveling (1 Kings 13:20-32).

3. Another lion killed a man who would not strike a young prophet with a sword as he had been commanded by the Lord to do (1 Kings 20:35,36).

4. A group of children made fun of Elisha, "and there came forth two she bears out of the wood, and tare forty and two children" (2 Kings 2:24).

5. "At the beginning of their dwelling there, ... they [foreigners who had moved into Samaria] feared not the Lord: therefore the Lord sent lions among them, which slew some of them" (2 Kings 17:24,25).

6. "The king commanded, and they brought those men which had accused Daniel, and they cast them into the den of lions, them, their children, and their wives; and the lions had the mastery of them" (Dan. 6:24).

135. The Ten Largest Mass Deaths

1. "Abijah and his people slew them with a great slaughter: so there fell down slain of Israel five hundred thousand chosen men" (2 Chron. 13:17).

2. "The angel of the Lord went out, and smote in the camp of the Assyrians an hundred fourscore and five thousand" (2 Kings 19:35).

The man who disobeyed a prophet is killed by a lion

3. Gideon and his men killed 120,000 Midianites (Judges 8:10).
4. King Pekah killed 120,000 men of Judah in one day because they had forsaken the Lord (2 Chron. 28:6).
5. "The children of Israel slew of the Syrians an hundred thousand footmen in one day" (1 Kings 20:29).
6. "The other Jews that were in the king's provinces gathered themselves together, . . . and slew of their foes seventy and five thousand" (Esther 9:15,16).
7. "The Lord sent a pestilence upon Israel from the morning even to the time appointed: and there died of the people from Dan to Beersheba seventy thousand men" (2 Sam. 24:15).
8. The Lord "smote the men of Beth-shemesh, because they had looked into the ark of the Lord, even he smote of the

people fifty thousand and three score and ten men" (1 Sam. 6:19).

9. "David slew of the Syrians seven thousand men which fought in chariots, and forty thousand footmen" (1 Chron. 19:18).

10. "The Philistines fought, . . . and there was a very great slaughter; for there fell of Israel thirty thousand footmen" (1 Sam. 4:10).

20

Interesting People

Over the past few years one of the most popular television themes has been that of discovering people who do unique things. The offshoot has been a number of programs which go anywhere to locate something that will catch the viewer's attention. The popularity of the *Guiness Book of Records* indicates that we enjoy hearing about people who do unique things. Regular publications in issues of the *Reader's Digest* under the heading of "My Most Unforgettable Character" also indicate the wide interest we have in people whom we will not forget for some particular reason.

Compiled below are seven Bible lists of interesting people. They are people who are still remembered for a particular reason. Something about their lives stands out as different from the ordinary. Especially interesting are the people who received their names from heavenly sources.

136. Five Insomniacs

1. Jacob said to Laban, "This twenty years have I been with thee; . . . in the day the drought consumed me, and the frost by night; and my sleep departed from my eyes" (Gen. 31:38,40).
2. On the night after Haman built a gallows for the purpose of hanging Mordecai, King Ahasuerus could not sleep (Esther 6:1).
3. The wicked "sleep not, except they have done mischief; and their sleep is taken away, unless they cause some to fall" (Prov. 4:16).

4. "Nebuchadnezzar dreamed dreams, wherewith his spirit was troubled, and his sleep brake from him" (Dan. 2:1).
5. While Daniel was in the lions' den, King Darius stayed up all night (Dan. 6:18).

137. Twenty-three References to Runners

1. Abraham ran to meet the Lord in the plains of Mamre (Gen. 18:1,2).
2. Abraham's servant ran to meet Rebekah (Gen. 24:17).
3. Laban ran to meet Abraham's servant at the well (Gen. 24:29).
4. "Jacob told Rachel that he was her father's brother, . . . and she ran and told her father" (Gen. 29:12).
5. When Jacob returned to his country, "Esau ran to meet him, and embraced him, and fell on his neck, and kissed him: and they wept" (Gen. 33:4).
6. Aaron ran into the midst of the congregation with incense to stay a plague (Num. 16:46-48).
7. Samson's mother ran to her husband Manoah to tell him that an angel had appeared to her a second time (Judges 13:10).
8. When the Lord called the child Samuel, he ran to Eli thinking that Eli had called him (1 Sam. 3:4,5).
9. A Benjamite man ran from the battlefield to tell Eli that the ark of the Lord had been captured by the Philistines (1 Sam. 4:12-18).
10. David ran toward the Philistine camp to meet Goliath and slew him (1 Sam. 17:48,49).
11. Joab sent Cushi to run to David with the news of Absalom's death. Ahimaaz later volunteered and, in spite of his late start, beat Cushi to David with the news (2 Sam. 18:19-23).
12. "Adonijah the son of Gaggith exalted himself, saying, I will be king: and he prepared him chariots and horsemen, and fifty men to run before him" (1 Kings 1:5).
13. Elijah "girded up his loins, and ran before Ahab to the entrance of Jezreel" (1 Kings 18:46).
14. Elisha ran after Elijah to accept the appointment as his successor (1 Kings 19:19-21).
15. Gehazi ran from Elisha to meet the Shunammite woman (2 Kings 4:25,26).
16. An angel told another angel to run to Zechariah and to

deliver him the message that Jerusalem would again be inhabited (Zech. 2:3,4).

17. One of the onlookers at Jesus' crucifixion ran and found a sponge to use for giving Jesus a drink (Matt. 27:46,48).

18. Mary Magdalene and the other Mary ran from the empty tomb to tell the disciples about it (Matt. 28:8).

19. When the Gadarene demoniac "saw Jesus afar off, he ran and worshipped him" (Mark 5:6).

20. People ran to hear Jesus teach and to see Him perform miracles (Mark 6:33,35).

21. Zacchaeus ran before the throng around Jesus and climbed up into a sycamore tree to see Him (Luke 19:4)

22. John outran Peter to see the empty tomb (John 20:4).

23. Philip ran to the Ethiopian eunuch's chariot (Acts 8:30).

138. Blind People

1. When the men of Sodom attacked Lot's house, the two angels "smote the men that were at the door of the house with blindness" (Gen. 19:11).

2. "When Isaac was old, . . . his eyes were dim, so that he could not see" (Gen. 27:1).

3. "The eyes of Israel were dim for age, so that he could not see" (Gen. 48:10).

4. "The Philistines took [Samson], and put out his eyes, and brought him down to Gaza" (Judges 16:21).

5. "Eli was ninety and eight years old; and his eyes were dim, that he could not see" (1 Sam. 4:15).

6. "Ahijah could not see; for his eyes were set by reason of his age" (1 Kings 14:4).

7. "Elisha prayed unto the Lord, and said, Smite [the Syrian army], I pray thee, with blindness. And he smote them with blindness" (2 Kings 6:18).

8. Nebuchadnezzar "put out Zedekiah's eyes, and bound him with chains to carry him to Babylon" (Jer. 39:7).

9. "Two blind men followed Jesus, crying, and saying, Thou son of David, have mercy on us. . . . Then touched he their eyes, saying, According to your faith be it unto you. And their eyes were opened" (Matt. 9:27-30).

10. Two blind men sat by the road and cried out to Jesus to have mercy on them. He restored their sight instantly (Matt. 20:30-34).

Zacchaeus in the sycamore tree

11. Jesus touched one blind man and the man said, "I see men as trees, walking." Jesus touched him again and he saw clearly (Mark 8:22-25).
12. Jesus healed a blind beggar named Bartimaeus near Jericho (Mark 10:46-52).
13. Jesus put mud on the eyes of one blind man and told him to go and wash in the pool of Siloam. He washed his eyes and saw again (John 9:1-7).

14. Saul was blind for three days after the Lord stopped him on the way to Damascus and spoke to him out of a great light (Acts 9:9).

15. Elymas the sorcerer stood against Paul and Barnabas as they told Sergius Paulus the Gospel. Paul pronounced God's judgment upon Elymas, and he immediately became blind (Acts 13:7-12).

139. Eighteen Sleepers

1. "And the Lord caused a deep sleep to fall upon *Adam*, and he slept: and he took one of his ribs" (Gen. 2:21).

2. God spoke to *Abram* while he was in a deep sleep (Gen. 15:12-16).

3. *Jacob* slept at Bethel and dreamed about angels (Gen. 28:11-15).

4. *Pharaoh* dreamed of cows and corn while he slept (Gen. 41:1-7).

5. "Jael Heber's wife took a nail of the tent, and took an hammer in her hand, and went softly unto [Sisera], and smote the nail into his temples . . . for he was fast asleep and weary" (Judges 4:21).

6. *Samson* slept while the Philistines cut off his hair (Judges 16:19).

7. David and Abishai sneaked into *Saul's* camp while he was asleep (1 Sam. 26:7).

8. *Uriah* slept at David's door while he was on leave from the battlefront (2 Sam. 11:9).

9. Elijah sarcastically suggested that *Baal* was asleep when Jezebel's priests could not get him to respond (1 Kings 18:27).

10. While *Nebuchadnezzar* slept, he had a troubling dream which he could not remember in the morning (Dan. 2:1-9).

11. *Jonah* slept in the bottom of the ship while it rolled in the storm (Jonah 1:5).

12. *Joseph* was sleeping when an angel of the Lord came to him in a dream (Matt. 2:13).

13. While the disciples sailed, *Jesus* fell asleep. A storm came and they anxiously woke Him up (Luke 8:23,24).

14. Jesus told the mourners that *Jairus' daughter* was not dead, but only sleeping (Luke 8:52).

15. While Jesus prayed in Gethsemane, His *disciples* slept (Luke 22:45).

16. *Peter* was sleeping between two soldiers in prison when an angel came to release him (Acts 12:6,7).
17. The *Philippian jailor* was awakened from a deep sleep by the earthquake that hit his prison (Acts 16:27).
18. *Eutychus* fell asleep and fell to the ground through a third-story window while Paul preached. Paul stopped the service long enough to raise him from the dead (Acts 20:9-12).

140. Laughers

1. "Abraham fell upon his face, and laughed, and said in his heart, Shall a child be born unto him that is an hundred years old? and shall Sarah, that is ninety years old, bear?" (Gen. 17:17).
2. When Sarah heard that she would have a son, she laughed (Gen. 18:10-12).
3. Hezekiah sent decrees that made an urgent plea for repentance "from city to city through the country of Ephraim and Manasseh even unto Zebulun: but they laughed them to scorn" (2 Chron. 30:10).
4. "When Sanballat the Horonite, and Tobiah the servant, the Ammonite, and Geshem the Arabian, heard [that Nehemiah and his group were going to rebuild Jerusalem], they laughed" (Neh. 2:19).
5. "When Jesus came into the ruler's house, and saw the minstrels and the people making a noise, he said unto them, Give place: for the maid is not dead, but sleepeth. And they laughed him to scorn" (Matt. 9:23,24).

141. Dancers

1. "Miriam the prophetess, the sister of Aaron, took a timbrel in her hand; and all the women went out after her with timbrels and with dances" (Ex. 15:20).
2. The children of Israel danced before the calf that Aaron made (Ex. 32:19).
3. After Jephthah's victory over the Ammonites, "his daughter came out to meet him with timbrels and with dances" (Judges 11:34).
4. The men of Benjamin took wives from among the dancers at Shiloh (Judges 21:20,23).
5. After David had returned from killing Goliath, the women

Jephthah is met by his dancing daughter

of Israel came out dancing with tabrets to meet Saul (1 Sam. 18:6,7).

6. When David finally caught up with the Amalekites, "they were spread abroad upon all the earth, eating and drinking, and dancing, because of all the great spoil that they had taken out of all the land of the Philistines" (1 Sam. 30:16-18).

7. When the ark of the Lord was brought into Jerusalem, "David danced before the Lord with all his might" (2 Sam. 6:14).

8. The daughter of Herodias so enchanted Herod with a dance at his birthday party that he promised her anything she wanted. She asked for the head of John the Baptist (Matt. 14:6-8).

9. When the prodigal son came back, his father held a feast with music and dancing (Luke 15:25).

142. People Named by God, Jesus, or Angels

1. God called His human creation Adam (Gen. 5:2).

2. "The angel of the Lord said to [Hagar], Behold, thou art with child and shalt bear a son, and shalt call his name Ishmael" (Gen. 16:11).

3. The Lord said, "Neither shall thy name be any more Abram, but thy name shall be Abraham" (Gen. 17:5).

4. God told Abraham, "Thou shalt not call her name Sarai, but Sarah shall her name be" (Gen. 17:15).

5. "God said, Sarah thy wife shall bear thee a son indeed; and thou shalt call his name Isaac" (Gen. 17:19).

6. The Lord declared, "Thy name shall be called no more Jacob, but Israel" (Gen. 32:28).

7. The Lord told David, "Behold, a son shall be born to thee, who shall be a man of rest; and I will give him a rest from all his enemies round about: for his name shall be Solomon" (1 Chron. 22:9).

8. The Lord commanded Isaiah to call his son Maher-shalal-hash-baz (Isa. 8:3).

9. Jeremiah said to Pashur, "The Lord hath not called thy name Pashur, but Magor-missabib" (Jer. 20:3).

10. When Hosea had a son, the Lord said, "Call his name Jezreel; for yet a little while, and I will avenge the blood of Jezreel upon the house of Jehu" (Hos. 1:4).

11. Hosea's wife "bare a daughter. And God said unto him, Call her name Lo-ruhamah: for I will no more have mercy upon the house of Israel" (Hos. 1:6).

12. After Hosea's second son was born, God said, "Call his name Lo-ammi: for ye are not my people, and I will not be your God" (Hos. 1:9).

13. "Thou shalt call his name Jesus: for he shall save his people from their sins" (Matt. 1:21).

14. "The angel said unto him, Fear not, Zacharias: for thy prayer is heard; and thy wife Elisabeth shall bear thee a son, and thou shalt call his name John" (Luke 1:13).

15. Jesus said, "Thou art Simon the son of Jona: thou shalt be called Cephas" (John 1:42).

21

Odds and Ends

It would be difficult to compile one hundred and forty-one lists without gathering some lists that don't fit under any specific heading. Though not related to each other, the following lists should be of interest to you.

Did you realize that there are some extremely important bones mentioned in the Bible? There are also at least twenty-nine important stones recorded for us. Did you know that some battles were won supernaturally? Do you know how many times God's name is mentioned in the Bible? Here's one you probably haven't considered: did you know that the New Testament alone includes at least thirty-one descriptions of non-Christians?

143. Important Bones

1. "And of the rib, which the Lord God had taken from man, made he a woman" (Gen. 2:21,22).
2. "The bones of Joseph, which the children of Israel brought up out of Egypt, buried they in Shechem" (Josh. 24:32).
3. Samson "found a new jawbone of an ass, and put forth his hand, and took it, and slew a thousand men therewith" (Judges 15:15).
4. The men of Jabesh-gilead rescued the bones of Saul and his sons from Beth-shan and buried them under a tree at Jabesh (1 Sam. 31:11-13).
5. "And it came to pass, as they were burying a man, that behold, they spied a band of [Moabites]; and they cast the man into the sepulchre of Elisha: and when the man was let

down, and touched the bones of Elisha, he revived, and stood up on his feet" (2 Kings 13:20,21).

6. King Josiah desecrated the heathen altar at Bethel by burning human bones on it (2 Kings 23:16).

7. Ezekiel saw a valley of dry bones in a vision (Ezek. 37:1-14).

8. "But when the soldiers came to Jesus, and saw that he was dead already, they broke not his legs. . . . For these things were done, that the scripture should be fulfilled, A bone of him shall not be broken" (John 19:33,36).

Ezekiel's valley of dry bones

144. The Number of Times God, Jesus, and Satan Are Mentioned

1. The capitalized word *God* appears in the Bible 4,395 times.
2. The name *Jesus* appears in the Bible 979 times.
3. The name *Satan* appears in the Bible 56 times.

145. Thirty Important Stones

1. Jacob used a stone for a pillow at Bethel and dreamed about the Lord. In the morning, he took the stone and set it up as a pillar of remembrance before the Lord (Gen. 28:11-22).
2. "When Jacob saw Rachel . . . Jacob went near and rolled the stone from the well's mouth, and watered the flock of Laban" (Gen. 29:10,11).
3. Jacob and Laban made a heap of stones as a witness to their covenant not to bother one another (Gen. 31:44-52).
4. "God appeared unto Jacob again, when he came out of Padan-aram, and blessed him. . . . And Jacob set up a pillar in the place where he talked with him, even a pillar of stone" (Gen. 35:9,14).
5. The Lord told Moses, "Thou shalt smite the rock, and there shall come water out of it, that the people may drink" (Ex. 17:6).
6. While Amalek fought Israel, Moses sat on a stone while Aaron and Hur held his hands up to God (Ex. 17:8-12).
7. "The Lord said unto Moses, Come up to me into the mount, and be there: and I will give thee tables of stone, and a law, and commandments which I have written" (Ex. 24:12).
8. Aaron's ephod held two onyx stones engraved with the names of the children of Israel (Ex. 28:9-12).
9. "The Lord said unto Moses, Hew thee two tables of stone like unto the first: and I will write upon these tables the words that were in the first tables" (Ex. 34:1).
10. Joshua had twelve stones taken from the dry pathway across the Jordan to be set in a heap in Canaan as a memorial. He also had twelve stones piled up where the priests had stood in the river (Josh. 4:4-8).
11. As Joshua pursued the Amorites, "the Lord cast down great stones from heaven upon them" (Josh. 10:11).
12. The five Amorite kings fled from Joshua and hid in a cave.

Jacob dreams while resting his head on a stone

He rolled large stones over the entrance to hold them in (Josh. 10:16-18).

13. After the children of Israel had covenanted to serve the Lord, Joshua set up a stone as a witness to all that had been promised (Josh. 24:27).

14. "A certain woman cast a piece of a millstone upon Abimelech's head, and all to brake his skull" (Judges 9:53).

15. After the Israelites had defeated the Philistines, Samuel raised a stone pillar "and called the name of it Ebenezer, saying, Hitherto hath the Lord helped us" (1 Sam. 7:12).

16. "David put his hand in his bag, and took thence a stone, and slang it, and smote [Goliath] in his forehead" (1 Sam. 17:49).

17. "King [Solomon] commanded, and they brought great stones, costly stones, and hewed stones, to lay the foundation of the house" of the Lord (1 Kings 5:17).

18. After the priests of Baal had failed, Elijah took twelve stones, built an altar, and laid a bullock on top. The fire of the Lord fell and consumed even the stones" (1 Kings 18:31-38).

19. Nebuchadnezzar dreamed about a great image and then "a stone was cut out without hands, which smote the image upon his feet that were of iron and clay, and brake them to pieces" (Dan. 2:34,35).

20. Daniel was thrown into the lions' den, and it was sealed with a stone and the king's own signet (Dan. 6:17).

21. Jesus said, "Thou art Peter, and upon this rock I will build my church; and the gates of hell shall not prevail against it" (Matt. 16:18).

22. "Jesus saith unto them, Did you never read in the scriptures, The stone which the builders rejected, the same is become the head of the corner?" (Matt. 21:42).

23. After laying Jesus in the tomb, Joseph of Arimathaea "rolled a great stone to the door of the sepulchre" (Matt. 27:59,60).

24. Jesus prophesied about the temple, saying, "There shall not be left one stone upon another that shall not be thrown down" (Mark 13:1,2).

25. The devil tempted Jesus, saying, "If thou be the son of God, command this stone that it be made bread" (Luke 4:3).

26. Jesus told the Pharisees that if the people did not hail Him king, the stones would cry out (Luke 19:40).

27. Before He called Lazarus from the grave, Jesus ordered that the stone be removed from the entrance of the tomb (John 11:38-40).

28. The children of Israel "drank of that spiritual rock that followed them: and that Rock was Christ" (1 Cor. 10:4).

29. "The Spirit saith unto the churches; To him that overcometh will I give . . . a white stone" (Rev. 2:17).

30. An angel took up a stone like a great millstone and threw it into the sea in John's vision (Rev. 18:21).

146. Lamps and Candles

1. Abraham set up a sacrifice to God to confirm the covenant, and God took a burning lamp through the midst of the sacrifice as a sign of His promise (Gen. 15:17).
2. The Lord commanded Moses to make a seven-branched candlestick to be placed within the tabernacle (Ex. 25:31-37).
3. Gideon's men "blew the trumpets, and brake the pitchers, and held the lamps in their left hands, . . . and they cried, The sword of the Lord, and of Gideon" (Judges 7:16-21).
4. David sang, "For thou art my lamp, O Lord: and the Lord will lighten my darkness" (2 Sam. 22:29).
5. "Thy word is a lamp unto my feet, and a light unto my path" (Ps. 119:105).
6. Jesus said, "Ye are the light of the world. A city that is set on a hill cannot be hid" (Matt. 5:14).
7. "Then shall the kingdom of heaven be likened unto ten virgins, which took their lamps, and went forth to meet the bridegroom" (Matt. 25:1).
8. "What woman having ten pieces of silver, if she lose one piece, doth not light a candle, and sweep the house, and seek diligently till she find it?" (Luke 15:8).
9. The Philippian jailor called for a light to see if his prisoners were still in the jail (Acts 16:29).
10. John saw Jesus walking among seven golden candlesticks in his vision on Patmos (Rev. 1:12).
11. John described the new Jerusalem, saying, "There shall be no night there; and they need no candle, neither light of the sun; for the Lord God giveth them light" (Rev. 22:5).

147. Ten Battles Won Supernaturally

1. The Lord destroyed the Egyptian army in the Red Sea (Ex. 14:13-31).
2. "And it came to pass, when Moses held up his hand, that Israel prevailed: and when he let down his hand, Amalek prevailed" (Ex. 17:11).
3. When Joshua fought the kings of the Amorites, the Lord caused the sun to stand still, and He threw large hailstones down from the sky to kill the fleeing Amorites (Josh. 10:6-13).

4. "The Philistines drew near to battle against Israel: but the Lord thundered with a great thunder on that day upon the Philistines, and discomfited them; and they were smitten before Israel" (1 Sam. 7:10).

5. Jonathan and his armor-bearer attacked the Philistines, and the Lord sent an earthquake that routed the enemy before them (1 Sam. 14:11-15).

6. "Israel won a battle against the Syrians when the Lord struck the Syrians blind at Elisha's word (2 Kings 6:18-23).

7. "The Lord had made the host of the Syrians to hear a noise of chariots, and a noise of horses, even the noise of a great host. . . . Wherefore they arose and fled in the twilight" (2 Kings 7:6-7).

8. The Lord saved Jerusalem from the Syrians when "the angel of the Lord went out, and smote in the camp of the Assyrians an hundred fourscore and five thousand" (2 Kings 19:35).

9. "As the men of Judah shouted, it came to pass, that God smote Jeroboam and all Israel before Abijah and Judah. And the children of Israel fled before Judah" (2 Chron. 13:15-16).

10. Jehoshaphat and Judah "began to sing and to praise, [and] the Lord set ambushments against the children of Ammon, Moab, and mount Seir, which were come against Judah; and they were smitten" (2 Chron. 20:22).

148. Thirty-one New Testament Descriptions of Sinful Mankind

1. Alienated from God (Eph. 4:18).
2. Blind (John 12:40; 2 Cor. 4:4; 1 John 2:11).
3. Carnally or fleshly minded (Rom. 8:6,13).
4. Corrupt (Matt. 7:17-18; 1 Tim. 6:5).
5. Darkened (Matt. 6:23; John 3:19; Rom. 1:21; Eph. 4:18; 1 John 1:6-7).
6. Dead in sin (John 5:24; Rom. 8:6; Col. 2:13; 1 Tim. 5:6; 1 John 3:14).
7. Deceived (Titus 3:3).
8. Defiled or filthy (Isa. 64:6; Titus 1:15; 2 Pet. 2:20; Rev. 22:11).
9. Destitute of truth (Rom. 1:18, 25; 1 Tim. 6:5).
10. Disobedient (Matt. 7:23; Eph. 2:3; Titus 3:3).

11. An enemy of God (James 4:4).
12. Evil (Matt. 6:22; 12:33-34; John 3:20).
13. Foolish (Matt. 7:26; Eph. 5:15; Titus 3:3).
14. Going astray (1 Pet. 2:25).
15. Hateful (Titus 3:3).
16. Hypocritical (Matt. 6:2,5,16; 23:13,28).
17. Impenitent (Rom. 2:5; Heb. 3:8).
18. Malicious and envious (Titus 3:3).
19. Pleasure or world-loving (2 Thess 2:12; 1 Tim. 5:6; 2 Tim. 3:4; Titus 3:3; 1 John 2:15).
20. Proud (Rom. 1:30; 1 Tim. 6:4; 2 Tim. 3:4; James 4:6; 1 Pet. 5:5).
21. Refusing belief (John 3:35; Titus 1:15).
22. Rejecting truth (2 Tim. 4:4).
23. Resisting God (Acts 7:51).
24. Guided by Satan (John 8:44; Eph. 2:3).
25. Lovers of self (2 Tim. 3:2).
26. Self-satisfied (Rev. 3:17).
27. A slave of sin (John 8:34; Rom. 6:16-17,20; Titus 3:3).
28. Subordinating God (Rom. 1:25).
29. Unconscious of bondage (John 8:33; Rom. 7:7).
30. Unrighteous (1 Cor. 6:9; Rev. 22:11).
31. Vain in their imaginations (Rom. 1:21).

149. Forty-two Parables of Jesus

1. "Ye are the salt of the earth: but if the salt have lost his savour, wherewith shall it be salted? it is thenceforth good for nothing, but to be cast out, and to be trodden under foot of men" (Matt. 5:13).
2. "Ye are the light of the world. A city that is set on an hill cannot be hid. Neither do men light a candle, and put it under a bushel, but on a candlestick; and it giveth light unto all that are in the house. Let your light so shine before men, that they may see your good works, and glorify your Father which is in heaven" (Matt. 5:14–16).
3. "Whosoever heareth these sayings of mine, and doeth them I [Jesus] will liken him unto a wise man, which built his house upon a rock: and the rain descended, and the floods came, and the winds blew, and beat upon that house; and it fell not: for it was founded upon a rock. And every one that heareth these sayings of mine, and doeth them not, shall be likened unto a foolish man, which built his house

upon the sand: and rain descended, and the floods came, and the winds blew, and beat upon that house; and it fell: and great was the fall of it" (Matt. 7:24–27).

4. "No man putteth a piece of new cloth unto an old garment, for that which is put in to fill it up taketh from the garment, and the rent is made worse" (Matt. 9:16).

5. "Neither do men put new wine into old bottles: else the bottles break, and the wine runneth out, and the bottles perish: but they put new wine into new bottles, and both are preserved" (Matt. 9:17).

6. "Behold, a sower went forth to sow; and when he sowed, some seeds fell by the way side, and the fowls came and devoured them up: some fell upon stony places, where they had not much earth: and forthwith they sprung up, because they had no deepness of earth: and when the sun was up, they were scorched; and because they had no root, they withered away. And some fell among thorns; and the thorns sprung up, and choked them: but other fell into good ground, and brought forth fruit, some an hundredfold, some sixty-fold, some thirtyfold. Who hath ears to hear, let him hear. Hear ye therefore the parable of the sower. When any one heareth the word of the kingdom, and understandeth it not, then cometh the wicked one, and catcheth away that which was sown in his heart. This is he which received seed by the way side. But he that received the seed into stony places, the same is he that heareth the word, and anon with joy receiveth it; yet hath he not root in himself, but dureth for a while: for when tribulation or persecution ariseth be-cause of the word, by and by he is offended. He also that received seed among the thorns is he that heareth the word; and the care of this world, and the deceitfulness of riches, choke the word, and he becometh unfruitful. But he that received seed into the good ground is he that heareth the word, and understandeth it; which also beareth fruit, and bringeth forth, some an hundredfold, some sixty, some thirty" (Matt. 13:3–9, 18–23).

7. "Another parable put he [Jesus] forth unto them saying, The kingdom of heaven is likened unto a man which sowed good seed in his field: but while men slept, his enemy came and sowed tares among the wheat, and went his way. But when the blade was sprung up, and brought forth fruit, then appeared the tares also. So the servants of the house-

holder came and said unto him, Sir, didst not thou sow good seed in thy field? from whence then hath it tares? He said unto them, An enemy hath done this. The servants said unto him, Wilt thou then that we go and gather them up? But he said, Nay; lest while you gather up the tares, ye root up also the wheat with them. Let both brow together until the harvest: and in the time of harvest I will say to the reapers, Gather ye together first the tares, and bind them in bundles to burn them: but gather the wheat into my barn. Then Jesus sent the multitude away, and went into the house: and his desciples came unto him saying, Declare unto us the parable of the tares of the field. He answered and said unto them, He that soweth the good seed is the Son of man; The field is the world; the good seed are the children of the kingdom; but the tares are the children of the wicked one; the enemy that sowed them is the devil; the harvest is the end of the world; and reapers are the angels. As therefore the tares are gathered and burned in the fire; so shall it be in the end of this world. The Son of man shall send forth his angels, and they shall gather out of his kingdom all things that offend, and them which do iniquity; and shall cast them into a furnace of fire: there shall be wailing and gnashing of teeth. Then shall the righteous shine forth as the sun in the kingdom of their Father. Who hath ears to hear, let him hear" (Matt. 13:24–30, 36–43).

8. "Another parable put he [Jesus] forth unto them, saying, The kingdom of heaven is like to a grain of mustard seed, which a man took, and sowed in his field: which indeed is the least of all seeds: but when it is grown, it is the greatest among herbs, and becometh a tree, so that the birds of the air come and lodge in the branches thereof" (Matt. 13: 31, 32).

9. "Another parable spake he [Jesus] unto them; The kingdom of heaven is like unto leaven, which a woman took, and hid in three measures of meal till the whole was leavened" (Matt. 13:33).

10. "The kingdom of heaven is like unto treasure hid in a field; the which when a man hath found, he hideth and for joy thereof goeth and selleth all that he hath, and buyeth that field" (Matt. 13:44).

11. "Again, the kingdom of heaven is like unto a merchant

man, seeking goodly pearls: who, when he had found one pearl of great price, went and sold all that he had, and bought it" (Matt. 13:45, 46).

12. "Again, the kingdom of heaven is like unto a net, that was cast into the sea, and gathered of every kind: which, when it was full, they drew to shore, and sat down, and gathered the good into vessels, but cast the bad away. So shall it be at the end of the world: the angels shall come forth, and sever the wicked from among the just, and shall cast them into the furnace of fire: there shall be weeping and gnashing of teeth" (Matt. 13:47–50).

13. "Every sribe which is instructed unto the kingdom of heaven is like unto a man that is an householder, which bringeth forth out of his treasure things new and old" (Matt. 13:52).

14. "How think ye? if a man have an hundred sheep, and one of them be gone astray, doth he not leave the ninety and nine, and goeth into the mountains, and seeketh that which is gone astray? And if so be that he find it, verily I say unto you, he rejoiceth more of that sheep, than of the ninety and nine which went not astray. Even so it is not the will fo your Father which is in heaven, that one of these little ones should perish" (Matt. 18:12–14).

15. "The kingdom of heaven [is] likened unto a certain king, which would take account of his servants. And when he had begun to reckon, one was brought unto him, which owed him ten thousand talents. But forasmuch as he had not to pay, his lord commanded him to be sold, and his wife, and children, and all that he had, and payment to be made. The servant therefore fell down, and worshipped him, saying, Lord, have patience with me, and I will pay thee all. Then the lord of that servant was moved with compassion, and loosed him, and forgave him the debt. But the same servant went out, and found one of his fellowservants, which owed him an hundred pence: and he laid hands on him, and took him by the throat, saying. Pay me that thou owest. And his fellowservant fell down at his feet, and besought him, saying, Have patience with me, and I will pay thee all. And he would not: but went and cast him into prison, till he should pay the debt. So when his fellowservants saw what was done, they were very sorry, and came and told unto their lord all that was done. Then his lord, after that he had called him, said unto him, O thou wicked servant,

I forgave thee all that debt, because thou desiredst me: shouldest not thou also have had compassion on thy fellowservant, even as I had pity on thee? And his lord was wroth, and delivered him to the tormentors, till he should pay all that was due unto him. So likewise shall my heavenly Father do also unto you, if ye from your hearts forgive not every one his brother their trespasses" (Matt. 18:23–35).

16. "The kingdom of heaven is like unto a man that is an householder, which went out early in the morning to hire labourers into his vineyard. And when he had agreed with the labourers for a penny a day, he sent them into his vineyard. And he went out about the third hour, and saw others standing idle in the marketplace, and said unto them; Go ye also into the vineyard, and whatsoever is right I will give you. And they went their way. Again he went out about the sixth and ninth hour, and did likewise. And about the eleventh hour he went out, and found others standing idle, and saith unto them, Why stand ye here all the day idle? They say unto him, Because no man hath hired us. He saith unto them, Go ye also into the vineyard; and whatsoever is right, that shall ye receive. So when even was come, the lord of the vineyard saith unto his steward, Call the labourers, and give them their hire, beginning from the last unto the first. And when they came that were hired about the eleventh hour, they received every man a penny. But when the first came, they supposed that they should have received more; and they likewise received every man a penny. And when they had received it, they murmured against the goodman of the house, saying, These last have wrought but one hour, and thou hast made them equal unto us, which have borne the burden and the heat of the day. But he answered one of them, and said, Friend, I do thee no wrong: didst not thou agree with me for a penny? Take that thine is, and go thy way: I will give unto this last, even as unto thee. Is it not lawful for me to do what I will with my own? Is thine eye evil, because I am good? So the last shall be first, and the first last: for many be called, but few chosen" (Matt.20:1–16).

17. "But what think you? [asked Jesus.] A certain man had two sons; and he came to the first, and said, Son, go work to day in my vineyard. He answered and said, I will not:

but afterward he repented and went. And he came to the second, and said likewise. And he answered and said, I go, sir: and went not. Whether of them twain did the will of his father? They say unto him, The first. Jesus saith unto them, Verily I say unto you, That the publicans and the harlots go into the kingdom of God before you. For John came unto you in the way of righteousness, and ye believed him not: but the publicans and the harlots believed him: and ye, when ye had seen it, repented not afterward, that ye might believe him" (Matt. 21:28–32).

18. "Hear another parable: There was a certain householder, which planted a vineyard, and hedged it round about, and digged a winepress in it, and built a tower, and let it out to husbandmen, and went into a far country: and when the time of the fruit drew near, he sent his servants to the husbandmen, that they might receive the fruits of it. And the husbandmen took his servants, and beat one, and killed another, and stoned another. Again, he sent other servants more than the first: and they did unto them likewise. But last of all he sent unto them his son, saying, They will reverence my son. But when the husbandmen saw the son, they said among themselves, This is the heir; come, let us kill him, and let us seize on his inheritance. And they caught him, and cast him out of the vineyard, and slew him. When the lord therefore of the vineyard cometh, what will he do unto those husbandmen? They say unto him, He will miserably destroy those wicked men, and will let out his vineyard unto other husbandmen, which shall render him the fruits in their seasons. Jesus saith unto them, Did ye never read in the scriptures, The stone which the builders rejected, the same is become the head of the corner: this is the Lord's doing, and it is marvellous in our eyes? Therefore say I unto you, The kingdom of God shall be taken from you, and given to a nation bringing forth the fruits thereof. And whosoever shall fall on this stone shall be broken: but on whomsoever it shall fall, it will grind him to powder" (Matt. 21:33–44).

19. "Jesus answered and spake unto them again by parables, and said, The kingdom of heaven is like unto a certain king, which made a marriage for his son, and sent forth his servants to call them that were bidden to the wedding: and they would not come. Again, he sent forth other servants,

saying, Tell them which are bidden, Behold, I have prepared my dinner: my oxen and fatlings are killed, and all things are ready: come unto the marriage. But they made light of it, and went their ways, one to his farm, another to his merchandise: and the remnant took his servants, and entreated them spitefully, and slew them. But when the king heard thereof, he was wroth: and he sent forth his armies, and destroyed those murderers, and burned up their city. Then saith he to his servants, The wedding is ready, but they which were bidden were not worthy. Go ye therefore into the highways, and as many as ye shall find, bid to the marriage. So those servants went out into the highways, and gathered together all as many as they found, both bad and good: and the wedding was furnished with guests. And when the king came in to see the guests, he saw there a man which had not on a wedding garment: and he saith unto him, Friend, how camest thou in hither not having a wedding garment? And he was speechless. Then said the king to the servants, Bind him hand and foot, and take him away, and cast him into outer darkness; there shall be weeping and gnashing of teeth. For many are called, but few are chosen" (Matt. 22:1–14).

20. 'Now learn a prable of the fig tree; When his branch is yet tender, and putteth forth leaves, ye know that summer is nigh: so likewise ye, when ye shall see all these things, know that it is near, even at the doors" (Matt. 24:32, 33).

21. "The kingdom of heaven [shall] be likened unto ten virgins, which took their lamps, and went forth to meet the bridegroom. And five of them were wise, and five were foolish. They that were foolish took their lamps, and took no oil with them   but the wise took oil in their vessels with their lamps. While the bridegroom tarried, they all slumbered and slept. And at midnight there was a cry made, Behold, the bridegroom cometh; go ye out to meet him. Then all those virgins arose, and trimmed their lamps. And the foolish said unto the wise, Give us of your oil; for our lamps are gone out. But the wise answered, saying, Not so; lest there be not enough for us and you: but go ye rather to them that sell, and buy for yourselves. And while they went to buy, the bridegroom came; and they that were ready went in with him to the marriage: and the door was shut. Afterward came also the other virgins, saying, Lord, Lord,

open to us. But he answered and said, Verily, I say unto you, I know you not. Watch therefore, for ye know neither the day nor the hour wherein the Son of man cometh" (Matt. 25:1–13).

22. "For the kingdom of heaven is as a man travelling into a far country, who called his own servants, and delivered unto them his goods. And unto one he gave five talents, to another two, and to another one; to every man according to his several ability; and straightway took his journey. Then he that had received the five talents went and traded with the same, and made them other five talents. And likewise he that had received two, he also gained other two. But he that had received one went and digged in the earth, and hid his lord's money. After a long time the lord of those servants cometh, and reckoneth with them. And so he that had received five talents came and brought other five talents, saying, Lord, thou deliveredst unto me five talents: behold, I have gained beside them five talents more. His lord said unto him, Well done, thou good and faithful servant: thou hast been faithful over a few things, I will make thee ruler over many things: enter thou into the joy of thy lord. He also that had received two talents came and said, Lord, thou deliveredst unto me two talents: behold, I have gained two other talents beside them. His lord said unto him, Well done, good and faithful servant: thou hast been faithful over a few things, I will make thee ruler over many things: enter thou into the joy of thy lord. Then he which had received the one talent came and said, Lord, I knew thee, that thou art a hard man, reaping where thou hast not sown, and gathering where thou hast not strawed: and I was afraid, and went and hid thy talent in the earth: lo, there thou hast that is thine. His lord answered and said unto him, Thou wicked and slothful servant, thou knewest that I reap where I sowed not, and gathered where I have not strawed: thou oughtest therefore to have put my money to the exchangers, and then at my coming I should have received mine own with usury. Take therefore the talent from him, and give it unto him which hath ten talents. For unto every one that hath shall be given, and he shall have abundance: but from him that hath not shall be taken away even that which he hath. And cast ye the unprofitable servant into outer darkness: there shall be weeping and

gnashing of teeth" (Matt. 25:14–30).

23. "When the Son of man shall come in his glory, and all the holy angels with him, then shall he sit upon the throne of his glory: and before him shall be gathered all nations: and he shall separate them one from another, as a shepherd divideth his sheep from the goats: and he shall set the sheep on his right hand, but the goats on the left. Then shall the King say unto them on his right hand, Come, ye blessed of my Father, inherit the kingdom prepared for you from the foundation of the world: for I was an hungred, and ye gave me meat: I was thirsty, and ye gave me drink: I was a stranger, and ye took me in: naked, and ye clothed me: I was sick, and ye visited me: I was in prison, and ye came unto me. Then shall the righteous answer him, saying, Lord, when saw we thee an hungred, and fed thee? or thirsty, and gave thee drink? When saw we thee a stranger, and took thee in? or naked and clothed thee? Or when saw we thee sick?, or in prison, and came unto thee? And the King shall answer and say unto them, Verily I say unto you, Inasmuch as ye have done it unto one of the least of these my brethren, ye have done it unto me. Then shall he say also unto them on the left hand, Depart from me, ye cursed, into everlasting fire, prepared for the devil and his angels: for I was an hungred, and ye gave me no meat: I was thirsty, and ye gave me no drink: I was a stranger, and ye took me not in: naked, and ye clothed me not: sick, and in prison, and ye visited me not. Then shall they also answer him, saying, Lord, when saw we thee an hungred, or athirst, or a stranger, or naked, or sick, or in prison, and did not minister unto thee? Then shall he answer them, saying, Verily I say unto you, Inasmuch as ye did it not to one of the least of these, ye did it not to me. And these shall go away into everlasting punishment: but the righteous into life eternal" (Matt. 25:31–46).

24. "And he [Jesus] said, So is the kingdom of God, as if a man should cast seed into the ground; and should sleep, and rise night and day, and the seed should spring and grow up, he knoweth not how. For the earth bringeth forth fruit of herself; first the blade, then the ear, after that the full corn in the ear. But when the fruit is brought forth, immediately he putteth in the sickle, because the harvest is come" (Mark 4:26–29).

25. "For the Son of man is as a man taking a far journey, who left his house, and gave authority to his servants, and to every man his work, and commanded the porter to watch. Watch ye therefore: for ye know not when the master of the house cometh, at even, or at midnight, or at the cockcrowing, or in the morning: lest coming suddenly he find you sleeping. And what I say unto you I say unto all, Watch" (Mark 13:34–37).

26. "And Jesus answering said unto him, Simon, I have somewhat to say unto thee. And he saith, Master, say on. There was a certain creditor which had two debtors: the one owed five hundred pence, and the other fifty, And when they had nothing to pay, he frankly forgave them both. Tell me therefore, which of them will love him most? Simon answered and said, I suppose that he, to whom he forgave most. And he said unto him, Thou hast rightly judged. And he turned to the woman, and said unto Simon, Seest thou this woman? I entered into thine house, thou gavest me no water for my feet: but she hath washed my feet with tears, and wiped them with the hairs of her head. Thou gavest me no kiss: but this woman since the time I came in hath not ceased to kiss my feet. My head with oil thou didst not anoint: but this woman hath anointed my feet with ointment. Wherefore I say unto thee, Her sins, which are many, are forgiven; for she loved much: but to whom little is forgiven, the same loveth little" (Luke 7:40–47).

27. "And Jesus answering said, A certain man went down from Jerusalem to Jericho, and fell among thieves, which stripped him of his raiment, and wounded him, and departed, leaving him half dead. And by chance there came down a certain priest that way: and when he saw him, he passed by on the other side. And likewise a Levite, when he was at the place, came and looked on him, and passed by on the other side. But a certain Samaritain, as he journeyed, came where he was: and when he saw him, he had compassion on him, and went to him, and bound up his wounds, pouring in oil and wine, and set him on his own beast, and brought him to an inn, and took care of him. And on the morrow when he departed, he took out two pence, and gave them to the host, and said unto him, Take care of him; and whatsoever thou spendest more, when I come again, I will repay thee. Which now of these three, thinkest thou, was neigh-

bour unto him that fell among the thieves? And he said,
He that shewed mercy on him. Then said Jesus unto him,
Go, and do thou likewise" (Luke 10:30–37).

28. "And he [Jesus] said unto them, Which of you shall have a
friend, and shall go unto him at midnight, and say unto
him, Friend, lend me three loaves; for a friend of mine in
his journey is come to me, and I have nothing to set before
him? And he from within shall answer and say, Trouble me
not: the door is now shut, and my children are with me in
bed; I cannot rise and give thee. I say unto you, Though he
will not rise and give him, because he is his friend, yet
because of his importunity he will rise and give him as
many as he needeth. And I say unto you, Ask, and it shall
be given you; seek, and ye shall find; knock, and it shall be
opened unto you. For every one that asketh receiveth; and
he that seeketh findeth; and to him that knocketh it shall
be opened. If a son shall ask bread of any of you that is a
father, will he give him a stone? or if he ask a fish, will he
for a fish give him a serpent? or if he shall ask an egg, will
he offer him a scorpion? If ye then, being evil, know how
to give good gifts unto your children: how much more shall
your heavenly Father give the Holy Spirit to them that ask
him?" (Luke 11:5–13).

29. "And he [Jesus] spake a parable unto them, saying, The
ground of a certain rich man brought forth plentifully: and
he thought within himself, saying, What shall I do, because
I have no room where to bestow my fruits? And he said,
This will I do: I will pull down my barns, and build greater;
and there will I bestow all my fruits and my goods. And I
will say to my soul, Soul, thou hast much goods laid up for
many years; take thine ease, eat drink, and be merry. But
God said unto him, Thou fool, this night thy soul shall be
required of thee: then whose shall those things be, which
thou hast provided? So is he that layeth up treasure for
himself, and is not rich toward God" (Luke 12:16–21).

30. "Let your loins be girded about, and your lights burning;
and ye yourselves like unto men that wait for their lord,
when he will return from the wedding; that when he cometh and knocketh, they may open to him immediately.
Blessed are those servants, whom the lord when he cometh
shall find watching: verily I say unto you, that he shall gird
himself, and make them to sit down to meat, and will come

forth and serve them. And if he shall come in the second watch, or come in the third watch, and find them so, blessed are those servants. And this know, that if the goodman of the house had known what hour the thief would come, he owuld have watched, and not have suffered his house to be broken through. Be ye therefore ready also: for the Son of man cometh at an hour when ye think not. Then Peter said unto him, Lord, speakest thou this parable unto us, or even to all? And the Lord said, Who then is that faithful and wise steward, whom his lord shall make ruler over his household, to give them their portion of meat in due season? Blessed is that servant, whom his lord when he cometh shall find so doing. Of a truth I say unto you, that he will make him ruler over all that he hath. But and if that servant say in his heart, My lord delayeth his coming; and shall begin to beat the menservants and maidens, and to eat and drink, and to be drunken; the lord of that servant will come in a day when he looketh not for him, and at an hour when he is not aware, and will cut him in sunder, and will appoint him his portion with the unbelievers. And that servant, which knew his lord's will, and prepared not himself, neither did according to his will, shall be beaten with many stripes. But he that knew not, and did commit things worthy of stripes, shall be beaten with few stripes. For unto whomsoever much is given, of him shall be much required: and to whom men have committed much, of him they will ask the more" (Luke 12:35–48).

31. "[Jesus] spake also this parable; A certain man had a fig tree planted in his vineyard; and he came and sought fruit thereon, and found none. Then said he unto the dresser of his vineyard, Behold, these three years I come seeking fruit on this fig tree, and find none: cut it down; why cumbereth it the ground? And he answering said unto him, Lord, let it alone this year also, till I shall dig about it, and dung it: and if it bear fruit, well: and if not, then after that thou shalt cut it down"(Luke 13:6–9).

32. "And [Jesus] put forth a parable to those which were bidden, when he marked how they chose out the chief rooms; saying unto them, when thou art bidden of any man to a wedding, sit not down in the highest room; lest a more honourable man than thou be bidden of him; and he that bade thee and him come and say to thee, Give this man

place; and thou begin with shame to take the lowest room. But when thou art bidden, go and sit down in the lowest room; that when he that badeth thee cometh, he may say unto thee, Friend, go up higher: then shalt thou have worship in the presence of them that sit at meat with thee. For whosoever exalteth himself shall be abased; and he that humbleth himself shall be exalted" (Luke 14:7–11).

33. "[Jesus said,] A certain man made a great supper, and bade many: and sent his servant at supper time to say to them that were bidden, Come; for all things are now ready. And they all with one consent began to make excuse. The first said unto him, I have bought a piece of ground, and I must needs go and see it: I pray thee have me excused. And another said, I have bought five yoke of oxen, and I go to prove them: I pray thee have me excused. And another said, I have married a wife, and therefore I cannot come. So that servant came, and shewed his lord these things. Then the master of the house being angry said to his servant, Go out quickly into the streets and lanes of the city, and bring in hither the poor, and the maimed, and the halt, and the blind. And the servant said, Lord, it is done as thou hast commanded, and yet there is room. And the lord said unto the servant, Go out into the highways and hedges, and compel them to come in, that my house may be filled. For I say unto you, That none of those men which were bidden shall taste of my supper" (Luke 14:16–24).

34. "Which of you, intending to build a tower, sitteth not down first, and counteth the cost, whether he have sufficient to finish it? Lest haply, after he hath laid the foundation, and is not able to finish it, all that behold it begin to mock him, saying, This man began to build, and was not able to finish. Or what king, going to make war against another king, sitteth not down first, and consulteth whether he be able with ten thousand to meet him that cometh against him with twenty thousand? Or else, while the other is yet a great way off, he sendeth an ambassage, and desireth conditions of peace. So likewise, whosoever he be of you that forsaketh not all that he hath, he cannot be my disciple" (Luke 14:28–33).

35. "What woman having ten pieces of silver, if she lose one piece, doth not light a candle, and sweep the house, and seek diligently till she find it? And when she hath found

it, she calleth her friends and neighbours together, saying, Rejoice with me; for I have found the piece which I had lost. Likewise, I say unto you, there is joy in the presence of the angels of God over one sinner that repenteth" (Luke 15:8–10).

36. "And [Jesus] said, A certain man had two sons: and the younger of them said to his father, Father, give me the portion of goods that falleth to me. And he divided to them his living. And not many days after the younger son gathered all together, and took his journey into a far country, and there wasted his substance with riotous living. And when he had spent all, there arose a mighty famine in that land; and he began to be in want. And he went and joined himself to a citizen of that country; and he sent him into the fields to feed swine. And he would fain have filled his belly with the husks that the swine did eat: and no man gave unto him. And when he came to himself, he said, How many hired servants of my father's have bread enough and to spare, and I perish with hunger! I will arise and go to my father, and will say unto him, Father, I have sinned against heaven and before thee, and am no more worthy to be called thy son: make me as one of thy hired servants. And he arose, and came to his father. But when he was yet a great way off, his father saw him, and had compassion, and ran, and fell on his neck, and kissed him. And the son said unto him, Father, I have sinned against heaven, and in thy sight, and am no more worthy to be called thy son. But the father said to his servants, Bring forth the best robe, and put it on him; and put a ring on his hand, and shoes on his feet: and bring hither the fatted calf, and kill it; and let us eat, and be merry: for this my son was dead, and is alive again; he was lost, and is found. And they began to be merry. Now his elder son was in the field: and as he came and drew nigh to the house, he heard musick and dancing. And he called one of the servants, and asked what these things meant. And he said unto him, Thy brother is come; and thy father hath killed the fatted calf, because he hath received him safe and sound. And he was angry, and would not go in: therefore came his father out, and entreated him. And he answering said to his father, Lo, these many years do I serve thee, neither transgressed I at any time thy commandment: and yet thou never gavest me a

kid, that I might make merry with my friends: but as soon as this thy son was come, which hath devoured thy living with harlots, thou hast killed for him the fatted calf. And he said unto him, Son, thou art ever with me, and all that I have is thine. It was meet that we should make merry, and be glad: for this thy brother was dead, and is alive again; and was lost, and is found" (Luke 15:11–32).

37. "And [Jesus] said unto his disciples, There was a certain rich man, which had a steward; and the same was accused unto him that he had wasted his goods. And he called him, and said unto him, How is it that I hear this of thee? give an account of thy stewardship; for thou mayest be no longer steward. Then the steward said within himself, What shall I do? for my lord taketh away from me the stewardship: I cannot dig; to beg I am ashamed. I am resolved what to do, that, when I am put out of the stewardship, they may receive me into their houses. So he called every one of his lord's debtors unto him, and said unto the first, How much owest thou unto my lord? And he said, An hundred measures of oil. And he said unto him, Take thy bill, and sit down quickly, and write fifty. Then said he to another, And how much owest thou? And he said, An hundred measures of wheat. And he said unto him, Take thy bill and write fourscore. And the lord commended the unjust steward, because he had done wisely: for the children of the world are in their generation wiser than the children of light. And I say unto you, Make to yourselves friends of the mammon of unrighteousness; that, when you fail, they may receive you into everlasting habitations. He that is faithful in that which is least is faithful also in much: and he that is unjust in the least is unjust also in much. If therefore ye have not been faithful in the unrighteous mammon, who will commit to your trust the true riches? And if you have not been faithful in that which is another man's, who shall give you that which is your own? No servant can serve two masters: for either he will hate the one, and love the other; or else he will hold to the one, and despise the other. Ye cannot serve God and mammon" (Luke 16:1–13).

38. "There was a certain rich man, which was clothed in purple and fine linen, and fared sumptuously every day: and there was a certain beggar named Lazarus, which was laid at his gate, full of sores, and desiring to be fed with the crumbs which fell from the rich man's table: moreoever the dogs

came and licked his sores. And it came to pass, that the
beggar died, and was carried by the angels into Abraham's
bosom: the rich man also died, and was buried; and in hell
he lift up his eyes, being in torments, and seeth Abraham
afar off, and Lazarus in his bosom. And he cried and said,
Father Abraham, have mercy on me, and send Lazarus,
that he may dip the tip of his finger in water, and cool my
tongue; for I am tormented in this flame. But Abraham
said, Son, remember that thou in thy lifetime receivedst
thy good things, and likewise Lazarus evil things: but now
he is comforted, and thou art tormented. And beside all
this, between us and you there is a great gulf fixed: so that
they which would pass from hence to you cannot; neither
can they pass to us, that would come from thence. Then he
said, I pray thee therefore, father, that thou wouldest send
him to my father's house: for I have five brethren; that he
may testify unto them, lest they also come into this place
of torment. Abraham saith unto him, They have Moses and
the prophets; let them hear them. And he said, Nay, father
Abraham: but if one went unto them from the dead, they
will repent. And he said unto him, If they hear not Moses
and the prophets, neither will they be persuaded, though
one rose from the dead" (Luke 16:19–31).

39. "Which of you, having a servant plowing or feeding cattle,
will say unto him by and by, when he is come from the field,
Go and seat down to meat? And will not rather say unto
him, Make ready wherewith I may sup, and gird thyself,
and serve me, till I have eaten and drunken; and afterward
thou shalt eat and drink? Doth he thank that servant because he did the things that were commanded him? I trow
not. So likewise ye, when ye shall have done all those things
which are commanded you, say, We are unprofitable servants: we have done that which was our duty to do" (Luke
17:7–10).

40. "And [Jesus] spake a parable unto them to this end, that
men ought always to pray, and not to faint; saying, There
was in a city a judge, which feared not God, neither re-
garded man: and there was a widow in that city; and she
came unto him, saying, Avenge me of mine adversary. And
he would not for a while: but afterward he said within himself, Though I fear not God, nor regard man; yet because
this widow troubleth me, I will avenge her, lest by her con-
tinual coming she weary me. And the Lord said, Hear what

the unjust judge saith. And shall not God avenge his own
elect, which cry day and night unto him, though he bear
long with them? I tell you that he will avenge them spee-
dily. Nevertheless when the Son of man cometh, shall he
find faith on the earth?" (Luke 18:1–18).

41. "And [Jesus] spake this parable unto certain which trusted
in themselves that they were righteous, and despised others: Two men went up into the temple to pray; the one a
Pharisee, and the other a publican. The Pharisee stood and
prayed thus with himself, God, I thank thee, that I am not
as other men are, extortioners, unjust, adulterers, or even
as this publican. I fast twice in the week, I give tithes of
all that I possess. And the publican, standing afar off, would
not lift up so much as his eyes unto heaven, but smote upon
his breast, saying, God be merciful to me a sinner. I tell
you, this man went down to his house justified rather than
the other: for every one that exalteth himself shall be abased;
and he that humbleth himself shall be exalted" (Luke 18:9–
14).

42. [Jesus] spake a parable, because he was nigh to Jerusalem,
and because they thought that the kingdom of God should
immediately appear. He said therefore, A certain nobleman went into a far country to receive for himself a kingdom, and to return. And he called his ten servants, and
delivered them ten pounds, and said unto them, Occupy till
I come. But his citizens hated him, and sent a message after
him, saying, We will not have this man to reign over us.
And it came to pass, that when he was returned, having
received the kingdom, then he commanded these servants
to be called unto him, to whom he had given the money,
that he might know how much every man had gained by
trading. Then came the first, saying, Lord, thy pound hath
gained ten pounds. And he said unto him, Well, thou good
servant: because thou hast been faithful in a very little,
have thou authority over ten cities. And the second came,
saying, Lord, thy pound hath gained five pounds. And he
said likewise to him, Be thou also over five cities. And another came, saying, Lord, behold, here is thy pound, which
I have kept laid up in a napkin: for I feared thee, because
thou art an austere man: thou takest up that thou layedst
not down, and reapest that thou didst not sow. And he saith
unto him, Out of thine own mouth will I judge thee, thou

wicked servant. Thou knewest that I was an austere man, taking up that I laid not down, and reaping that I did not sow: wherefore then gavest not thou my money into the bank, that at my coming I might have required my own with usury? And he said unto them that stood by, Take from him the pound, and give it to him that hath ten pounds. (And they said unto him, Lord, he hath ten pounds.) For I say unto you, That unto every one which hath shall be given; and from him that hath not, even that he hath shall be taken away from him. But those mine enemies, which would not that I should reign over them, bring hither, and slay them before me" (Luke 19:11–27).

150. Three Other Parables of Jesus

1. "And [Jesus] called the multitude, and said unto them, Hear, and understand: not that which goeth into the mouth defileth a man; but that which cometh out of the mouth, this defileth a man. Then came his disciples, and said unto him, Knowest thou that the Pharisees were offended, after they heard this saying? But he answered and said, Every plant, which my heavenly Father hath not planted, shall be rooted up. Let them alone: they be blind leaders of the blind. And if the blind lead the blind, both shall fall into the ditch. Then answered Peter and said unto him, Declare unto us this parable. And Jesus said, Are ye also yet without understanding? Do not ye yet understand, that whatsoever entereth in at the mouth goeth into the belly, and is cast out in the draught? But those things which proceed out of the mouth come forth from the heart; and they defile the man. For out of the heart proceed evil thoughts, murders, adulteries, fornications, thefts, false witness, blasphemies: these are the things which defile a man: but to eat with unwashen hands defileth not a man" (Matt. 15:10–20).
2. "And [Jesus] spake a parable unto them, Can the blind lead the blind? shall they not both fall into the ditch? The disciple is not above his master: but every one that is perfect shall be as his master" (Luke 6:39, 40).
3. "Verily, verily, I say unto you, He that entereth not by the door into the sheepfold, but climbeth up some other way, the same is a thief and a robber. But he that entereth in by the door is the shepherd of the sheep. To him the porter

openeth; and the sheep hear his voice: and he calleth his own sheep by name, and leadeth them out. And when he putteth forth his own sheep, he goeth before them, and the sheep follow him: for they know his voice. And a stranger they will not follow, but will flee from him: for they know not the voice of strangers. This parable spake Jesus unto them: but they understood not what things they were which he spake unto them. Then said Jesus unto them again, Verily, verily, I say unto you, I am the door of the sheep. All that ever came before me are thieves and robbers: but the sheep did not hear them. I am the door: by me if any man enter in, he shall be saved, and shall go in and out, and find pasture. The thief cometh not, but for to steal, and to kill, and to destroy: I am come that they might have life, and that they might have it more abundantly. I am the good shepherd: the good shepherd giveth his life for the sheep. But he that is an hireling, and not the shepherd, whose own the sheep are not, seeth the wolf coming, and leaveth the sheep, and fleeth: and the wolf catcheth them, and scattereth the sheep. The hireling fleeth, because he is an hireling, and careth not for the sheep. I am the good shepherd, and know my sheep, and am known of mine. As the Father knoweth me, even so know I the Father: and I lay down my life for the sheep. And other sheep I have, which are not of this fold: them also I must bring, and there shall be one fold, and one shepherd. Therefore doth my Father love me, because I lay down my life, that might take it again. No man taketh it from me, but I lay it down of myself. I have power to lay it down, and I have power to take it again. This commandment have I received of my Father" (John 10:1–18).

151. Ten Mountaintop Experiences

1. Noah's ark came to rest upon the mountains of Ararat (Gen. 8:4).
2. Abraham offered up Isaac upon a mountain in the land of Moriah (Gen. 22:2).
3. The angel of the Lord appeared to Moses in the burning bush at Mount Horeb (Ex. 3:2).
4. Moses received the ten commandments atop Mount Sinai (Ex. 19:20).

5. Aaron died upon Mount Hor (Num. 20:22–28).
6. The Lord showed Moses the promised land from the top of Mount Pisgah (Deut. 34:1–4).
7. Satan took Jesus "up into an exceeding high mountain, and sheweth him all the kingdoms of the world, and the glory of them; and saith unto him, All these things will I give thee, if thou wilt fall down and worship me. Then saith Jesus; Get thee hence, Satan: for it is written, Thou shalt worship the Lord thy God, and him only shalt thou serve" (Matt. 4:8–10).
8. Jesus went up into a mountain and delivered the sermon on the mount (Matt. 5–7).
9. Jesus was transfigured in front of Peter, James, and John up in a high mountain (Matt. 17:1–9).
10. Jesus was betrayed and arrested on the Mount of Olives (Matt. 26:30–57).

152. The Fatherless and the Motherless (Orphans in the Bible)

1. Benjamin and Joseph lost their natural mother when Rachel died while giving birth to Benjamin (Gen. 35:16–18).
2. About four hundred young virgins from Jabeshgilead were orphaned all about the same time (Judges 21:1–12).
3. Ichabod was born a full fledged orphan (1 Sam. 4:19–22).
4. Mephibosheth lost his father (Jonathan) when he was just a child (2 Sam. 4:4).
5. The nameless young son of a widow was raised from the dead by Elijah (1 Kings 17:8–23).
6. Joash was only one year old when his father, Ahaziah was slain (2 Kings 11:1–21).
7. Azariah was left fatherless at age sixteen when his father, King Amaziah was murdered (2 Kings 14:17–21).
8. Manasseh was twelve years old when his father, King Hezekiah died (2 Kings 20:21, 21:1).
9. Josiah was only eight years old when his father was murdered (2 Kings 21:23–26, 22:1).
10. Jehoiachin was eighteen when his father died (2 Kings 24:6–8).
11. Esther was orphaned when she was a young girl and was raised by her cousin, Mordecai (Esther 2:5–7).
12. Daniel, Shadrach, Meshach, and Abednego were probably all orphans (Dan. 1:1–17).

Bibliography

Abbreviated Bible, The—with the Apocrypha
 by James Leslie McCary and Mark McElhaney
 Published by Van Nostrand Reinhold Co.
 Copyright 1971
Aids to Understanding the Holy Bible—
Appendix to *Family Bible*
 General Editor John Rea
 Published by the World Publishing Co.
 Copyright 1968
All the Men of the Bible
 by Herbert Lockyer
 Published by Zondervan Publishing House
 Copyright 1958, 26th printing, January 1979
Bible Dictionary—Concordance to Holy Bible,
Appendix to King James Version
 Published by A. J. Holman Co.
 Copyright 1942
Halley's Bible Handbook
 by Henry H. Halley
 Published by Zondervan Publishing House
 Copyright 1965, 24th edition
Interlinear Greek-English New Testament
 by Rev. Alfred Marshall D. Litt
 Published by Zondervan Publishing House
 Copyright 1958, 2nd edition, June 1969 reprint
Meredith's Book of Bible Lists
 By J. L. Meredith
 Published by Bethany House Publishers
 Copyright 1980
Strong's Exhaustive Concordance of the Bible
 by James Strong
 Published by Abingdon Press
 Copyright 1890, 25th printing, 1963
Unger's Bible Dictionary
 by Merrill F. Unger
 Published by Moody Press
 Copyright 1957, 1961, 1966, 3rd edition, 33rd printing, 1981
Universal Bible Dictionary, The
 Edited by A. R. Buckland & Assisted by A. Luky Williams
 Published by Fleming H. Revell Co.
 No Copyright, 1951 edition
Wycliffe Bible Commentary, The
 Edited by Charles F. Pfeiffer (O.T.) & Everett F. Harrison (N.T.)
 Published by Moody Press
 Copyright 1962, 7th printing, 1972